Frommer's®

P9-BIG-843

Vancouver Island, the Gulf Islands & the San Juan Islands

3rd Edition

by Chris McBeath

WILEY

John Wiley & Sons Canada, Ltd.

Published by:

JOHN WILEY & SONS CANADA, LTD.

6045 Freemont Blvd.
Mississauga, ON
L5R 4J3

ISBN 978-0-470-68170-1 (paper); 978-1-118-04594-7 (ebk); 978-1-118-04593-0 (ebk); 978-1-118-04592-3 (ebk)

Editor: Gene Shannon
Developmental Editor: William Travis
Production Editor: Lindsay Humphreys
Cartographer: Tim Lohnes
Photo Editor: Richard Fox
Production by Wiley Indianapolis Composition Services
Front cover photo: ©R. Breucker / AGE Fotostock, Inc.
Description: Sea Stars at flow at the west coast of Vancouver Island, Canada, Vancouver Island
Back cover photo: ©Performance Image / Alamy Images
Description: Tofino, British Columbia: Canada Pacific Rim National Park Rain Forest Trail, person on pathway in distance

For information on our other products and services or to obtain technical support, please contact our Customer Care Department within the U.S. at 877/762-2974, outside the U.S. at 317/572-3993 or fax 317/572-4002.

Wiley also publishes its books in a variety of electronic formats. Some content that appears in print may not be available in electronic formats.

Printed in the United States

1 2 3 4 5   RRD   15 14 13 12 11

WILEY

CONTENTS

LIST OF MAPS

HOW TO CONTACT US

In researching this book, we discovered many wonderful places—hotels, restaurants, shops, and more. We're sure you'll find others. Please tell us about them, so we can share the information with your fellow travelers in upcoming editions. If you were disappointed with a recommendation, we'd love to know that, too. Please write to:

Frommer's Vancouver Island, the Gulf Islands
& the San Juan Islands, 3rd Edition
John Wiley & Sons Canada, Ltd. • 6045 Freemont Blvd.
Mississauga, ON • L5R 4J3

AN ADDITIONAL NOTE

Please be advised that travel information is subject to change at any time—and this is especially true of prices. We therefore suggest that you write or call ahead for confirmation when making your travel plans. The authors, editors, and publisher cannot be held responsible for the experiences of readers while traveling. Your safety is important to us, however, so we encourage you to stay alert and be aware of your surroundings. Keep a close eye on cameras, purses, and wallets, all favorite targets of thieves and pickpockets.

ABOUT THE AUTHOR

A full-time writer who globe-trots and scribes for a living, Chris McBeath makes her home in these islands of the Pacific Northwest. Because she has worked in so many facets of the tourism industry, from chambermaid to management, aboard cruise ships and in top-ranked hotels, she has an insider's eye for what makes a great travel experience. Chris tweets, blogs, and maintains a travel website (www.greatestgetaways.com) on her various travels. Although she contributes to publications worldwide, this book represents a part of the world that is closest to her heart.

ACKNOWLEDGEMENTS

Updating the contents of this book is a pleasure, because the entire experience hits the pulse of the islands' people, places, and landscapes. Every day is an adventure and never disappoints. Islanders are resourceful, creative, and hospitable, so there's always something new to discover. My grateful thanks go to Frommer's editor Gene Shannon, production editor Lindsay Humphreys, and copy editor Laura Miller for their efforts in making this edition of the guide the finest yet. Thanks, also, to the Tourism folks for being such terrific allies in my quest to bring you the best. And, most especially, my heartfelt appreciation goes to readers and travelers alike. Your feedback and opinions are part of this book and certainly contributed to the fun I had exploring the region. Now it's your turn. Enjoy.

FROMMER'S STAR RATINGS, ICONS & ABBREVIATIONS

Every hotel, restaurant, and attraction listing in this guide has been ranked for quality, value, service, amenities, and special features using a **star-rating system.** In country, state, and regional guides, we also rate towns and regions to help you narrow down your choices and budget your time accordingly. Hotels and restaurants are rated on a scale of zero (recommended) to three stars (exceptional). Attractions, shopping, nightlife, towns, and regions are rated according to the following scale: zero stars (recommended), one star (highly recommended), two stars (very highly recommended), and three stars (must-see).

In addition to the star-rating system, we also use **seven feature icons** that point you to the great deals, in-the-know advice, and unique experiences that separate travelers from tourists. Throughout the book, look for:

special finds—those places only insiders know about

fun facts—details that make travelers more informed and their trips more fun

kids—best bets for kids and advice for the whole family

special moments—those experiences that memories are made of

overrated—places or experiences not worth your time or money

insider tips—great ways to save time and money

great values—where to get the best deals

The following **abbreviations** are used for credit cards:

AE	American Express	DISC	Discover	V	Visa
DC	Diners Club	MC	MasterCard		

TRAVEL RESOURCES AT FROMMERS.COM

Frommer's travel resources don't end with this guide. Frommer's website, **www.frommers. com,** has travel information on more than 4,000 destinations. We update features regularly, giving you access to the most current trip-planning information and the best airfare, lodging, and car-rental bargains. You can also listen to podcasts, connect with other Frommers. com members through our active-reader forums, share your travel photos, read blogs from guidebook editors and fellow travelers, and much more.

THE BEST OF VANCOUVER ISLAND, THE GULF ISLANDS & THE SAN JUAN ISLANDS

There's a geological reason, having to do with movement of the various layers of the Earth's crust, that explains why these islands on the Northwest coast of the North American continent came into being. But to my mind, it is the words of one island resident that best describe this creation of nature: "When God made this continent, He finished up with Vancouver Island," he explains. "But there was a little material left, so God stood up, and brushed off His hands. The results are jewels in the water that we know today as the San Juans and the Gulf Islands."

However it happened, these islands in the Pacific Northwest are home to some of the most beautiful and pristine wilderness on Earth today. An archipelago that stretches along the coastline of both sides of the 49th parallel, the islands number in the hundreds. Some are large enough to sustain small communities as diverse as the islands themselves, while others are no more than seagull perches that disappear at high tide.

Vancouver Island is the largest. Separated from the British Columbia mainland by the Georgia Strait, the island offers the best of all worlds. In the south, the city of Victoria has the urban sophistication of a cosmopolitan center and lies within easy reach of soft adventure activities such as hiking, whale-watching, and cycling. In the north, the countryside grows untamed, opening a door to exhilarating eco-adventures such as mountaineering, spelunking, surfing, and canoeing. This diversity consistently earns Vancouver Island high marks from leading travel publications.

The smaller Gulf Islands and San Juan Islands are equally appealing, and their communities reflect the isolation of their water-bound environments. Each has a different history and ambience, whether it is sleepy Lopez Island or eclectic Galiano Island. It's a sense of magic, though, that is their charm. Island residents prefer to live outside the mainstream: They are writers, artists, and craftspeople, city retirees looking for a sense of community, or specialty producers farming everything from llama and sheep to organic orchards and cottage dairies. They've chosen to live on "island time," an easygoing tempo that bewitches visitors the moment they set foot on the soil. Although visitors are certainly welcome (in summer, they swell island populations tenfold), islanders like to keep outside influences at arm's length, lest they change that special way of life too dramatically. Islanders are self-professed stewards of the land and, as such, keepers of the island faith. When writer James Michener wanted to describe his love of islands, he made up a word for it: *nesomania,* from the Greek *neso* (island) and *mania* (extreme enthusiasm). Explore these islands, and you'll discover that nesomaniacs abound—you might even become one yourself!

THE best FAMILY EXPERIENCES

- o **Visiting the Royal British Columbia Museum** (Victoria; ✆ **250/356-7226**): This place is so diverse and inspiring that kids may want to stay all afternoon. How often can you say *that* about a museum? See p. 85.
- o **Actually enjoying having stick insects navigate their way up your arm at the Victoria Bug Zoo** (Victoria; ✆ **250/384-2847**): The interaction with insects takes the creepy out of crawly. See p. 85.
- o **Exploring at Horne Lake Caves Provincial Park** (near Qualicum Beach): Armed with flashlights, helmets, and good shoes, you'll feel like intrepid adventurers, even though the darkened path has been well scouted. One of the most accessible networks of caverns on the island, the caves can also accommodate extreme spelunkers. See p. 148.
- o **Trolling your curiosity through the Salish Sea at Shaw Discovery Centre** (Sidney; ✆ **250/665-7511**): Whatever your age, you'll enjoy the showmanship, staged as an intriguing blend of seabed-to-seashore displays alongside innovative high-tech, touchy-feely exhibits. See p. 108.
- o **Wading through minnows and searching out sand dollars at Rathtrevor Beach Provincial Park** (Parksville): This is one of the most family-friendly parks in British Columbia. The warm, ankle-deep waters seem to go on forever. So does the sand. See p. 146.
- o **Investigating the sandstone-sculpted tide pools at Botanical Beach** (Port Renfrew): Discover hundreds of different species of intertidal life, including congregations of sea stars, chitons, anemones, purple sea urchins, barnacles, snails, and mussels. Ridges of shale and quartz jut through the black basalt cliffs, creating some of the most photogenic landscapes on the island. See p. 116.
- o **Harnessing up to zip along cables from one Douglas fir to another at Wild Play at the Bungy Zone** (Nanaimo; ✆ **888/716-7374**): Zip trips can reach speeds of up to 100kmph (62 mph), and there's no age limit. See p. 136.

o **Wandering through the Victoria Butterfly Gardens** (Victoria; ℂ 250/652-3822): Very few things top the feel of a butterfly's kiss on your cheek. See p. 108.

o **Playing with sea slugs and urchins at the Ucluelet Mini Aquarium** (Ucluelet; ℂ 604/987-6992): Students of marine biology share little-known facts and folklore about local underwater wildlife with infectious enthusiasm that will captivate youngsters and charm oldsters! See p. 161.

o **Digging for fossils with the Courtenay & District Museum and Palaeontology Centre** (Courtenay, along the Puntledge River; ℂ 250/334-3611): It's a dirty business (which kids love), and you get to keep any fossils you find. See p. 180.

THE best ADVENTURES

o **Kayaking through the Broken Group Islands** (Pacific Rim National Park): It's an oasis of calm waters, seal colonies, and other Pacific Ocean marine life. Better yet, travel there aboard the freighter MV *Frances Barkley*. See p. 163.

o **Honing a new outdoor skill at Strathcona Park Lodge** (Strathcona Provincial Park; ℂ 250/286-3122): Everything from hiking to rappelling is on offer here, for both novice and extremist. See p. 183.

o **Learning to surf on Long Beach:** The waves just keep coming, and whether or not you manage to stand, it's a long and exhilarating ride to shore. See p. 165.

o **Navigating a canoe through The Sayward Forest** (Gold River): There's plenty of portaging for experienced paddlers who want to do the full 50km (31-mile) circuit. See p. 202.

o **Scuba diving the "Emerald Sea"** (Nanaimo): The Cousteau Society ranks these waters one of the top dives sites in the world for its reef of sunken wrecks and other marine treasures. See p. 134.

o **Exploring Broughton Inlet's narrow fjordic waterways** (Port McNeil): While aboard the heritage vessel *Columbia III*, you'll paddle along two-kayak-wide channels and coves by day and enjoy ship comforts by night. Expect to see whales, eagles, and sea lions just a few paddle-lengths away. See p. 209.

o **Catching the updrafts with Vancouver Island Soaring** (Port Alberni; ℂ 250/667-3591): With nothing but the wind to keep you airborne, gliding is the nearest thing to natural flying as you can get. See p. 154.

THE best LEISURE ACTIVITIES

o **Teeing off with kindred spirits:** Both **Crown Isle Resort** (Comox/Courtenay; ℂ 888/338-8439) and Westin **Bear Mountain Resort** (Victoria; ℂ 888/533-2327) are deliciously golf-nutty. Bear Mountain has two Jack Nicklaus–designed courses, and Crown Isle is one of more than 20 courses you'll find in the Central Island. See p. 182 and 72.

o **Cruising on the *Aurora Explorer*** (Campbell River; ℂ 250/286-3347): This 12-passenger packet freighter works her way up and down some of the most beautiful coastal inlets in British Columbia. Although cargo is priority, passengers are a lucrative sideline. A casual, offbeat way to travel. See p. 191.

o **Scooting around San Juan Island in a Scootcar** (Friday Harbor; ✆ **800/532-0087**): A Scootcar is a hybrid vehicle that shuttles along at a low speed, giving you all the fun of a moped and the cover of a car. See p. 250.

o **Storm-watching** (Tofino/Ucluelet): Pick a spot from anywhere along Vancouver Island's westernmost coast that's open to the fury of the Pacific Ocean and get set for an OMNIMAX-style show. See chapter 7.

o **Day tripping to Bamfield aboard the MV *Frances Barkley*** (Port Alberni; ✆ **250/723-8313**): Water is the most scenic route to get to the famous boardwalks of Bamfield, a village originally built on stilts above the tidal currents. See p. 155 and 157.

o **Wining (and dining) through the Cowichan Valley:** The wine scene here is as diverse as it is sophisticated; be sure to eat en route. This is the heart of Cittaslow country; most menus feature local, organic, artisan foods. See p. 124.

o **Day sailing aboard MV *Uchuck III*** (Gold River; ✆ **250/283-2515**): A day trip with this converted minesweeper takes you to some of Vancouver Island's most isolated (and picturesque) communities, from logging camps to water-bound hamlets. It's a great value cruise. Bring your binoculars. See p. 197.

THE best HIKING TRAILS

o **The boardwalks of the Wild Pacific Trail** (Ucluelet): You can make believe you're in training for the West Coast Trail or a trek to Cape Scott. Great for 8- and 80-year-olds alike, the trail has all the dramatic views with absolutely none of the true-grit challenges. See p. 161.

o **The West Coast Trail** (Pacific Rim National Park): This trek is one of the world's best to test the mettle of the hardiest and most experienced hiker. Many don't make the grade. But if you do, you'll have some of the most spectacular coastal scenery shots to prove it. See p. 164.

o **The Cape Scott Trail (North Island):** A West Coast Trail alternative, this trail sees you through marshland, across beaches, and over suspension bridges, with turn-back points to suit your stamina level. Choose the moderate 3-hour round trip to San Josef Bay or the full 8-hour trek to Cape Scott. There's also a new North Coast Trail that's a part of a larger plan to construct a trail all the way from Cape Scott to Port Hardy. See p. 211.

o **The Juan de Fuca Trail** (Sooke–Port Renfrew): Here's another West Coast Trail alternative with (almost) equally impressive scenic beauty, wildlife viewing, and roaring surf crashing against the coast. Moderate 1-day hikes string together for a multiday excursion that's a good rehearsal for more grueling expeditions. See p. 114.

o **Cathedral Grove** (Coombs–Port Alberni): This ancient stand of Douglas firs grows so close to the heavens, you feel you're in a medieval cathedral. The trails are easy—at the very least, pull into the parking lot to understand why tree-huggers fought so hard to save this area from logging. See p. 154.

o **Galloping Goose Trail** (Victoria–Sooke): A great trail for walking and better still if you're on wheels—in-line skates or a bicycle. The Goose is mostly graded, relatively level, and passes through some of Victoria's most picture-perfect neighborhoods and urban wilderness—all the way to Sooke. See p. 114.

○ **East Sooke Coast Trail** (Sooke): It can be challenging in places (think coastal rain-forest to surf-beaten rocks), but this kind of wilderness hiking within a half-hour's drive of a major city is what makes Vancouver Island an eco-adventurer's dream destination. See p. 116.

○ **Brookes Point Bluff** (South Pender Island): If you're prepared to scramble up a small rock face from Gowland Point, you can walk through waist-high dried grasses along the edge of the bluff to Brookes Point. The views are stunning, mak-ing it an intimate spot for a romantic picnic. See p. 231.

○ **The trail to Iceberg Point** (Lopez Island): Cutting through private property, this trail delivers you to a windy walk along the cliff's edge. Good walking shoes, and perhaps a picnic, are all anyone needs to enjoy the bluffy landscape. See p. 268.

THE best SCENIC DRIVES

○ **Following the shoreline between Sooke and Port Renfrew:** The views are expan-sive, and the beaches along the way provide an excellent excuse to pull over and stretch your legs. If you can't make it all the way to Botanical Beach Provincial Park (well worth the effort), the restaurant at the **Point No Point Resort** (② **250/646-2020**) is a good point to refresh and turn around. See chapter 6.

○ **Driving the scenic route from Victoria to Swartz Bay:** Highway 17A runs along the western shores of the Saanich Peninsula. It's only about 42km (26 miles), but with wineries, U-Pick flower fields, and roadside stands selling produce, eggs, and homemade jams, the 45-minute drive can easily take hours, especially if you "do lunch" en route or spend half a day at Butchart Gardens. See chapter 6.

○ **Highway 4 across Vancouver Island, from Parksville to Tofino:** Bisecting the island east to west is a topographical treasure. You'll pass through forests, rivers, and snow-capped mountains before hitting the windswept shores and beaches of the west coast. See chapter 7.

○ **Checking out Washington State's Scenic Byway:** Travel the ferry from Anacortes to the San Juan Islands, once an Indian canoe route, and track the byway around historical San Juan Island and pretty Orcas Island. See chapter 10.

○ **Follow the starfish signs along Highway 19A, the Oceanside Route:** Take any exit off Highway 19 near Parksville and weave up to Campbell River through seaside communities overlooking the Georgia Strait, past artisan studios, and across lush farmlands. A sage farmer once said that if the cows are lying down, inclement weather is brewing. Keep an eye open and check the theory out. See chapter 7.

○ **Detouring across Denman and Hornby islands:** This meandering drive through island countryside and along a shoreline will leave you awestruck with the random beauty of sculpted rock and mountain panoramas. See chapter 9.

○ **Cruising the Coastal Circle Route:** The drive from Victoria to Courtenay, over the Malahat, takes you from urban charm to mountain vistas and then down into a valley of wineries. From Courtenay, take the car ferry across to Powell River for a drive down along coastal rainforest to more ferry connections heading for Horse-shoe Bay and Vancouver. See chapter 8.

THE best WILDLIFE VIEWING

o **Spotting bald eagles at Goldstream Provincial Park** (Victoria): When the salmon run ends, thousands of eagles come to feast on the carcasses. From early December until late February, the park puts on eagle-oriented programs, including a daily count that has reached as many as 276 sightings in 1 day. See p. 115.

o **Whale-watching at Robson Bight** (Port McNeil): There are many whale-watching opportunities throughout the islands, including a grey whale migration that passes by the West Coast. But nothing beats the orcas in Robson Bight (p. 207), a one-of-a-kind ecological whale preserve. **Lime Kiln Point Park** (San Juan Island, p. 254) is a hot contender, as well. Whale-watching and research takes place formally in the lighthouse and informally on the bluffs below.

o **Catching up with marmots** (Nanaimo): The Vancouver Island marmot has the dubious distinction of being Canada's most critically endangered species. Take a hike into the wilds surrounding Nanaimo, and you might get lucky and see these highly inquisitive creatures popping up from their underground burrows. See p. 144.

o **Seeing birds of prey up close at Pacific Northwest Raptors** (Duncan): It's one of the few places you can have eyeball contact with a raptor outside of caged environs, and even learn falconry skills. See p. 122.

o **Hearing the breeding call of a bull Roosevelt elk** (San Juan River): It's a haunting refrain, heard every fall, as the bull searches out new females to add to his harem. Roosevelt elk are a formidable sight anytime of year, and finding their shed antlers is a fine reward for a hike. This species of elk is found only on Vancouver Island and the Queen Charlotte Islands; herds hang out near Gold River and the Jordan River meadows, and in the Nanaimo Lake region.

o **Spying upon noisy nesting birds** (Hornby Island): The cliffs of Helliwell Park provide some of the most prolific nesting habitats for Pelagic cormorants, as well as for Harlequin duck, surf scoter, pigeon guillemot, marbled murrelet, and ancient murrelet. An excellent starting point for beginner birders. See p. 187.

o **Venturing into the Great Bear Rainforest:** In one of the largest remaining tracts of pristine rainforest in the world, grizzlies roam the undergrowth and shore-sides, as do cougars and wolves. The hope is that you'll see a Kermode ("spirit") bear, a white-coloured member of the black bear family. See p. 201.

THE best FIRST NATIONS EXPERIENCES

o **Quw'utsun' Cultural Centre** (Duncan; © 877/746-8119): Owned and operated by the Cowichan Band, the center shares the band's cultural heritage through live demonstrations, dance, Native food, and the knitting of its famous Cowichan sweater. See p. 123.

o **Eagle Aerie Gallery** (Tofino; © 250/725-3235): Acclaimed artist Roy Vickers owns this stunningly moody and inspiring gallery, primarily a showcase for his own work, as well as a chosen few other artists. See p. 159. Henry Vickers, Roy's brother, is also an acclaimed artist with his **Shipyard Gallery** in Cowichan Bay.

○ **Nuyumbalees Cultural Centre** (Quadra Island; ✆ 250/285-3733): Small but insightful, the center is home to a collection of potlatch treasures, a petroglyph rubbing gallery, and an *Ah-Wah-qwa-dzas* (meaning "a place to relax and tell stories") on the waterfront. See p. 200.

○ **U'Mista Cultural Centre** (Alert Bay; ✆ 250/974-5403): Even if you're not an aficionado of aboriginal art, a guided tour around the center's collection provides an invaluable perspective on First Nations culture. See p. 207.

○ **Eagle Feather Gallery** (Victoria; ✆ 250/388-4330): Although you'll find many small studios scattered throughout Vancouver Island, if you're staying south and you have time for only one stop, this shop carries some of the best jewelry, arts, and crafts. See p. 95.

THE best SPAS

○ **The Ancient Cedars Spa** (Wickaninnish Inn; ✆ 250/725-3100): This spa offers hot stone massages in a little cedar hut perched on the rocks as the Pacific Ocean crashes below. A very sensual experience. See p. 169.

○ **Willow Stream Spa** (Fairmont Empress; ✆ 250/384-8111): Regardless of what type of service you've booked, this spa throws in time in the steam room and its mineral pool so that you can turn a manicure into an afternoon event. See p. 99.

○ **The Madrona del Mar Spa** (Galiano Inn; ✆ 250/539-3388): The concept of a healing sanctuary rises to new levels with private glass-and-marble steam rooms, a sea-flotation bath, and guest rooms that even have a Murphy bed–style massage table for fireside treatments. See p. 236.

○ **The Spa at Ocean Pointe** (✆ 800/575-8882): Prepare yourself for upscale pampering all the way, all the time, with a sauna, pool, and complete fitness facility thrown in for good measure. See p. 99.

○ **The Grotto Spa** (Tigh-Na-Mara Resort; ✆ 250/248-2072): British Columbia's largest resort spa features a sizeable cave-like mineral pool and two-story waterfall. See p. 151.

○ **The Kingfisher Oceanside Spa** (Courtenay; ✆ 800/663-7929): One of the first destination resort spas on the island, this is a great spot for group spa getaways. It offers the only Pacific Mist Hydropath in North America (a kind of "walking hydrotherapy"), as well as tidal baths carved out of rock, mineral soaks, and a steam cave. See p. 180.

○ **Essence of Life Spa** (Brentwood Bay Lodge; ✆ 888/544-2079): The couples massage here is just one more great reason why you won't want to leave this contemporary, and very romantic, sanctuary. See p. 99.

○ **Sante Spa** (Bear Mountain; ✆ 888/533-2327): Its mountaintop location and organic, healthful treatments earn Sante enough kudos to warrant a spa stopover for more than just an hour or two. See p. 99.

THE best HOTELS & RESORTS

- **The Fairmont Empress** (Victoria; ℂ 800/441-1414): Like a grand old dowager, this magnificent hotel commands the Victoria Inner Harbour as her fiefdom and beckons her audience inside. If you're going for broke, stay here; the experience is what North Americans think England is all about. See p. 64.

- **Brentwood Bay Lodge & Spa** (Brentwood Bay; ℂ 888/544-2079): This contemporary lodge boasts an oceanfront location and a service ratio nearing three staff per one guest room. Expect all the amenities of a five-star resort. See p. 109.

- **Magnolia Hotel & Spa** (Victoria; ℂ 877/624-6654): With a quiet, European elegance, this boutique hotel is everything you would find in a ritzy neighborhood in London or Monaco. Style, grace, service, and discretion, and it's so close to great shopping, who cares about being set back from the harbor? See p. 68.

- **Clayoquot Wilderness Resort** (Clayoquot Sound; ℂ 888/333-5405): Accessible only by water, the resort is quite isolated, so you feel as if you're completely one with the wilderness. But it's the luxurious safari-style campsites that steal the show. See p. 166.

- **Rosario Resort** (Orcas Island; ℂ 800/562-8820): Situated on a peninsula, Rosario emanates an air of 1920s grace. Listed on the National Register of Historic Places, this beautifully refurbished resort has everything: elegant dining, spa services, and a see-it-to-believe-it, 1,972-pipe Aeolian organ. See p. 262

- **Sidney Pier Hotel** (Sidney; ℂ 866/659-9445): This youthful hotel mixes superb customer service with a casual, beachside ambiance. Look out for "Dave", the dog ambassador. See p. 110.

- **Sonora Resort** (Sonora Island; ℂ 888/576-6672): Accessible only by air (the resort has its own state-of-the-art helicopter) or by boat, getting there is half the fun. Fishing is the number-one activity, though visiting the spa, hiking, and going on wildlife excursions are catching up quickly. The private lounge theater is like something made for reclusive movie moguls. See p. 193.

- **Poets Cove** (Pender Island; ℂ 888/512-POET [888/512-7638]): This resort offers a wide variety of accommodations that beckons families (and boaters) in the summer and romantics at every other time of the year. It's so self-contained, you can eat, sleep, spa, and cocoon—all in one place. See p. 232.

- **Beach Club Resort** (Parksville; ℂ 888/760-2008): There are plenty of beachside resorts in this seaside community, but here, the views from the oceanfront suites are the best for the "Wow" factor, especially from the upper floors. See p. 149.

- **Painter's Lodge Holiday & Fishing Resort** (Campbell River; ℂ 800/663-7090): This is *the* place for fishing enthusiasts. These folks also own activity-oriented April Point Lodge & Spa across the channel, and because guest privileges flow from one to the other, it's almost like staying in two resorts for the price of one. See p. 193.

THE best B&BS & INNS

- **Abigail's Hotel** (Victoria; ℂ 800/561-6565): This inn is an indulgent essence of old-world charm and hospitality in a phenomenal downtown Victoria location. See p. 68.

- **Albion Manor** (Victoria; ☎ 877/389-0012): Refurbished to enhance its turn-of-the-century glory, the inn is a mosaic of striking heirloom pieces, outlandish art sculptures, antiques, and comfortable kitsch. See p. 67.
- **Blackberry Glen** (Salt Spring Island; ☎ 877/890-0764): One of the newest inns on the island set in gorgeous gardens. Rooms are lovely, though the float home on the pond is the fairest—and quirkiest—of them all. See also p. 224.
- **Hastings House** (Ganges, Salt Spring Island; ☎ 800/661-9255): Everything you would want in an English country inn is here, but so much better. Expect wonderful gardens, inspired guest rooms, and world-renowned cuisine. Catching your own crab dinner is *the* most fun eating experience. See p. 225.
- **Friday Harbor House** (Friday Harbor, San Juan Island; ☎ 360/378-8455): This is a modern, beautifully furnished inn sitting high above busy Friday Harbor. The views are outstanding. At night, the twinkling lights make the inn's restaurant a really romantic spot. See p. 256.
- **Free Spirit Spheres** (Qualicum Beach; ☎ 250/757-9445): If there's a gale, your orb bedroom in the trees may sway a shade, but these ingenious spheres are absolutely unique, conjuring up images of *Swiss Family Robinson,* but with a West Coast flavor. See also p. 150.
- **Oceanwood Country Inn** (Dinner Bay, Mayne Island; ☎ 250/539-5074): If you're lucky, from the dining room, you'll see whales passing up Navy Channel. The inn offers a range of top-quality guest rooms, extravagant gardens, and lounges featuring a contemporary, country charm. See p. 240.
- **Crown Mansion** (Qualicum Beach; ☎ 250/752-5776): Overlooking the community's most established golf course, this Art Deco home radiates an understated comfort. See p. 150.
- **Wildwood Manor B&B** (San Juan Island; ☎ 877/298-1144): Staying here is like being an honored house guest. The proprietors' attention to detail is extraordinary, and hospitality is so genuine that you'll feel you've made lifetime friends. See p. 257.
- **Turtleback Farm Inn** (Orcas Island; ☎ 800/376-4914): Set on a private 32 hectares (79 acres), this 1800s green clapboard farmhouse has been lovingly restored. The pastoral views lull you into a relaxed state of nirvana. See p. 264.
- **Wickaninnish Inn** (Tofino; ☎ 800/333-4604): With only floor-to-ceiling triple-glazed windows standing between you and the churning Pacific Ocean, this Relais & Châteaux property elevates storm-watching to an art, and a whole lot more. See p. 168.
- **Villa Marco Polo** (Victoria; ☎ 877/601-1524): Lavish in style and hospitality, influences of Venetian traveler Marco Polo exude an exotic touch to this (not inexpensive) manor house. Definitely a place for special occasions. See p. 72.

THE best CULINARY INNS

- **Sooke Harbour House** (Vancouver Island; ☎ 800/889-9688): Beyond its reputation as a hideaway for Hollywood's beautiful people, this place offers so much more. Many come for the Wine Spectator Grand Award–winning wine cellar and the food—an epicurean feast of local and organic fare that seems to go on for as long as you can eat. Be prepared to make reservations at the restaurant, sometimes weeks in advance. See p. 118.

o **Coopers Cove** (Sooke; © 877/642-5727): *The Oprah Winfrey Show* has featured the Cove's ex-Olympiad chef Angelo Prosperi-Porta, who teams up with his guests to create mouth-watering interactive dinners. He claims you'll forge a "spiritual connection to the food you eat." However you interpret that, the results taste heaven-sent! See p. 117.

o **Fairburn Farm Culinary Retreat & Guesthouse** (Duncan; © 250/746-4637): Part farm, part cooking school, and part country inn, Fairburn exemplifies what the Slow Food movement is all about. Chef Mara Jernigan creates a delicious experience that really raises your consciousness about foods of the land. See p. 125.

THE best RESTAURANTS

o **Aura** (Victoria, © 250/414-6739): The chefs here are in training to represent Canada at the 2012 World Culinary Olympics. In addition to fantastic food, Aura has the city's most dramatic, view-filled patio. See p. 73.

o **Blue Crab Bar & Grill** (Victoria; © 250/480-1999): This restaurant serves the best seafood in Victoria, along with fabulous views of the harbor. See p. 74.

o **Smoken Bones Cookshack** (Victoria; © 250/391-6328): Finger-lickin' BBQ ribs and much more, done southern style in both taste and massive servings. See p. 82.

o **Amuse Bistro** (Victoria; © 250/743-3667): A former home now turned restaurant, dining here is like being a member of an exclusive supper club, especially when everything on the menu is geared to amuse your palate with a range of locally produced fare such as roasted venison, chanterelles with brandy and veal jus, and heritage carrots. See p. 127.

o **Deep Cove Chalet** (Saanich Inlet, near Victoria; © 250/656-3541): This place makes the list for its caviar: Beluga, Ocietra, and Sevugra, from Russia, Iran, and China, which helps make the elegant French menu a standout. The wine reserve of 18,000 bottles is remarkable, too. See p. 110.

o **Fox & Hounds** (Nanaimo; © 250/740-1000): Even the Brits would have to take their hats off to this pub-style drinking establishment. The steak and kidney pie is as good as it gets, and the Guinness is just one of many British Isles imports, a number of which you won't easily find elsewhere. See p. 140.

o **Foo Asian Street Food** (Victoria; © 250/383-3111): Whether you eat in or take out, you'll wonder how the inventive fusion dishes created here can taste so good. Either way, we're talking food in a carton. See p. 79.

o **The Sushi Bar at the Inn at Tough City** (Tofino; © 250/725-2021): Surrounded by the bounty of the sea, you would think there would be a proliferation of sushi restaurants on the west coast of Vancouver Island. Not so, which is why this tiny cafe at the Inn at Tough City is such a treat. See p. 172.

o **House Piccolo** (Ganges; © 250/537-1844): The restaurant inside this tiny farmhouse is consistently recognized by the prestigious Chaine des Rôtisseurs, (a gastronomic society) so you know the cuisine is top-notch. Many dishes have a Scandinavian twist, as in spiced herring or scallop ceviche. The gorgonzola cheese tart with red-onion marmalade is an example of Piccolo's creativity. See p. 228.

o **Prima Strada Pizzeria** (Victoria, © 250/590-8595): This Neapolitan, wood-fired-oven pizza bistro blows all other pizza parlors out of the water. See p. 80.

- **Pointe Restaurant** (Tofino; ✆ **250/725-3100**): The food is as spectacular as its location, perched on a craggy bluff. This is where you come for an amazing multi-course, gourmet, culinary experience—albeit with gourmet prices to match. See p. 171.

- **Shelter Restaurant** (Tofino; ✆ **250/725-3353**): This upbeat restaurant gives the Pointe a run for its money, only here you'll save a few dollars. Perhaps that's because there's no view. But with such fresh and imaginatively blended flavors before you, you probably won't even notice. See p. 172.

- **Hastings House** (Ganges; ✆ **250/537-2362**): It's at the top of the food chain in terms of fine dining, exquisite service, and poshness. From the hand-crafted butters and personalized menus to a glass of port by the log fire, the attention to detail here is unmatched. See p. 225.

- **Duck Soup Inn** (San Juan Island; ✆ **360/378-4878**): The artsy decor and off-beat paraphernalia is second only to the ever-changing menu, which is created on the fly, depending on what the garden is producing at any given moment. The results are imaginative pairings such as lamb with sour cherry port, homemade lemon linguini, and lavender-thyme roasted chicken, all served with spiced, herbed, or nutty breads. See p. 258.

- **Bruce's Kitchen** (Ganges; ✆ **250/931-3399**): The informality of your own kitchen is right here, seated around communal tables, as Big Bruce creates magic behind a hot stove. See p. 227.

VANCOUVER ISLAND, THE GULF ISLANDS & THE SAN JUAN ISLANDS IN DEPTH

2

t's no advertising hype when you hear that these islands can be all things to all people. Their coastlines are the envy of sailors from all over the world, and their landscapes are lush with the promises of extraordinary soft adventure, mouthwatering organic produce, and a rich cultural history—a mosaic of ancient Native Canadian settlements, Spanish exploration, trappers and traders, opium dens, and pioneers who believed they had found their Eden.

Magazines such as Conde Nast's *Traveler* and *Travel & Leisure* consistently rank Victoria and Vancouver Island among the world's finest visitor destinations. And little wonder. They offer activities at both ends of the spectrum. The islands' home-grown, organic food scene is phenomenal, giving rise to a terrific selection of restaurants and inns (especially in Victoria), so you can literally graze your way from point A to point B. Or you can simply pitch a tent in the rainforest and hike, spelunk, and sea kayak in and around protected inlets, craggy shores, and windswept beaches.

Although tourism is the largest sector of the local economy—it's virtually the only industry on the Gulf and San Juan islands—the tourism scene is only just now hitting its stride. Oceanfront lodges and snazzy boutique hotels are certainly upping the ante in terms of the visitor experience, and they are juxtaposed against a laid-back pastoral charm—sheep dotting the hillsides, cottage wineries, and picturesque communities—that's usually hard to find in such close proximity to sophisticated centers like Seattle and Vancouver. Even Victoria, which is unabashedly touristy with its ornamental architecture, abundant gardens, and horse-drawn carriages, maintains its "Victorian-ness" in an absolutely authentic way.

THE ISLANDS TODAY

While farmers, fishermen, and seafarers were the settlers of these islands, in the 1970s, they were joined by hippies, draft dodgers, and those seeking alternative lifestyles to urban living. As demographics began to change, traditional occupations became less profitable; and as more and more artists, writers, and retirees escaped to the islands, the economic profile, now largely dependent on tourism, began to shift.

Regardless, most residents still choose to live here on island time and tend to resent any progress or development that might counter their rural tranquility. But affluent professionals, retired executives, dot.com millionaires, and others are seeking to put their money into vacation properties. Rest assured, the islands are terrific places to visit, and seldom will a visitor come across some of the beneath-the-surface controversial issues of island living. For example, because many new homes are built to comfort-driven specs with spa-like bathrooms, dishwashers, and hot tubs, water usage is a huge issue. City migrants aren't always connected to the islands' conservation efforts and, while their awareness may stretch to the installation of things like low-flush toilets, such token efforts are often negated when a home has multiple bathrooms. Furthermore, although every property has its own well, few homeowners realize that individual wells actually share the same underground aqueduct, so when water spews up mud and silt early on in the summer, it quickly puts a strain on neighborly relations.

Economic sustainability is another issue that divides the old and new. Construction might benefit the local economy in the short term, but the long-term implications are proving to be a different reality. Because homes are purchased as vacation properties, owners are rarely resident and, as such, do not participate in community-sustaining activities such as volunteering for the local fire department or helping run the library. And, as buying sprees push the price of real estate upwards, it becomes less affordable for people to live and work on the islands. Consequently, there's an underlying "them versus us" mentality, though locals may not be eager to let you know that. Islanders need the dollars that vacation-home owners bring, and the construction industry, in particular, is more than willing to take their money. They'll juggle one project with another, and yet another, until completion deadlines come and go, resulting in some new property owners shipping in entire crews from the mainland just to get the job done on time and on budget. Much to the further chagrin of islanders, of course.

Vancouver Island is quite distinct from its smaller cousins. With a broader population base and a diverse economy of its own, this island is in the throes of change and exceptional growth, in spite of the recession—islanders have a knack for reinventing themselves, so it's not unusual to find ex–commercial fishermen and lumberjacks now guiding or running B&Bs. Tourism is taking off into the stratosphere. Like the rest of British Columbia, there are still many wilderness areas flying below the radar, but the flood of adventurous spirits is dragging them into the mainstream. You need look no farther than the quota system now in place for the West Coast Trail. Families, retirees, and wealthy Albertans are the main thrust of the island's population growth, first in Victoria and then, driven by affordability, in communities such as Nanaimo, Port

Alberni, and Parksville. They are discovering a kinder place to live than hard-edged Toronto or cliquey Vancouver.

If Vancouver Island is becoming the trendy place to live, Victoria has become chic. No longer is the city filled solely with pensioners and civil servants. That said, this is the provincial capital, and British Columbia politics have a time-honored tradition of being anything but dull.

In spite of the many sandal-clad people you'll meet on the islands, and the left-wing discourse of many citizens, British Columbia is surprisingly fond of right-wing parties. Only 14 years of the last 50 have favored left-leaning governments from the New Democratic Party, likely due in part to three scandalous Premier resignations. Although the "Liberal Party" is currently in government, it is in fact mostly made up of right-wingers who migrated to the party when their own went defunct a few years back.

The result? The lawns of the legislature host frequent rallies against poverty, homelessness, and forest clear-cuts, or groups supporting the legalization of marijuana or a woman's right to choose such things as an abortion. Aboriginal rights, particularly settling land claims, which British Columbia continues to pioneer, are a long-standing issue that usually draws a crowd. But remember, this is Canada, where "niceties" prevail, so even though you now have the inside track on issues, most protests are polite, well-mannered affairs where encounters in civil disobedience are handled with decorum and a handshake! Besides, isn't it this confluence of diversity—in its people, creative make-up, and geography—that makes this part of the world so richly appealing?

LOOKING BACK AT ISLAND HISTORY

The histories of these Pacific Northwest islands are inextricably linked. Geographically, the islands are part of the same archipelago that runs up the western-most coast of the continent, tucked against mainland British Columbia and the north shore of Washington State's Olympic Peninsula. Only climate and formal boundaries have evolved to take on particular characteristics that now set them apart, whether they are the mists that cling to the northerly Queen Charlottes, or the American-British story that textures much of San Juan Island.

The Early Years

If you were on a boat and oblivious to any bureaucratic boundaries, you would be traveling in and around islands in much the same way as their earliest inhabitants. Native Americans (referred to as First Nations in Canada), such as the Coast Salish, Samish, and Lummi peoples, led a semi-nomadic life here, harvesting the abundant supplies of salmon, growing crops in the protected landscapes, and sourcing supplies of wild berries. Throughout the islands, the Native influence is still evident. Middens of oyster shells, charcoal, and fish bone mark the site of many a summer camp, petroglyphs can be seen on rock faces, and burial sites are still being discovered.

Archaeologists date these early inhabitants to as far back as 9,000 years ago; by the time European contact was made in the mid–18th century, these peoples had developed a sophisticated social system with elaborate rituals, art, and spiritual beliefs that represented a way of life in harmony with their natural, wild surroundings.

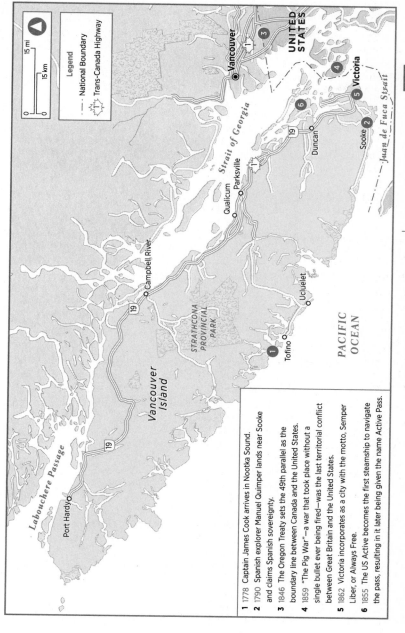

Legend
- National Boundary
- Trans-Canada Highway

United States

Vancouver

Victoria

Sooke

Duncan

Qualicum

Parksville

Campbell River

Ucluelet

Tofino

Port Hardy

Strait of Georgia

Juan de Fuca Strait

Vancouver Island

STRATHCONA PROVINCIAL PARK

PACIFIC OCEAN

Labouchere Passage

1 1778 Captain James Cook arrives in Nootka Sound.

2 1790 Spanish explorer Manuel Quimper lands near Sooke and claims Spanish sovereignty.

3 1846 The Oregon Treaty sets the 49th parallel as the boundary line between Canada and the United States.

4 1859 "The Pig War"—a war that took place without a single bullet ever being fired—was the last territorial conflict between Great Britain and the United States.

5 1862 Victoria incorporates as a city with the motto, Semper Liber, or Always Free.

6 1855 The US Active becomes the first steamship to navigate the pass, resulting in it later being given the name Active Pass.

The farther north you travel, the more evidence remains, especially in places such as Duncan, Alert Bay, and the Queen Charlottes. Here, ancient Haida totem poles sink under the weight of heavy moss, their history returning to the earth just as the Haida pit houses have already done. Little attempt is being made to restore them, since the Haida consider their slow, natural demise to be a part of the life cycle. *Aho* (and so it is).

European Exploration

Although the *Golden Hind* is rumored to have visited the region during Sir Francis Drake's circumnavigation of the world in the 16th century, serious exploration didn't commence until some 200 years later. The Spanish who had long been present in Mexico and Central America, started to spread their territorial claims north.

The Spanish frigate *Santiago* was the first to venture up the coast, in 1774, traveling as far as the Queen Charlottes. Although none of her crew set foot on shore (this was to happen on a return trip with the *Sonora* the following year), they traded goods with the Haida peoples there, ship to canoe. Storms forced the ship to take shelter in the protected waters of Nootka Sound, which 16 years later would become a focal point in history. Trading with members of the Nuu-chah-nulth and Nootka peoples, the Spanish left behind four silver spoons, which in 1790 Spain would cite as evidence that they had reached the region before the arrival of Captain James Cook in 1778.

During the late 1700s, European exploration of the area was particularly frenetic. By then, it involved a competitive quest to find the Northwest Passage as much as claiming sovereignty. They were turbulent times: Spain had sided with France against Britain in the fight for American independence; the French Revolution was in full throttle; and the Russians were growing their fur trading interests through the Clayoquot and Queen Charlottes. Consequently, claims to Nootka Sound were never far from mind, especially for long-standing rivals Spain and Britain.

With relations between the two nations as tense as ever, Britain dispatched Captain George Vancouver to represent British interests. In 1792, he traveled up from the Gulf Islands, charting the region en route while his Spanish counterparts, Galiano and Valdes, were doing the same. It wasn't long before the three parties were sharing information, and their work formed the basis of a series of Nootka Conventions which, eventually, led to the negotiation of a mutual withdrawal from the region.

Collaboration was also expediently practical: The British ships were large and quick, so they covered more territory, while the small, Spanish ships could maneuver narrow inlets and shallow waters. But still, the prevailing distrust caused each to double-check the other's work and, often, a topographical feature that was named by one was then renamed by the other. When American explorer Charles Wilkes arrived some time later (1841), he added to the confusion. Armed with only British maps, he revised most of the Spanish names to bear patriotically American names, mostly for heroes of the War of 1812. By 1847, map names were such a muddle that the British Admiralty reorganized and created official charts of the region—keeping most of the British and Spanish names, and removing most of Wilkes's, save for a few such as Chauncey, Shaw, Decatur, Lawrence, and Percival.

Commercial Expansion

The gold rushes of 1858 (Fraser River), 1862 (the Cariboo), and 1898 (the Yukon) really put the Pacific Northwest on the map. Hopeful pioneers started to settle the larger islands, and still today, there is many an old orchard and early homestead that

Name That Island

- The San Juan Islands were given the name by the Spanish explorer Francisco de Eliza, who charted the islands in 1791.
- The Gulf Islands were named in 1792 for Captain Vancouver's belief that they were located in a gulf, and although he was later proven wrong, the name stuck.
- Vancouver Island was originally called Quadra and Vancouver's island, in recognition of the joint explorations of Captain Vancouver and Captain Bodega y Quadra.
- When he returned to the region in 1794, Captain Cook was the first to circumnavigate Vancouver Island, thus proving it to be an island.
- In 1846, the Oregon Treaty established the 49th parallel as the boundary between Canada and the United States. Although both sides agreed Vancouver Island would remain British, jurisdiction was vague regarding the San Juans. Tensions exploded when an American farmer, Lyman Cutler, shot a British-owned pig that was overly partial to his potato patch (settlers had to row 24km/15 miles across the Strait of Juan de Fuca to the Olympic Peninsula to get seed for crops, so pork rustling was no small matter). Troops were readied, British war ships gathered, and conflict seemed imminent. The Kaiser of Germany eventually arbitrated that the Americans had a stronger claim to the islands. The Pig War is the only war to occur without a shot ever being fired, and was the last territorial conflict between the United States and Great Britain.

bear testimony to these once-thriving communities. Because of its location, midway between Victoria and the mainland, Miners Bay on Mayne Island became a resting point before crossing the Strait of Georgia. It was the commercial hub for all of the islands, and for years afterwards, the postmasters from Galiano and Pender islands had to row to Mayne Island to collect the mail.

Meanwhile, American blacks, Germans, Scandinavians, and Portuguese established produce farms on the San Juans and Salt Spring; the Japanese came with their salteries; and the Hawaiians, working for the Hudson's Bay Company, also settled here—St. Paul's Catholic Church in Fulford Harbour on Salt Spring was built largely with Hawaiian labor. In the Queen Charlottes, whaling stations employed Native Canadians and hundreds of Chinese who migrated here after the completion of Canada's trans-Canada railroad in 1869. Whaling continued through to the 1930s, leaving behind both commercial remnants and beachcombing treasures of whale teeth and bone.

As with so much of Canada, the most significant settlement in this region was the Hudson Bay community in Victoria on Vancouver Island. First established in 1843, it became an important center for trading furs and a supply center for the thousands of prospectors en route to the mainland's gold. Intent on securing an empire where "the sun never set," Victorian Britain coveted this westernmost outpost of the Americas and its new Dominion of Canada, and set out to carve its likeness out of the coastal wilderness. Today, that British influence permeates a palpable charm throughout the peninsula; although, like all these island destinations, it is enjoying a far quieter pace than its rough-and-tumble beginnings.

THE LAY OF THE LAND

Although many of the 700 or so islands in the archipelago disappear at high tide, there are still about 400 or so to explore. Some are no more than a raised tuft of land; others are wildlife sanctuaries or privately owned paradises.

The largest, Vancouver Island, seems to capture the essence of all its smaller counterparts. Stretching 520km (323 miles) southeast to northwest, and with an average width of 100km (62 miles), it covers an area comparable to countries such as the Netherlands or Taiwan, yet the population is under 1 million. Greater Victoria, the largest community, has approximately 350,000; the second largest city is Nanaimo, with a regional district population nearing 132,000. Down its spine, mountains divide the island into two distinct areas, and the result is a glorious mix of urban sophistication; busy fishing; market and logging towns; and most especially, a coast and wilderness as rugged as they were so long ago.

Vancouver Island, the Gulf Islands, and the San Juan Islands are actually the remaining mountain tops of a receding continent much older than the American mainland. Consequently, islands are generally quite hilly, with some flat areas and fertile valleys in between featuring plenty of old-growth forests. Look for cedar; Douglas fir; hemlock; spruce; yew; and most especially, *madrona* (also known as arbutus), which cling to the cliffs at precarious 45-degree angles. Coastlines are a mix of reef-studded bays, and sandy and rock-strewn beaches, which make for great clambering adventures and tidal pools.

Because of the protective shadowing of the nearby American and Canadian mountain ranges, the islands get less rainfall than Vancouver or Seattle. The Gulf Islands, in particular, can get less than 30 inches of rain a year, so water shortages are not uncommon in summer, and even though temperatures don't reach sizzling heights, fire-hazard signs move quickly from no-risk green to high-alert red in the space of a few days.

DATELINE

1790 On June 30, the native people of Albert Head (now part of Sooke) discover Spanish explorer Manuel Quimper on their beach, claiming the land in the name of the king of Spain.

1842 James Douglas, Chief Factor, the Hudson's Bay Fur Trading Company, selects Victoria as the site for the company's new depot.

1843 Douglas decides to build a fort at the Inner Harbour, and it is eventually named Fort Victoria (now Bastion Square).

1846 On June 15, the Oregon Treaty sets the boundary line with the United States as the 49th parallel.

1849 The British government grants Vancouver Island to the Hudson's Bay Company for 7 shillings a year, stipulating that it must establish settlements of colonists on the island within 5 years.

1850 Richard Blanshard becomes Vancouver Island's first governor.

1858 The mainland's gold rush turns Victoria into an important community, funneling some

Conservation

The San Juans together comprise San Juan County, one of the smallest counties in Washington State. The county seat is at Friday Harbor, the islands' largest and only incorporated town; despite their size, the San Juans boast over 15 parks and nature preserves, and almost as many national sites. In total, the county claims to have approximately 27% of its land area protected.

The Gulf Islands, on the other hand, are partially governed by the Islands Trust, a government-related bureaucracy, which has a unique legislated mandate for protecting and preserving the islands, primarily through land-use planning and regulation. As island commerce increases, the Trust becomes the bane of their existence; for example, Salts Spring Island Coffee has moved its headquarters to Vancouver in order to expand. Protected areas in the Islands Trust Area now constitute over 15% of the area's land base—more than 987 hectares (2,439 acres). On some islands, landowners can even register a conservation covenant and benefit from reduced property taxes. One of the Trust's most recent and significant accomplishments has set an example to be modeled for the province. Working with the Hul'qumi'num Treaty Group, the Trust has helped negotiate a one-of-a-kind agreement to protect aboriginal "sacred" or "spiritual" places, in addition to and apart from archaeological sites that already receive protection. Such an agreement could have prevented the destruction of such First Nations treasures as the spirit caves at Bear Mountain Resort on Vancouver Island.

Since the population is predicted to increase by 35% over the next decade, it will become more and more difficult to maintain such unspoiled environs. Already, ecosystems and special habitats are threatened, with water usage being the most obvious problem.

25,000 miners and their supplies to the gold camps—giving rise to Market Square and Victoria's tiny, bustling Chinatown, one of North America's oldest.

1862 Victoria incorporates as a city; the first gas lights go up over the front doors of the saloons; and in September, the Tynemouth, a "bride ship" from England, arrives carrying 61 "well-built, pretty-looking young women, ages varying from 14 to an uncertain figure; a few are young widows who have seen better days" (*Victoria Press*).

1871 British Columbia enters Confederation; Victoria is named the provincial capital; and in December, Emily Carr is born at Carr House at the northeast corner of Government and Simcoe streets.

1882 The Hudson's Bay Company gifts Beacon Hill Park to the City of Victoria.

1895 Fort Rodd Hill is established as a military outpost, where gun batteries are built to protect the Royal Navy base on Esquimalt Harbour from the Americans.

continues

2

THE ISLANDS IN DEPTH | The Lay of the Land

ONE smart TREE

The arbutus, also known as the strawberry tree for its reddish bark, is the only deciduous tree that does not lose its leaves in winter. Rather, new leaves grow each spring and the old ones fall off, similar to pine needles, but the tree is never naked. The *madrona*, as it is also called, is never far from the ocean, growing to over 30m (98 ft.) and living to 500 years old. Because it tends to choose rough terrain and rocky cliffs, where water runoff is rapid, it stores water in its burls and grows at extraordinary angles, constantly bending in search of light. The Salish peoples honor it as their Tree of Knowledge because it knows how to find the sun.

Natural Resources

Wherever you are on the islands, you're likely to come across designated national wildlife refuges, and just as likely to notice the number of bird species—more than 250 of them! Situated on the Pacific Flyway, a major bird migration route, you have the opportunity to see bald eagles, hawks, ospreys, woodpeckers, and hummingbirds, as well as shorebirds such as blue herons, oystercatchers, snow geese, and trumpeter swans. These inland waters also are one of the richest marine environments in the world. In addition to harbor seals, Steller sea lions, Dall porpoises, and sea otters, there are resident and transient whale pods that can be seen year-round.

Exploring or exploiting the islands' natural attributes is a double-edged sword for tourism. Sea kayaking, spelunking, wilderness hikes, and wildlife safaris depend on maintaining the islands' fragile ecosystem which, to date, is showing remarkable resilience. The endangered Vancouver Island marmot is making a comeback, as are the Roosevelt deer. Offshore, the story is less optimistic. The rich fishing grounds up around the Queen

1898 The Provincial Legislature Buildings are completed.

1908 The Canadian Pacific Railway completes the Empress Hotel.

1910 William Gibson becomes the first person in Canada to design, build, and fly his own aircraft when he takes to the air at Mount Tolmie.

1914 World War I breaks out. The Patricia Bay Airport is constructed as a training site for the Allied forces. Today, it operates as Victoria International Airport.

1918 The Dominion Astrophysical Observatory on Little Saanich Mountain showcases the largest telescope in the world at that time.

1932 The first Sidney-to-Anacortes ferry, the *City of Angels*, makes its inaugural run.

1962 The Trans-Canada Highway finishes at Victoria, establishing Mile 0.

1986 Victoria experiences the longest period of rainfall of any Canadian city: 33 consecutive days.

1994 Victoria hosts the XV Commonwealth Games.

Charlottes are showing strain; runs are down, and fish farms breeding Atlantic salmon in Pacific salmon waters are a contentious issue. Sea lice are an epidemic.

Logging, too, continues to be a debatable hot button. The smaller islands (Galiano being a prime example) have managed to reclaim much of their territory from timber companies, but on northern Vancouver Island and in the back waters near Clayoquot Sound (a UNESCO-protected biosphere), logging is still a mainstay of the economy and a rich resource for the province. Although current logging practices include a comprehensive re-plantation program, there remains an innate distrust between tree-hugger and logging company which, every so often, spawns a protest or two when virgin timber comes under threat.

THE ISLANDS IN POPULAR CULTURE: BOOKS, FILM & TV

Detour down the most unlikely country lane, and you're liable to find a barn transformed into a potter's studio or a garden shed converted into a painter's workspace. And once you've visited the islands, you'll start to recognize just how many books and movies use their diverse landscapes as backdrops.

Books

If there is one title that epitomizes the juxtapositions you'll find in this part of the world, it's the book *Fishing with John* (Harbour Publishing), an unusual West Coast love story of a sophisticated New York journalist who gives it all up to marry an impassioned and greatly talented coastal fisherman with a particular distaste for pretension. Although true, the story reads like fiction, and established its author, Edith Iglauer, as one of BC's most popular writers. It was later made into a movie: *Navigating the Heart,* starring Jaclyn Smith and Tim Matheson.

Vancouver Island resident John Hodgins has a battery of books to his name, many of which are set on and around the island, from *Innocent Cities* (Emblem Editions), based in Victoria, to others that take place in the lush green forests, pulp mills, and seas. *Spit Delaney's Island* (Macmillan of Canada) is a compelling collection of short fiction and a good introduction to the author's ability to mingle history, personal experience, and imagination. His other island-based, award-winning titles include *Resurrection of Joseph Byrne* (Macmillan of Canada; Governor General's Award for Fiction); *Invention of the World* (Ronsdale Press; Gibson's First Novel Award); and *Honorary Patron* (McClelland & Stewart; Commonwealth Regional Prize).

More books that touch on island culture include *The Darkening Archipelago* (NeWest Press), by Victoria writer-activist Stephen Legault, who stages this environmental mystery thriller, the second in a series, around salmon farming. *The Cardinal Divide* (NeWest Press) was his first. In *The Empress Letters* (Cormorant Books), by Linda Rogers, Victoria's poet laureate until November 2011, you'll find a sea voyage in the '20s mixed with opium secrets and a few cameos by island notables like Emily Carr and frequent visitor Tallulah Bankhead. And where else but Victoria would you expect to find a hard-boiled Coast Salish aboriginal detective? In Stanley Evans' *Seaweed* series (TouchWood; five titles to date and counting), Silas Seaweed is on the case, keeping city streets and island regions safe with a trademark blend of Coast Salish mythology and mysticism.

If the written word is love, then Patrick Lane's critically acclaimed *There Is a Season* (McClelland & Stewart) is a must-read. Although the book is a memoir about the author's relationship between his garden and his own recovery from alcoholism, the words are so beautifully crafted, they read more like poetry and come together as perhaps the definitive book about the Victoria, aka the Garden City.

With an eye on the capitol, nothing helps you understand a place better than getting a sense of how it has grown up. In *My Turquoise Years* (Greystone Books), M.A.C. Farrant remembers the region in the '50s and '60s with sweet nostalgia, without ever becoming cloying. Then there's Tara Saracuse's *Island Kids* (Brindle & Glass), great because it's all about how kids helped shaped Vancouver Island's collective history, from its aboriginal origins to some lesser-known moments of the 20th century. It's a charming read that will appeal to both young and old readers alike.

As for resource titles, the following suggestions will broaden your experience of the islands, depending on your interests. Poet Don McKay's *Deactivated West 100* (Gaspereau) follows the landscapes of a deactivated logging road (hence the title) in what has been described as a "geo-poetic" exploration. *Whales of the West Coast* (Harbour), by David A. E. Spalding, answers every question you ever had about whales and dolphins of the West Coast, including their natural history, aboriginal and commercial whaling practices, current conservation issues, and a month-by-month list of when and where whales regularly appear.

When you're on the San Juan Islands, look for *Magic Islands: A Treasure-Trove of San Juan Islands Lore* (Orcas Publishers), by David Richardson, and *San Juan: The Powder-Keg Island: The Settler's Own Stories* (Beach Combers), by Jo Bailey-Cummings and Al Cummings. Both titles offer the flavor of cultural and anecdotal history of the islands' earliest settlers and their families. One of the most inspired coffee-table books about the Gulf Islands is *Enchanted Isles: The Southern Gulf Islands* (Harbour), by author David A. E. Spalding and photographer Kevin Oke—it's packed with history, information, and stunning photography.

Films

In terms of movies, *Double Jeopardy* (starring Tommy Lee Jones and Ashley Judd) manages to incorporate many of the islands' attributes—stunning scenery from oceanfront homes, misty coastlines, and passenger ferry "chases"—while other films use the area

Famous Islanders

The islands have a remarkable collection of celebrities, past and present, who either grew up here or have decided to make this their home.

- Robert Bateman, painter: lives on Salt Spring Island
- Rick Hansen, wheelchair athlete: born in Port Alberni
- Pamela Anderson, actor: born in Ladysmith
- Randy Bachman, musician: lives on Salt Spring Island
- Diana Krall, jazz musician: born in Nanaimo
- Kim Cattrall, actor: raised in the Comox Valley
- Alex Shapiro, singer/composer: lives in the San Juan Islands
- Warren Miller, filmmaker and ski/snowboard legend: lives on Orcas Island

more generically. A sampling of movies filmed here include *Insomnia* (Robin Williams, Al Pacino); *Clan of the Cave Bear* (Darryl Hannah); *Cats & Dogs* (Jeff Goldblum, Elizabeth Perkins); *Lake Placid* (Bill Pullman, Bridget Fonda); *Little Women* (Winona Ryder, Gabriel Byrne, Kirsten Dunst); *The Scarlet Letter* (Demi Moore, Gary Oldman, Robert Duvall); *X2* and *X-Men: The Last Stand* (Patrick Stewart, Ian McKellen, Halle Berry); *Chronicles of Narnia: Prince Caspian* (Ben Barnes); *Fierce People* (Diane Lane, Donald Sutherland); and *The 13th Warrior* (Antonio Banderas).

EATING & DRINKING IN THE ISLANDS

The 100-mile diet—a philosophy of eating based on consuming only what originates within that radius—started in Vancouver, so it is little wonder that the West Coast has taken to the concept with almost obsessive ownership. And this becomes all the more evident once you set foot on any of the islands which, by their very nature, have always tried to practice self sufficiency. Put the two dynamics together, and you have an agritourism scene that—in the last 5 years, in particular—is taking the region by storm. Local food is not just a fad, it is part of a 130-country-strong Slow Food movement, and Vancouver Island is one of its epicenters—Cowichan Bay is even named as North America's first certified CittaSlow (as in Slow City) community.

Vancouver Island has set the pace, largely because it has the climate, resources, and population base to sustain an agricultural economy made up of an enviable wine scene (including meaderies and artisan distilleries) and fresh produce farms that run the gamut from raising alpaca llamas for handmade cloth to venison and bison for smoked meats, hand-crafted cheeses, and more. Add to this the natural bounty of the land—rainforests filled with chanterelle mushrooms, beaches awash with healthful seaweed, and oceans abundant with salmon, halibut, oysters, and crab—and you quickly realize why islanders have adapted the 100-mile diet to an all-islands enclave (a diet inclusive of all growers and food producers on Vancouver Island and the Gulf Islands). In fact, Seattle and Vancouver are so close, and the exchange of goods between island and mainland so great, that it's estimated that if ever Vancouver Island was left to its own devices, it would have only a 3-day food supply for islanders, even though it has the resources to be agriculturally independent.

Enter the Island Chefs Collaborative (ICC), a group of like-minded Vancouver Island chefs who shared the vision to create a sustainable food and agricultural system on Vancouver Island and the Gulf Islands. When they visited farms and producers, chefs were amazed at what was available, and in turn, local farmers were often surprised by what chefs wanted to cook with. The result? Competing chefs readily share knowledge and sources with one another, and farmers have become both niche-market savvy and creative. The partners often sit down with seed catalogues together to choose what should be grown for the following year, and it is the reason why more and more menus are able to include items such as prosciutto from locally-raised pigs, heirloom tomato varieties, and exotic chards. Since establishing itself in 1999, the ICC movement has done much to make food from local farmers, fishers, and foragers an integral part of the islands' experience. It even sponsors a new food celebration: **Defending our Backyard Local Food Festival** at Fort Rodd Hill and Fisgard Lighthouse in May, a combination tasting and education event to raise awareness about on-island food sources and how they make their journey to the table. There's everything from oyster shucking and slurping to spit-roasting a pig, alongside wine tasting and interesting specialty products. The island's strong food ethos has also helped to create the **Culinary Tourism Society of BC** (www.bcculinarytourism.com), whereby restaurants earn certification for their culinary excellence, service, and support of local suppliers. To date, it is the first program of its kind in the world. A helpful guide to the island's food culture is Rosemary Neering's book *Eating Up Vancouver Island* (Whitecap Books); while a few years old now, it's still a relevant (and humorous) resource describing the islands' more established farms, wineries, craft breweries, and seafood markets.

The San Juan and Gulf islands may not be as lushly diverse as Vancouver Island, but they still pride themselves on colorful farmers' markets and a buy-direct mentality that supports local fishermen, cheese makers, vineyards, and farms producing organic herbs and edible flowers, greens, meats, and other culinary delights. Heritage and organic fruit orchards dot the countryside on all the islands (tours and visits are often available), and local producers are the primary source for most island restaurants. In the San Juans, many suppliers and restaurants participate in an Islands Certified Local program (the longest transport time between any of the islands is only 1 hour, so food is certainly fresh). Look for the ICL emblem in restaurant windows. Check out **Farm Products Guides** for Lopez, Orcas, and San Juan, which describe those farms and orchards open to the public. Downloadable guides are available on the WSU Cooperative Extension/San Juan County website: http://sanjuan.wsu.edu/agriculture.

PLANNING YOUR TRIP TO VANCOUVER ISLAND, THE GULF ISLANDS & THE SAN JUAN ISLANDS

The islands of the Pacific Northwest are captivating, and their charm certainly invites impromptu getaway visits. Advance planning, however, will save you time, money, and worry, and is what this chapter is all about. It covers the necessary nuts and bolts to help you plan a successful trip.

For additional help in planning your trip, and for more on-the-ground resources in Vancouver Island, the Gulf Islands, and the San Juan Islands, please turn to "Fast Facts," on p. 270.

WHEN TO GO

There's a reason for the lush, green landscape, bountiful flowers, and rich agricultural fields in the Pacific Northwest. It's called rain. So, while you're enjoying the milder temperatures, always tote an umbrella.

In **March,** Victoria boasts the first spring blooms in Canada, parading its daffodils on television newscasts across a country still bound in much chillier climes. It's also a signal for travelers to hit the road. Although weather can still be a little unsettled, the deals on accommodations and uncrowded restaurants are worth the effort of carrying an umbrella. By

May, cherry blossoms and tulips dot the islands, leading the way to a summer that enjoys at least 16 hours of daylight per day, temperatures that push the mercury to around 77°F (25°C), and a monthly rainfall that averages barely 2.5cm (1 in.). This is **high season,** when the islands seem on perpetual parade. **September** or **October** is a golden time to visit. The days are still long, there's warmth in the air, and the leaves turn to hues of yellow, gold, and red. With the kids back in school, attractions aren't as jam-packed; getaway packages offer great savings. The winter season, from **November** to **February,** sees more rain than snow, which, if it falls at all, dissolves into the atmosphere within hours. But snow does settle in the mountains and on Vancouver Island's northernmost reaches, making skiing and snowboarding popular pastimes. Along the westernmost coast of Vancouver Island, **winter storms** from the open Pacific Ocean are so dramatic that savvy marketers have successfully created a new high season specifically geared to storm watchers. Yet, for all the rain, gray days are still outnumbered by beautiful, crisp weather, especially in the San Juan Islands.

Vancouver Island's Average Temperature & Precipitation

	JAN	FEB	MAR	APR	MAY	JUNE	JULY	AUG	SEPT	OCT	NOV	DEC
Temp. (°F)	39°	41°	45°	46°	52°	61°	66°	66°	63°	45°	45°	41°
Temp. (°C)	4°	5°	7°	8°	11°	16°	19°	19°	17°	7°	7°	5°
Precip. (in./cm)	3.6/9.1	2.6/6.6	1.7/4.3	1.5/3.8	.9/2.3	.7/1.8	.6/1.5	0.8/2	1.3/3.3	2.3/5.8	3.6/9.1	3.9/9.9

Note: Temperature may vary among different parts of Vancouver Island by as much as 7.2° to 9°F (4°–5°C); precipitation varies, as well. For example, you can expect the northern regions to be the coolest and the Cowichan Valley to be the warmest. Also, the west coast usually gets more precipitation than the east coast. The above chart can be used as a general gauge for conditions on the Gulf and San Juan islands, as well. For island-specific readings, contact the local chambers of commerce or visitor information centers.

Calendar of Events

Island events tend to be community oriented and not as finessed as you would find in big city centers. Weather dictates that most activities take place in the summer months, except for those celebrating wildlife migrations. Victoria and Nanaimo stage the most special events, though you're likely to find small festivities, such as outdoor summer concerts and fall agricultural fairs, on any one of the Gulf and San Juan islands, as well as in Vancouver Island's rural communities. The San Juan Islands Visitors Bureau (✆ **360/378-6822;** www.visit sanjuans.com) or Tourism Vancouver Island (✆ **250/754-3500;** www.vancouverisland.travel), which also covers the Gulf Islands, can provide further details. For an exhaustive list of events beyond those listed here, check http://events.frommers.com, where you'll find a searchable, up-to-the-minute roster of what's happening in cities and communities all over the world.

JANUARY

Annual Bald Eagle Count, Goldstream Provincial Park, Vancouver Island. When the salmon swim up Goldstream Provincial Park's spawning streams, more than 300 bald eagles take up residence with an eye to a month-long feast. Call ✆ **250/478-9414** for exact dates and events.

FEBRUARY

Chinese New Year, Victoria, Vancouver Island. This is when the Chinese traditionally pay their debts and forgive old grievances to start the new lunar year with a clean slate. The Chinese community rings it in with firecrackers, dancing dragon parades, and other festivities. Late January or early February.

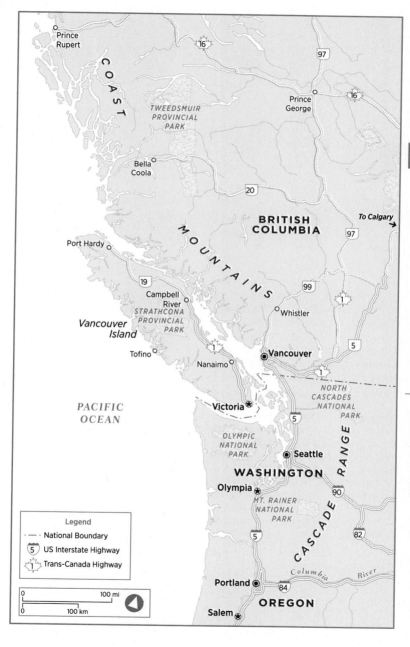

Prince
Rupert

16

97

C O A S T

TWEEDSMUIR
PROVINCIAL
PARK

Prince
George

16

Bella
Coola

20

BRITISH
COLUMBIA

To Calgary

97

Port Hardy

M O U N T A I N S

99

1

19

Campbell
River

STRATHCONA
PROVINCIAL
PARK

Whistler

Vancouver
Island

Tofino

1

Nanaimo

Vancouver

5

1

Victoria

PACIFIC
OCEAN

NORTH
CASCADES
NATIONAL
PARK

5

OLYMPIC
NATIONAL
PARK

C A S C A D E   R A N G E

Seattle

WASHINGTON

Olympia

MT. RAINER
NATIONAL
PARK

90

5

82

Legend

------ National Boundary

5 US Interstate Highway

1 Trans-Canada Highway

Columbia   River

Portland

84

0   100 mi

0   100 km

Salem

OREGON

Literary Festival, Galiano Island. It's still somewhat embryonic, but local luminaries of all writing genres give clout to this mid-winter gathering of readings, workshops, and socializing with your favorite authors. For information, contact ☏ **250/539-3340** or www.galianoislandbooks.com.

Trumpeter Swan Festival, Comox Valley, Vancouver Island. A weeklong festival celebrating these magnificent white birds that gather in the Comox Valley. Call the **Tourism Association of Vancouver Island** (☏ **250/754-3500**) for exact dates.

MARCH

Pacific Rim Whale Festival, Pacific Rim National Park Region, Vancouver Island. Every spring, mid-March through early April, more than 20,000 grey whales migrate past Vancouver Island's west coast, attracting visitors from all over the world. It's a colorful celebration featuring live crab races, storytelling, parades, art shows, guided whale-spotting hikes, and whale-watching excursions in zippy Zodiacs. For information, call Tourism Ucluelet (☏ **250/726-4641**) or Tourism Tofino (☏ **250/725-3414**), or visit www.pacificrimwhalefestival.com.

APRIL

Brant Wildlife Festival, Parksville/Qualicum Beach, Vancouver Island. A birder's nirvana, this 3-day celebration focuses on the annual black brant migration through the area from Mexico to Alaska (20,000 birds). The event includes guided walks through old-growth forest, and saltwater and freshwater marshes; goose-viewing stations; a birding competition; art, photography, and carving exhibitions; and numerous children's activities. For exact dates, contact ☏ **866/288-7878** or www.brantfestival.bc.ca.

Victoria Hot Jazz Jubilee, Sidney, Vancouver Island. A small, 3-day seaside festival that attracts traditional jazz, swing, bebop, fusion, Dixie, and blues musicians from all over North America. It offers top music with a parochial charm. Call ☏ **250/882-JAZZ** (250/882-5299) for performance venues and schedules.

Victoria Harbour Floating Boat Show, Victoria, Vancouver Island. If boating is your thing, this floating show takes up most of the harbor with more than 150 new and pre-owned boats on display, as well as numerous marine-related products, from electronics and diving gear to dinghies. Call ☏ **250/416-0097** for details.

MAY

Swiftsure Weekend, Victoria and Vancouver Island. More than 200 vessels navigate the unpredictable coastal waters in this, the oldest and largest offshore overnight sailing race in the Pacific Northwest. In 2008, it celebrated its 65th anniversary. It is as exciting to watch as it is to participate. Call the **Royal Victoria Yacht Club** (☏ **250/592-2441**) for information.

Artists' Studios Open House, San Juan Island. An island-wide open house featuring weavers, potters, and other craftspeople. Call ☏ **360/378-5594** for information. Last weekend in May or early June.

Scottish Highland Games, Victoria. It's everything you might expect from bonny Scotland: the caber toss and haggis hurl; the kilted mile; and pipe band, drumming, and dancing competitions. Athletes come from countries worldwide. Contact www.victoria highlandgames.com for details. Mid-May.

JUNE

Boat Festival, Cowichan Bay, Vancouver Island. Classic boats, a boat-building house for children, Dragon Boat races, folk singers, and dancing are some of the fun activities of this festival. The Fast-and-Furious Boat Building Contest is a highlight: Entrants build a boat and race it within 4 hours! Call the **Cowichan Bay Maritime Centre** for exact dates (☏ **250/746-4955**).

Multicultural Festival, Nanaimo, Vancouver Island. Since its inaugural festival in 2005, Nanaimo has earned the title of Cultural Capital of Canada, and this event is the official celebration of the city's international mosaic. It starts with Aboriginal Day and ends on Canada Day, July 1, in between which the downtown core features live entertainment, ethnic foods, information exhibits, a children's area, contests, and prizes. ☎ **250/754-8141.**

TD Victoria International JazzFest, Victoria. More than 90 performances take place in 13 of the coolest venues around Victoria. Watch for artists like Grammy winner George Benson and others. Jazz Victoria also organizes **Blues Bash** every Labor Day weekend in the Inner Harbour. Contact ☎ **250/388-4423** or www.jazzvictoria.ca for details.

JULY

Nanaimo Marine Festival, Nanaimo, Vancouver Island. Lots of activities take place around the harbor, culminating in the famous Bathtub Race between the city of Nanaimo and Kitsilano Beach, in Vancouver. Yes, it's exactly what it sounds like—racers scrunched up in racer-designed bathtub look-alikes that may or may not make it across the chop. Contact **Tourism Nanaimo** (☎ **800/663-7337**) or the **Loyal Nanaimo Bathtub Society** (☎ **250/753-7223**) for information.

Organic Islands Festival & Sustainability Expo, Glendale Gardens, Victoria. Learn more about healthy lifestyle choices from an array of organic companies, sustainability advocates, green businesses, fair traders, food producers, health practitioners, restaurateurs, and vintners. Details at ☎ **250/479-6162** and www.organicislands.ca.

Rodeo Days & KiteFest, Coombs & Parksville, Vancouver Island. Bull riding, steer wrestling, roping, and traditional barn dancing make up this western-style family event. Call ☎ **250/248-1009** for details. The dates always coincide with a community Kite Festival in nearby Parksville, where kite flying and championship flight rallies create quite a sky-spectacle. Call ☎ **250/248-6300.**

Lavender Festival, Salt Spring Island. Set amidst rolling hills of lavender, atop Sacred Mountain, this festival features all manner of lavender-related arts, from cheesecake to ice creams and hand-crafted soap, scented wands, and oils. Artists set up shop, too, as do Morris Dancers. Call ☎ **250/653-2315** for dates and details. Early July.

Festival of Murals, Chemainus, Vancouver Island. Chemainus is known worldwide for its ever-changing murals. During the festival, visitors have the opportunity to see local and international artists "decorate" the sides of buildings, walls, and more with new murals—pictorials that have included turn-of-the-20th-century farming scenes, wildlife, aboriginal profiles, and whimsical townspeople characters. From mid-July to mid-August.

AUGUST

Parksville Beach Festival, Parksville, Vancouver Island. From late July through most of August, the wide, sandy beaches are transformed with sandcastles of imagination and creativity, alongside a myriad of family activities. This event attracts more than 40,000 people. Call ☎ **250/951-2678** for exact dates and information.

Filberg Festival, Comox, Vancouver Island. Widely considered one of the finest arts festivals in BC, this outdoor art exhibition presents the work of more than 150 artisans from throughout British Columbia and includes entertainment. For ticket information contact ☎ **866/898-8499** or 250/338-2430, or visit www.filbergfestival.com. Early August.

Victoria Dragon Boat Festival, Victoria, Vancouver Island. Traditional dragon-boat races take place in the Inner Harbour, where 120 local and international teams compete. For details, contact ☎ **250/704-2500** or visit www.victoriadragonboat.com. Mid-August.

Symphony Splash, Victoria, Vancouver Island. It lasts only 1 day, but this free event draws a crowd of 40,000 people to hear the Victoria Symphony play from a barge moored in the middle of Victoria's picturesque Inner Harbour. Traditionally, Tchaikovsky's 1812 Overture closes the concert, accompanied by fireworks. Call ☎ **250/385-9771** for details. Early August.

Summertime Blues Festival, Nanaimo and Coombs, Vancouver Island. Usually scheduled one after the other, these bluegrass and blues festivals feature Canada's best artists who play at various venues along Nanaimo's harbor front and in Coombs.

Old-time fiddlers are always headliners. Call Tourism Vancouver Island ℭ **250/754-3500** for dates and specific locations.

Art in the Park, Orcas Island. Held at Moran State Park, this annual event brings together displays by local artists and traditional craftspeople who are normally scattered throughout the San Juan Islands. For information, call ℭ **360/376-2273.**

Saanich Fall Fair, Saanichton, Vancouver Island. The oldest agricultural fair in Western Canada showcases livestock, sheep shearing, show jumping, crafts, produce, home baking, and more. Lots of candy floss and old-style country fun, including a fiddle competition. Call ℭ **250/652-3314** for information. Early September.

Classic Boat Festival, Victoria. For boat lovers, this is a showcase of maritime heritage, when as many as 140 classically restored boats moor in the Inner Harbour and vie for prizes such as the Best Restored Sail award and the Best Restored Power award. Contact ℭ **250/953-2033** or www.classicboatfestival.ca for information.

The Great Canadian Beer Festival, Victoria, Vancouver Island. Held at the Royal Athletic Park, this outdoor event draws some of British Columbia's best microbreweries in a sampling extravaganza of beers from across Western Canada. Call ℭ **250/383-2332** or visit www.gcbf.com for information. Second week in September.

Harvest of Music, Qualicum Beach, Vancouver Island. Musicians from all over the world, playing everything from Gypsy jazz to Japanese *taiko* drumming, gather for 9 days of performances and workshops. Call ℭ **250/752-6133** for information.

Fall Fair, Salt Spring Island. Originated in 1896, this fair is less sophisticated than the one at Saanich and epitomizes island living as no other. Competition for the biggest dahlias and tastiest pies is hot and heavy; the gymkhana is a hybrid of sheepdog trials

and a pony obstacle course; the exotic range of poultry on show is worth the price of admission; and listening to local musicians while sitting on bales of hay is a throwback to yesteryear. Call ℭ **250-537-5252.**

Cowichan Wine & Culinary Festival, Cowichan Valley, Vancouver Island. As the fastest growing wine region in Canada, the range of fruit-filled wines, cider, and mead you'll find in these islands is matched only by the variety of artisan cheeses, fresh produce, seafood, and herbs. This 3-day annual festival started in 2005 and is already among the top events for food and wine aficionados. Call Tourism Cowichan for details at ℭ **888/303-3337** or visit www.saanichfair.ca. Last weekend in September.

Royal Victorian Marathon, Victoria, Vancouver Island. This annual race attracts runners from around the world. The air is fresh, and the temperature is usually just cool enough to keep the runners moving along a course that's not too strenuous. It's good trainer for the Boston Marathon course, for which it is a qualifier. 2009 represented the run's 30th annual celebration. Call ℭ **250/658-4520** for information. Canadian Thanksgiving weekend (second weekend in Oct).

Savor the San Juans, Lopez, Orcas and San Juan islands. Started in 2008, the islands come together for a month-long medley of culinary and cultural events, such as specialty winemaker dinners, cooking classes, art gallery events, theater performances, and presentations. For information, call ℭ **360/378-6822** or visit www.visitsanjuans.com.

Oyster Festival, Tofino, Vancouver Island. It seems that every chef in the region gets into the act of shucking, slurping, sampling, and pulling together all manner of culinary delights alongside exceptional regional wines and music. During the festival, some 4,000 oysters are consumed. Call Tourism Tofino for details ℭ **250/725-3414.**

The Finale, Nanaimo, Vancouver Island. Unfortunately, most cities found that despite a no-alcohol policy, First Night celebrations encouraged rowdy crowds, and so they shelved them all together.

Nanaimo, however, has modified the concept to create a small family-style gathering at Beban Park with performing arts, fireworks, food stalls, and more. Activities vary each year. Call ℂ **250/756-5200** for details. December 31.`

ENTRY REQUIREMENTS
Passports

It is no longer possible to enter Canada and return to the U.S. by showing a government-issued photo ID (such as a driver's license) and proof of U.S. citizenship (such as a birth or naturalization certificate). The **Western Hemisphere Travel Initiative (WHTI),** which took full effect in 2009, requires all U.S. citizens returning to the U.S. from Canada to have a U.S. passport (this includes children under age 18).

In other words, if you are a U.S. citizen traveling to Canada by air, sea, or land, you must have a valid U.S. passport or a new passport card (see box below) in order to get back into the U.S.

You'll find current entry information on the website of the U.S. State Department at **www.travel.state.gov** and on the Canada Border Services Agency website, **www.cbsa-asfc.gc.ca**.

PASSPORT CARDS: THE new way TO ENTER CANADA FOR U.S. CITIZENS

If you are an American traveling to and from Canada by land or sea in 2010 or 2011, you can do so with the new **passport card** issued by the U.S. Department of State. The department adopted this idea in 2008 after vociferous complaints by border communities that requiring expensive passports for all visitors would harm local businesses dependent on easy cross-border access. Less expensive and more portable than the traditional passport book, the wallet-size passport card has the same validity period as a passport book: 10 years for an adult, 5 years for children 15 and younger. Adults who already have a passport book may apply for the card as a passport renewal and pay only $20. First-time applicants are charged $45 for adult cards and $35 for children.

The passport card contains a vicinity-read radio frequency identification (RFID) chip that links the card to a stored record in government databases. No personal information is written to the RFID chip itself. Note that **the passport card is valid for entry by land or sea only;** air travelers must have a valid U.S. passport. If you already have a passport, you may, of course, use that to enter Canada by land or sea. The passport card cannot be used for other international travel. First-time applicants can apply at any one of the 9,300 Passport Acceptance Facilities across the U.S. For more information on passport cards and to locate the application office nearest you, visit http://travel.state.gov.

Permanent U.S. residents who are not U.S. citizens should carry their passport and Resident Alien Card (U.S. form I-151 or I-551). Foreign students and other noncitizen U.S. residents should carry their passport, a Temporary Resident Card (form 1688) or Employment Authorization Card (1688A or 1688B), a visitor's visa, an I-94 arrival-departure record, a current I-20 copy of IAP-66 indicating student status, proof of sufficient funds for a temporary stay, and evidence of return transportation.

Visitors arriving by ferry from the U.S. must fill out International Crossing forms, which are collected before boarding.

Visas

For information on obtaining a Visa, visit "Fast Facts," on p. 274.

Customs

You'll pass through **Canadian Customs** (*C* 800/461-9999 in Canada or 204/983-3500) upon arrival and **U.S. Customs** (*C* 360/332-5771), if you are traveling through the U.S., on your departure.

If you're **driving** from Seattle, you'll enter British Columbia, Canada, at the Peace Arch crossing (open 24 hr.; often, there's a 30-min. or longer wait) in Blaine, Washington. You'll go through Customs when you cross the border into Canada and show your passport.

Arriving by air, you'll go through Customs at the airport once you clear passport control. (Even if you don't have anything to declare, Customs officials randomly select a few passengers and search their luggage.)

Visitors arriving by **train, ferry,** or **cruise ship** from the U.S. pass through U.S. Customs before boarding and Canadian Customs upon arrival.

WHAT YOU CAN BRING INTO CANADA

Your personal baggage can include the following: boats, motors, snowmobiles, camping and sports equipment, appliances, TV sets, musical instruments, personal computers, cameras, and other items of a personal or household nature. If you are bringing excess luggage, be sure to carry a detailed inventory list that includes the acquisition date, serial number, and cost or replacement value of each item. It sounds tedious, but it can speed things up at the border. Customs will help you fill out the forms that allow you to temporarily bring in your effects. This list will also be used by U.S. Customs to check off what you bring out. You will be charged Customs duties for anything left in Canada.

A few other things to keep in mind:

o If you're over 18, you're allowed to bring in 1.2L (40 oz.) of liquor and wine, or 24 .4L (12-oz.) cans or bottles of beer and ale, and 50 cigars, 400 cigarettes, or 397g (14 oz.) of manufactured tobacco per person. Any excess is subject to duty.

o Gifts not exceeding C$60 and not containing tobacco products, alcoholic beverages, or advertising material can be brought in duty-free. Meats, plants, and vegetables are subject to inspection on entry. There are restrictions, so contact the Canadian Consulate for more details if you want to bring produce into the country, or check the Canada Border Services Agency website, www.cbsa-asfc.gc.ca.

o If you plan to bring your dog or cat, you must provide proof of rabies inoculation during the preceding 36-month period. Other types of animals need special clearance and health certification. (Many birds, for instance, require 8 weeks in quarantine.)

If you need more information concerning items you wish to bring into and out of the country, contact **Canada Border Services** (✆ **800/461-9999** in Canada or 204/983-3500; www.cbsa-asfc.gc.ca).

WHAT YOU CAN TAKE HOME FROM CANADA

For information on what you're allowed to bring home, contact one of the following agencies:

U.S. Citizens: U.S. Customs & Border Protection (CBP; 1300 Pennsylvania Ave., NW, Washington, DC 20229; ✆ **877/227-5511;** www.cbp.gov)

U.K. Citizens: HM Customs & Excise (✆ **0845/010-9000,** or 020/8929-0152 from outside the U.K.; www.hmrc.gov.uk).

Australian Citizens: Australian Customs Service (✆ **1300/363-263;** www.customs.gov.au).

New Zealand Citizens: New Zealand Customs (The Customhouse, 17–21 Whitmore St., Box 2218, Wellington; ✆ **04/473-6099** or 0800/428-786; www.customs.govt.nz).

GETTING THERE & AROUND

Getting There

BY PLANE

The Western United States is linked with Canada, Europe, and Asia by frequent nonstop flights. Seattle's **Seatac International Airport** (✆ **206/787-5388;** www.portseattle.org; SEA) and **Vancouver International Airport** (✆ **604/207-7077;** www.yvr.ca; YVR) are major hubs; regional airlines connect to Victoria (YYJ), Bellingham (BLJ), and smaller centers throughout the islands. Major carriers include **Air Canada** (✆ **888/247-2262;** www.aircanada.ca), **WestJet** (✆ **800/538-5696** or 888/937-8538; www.westjet.com), **American Airlines** (✆ **800/443-7300;** www.aa.com), **Continental** (✆ **800/231-0856;** www.continentalairlines.com), **Delta Airlines** (✆ **800/221-1212;** www.delta.com), and **United Airlines** (✆ **800/241-6522;** www.united.com).

Air Canada and **Horizon Air** (✆ **800/547-9308;** www.horizonair.com or www.alaskaair.com), Alaska Airlines' connector, offer direct connections from several U.S. and Canadian cities such as Washington, D.C., Anchorage, San Francisco, and Calgary, to Vancouver, Victoria, and Seattle.

Commercial air carriers between the Seattle area and the San Juan Islands include **Island Air** (charter only; ✆ **360/378-2376;** www.sanjuan-islandair.com), **Kenmore Air** (seaplanes; ✆ **866/435-9524;** www.kenmoreair.com), **Northwest Seaplanes** (✆ **800/690-0086;** www.nwseaplanes.com), and **San Juan Airlines** (✆ **800/874-4434;** www.sanjuanairlines.com).

On the Canada side, regional commuter airlines, including floatplanes and helicopters that fly between Vancouver Harbour on the mainland and Victoria's Inner Harbour, also serve the Gulf Islands. They include **Air Canada Jazz** (a subsidiary of Air Canada; ✆ **888/247-2262;** www.flyjazz.ca), **Harbour Air Sea Planes** (✆ **800/665-0212** or 604/274-1277; www.harbour-air.com), **Helijet Airways** (✆ **800/665-4354;** www.helijet.com), **Kenmore Air** (✆ **800/543-9595;** www.kenmoreair.com), **Pacific Coastal Airlines** (✆ **800/663-2872,** or 604/273-8666 in Vancouver; www.pacific-coastal.com), and **West Coast Air** (float planes; ✆ **800/ 347-2222;** www.westcoastair.com).

Overseas visitors can take advantage of the APEX (Advance Purchase Excursion) reductions offered by all major Canadian, U.S., and European carriers. In addition, some large U.S. airlines offer transatlantic or transpacific passengers special discount tickets under the name **Visit USA,** which allows mostly one-way travel from one U.S. destination to another at very low prices. Unavailable in the U.S., these discount tickets must be purchased abroad in conjunction with your international fare. This system is the easiest, fastest, cheapest way to see the country.

IMMIGRATION & CUSTOMS CLEARANCE   Visitors arriving by air, no matter what the port of entry, should cultivate patience and resignation before setting foot on U.S. soil. Since the terrorist attacks of September 11, 2001, getting through immigration control can take as long as 2 hours on some days, especially on summer weekends, so be sure to carry this guidebook or something else to read.

People traveling by air from Canada, Bermuda, and certain countries in the Caribbean can sometimes clear Customs and Immigration at the point of departure, which is much quicker.

Visitors traveling into Canada may experience the same time-consuming wait, depending on your point of entry.

BY CAR

If you're visiting from abroad and plan to rent a car in the United States or Canada, keep in mind that foreign driver's licenses are usually recognized in both countries; but you should get an international one if your home license is not in English. Both the major centers of Victoria and Seattle have a wide selection of rental agencies (and vehicles). Once on the Gulf or San Juan islands, however, the choice of vehicles is much more limited.

Check out **Breezenet.com,** which offers car-rental discounts with some of the most competitive rates around. Also worth visiting are Orbitz.com, Hotwire.com, Travelocity.com, and Priceline.com, all of which offer competitive online car-rental rates. International visitors should note that insurance and taxes are almost never included in quoted rental car rates. Be sure to ask your rental agency about additional fees for these. They can add a significant cost to your car rental.

BY TRAIN

International visitors (excluding those from Canada) can buy a **USA Rail Pass,** good for 15 or 30 days of unlimited travel on Amtrak (✆ **800/USA-RAIL** [800/872-7245]; www.amtrak.com). The pass is available through many overseas travel agents. Current prices for a 15-day pass is US$389, a 30-day pass costs US$579, and a 45-day pass is US$749. With a foreign passport, you can also buy passes at some Amtrak offices in the United States, including locations in San Francisco, Los Angeles, Chicago, New York, Miami, Boston, and Washington, D.C. Reservations are generally required and should be made for each part of your trip as early as possible. If a stopover to the islands is in your overall touring plans, such a pass is a good option. Because **Amtrak** services, and Canada's VIA Rail services across Canada, end in Vancouver, travel to Victoria and Vancouver Island requires connecting to either ferry or plane transportation. **VIA Rail** (✆ **800/561-8630;** www.viarail.com) connects Vancouver to the rest of Canada. **Amtrak** (© 800/872-7245; www.amtrak.com) offers a daily service (a combination of train and coach) between Seattle and Vancouver. Schedules for both VIA Rail and Amtrak are posted at **Pacific Central Station,** 1150 Station St. (at the corner of Main St. and Terminal Ave.), Vancouver, and at King Street Station, 303 South Jackson St., Seattle.

Getting Around

If you're planning to stay in Victoria, you can consider leaving your car parked. Public transit is good, and when you tire of walking around this very walk-able city, there are plenty of getting-around options such as mini-ferry rides across the harbor, horse-drawn carriages, and kabuki pedal cabs. Once you're out of the city, or on one of the islands, public transit is far less conducive to seeing the sights. See the "Getting Around" sections in the respective chapters.

BY PLANE

There are several regional carriers that commute between the major centers of Victoria, Nanaimo, and San Juan, and other coastal communities and specific resorts (see "Getting There," above). Some areas have private landing strips, often grass. Upon arrival, however, car travel is still the best way to explore the area, although if you plan to stay put at a specific resort, bike rentals and mopeds are fun options to consider—yes, some of the islands are that small!

BY CAR

All the islands are a pleasure to explore and best done by car. In Victoria and Nanaimo, you'll find a number of rental car companies, including **Avis** (© 800/879-2847; www.avis.com), **Budget** (© 800/268-8900; www.budget.com), and **Hertz** (© 800/263-0600; www.hertz.com).

ON VANCOUVER ISLAND   Although highways are well maintained on Vancouver Island, getting from point A to point B can take longer than anticipated. Traffic in and around Victoria tends to be heavy and frustratingly slow—perhaps because so many drivers appear to be cautious retirees. Also, many of the region's more interesting attractions are off the highway on roads that twist and turn through picturesque communities. If you have the time, this beats highway asphalt. Gas is sold by the liter, and was averaging around C$1.15 a liter at press time, but can vary considerably. Speeds and distances are posted in kilometers (1km = 0.6 miles). Logging roads lead to some of the best places on the island, but if you drive on one, remember that logging trucks have absolute right-of-way. Members of the **American Automobile Association (AAA)** can get emergency assistance from the **British Columbia Automobile Association (BCAA;** © 800/222-4357; www.bcaa.com).

IN VICTORIA   This is a walking city, so don a good pair of shoes and park your car. Those few attractions that are not close to the city core are only a short taxi ride away. Victoria also has a comprehensive public transit system (see "Essentials," in chapter 5).

ON THE GULF & SAN JUAN ISLANDS   The easiest way to tour these islands is by car, although some communities have rental scooters, mopeds, and bicycles. With that in mind, be aware that driving here takes extra care. Roads are shared with pedestrians taking leisurely strolls, bikers, and deer (which are especially prevalent

- Victoria to Sidney: 26km (16 miles), approximately ½ hour
- Victoria to Nanaimo: 111km (69 miles), approximately 1¾ hours
- Victoria to Port Alberni: 195km (121 miles), approximately 3 hours
- Victoria to Campbell River: 264km (164 miles), approximately 4 hours
- Victoria to Tofino: 316km (196 miles), approximately 4¾ hours
- Victoria to Port Hardy: 502km (312 miles), approximately 7 hours

at dawn and dusk). Rarely is anyone in a rush to get anywhere. (For details, see "Essentials," in chapter 9 or 10, for the specific island.)

BY TRAIN

VIA Rail's Malahat (© 888/842-7245; www.viarail.ca) travels between Victoria and Courtenay, winding through the Cowichan River Valley and Goldstream Provincial Park. Travelers on the Horseshoe Bay–Nanaimo ferry board the train in Nanaimo. It departs from Victoria's **VIA Rail Station** (450 Pandora Ave.). The service runs Monday through Saturday, and the trip takes about 4½ hours. One-way fares from Victoria to Courtenay are C$30 adults, (discounts with advance reservations), discounts for children, students, and seniors. Seniors should check into "buy one ticket and travel with a companion for free" promotions.

BY BUS & FERRY

Bus travel is often the most economical form of public transit for short hops between cities, but it's certainly not an option for everyone.

Greyhound (© 800/231-2222; www.greyhound.com) is the sole nationwide bus line and offers a Discovery Pass in increments of 7-, 15-, 30-, and 60-day passes for unlimited travel and stopovers in the U.S. and Canada. They range from C$239 (7-day) to C$539 (60-day). The pass can be purchased online through www.discovery pass.com and must be ordered at least 21 days before your departure.

TO VICTORIA Pacific Coach Lines (© 800/661-1725 or 604/662-7575; www.pacificcoach.com) operates bus service between Vancouver and Victoria. The 4-hour trip from the **Vancouver bus terminal** (Pacific Central Station, 1150 Station St.) to the **Victoria Depot** (700 Douglas St.) includes passage on the **Tsawwassen–Swartz Bay ferry.** One-way fares are C$43 adults, C$22 children 5 to 11, C$29 for BC seniors; return fares are C$84 adults, C$42 children 5 to 11, C$55 for BC seniors. Discounts are not offered to out-of-province seniors. Departures are daily every 2 hours (hourly June to early September) between 5:45am and 7:30pm.

The Victoria Express (© 800/633-1589 in season, year round © 360/452-8088 from the U.S. or 250/361-9144 from Canada; www.victoriaexpress.com) operates a seasonal passenger-only ferry service, June through September, between Port Angeles and Victoria. Crossing time is 1 hour. There are two crossings per day. Reservations are available. Fares are US$13 adults; children 1 year and under travel for free. Bikes and kayaks are US$5 each.

Clipper Vacations (© 800/888-2535; www.victoriaclipper.com) runs a year-round passenger-only service between Seattle and Victoria aboard a high-speed catamaran called the **Victoria Clipper.** From mid-May to mid-September, there are up to three crossings per day. The rest of the year, this is reduced to one crossing per day. The trips are approximately 3 hours. One-way fares mid-May through mid-September are US$93 adults; return fares are US$155 adults. From mid-September to mid-May, in the off season, one-way fares are US$85 adults; return fares are US$134 adults. From mid-May to mid-September, there is one daily crossing aboard the Victoria Clipper from Seattle to Friday Harbor, on San Juan Island. Return fares are from US$70 adults. Reservations are recommended.

TO THE GULF ISLANDS Travelers should take the **Pacific Coach Lines coach** from Vancouver to Victoria, as mentioned above, but disembark in **Tsawwassen,** where **BC Ferries** (© **888/BCFERRY** [888/223-3779] or 250/386-3431; www.bcferries.com) sails year-round to the island of your choice. On Vancouver Island, BC Ferries departs from **Swartz Bay,** north of Victoria. Fares and sailing times range from 1 to 3 hours, depending on your final island destination. See "Getting There," in chapter 9, for information about schedules and fares to specific islands.

TO THE SAN JUAN ISLANDS From Seattle's **Seatac International Airport** (© **206/787-5388;** www.portseattle.org) and from the **Bellingham Airport** (© **360/671-5674,** www.portofbellingham.com), **Airporter Shuttle** (© **800/235-5247;** www.airporter.com) and **Skagit County Bus** (© **360/757-4433;** www.skagit transit.org) transport passengers to Anacortes, north of Seattle on the Olympic Peninsula, just east of the San Juans. Connections can be made between Bellingham Airport and Vancouver on **Quick Shuttle** (© **800/665-2122;** www.quickcoach.com). There is no bus transportation for travelers from Anacortes to the San Juans; you travel either on foot or in your own vehicle. Once there, visitors traveling on foot have a choice of taxis, car rentals, moped rentals, or bicycle rentals. See chapter 10.

BY CAR & FERRY

Car travel is the most cost-effective, convenient, and comfortable way to travel around this westernmost part of North America. The inter-provincial highway system connects cities and towns all over the country; in addition to these high-speed, limited-access roadways, there's an extensive network of federal, provincial, and local highways and roads. Some of the national car-rental companies include **Alamo** (© **800/462-5266;** www.alamo.com), **Avis** (© **800/230-4898;** www.avis.com), **Budget** (© **800/527-0700;** www.budget.com), **Dollar** (© **800/800-3665;** www. dollar.com), **Hertz** (© **800/654-3131;** www.hertz.com), **National** (© **800/227-7368;** www.nationalcar.com), and **Thrifty** (© **800/847-4389;** www.thrifty.com).

If you plan to rent a car in either the United States or Canada, you probably won't need the services of an additional automobile organization. If you're planning to buy or borrow a car, automobile-association membership is recommended. **British Columbia Automobile Association** (© **877/268-5500** in B.C.; 604/268-5500; www. bcaa.com) is the province's largest auto club and supplies BCAA members with maps, insurance, and, most importantly, emergency road service. The cost of joining runs from C$85 to C$130, depending on packaged benefits, but if you're a member of another auto club with reciprocal arrangements, you can enjoy free BCAA service.

TO VANCOUVER ISLAND Hopping across the United States/Canadian border by car is easy, with the main crossing located right on the **I-5 at Peace Arch Park,** just north of **Blaine.** Once in Canada, drive to **Tsawwassen** to catch any number of ferries leaving for Vancouver, Nanaimo, and the Gulf Islands.

From the United States, daily ferry services link Port Angeles, Seattle, and Ana-cortes (all in Washington) with port facilities near Victoria. These include **Blackball Transport** (📞 **360/457-4491** in Washington or 250/386-2202 on Vancouver Island; www.cohoferry.com), which runs a year-round reserved and a first-come, first-served car and passenger service aboard the MV *Coho* between Port Angeles and Victoria. One-way fares are US$53 for a standard-size vehicle and driver, US$15 adults, and US$7.25 children. There are four 1½-hour daily crossings from June to mid-September. There is one crossing daily from October to January and two cross-ings daily from February to May.

Washington State Ferries (📞 **800/843-3779** in Washington, 888/808-7977 in Canada, or 206/464-6400; www.wsdot.wa.gov/ferries) runs a passenger and car ferry service from Anacortes, through the San Juan Islands, to Sidney (26km/16 miles north of Victoria), and back again. There are two crossings daily, and vehicle reservations are strongly recommended in summer. Reservations must be made by 5:30pm the day prior to travel. Year round, one-way fares are US$16 adults, US$8 seniors, US$13 children 6 to 18, and US$55 for a standard-size vehicle and driver. Crossing time is 3 hours.

Alternatively, you can choose to cross the border just north of Blaine and catch a **BC Ferries** vessel from Tsawwassen on the mainland to Swartz Bay, a 32km (20-mile) drive from Victoria's city center, or to Duke Point Terminal, near Nanaimo. Ferries leave every hour on the hour during the summer season, June through Labor Day, and on the odd hour for the rest of the year. Extra sailings are often added for holiday periods. Reservations are available but not always necessary if you're traveling outside of the Friday escape/Sunday night return rush hour. One-way fares average C$14 adults, C$7 children 5 to 11, and C$47 for a standard-size vehicle. BC seniors travel free Monday through Thursday, except on holidays. All BC Ferries have a restaurant and/or coffee bar on board, serving a wide range of soups, sandwiches, burger platters, salads, and snack food.

TO THE GULF ISLANDS   BC Ferries (📞 **888/BCFERRY** [888/223-3779] or 250/386-3431; www.bcferries.com) operates an extensive network of ferries to the Gulf Islands, linking the islands to one another, to the BC mainland, and to Vancou-ver Island. There are at least two crossings daily, year round, to each of the Gulf Islands, but departure times vary according to your destination. Ferry travel can be expensive if you're taking a vehicle, and long boarding waits are not uncommon. Ticket prices vary seasonally; midweek travel is slightly less than on weekends and holidays. During these peak periods, book at least 3 weeks in advance to avoid disap-pointment. Reservations can be made by phone or online. One-way fares from Tsaw-wassen average C$16 adults and C$58 for a standard-size vehicle. One-way fares from Swartz Bay average C$11 adults, C$33 for a standard-size regular vehicle. Return fares are less and vary according to which island you are returning from. Return fares from the islands to Swartz Bay are free. Inter-island trips average C$5 adults, C$10 for a standard-size vehicle.

TO THE SAN JUAN ISLANDS   From mid-May to September, **Clipper Vacations** (📞 **800/888-2535;** www.clippervacations.com) runs one crossing daily from Seattle to Friday Harbor, on San Juan Island, aboard the **Victoria Clipper III** passenger-only ferry. Return fares run from US$70 to US$120 adults, depending on the day traveled. Fares for children 1 to 11 are 50% less. Day returns are US$100. The ferry departs Seattle at 7:45am and returns at 7:15pm daily. Crossing time is 2½ hours. Reservations are recommended. **Washington State Ferries** (© **888/808-7977** or 206/464-6400; www.wsdot.wa.gov/ferries) provides multiple crossings daily between Anacortes and each of the larger San Juan Islands. No reservations are available. If you're taking a vehicle, you should arrive at least an hour before scheduled sailings, up to 3 hours beforehand at peak travel times on summer and holiday weekends. Some food service and a picnic area are available near the terminal. Check out **www.ferrycam.net** to see live images of the ferry lanes. One-way fares Wednesday through Saturday top out during peak season at US$13 adults. Children's tickets are about US$2 less, and seniors are approximately half-price. Passage for a standard-size vehicle and driver is US$53. Fares are lower in the off season and for traveling earlier in the week. Inter-island travel is US$23 for a standard-size vehicle and driver; passengers and bicycles are free.

MONEY & COSTS

THE VALUE OF THE CANADIAN DOLLAR VS. OTHER POPULAR CURRENCIES

US$	UK£	Euro (€)	Aus$	NZ$
$1	£0.80	€0.70	A$1	NZ$1.30

Frommer's lists exact prices in the local currency. The currency conversions quoted above were correct at press time. However, rates fluctuate, so before departing, consult a currency exchange website such as www.oanda.com/convert/classic to check up-to-the-minute rates.

The favorable exchange rate of the Canadian dollar against the U.S. dollar, the British pound, and the euro gives added value to whatever you buy. In 2010, the Canadian dollar grew considerably stronger, and at press time was virtually at par with the U.S. dollar. The Canadian dollar also gained strength against the British pound, the euro, and the Australian and New Zealand dollars. To offset this change, and because of the recession, hotels and restaurants have generally reduced their prices or kept them the same as last year.

It's always advisable to bring money in a variety of forms on a vacation: A mix of cash and credit cards is most convenient for most travelers today. You can exchange currency or withdraw Canadian dollars from an ATM upon arrival in Vancouver or Victoria. ATMs offer the best exchange rates and 24-hour access. Avoid exchanging money at commercial exchange bureaus and hotels, which often have the highest transaction fees.

Currency

Canadian monetary units are dollars and cents, with dollar notes issued in different colors. The standard denominations are C$5, C$10, C$20, C$50, and C$100. The "loonie" (so named because of the loon on one side) is the C$1 coin that replaced the C$1 bill. A C$2 coin, called the "toonie" because it's worth two loonies, has replaced the C$2 bill. **Note:** If you're driving, it's a good idea to have a pocketful of toonies and loonies for parking meters. Avoid C$100 bills when exchanging money, as many stores refuse to accept these bills. Almost all stores and restaurants accept American currency, and most will exchange amounts in excess of your dinner check or purchase. However, these establishments are allowed to set their own exchange percentages and generally offer the worst rates of all.

ATMs

The easiest and best way to get cash away from home is from an ATM (automated teller machine), sometimes referred to as a "cash machine," or a "cashpoint." The **Cirrus** (© **800/424-7787**; www.mastercard.com) and Visa (© **800/336-3386**; www.visa.com/mobileatm) networks span the globe; look at the back of your bank card to see which network you're on, then call or check online for ATM locations at your destination. Be sure you know your personal identification number (PIN) and daily withdrawal limit before you depart. *Note:* Remember that many banks impose a fee every time you use a card at another bank's ATM, and that fee can be higher for international transactions (up to C$5 or more) than for domestic ones (where they're rarely more than C$2). In addition, the bank from which you withdraw cash may charge its own fee. For international withdrawal fees, ask your bank.

Tip: Although ATMs are widespread on Vancouver Island, they are less prevalent on the Gulf and San Juan islands. Some of the Gulf Islands don't even have banks! If you plan to tour the Gulf and San Juan islands, be sure to travel with a **major credit card,** a **direct debit card,** or **traveler's checks,** and of course, **cash.** Visa and MasterCard are accepted at most locations. Not as many businesses accept American Express.

Credit Cards

Credit cards are another safe way to carry money. They also provide a convenient record of all your expenses, and they generally offer relatively good exchange rates. You can withdraw cash advances from your credit cards at banks or ATMs, provided you know your PIN. Keep in mind that you'll pay interest from the moment of your withdrawal, even if you pay your monthly bills on time. Also, note that many banks now assess a 1% to 3% "transaction fee" on **all** charges you incur abroad (whether you're using the local currency or your native currency).

Canadian businesses honor the same credit cards as do those in the U.S. Visa and MasterCard are the most common, though American Express is often accepted in only hotels and restaurants catering to tourists. Discover and Diner's Club cards are accepted less frequently.

Beware of hidden credit-card fees while traveling. Check with your credit or debit card issuer to see what fees, if any, will be charged for overseas transactions. Recent reform legislation in the U.S., for example, has curbed some exploitative lending practices. But many banks have responded by increasing fees in other areas, including fees for customers who use credit and debit cards while out of the country—even if those charges were made in U.S. dollars. Fees can amount to 3% or more of the purchase price. Check with your bank before departing to avoid any surprise charges on your statement.

STAYING HEALTHY

Victoria and most of the major towns in the region have hospitals, but some of the Gulf and San Juan islands operate only clinics. These are well equipped for most medical needs, but for life-threatening emergencies, airlift services are used. More often than not, medical issues you'll encounter in this area are related to ailments such as allergies to bee stings, horsefly bites, and mosquitoes; sprained ankles and broken limbs from underestimating some of the hikes (and wearing improper foot-wear); and sunburns. Forewarned is forearmed—travel with appropriate repellents and gear that befits your itinerary. If you become ill, we list additional **emergency numbers** in "Fast Facts", p. 271.

CRIME & SAFETY

Because these islands are more laid-back than many other travel destinations, they have a stronger sense of community that is safe and genuinely friendly. This is espe-cially true of the Gulf and San Juan islands. That said, you should still use your common sense and discretion. Avoid hitchhiking; stow things in the trunk of your car, out of sight; hold onto your pocketbook when in a crowd; and keep expensive cameras or electronic equipment bagged up or covered when not in use. Vancouver Island, too, is regarded as pretty safe, including for women solo travelers, though you might find Victoria busy enough to attract pickpockets and petty thieves. Further north, however, the population thins, and some roads are fairly remote. Be sure that your gas tank is full and take along water and a snack because if you get into trouble, help may take a few hours to arrive. For these reasons, travel with a companion or group. The northerly communities tend to be more conservative, too, so while gay and lesbian travelers are unlikely to experience discrimination, an overly affectionate display between couples may draw unwanted attention and derogatory comments.

SPECIALIZED TRAVEL RESOURCES

The multicultural population base of the Pacific Northwest, on both sides of the border, makes for a relaxed, tolerant, and safe environment. Whether traveling solo or as part of a group, you'll find many facilities catering specifically to families, seniors, gay and lesbian travelers, and outdoorsy adventurers. In addition to the destination-specific resources listed below, please visit Frommers.com for other specialized travel resources.

LGBT Travelers

The larger cities in Western Canada are gay-tolerant, with a number of gay bars, gay-owned businesses, and after-hours clubs. In fact, same-sex union celebrations are one of Canada's hottest tourism products. In Victoria, Gay Pride stages an annual parade in early July, where transvestites and others really strut their stuff. The gay lifestyle is widely accepted throughout the islands, on either side of the border, although in some of the small, northernmost communities on Vancouver Island, discretion is advised. Public displays of affection will not be appreciated. Log into the chat channel at **www.gayvictoria.ca** for updates on events and resources around the region.

The International Gay and Lesbian Travel Association (IGLTA; ✆ 800/448-8550 or 954/776-2626; www.iglta.org) is the trade association for the gay and lesbian travel industry and offers an online directory of gay- and lesbian-businesses.

Many agencies offer tours and travel itineraries specifically for gay and lesbian travelers. Among them are **Above and Beyond Tours** (© 800/397-2681; www.abovebeyondtours.com); **Now, Voyager** (© 800/255-6951; www.nowvoyager.com); and **Olivia Cruises & Resorts** (© 800/631-6277; www.olivia.com).

Travelers with Disabilities

Most disabilities shouldn't stop anyone from traveling in the U.S. and Canada. Indeed, the law on both sides of the border requires that most public places comply with disability-friendly regulations. Almost all public establishments (including hotels, restaurants, museums, etc., but not including certain National Historic Landmarks) and at least some modes of public transportation provide accessible entrances and other facilities for those with disabilities. However, the nature of certain buildings and small-town layouts makes their compliance inconsistent, especially in the Gulf Islands and the San Juans. Except in towns like Ganges (on Salt Spring Island) and Friday Harbor (on San Juan Island), most streets are like country lanes. The charm or historical ambience of a building often means that access routes are difficult, which doesn't make for easy maneuverability. The **"British Columbia Accommodations Guide"** details accessibility options at lodgings throughout Western Canada. Contact **Tourism British Columbia** (P.O. Box 9820, Station Prov. Govt., 1803 Douglas St., Victoria, BC VAW 9W5; © **800/HELLOBC** [800/435-5622]; www.hellobc.com). For accessibility advice in the San Juans, contact the San Juan Islands Visitors Bureau (P.O. Box 1330, Friday Harbor, San Juan Island, WA 98250; © **888/468-3701** or 360/378-9551; www.visitsanjuans.com).

Many travel agencies offer customized tours and itineraries for travelers with disabilities. Among them are **Flying Wheels Travel** (© **507/451-5005;** www.flyingwheelstravel.com); **Access-Able Travel Source** (© 303/232-2979; www.access-able.com); and **Accessible Journeys** (© 800/846-4537 or 610/521-0339; www.disabilitytravel.com). **Avis Rent a Car** has an "Avis Access" program that offers such services as a dedicated 24-hour toll-free number (© **888/879-4273**) for customers with special travel needs; special car features such as swivel seats, spinner knobs, and hand controls; and accessible bus service.

Organizations that offer assistance to travelers with disabilities include **MossRehab** (© **215/663-6000** or 456-9900; www.mossresourcenet.org); the **American Foundation for the Blind** (**AFB;** © **800/232-5463;** www.afb.org); and **SATH** (Society for Accessible Travel & Hospitality; © **212/447-7284;** www.sath.org). **AirAmbulance Card.com** is now partnered with SATH and allows you to preselect top-notch hospitals in case of an emergency.

For more on organizations that offer resources to travelers with disabilities, go to www.frommers.com/planning.

Family Travel

Victoria is one of the most child-friendly, cosmopolitan cities on Vancouver Island, offering a great selection of family activities to enjoy. **Tourism Victoria** (812 Wharf St.; © **250/953-2033;** www.tourismvictoria.com) publishes a good guide for parents, called "Things to Do with Kids."

To locate accommodations, restaurants, and attractions that are particularly kid-friendly, refer to the "Kids" icon throughout this guide.

Women Travelers

British Columbia and the entire Pacific Northwest are safe, polite, and a great place for female travelers. As with any destination, common sense should dissuade you from hitchhiking or walking alone late at night in a city. Otherwise, traveling should be a delight. If you're heading off the beaten track and into the wilds, hike or camp with a friend. A number of Canadian outfitters offer women-only adventure tours.

Check out the award-winning website **Journeywoman** (www.journeywoman.com), a "real life" women's travel-information network where you can sign up for a free e-mail newsletter and get advice on everything from etiquette and dress to safety; or the travel guide *Safety and Security for Women Who Travel* (Travelers' Tales, Inc.), by Sheila Swan and Peter Laufer, offers common-sense tips on safe travel.

Senior Travel

Travelers 65 years of age and over often qualify for discounts at hotels and attractions, so don't be shy about asking. Just be sure to always carry some kind of ID— such as a driver's license—that shows your date of birth. In Victoria and Nanaimo, seniors receive **discounts on public transit.** Passes for persons over 65 (with proof of age) may be purchased at shops in Victoria that display a FareDealer sign (7-Eleven stores are a good bet, as are most newsstands). To locate a FareDealer vendor, contact **BC Transit** (520 Gorge Rd., Victoria, BC V8W 2P3; ℂ **250/382-6161;** www.bctransit.com).

Members of AARP (601 E. St. NW, Washington, DC 20049; ℂ **800/424-3410** or 202/434-2277; www.aarp.org), can get discounts on hotels, airfares, and car rentals. Anyone over 50 can join; members receive a wide range of benefits, including a monthly newsletter. The Canadian equivalent can be reached at www.carp.ca.

Many reliable agencies and organizations target the 50-plus market. **Elderhostel** (ℂ **877/426-8056;** www.elderhostel.org) arranges study programs for those aged 55 and over. **ElderTreks** (ℂ **800/741-7956;** www.eldertreks.com) offers small-group tours to off-the-beaten-path or adventure-travel locations, restricted to travelers 50 and older. **INTRAV/Only the Best Travel** (ℂ **888/224-5685;** www.onlythebesttravel. com) is a high-end tour operator that caters to the mature, discerning traveler (not specifically seniors), with trips around the world that include guided safaris, polar expeditions, private-jet adventures, and small-boat cruises down jungle rivers.

RESPONSIBLE TOURISM

Western Canada—specifically, British Columbia—is the birthplace of consciousness-raising organizations such as Greenpeace, Westcoast Wilderness Society, and the David Suzuki Foundation. Residents throughout these islands are activists when it comes to green-living, saving whales, and adopting orphaned sea lions and other wildlife. The days of tree-huggers chaining themselves to old-growth cedars may be history, but the memory evokes considerable community pride. The hippies of yore still call these islands home, and it's their children who have picked up the conservation gauntlet. The 100-Mile Diet, which originated in British Columbia, is a way of life for many islanders, as is ardent water management, composting, recycling, and re-using. Islanders are equally conscientious about ethical tourism issues, which is not only pushing more aboriginal ventures to the forefront, but fine-tuning wildlife management programs.

GENERAL RESOURCES FOR responsible TRAVEL

In addition to the resources for **Vancouver Island, the Gulf Islands,** and **the San Juan Islands** listed above, the following websites provide valuable wide-ranging information on sustainable travel:

○ **Responsible Travel** (www.responsibletravel.com) is a great source of sustainable travel ideas; the site is run by a spokesperson for ethical tourism in the travel industry. **Sustainable Travel International** (www.sustainabletravelinternational.org) promotes ethical tourism practices and manages an extensive directory of sustainable properties and tour operators around the world.

○ **Carbonfund** (www.carbonfund.org), **TerraPass** (www.terrapass.org), and **Cool Climate** (http://coolclimate.berkeley.edu) provide info on "carbon offsetting," or offsetting the greenhouse gas emitted during flights.

○ **Greenhotels** (www.greenhotels.com) recommends green-rated member hotels around the world that fulfill the company's stringent environmental requirements. **Environmentally Friendly Hotels** (www.environmentallyfriendlyhotels.com) offers more green accommodation ratings.

○ **Sustain Lane** (www.sustainlane.com) lists sustainable eating and drinking choices around the U.S.; also visit **www.eatwellguide.org** for tips on eating sustainably in the U.S. and Canada.

○ **Volunteer International** (www.volunteerinternational.org) has a list of questions to help you determine the intentions and the nature of a volunteer program. For general info on volunteer travel, visit **www.volunteerabroad.org** and **www.idealist.org**.

STAYING CONNECTED
Mobile Phones

The three letters that define much of the world's wireless capabilities are GSM (Global System for Mobiles), a big, seamless network that makes for easy cross-border cellphone use throughout Europe and dozens of other countries worldwide. In the U.S., T-Mobile and AT&T Wireless use this quasi-universal system; in Canada, Rogers customers are GSM. If your cellphone is on a GSM system and you have a world-capable multiband phone, such as many Sony Ericsson, Motorola, or Samsung models, you can make and receive calls across civilized areas around much of the globe. Just call your wireless operator and ask for "international roaming" to be activated on your account. None of the islands mentioned in this book offer any cellphone rental services. *Note:* Other than in the major centers, cellphone signals may vary in strength in different areas of all these islands, ranging from nonexistent to mediocre.

Buying a phone can be economically attractive, as both Canada and the U.S. have cheap prepaid phone systems. Once you arrive at your destination, stop by a local cellphone shop and get the cheapest package; you'll probably pay less than C$100 for a phone and a starter calling card. Local calls may be as low as 10¢ per minute. Outlets include **Future Shop** (102-805 Cloverdale Ave., Victoria; © **250/380-9338**).

Wilderness adventurers might consider renting a **satellite phone** ("satphone"). It's different from a cellphone in that it connects to satellites and works where there's no cellular signal or ground-based tower. You can rent satellite phones from RoadPost (www.roadpost.com). InTouch USA (www.intouchusa.com) offers a wider range of satphones but at higher rates. Per-minute call charges can be even cheaper than roaming charges with a regular cellphone, but the phone itself is more expensive.

Internet & E-Mail

WITH YOUR OWN COMPUTER

More and more hotels, cafes, and retailers are signing on as Wi-Fi (wireless fidelity) "hotspots." **T-Mobile Hotspot** (www.t-mobile.com/hotspot) serves up wireless connections at more than 1,000 Starbucks coffee shops nationwide. **Boingo** (www. boingo.com) and **Wayport** (www.wayport.com) have set up networks in airports and high-class hotel lobbies. IPass providers (see below) also give you access to a few hundred wireless hotel lobby setups. To locate other hotspots that provide **free wireless networks** in cities around the world, go to **www.personaltelco.net/ index.cgi/WirelessCommunities**.

For dial-up access, most business-class hotels offer dataports for laptop modems, and many now offer free high-speed Internet access. In addition, major Internet Service Providers (ISPs) have **local access numbers** around the world, allowing you to go online by placing a local call. The **iPass** network also has dial-up numbers around the world. You'll have to sign up with an iPass provider, who will then tell you how to set up your computer for your destination(s). For a list of iPass providers, go to www.ipass.com.One solid provider is **i2roam** (© **866/811-6209** or 920/235-0475; www.i2roam.com).

In Victoria, the larger hotels are likely to have Wi-Fi and bedroom dataports, as well. This cannot be said for inns on the San Juan or Gulf islands. While services have now arrived in this part of the world, reception is sporadic and/or slow.

Wherever you go, bring a **connection kit** of the right power and phone adapters, a spare phone cord, and a spare Ethernet network cable—or find out whether your hotel supplies them to guests.

WITHOUT YOUR OWN COMPUTER

Most major airports have **Internet kiosks** that provide basic Web access for a per-minute fee that's usually higher than cybercafe prices. Check out copy shops like **FedEx Kinko's,** which offers computer stations with fully loaded software (as well as Wi-Fi).

In Victoria, most hotels have wireless access either in the lobby or lounge. Don't expect to come across very many, if any, cybercafes. So, if living "wired" is essential, call ahead to check. To find public Wi-Fi hotspots, go to www.jiwire.com; for help locating cybercafes and other establishments where you can go for Internet access, check **www.cybercaptive.com** and **www.cybercafe.com**. Aside from formal cybercafes, most **youth hostels** and **public libraries** have Internet access. Avoid **hotel business centers** unless you're willing to pay exorbitant rates. Please see "Internet Access" in the **"Fast Facts"** appendix (p. 272).

Newspapers & Magazines

For regional and world news, Gulf Islanders have access to Victoria's major newspaper, *The Victoria Times-Colonist* and to the *Vancouver Sun. The Gulf Islands Driftwood* is a small community newspaper published every Wednesday. Local papers on the San Juans include *The Journal* (San Juan Island), *The Sounder* (Orcas Island), and the *Islands Weekly* (Lopez Island), all owned by the same publisher but each reporting on their specific island's news.

Telephones

Although the Canadian and U.S. phone systems are the same, the systems are run by private companies, so rates, especially for long-distance service and operator-assisted calls, can vary widely. Generally, hotel surcharges on long-distance and local calls are astronomical, so you're usually better off using a public pay telephone, which you'll find clearly marked in most public buildings and private establishments, as well as on the street. Most public phones accept prepaid phone cards, sold at drugstores and convenience stores. Many public phones also accept American Express, MasterCard, and Visa credit cards. Numbers are made up of the 3-digit area code and the 7-digit local number. On Vancouver Island and the Gulf Islands, this prefix is 250. For the San Juan Islands, the area code is 360. The long-distance prefix is 1. For directory assistance within Canada, dial © **411;** in the U.S., dial **1 + area code + 555-1212.**

TIPS ON ACCOMMODATIONS

Between the large hotels in Victoria and the picturesque B&Bs and inns in the rest of the region, there really is something for everyone in terms of charm, character, and comfort. Other than in Victoria, you won't come across major chains. The inns and B&Bs on the islands have a special appeal because they're far from cookie-cutter guesthouses. Be aware, however, that accommodations tend to get a little more basic the farther north you travel. In Canada, a big deal is made about the term "Canada Select," which refers to a provincial rating program. If a place is part of the program, then you know to expect a level of cleanliness and service that won't disappoint. Hence, most don't advertise their rating until it reaches in excess of 2—the top being "we've got absolutely everything" 5 stars. That includes having a paved driveway, which some rural destinations have forgone for the sake of ambience, costing themselves half a star in the process.

SUGGESTED ITINERARIES

The coastal islands of the Pacific Northwest are almost as diverse as they are numerous, so explorations can be virtually custom-created according to mood and preference. City lovers can hover around Victoria, urban escapees will likely enjoy touring the San Juan and Gulf islands, while outdoor devotees should head for Vancouver Island's westernmost coast or to its most northern regions. The best thing about this part of the world, though, is that you can mix and match activities to get a little of everything.

THE REGIONS IN BRIEF

As the largest of all the islands along the Pacific Northwest coast, **Vancouver Island** offers both urban sophistication and wilderness adventure; it can be as cosmopolitan or extreme as you want.

Victoria, the provincial capital of British Columbia, lies on the southern tip of Vancouver Island, not far from the international boundary. In fact, the U.S. border scoops below the 49th parallel, keeping the island—in its entirety—in Canada. With an ambience that's more English than England ever was, Victoria's beautifully preserved turn-of-the-20th-century buildings dominate its harbor. The city's picturesque charm draws visitors in droves, especially in summer. Shopping, dining, and urban attractions, such as the **Royal BC Museum,** make the city a first-class family destination. From Victoria, there are a number of pleasant day and half-day trips around the southern part of Vancouver Island, including to the famed **Butchart Gardens.** It is also an ideal starting point for exploring farther afield.

As you travel north, the rest of Vancouver Island ranges from rural to wild, and nowhere is this better seen than in the central part of the island. Holiday resorts line the east coast overlooking the protected Georgia Strait, while the open Pacific Ocean pounds against Canada's wildest and most westerly coast. This is where to find the unpredictable **West Coast Trail,** the awe-inspiring **Pacific Rim National Park,** and some of the untouched wilderness areas of **Clayoquot Sound.** Much of the island is home to dozens of First Nations Canadian bands; throughout your travels there'll be opportunities to shop for Native arts and to experience the many different cultures.

At **Port Hardy,** Vancouver Island's most remote and northerly community, you can board a BC Ferries vessel and take a 15-hour trip through the famed **Inside Passage** to Prince Rupert, a port town on the mainland just shy of the Alaska Panhandle. A cruise aboard BC Ferries doesn't compare with the luxurious cruise ships that ply these waters, but you'll save yourself thousands of dollars and still travel through the same spectacular scenery. It's also the starting point for the **Queen Charlotte Islands**, where vestiges of Haida history lay hidden among ancient cedars and beneath blankets of Spanish moss.

The **Gulf Islands** and the **San Juan Islands** are actually a part of the same archipelago, yet, surprisingly, each group of islands has its individual appeal. While all are rural in character, each one offers a slightly different experience. For example, Galiano and Gabriola islands feel as if they're still hanging out in the '60s; Saturna Island is like a rainforest retreat; and in summer, Hornby and Denman islands are a bit like holiday camps, as holiday-makers and day-trippers throng to these sun-drenched havens. The two most sophisticated islands are San Juan—it has a "real" town with a decent range of services, save for big box stores—and Salt Spring Island, which is by far the most arts-oriented of all the islands (although Orcas Island gives it a run for its money).

That said, all the islands are very rural. Many of the smaller ones are limited in the number of services they can provide (i.e., don't expect bank machines, let alone banks). The one thing they do share is a milder climate than the rest of BC or Washington State, in large part because they are protected by the coastal mountains, which means more sunshine and less rain than even Vancouver Island.

THE SAN JUAN SHUFFLE

Whether you arrive by ferry from Sidney or Anacortes, this short getaway beginning on San Juan Island feels like a world away, which is, of course, the islands' main attraction. This itinerary is for a low-key, modestly paced, get-away-from-it-all vacation. Island hopping gives you a real feel for the Pacific Northwest—chances are you'll see whales en route, and it is certainly the only way to appreciate the bucolic diversity of each island, whether it's history-laden San Juan Island, the evolving gentrification of Orcas Island, or the wilder isolation of the smaller isles. If you head for San Juan Island from Anacortes, you can work your way back through the other islands with free inter-island ferry trips. Traveling to and from Sidney on Vancouver Island means you can spend extra days in and around Victoria.

Day 1: San Juan Island

After stopping off at **Friday Harbor** (p. 250) to see the sights and shops, take the perimeter road south to **American Camp** (p. 252). It's a long stretch of road (watch out for cyclists) with expansive views. On your return, take a slight detour to the **Pelindaba Lavender Farm** (p. 255) before heading along the westerly coast road to **English Camp** (p. 253). Farther along the road, you'll come to the new **Westcott Bay Sculpture Park** (p. 255). From there, you can either walk or drive down to **Roche Harbor** (p. 254)—a good stop for the evening, if only to enjoy the nightly sunset Taps ceremony.

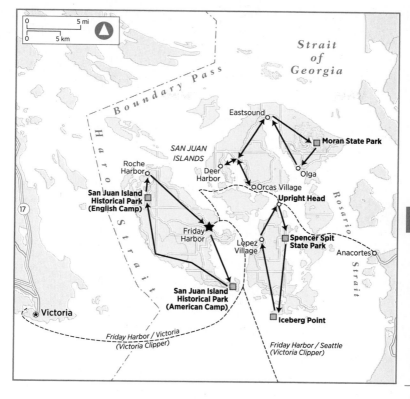

Day 2: Orcas Island

Hop onto an early morning inter-island ferry, and 35 minutes later, you'll arrive at Orcas Island. Local traffic tends to head straight up the main road to Eastsound, but since you're a visitor, take the picturesque, winding drive west to **Deer Harbor** (p. 261) to get a sense of how pretty parts of this island can be. Then head north to **Eastsound** (p. 260), where you can browse specialty shops and enjoy lunch. Exploring the eastern arm of Orcas Island, including **Moran State Park** and **Olga** (p. 260), will take the better part of your afternoon. Be sure to drop by **Rosario Resort** (p. 262), as much for its intriguing history as for its lovely marina location.

Day 3: Shaw Island/Lopez Island

Shaw Island (p. 265) is a pleasant morning detour en route to Lopez Island, although you'll need to coordinate your day carefully around sailing times. Once on Lopez, there's little left to do but kick back and relax. Enjoy the bucolic atmosphere and go on rambles along the bluff at **Iceberg Point** (p. 268) and around **Spencer Spit State Park** (p. 266).

Day 4: Return Options

Take the return ferry to Anacortes or plan to sail to Sidney to continue your adventure on Vancouver Island.

GULF ISLANDS GETAWAY IN 1 WEEK

Island-hopping around the southern Gulf Islands will treat you to scenery that's breathtakingly beautiful: dense rainforest, wild shorelines, pretty coves, and pastoral landscapes. Every island has a distinct charm. Bring along a book or crossword puzzle to help wile away the inevitable hours you have to linger waiting for your ferry to come in! Ferry connections aren't always back to back, and ferries can run later than scheduled. This itinerary assumes you're starting from Vancouver. Reverse it for Victoria departures.

Day 1: Galiano

Although Galiano is the closest island from Vancouver, it's a laid-back community that's worked hard to maintain its rural roots. The road that runs the length of the island's long, skinny shape takes you from a cluster of buildings near the ferry terminal, past pretty coves and marinas, and up to densely packed forests. There are wonderful walks in and around **Galiano Bluffs Park** and **Montague Provincial Park** (p. 234). Head north to experience the island's "wild" side in and around **Dionisio Point Provincial Park.** Kayaking out of **Montague Harbour** (p. 234) is another great way to fully appreciate the gentleness of this island.

Day 2: Mayne Island

The small village area around **Miners Bay** (p. 238) boasts a bakery, a few worthwhile eateries and country inns, and sandy beaches. Of all the islands, this one is where you'll find the most accessible history: visit the tiny church, **St. Mary Magdalene** (p. 238); **Active Pass Lighthouse** (p. 239); **Mayne Island Museum,** which is housed in an historic jail; and the **Agricultural Hall** (p. 238), where you can still see island amateur thespians strut their stuff across the stage. The much newer Community Centre is quickly gaining status as *the* gathering spot for local dances, Saturday-night bingo, and second-run movies, for those seeking true local flavor.

Day 3: The Penders

The marinas and coves here make the Penders a favorite destination for sailors, and with a permanent population base of approximately 2,000, these hilly islands have lots for you to see and do. **Beaumont Marine Provincial Park** (p. 231) is one of the prettiest destinations for hiking. It's also ideal for a picnic—pick up a bottle of wine from **Morning Bay Vineyard** (p. 230). If you're interested in **kayaking** (p. 230), it's especially easy to reach neighboring Saturna and Mayne islands from here. **Poets Cove** (p. 232) is one of the best destination resorts in the Gulf Islands archipelago. If you have time, take a mini wildlife cruise; some go over to Saturna Island.

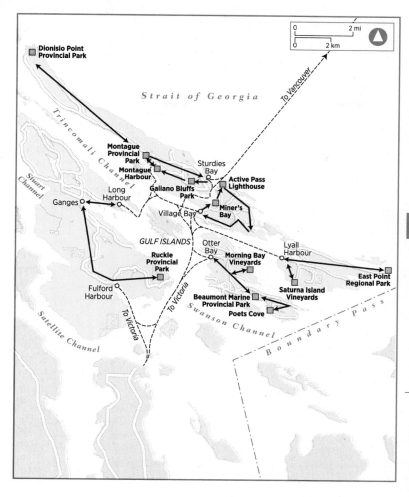

Day 4: Saturna

You can tour around Saturna in less than a day; but staying longer means you have time to really appreciate the remote tranquility of this rainforested island. **East Point Regional Park** (p. 243) is a beautiful spot to picnic; en route, you can pick up some wine at the **Saturna Island Vineyards** (p. 242).

Days 5 & 6: Salt Spring

As the largest and most commercial of all the southern Gulf Islands, Salt Spring's proximity to Victoria makes it a popular weekend escape. Although developers are catching the wave of recreational property seekers, they haven't yet affected the pastoral and artsy charm of Salt Spring. This is especially true of the island's southern half. The **shops, galleries,** and **pubs** in Ganges (p. 219) alone will take at least a half-day to explore (longer if it's **market day** [p. 222]). Take the second day to tour the island's art studios, galleries, farms, and parks (**Ruckle Provincial Park** [p. 222] being the prettiest).

Day 7: Victoria/the Inner Harbour

Park the car and enjoy the more refined atmosphere of Victoria's Inner Harbour. Here's where you'll find the **Provincial Legislature** (p. 85) and the ivy-clad **Fairmont Empress** (p. 64), both landmark buildings that, not surprisingly, conjure up the era of the city's Victorian namesake. Fun attractions, particularly if you're traveling with children, include **Miniature World** (p. 84), **Pacific Undersea Gardens** (p. 84), and the terrific-at-any-age **Royal BC Museum** (p. 85). When your feet have had enough, hop into a **horse-drawn carriage** (p. 90) for a trip through **Beacon Hill Park** (p. 87), or simply take a **Kabuki Cab** to **Fisherman's Wharf** (p. 87) for a meal of chips and just-caught fish, served in newspaper with salt and traditional malt vinegar.

THE WILD WEST COAST IN 1 WEEK

To follow this itinerary, you'll need a car; it's the only way to experience the full diversity of what Vancouver Island has to offer. Your trip starts in Victoria, with the option to stay in the urban center or venture into the surrounding countryside. Think of it as a teaser of what's to come on the wild west coast, where nature still has the upper hand. The changes in countryside during the drive from Victoria to Tofino, over mountains, through orchards, by seashores, and past fast-moving rivers, are mesmerizing.

Day 1: Victoria

If you've already enjoyed Victoria's main attractions (described in day 7 of the previous itinerary), explore some of those attractions away from the Inner Harbour, such as **Craigdarroch Castle** (p. 83) and **Butchart Gardens** (p. 107). If you've been to Victoria before, try going farther afield: Count eagles at **Goldstream Provincial Park** (p. 115), cycle the **Galloping Goose Trail** (p. 114), or make a day trip of hiking and tide-pool exploring along the **Juan de Fuca Trail** (p. 114) to **Botanical Beach** (p. 116). The latter two suggestions are great family excursions.

Day 2: Cowichan Valley/Duncan

The drive north from Victoria takes you over the vista-filled Malahat before descending into the Cowichan Valley, one of Canada's fastest growing agritourism regions. Explore the back roads, and you'll be rewarded with a range of small, quality **wineries** (p. 124), orchards, specialty farms, and dairies. If time runs short, you can always plan to see some of these on the return trip. You get a good impression of the island's Native culture in Duncan with its host of totem poles. Nearby Cowichan is home of the must-see **Quw'utsun Cultural Centre** (p. 123), which illustrates the story of the Cowichan people, the original inhabitants of the valley.

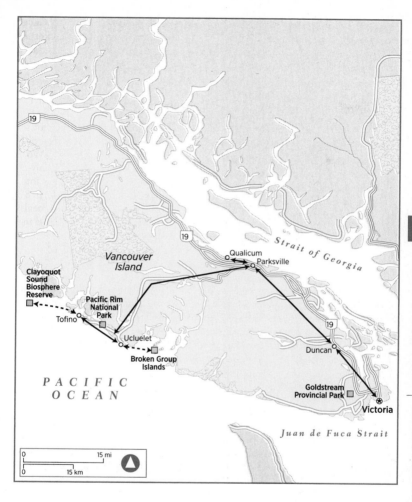

Days 3 & 4: Tofino/Long Beach

From Duncan, continue north to Parksville and the junction with Highway 4, the start of the beautiful, windy, and mountainous drive west. Allow 3 hours to cross the island—longer if you stretch your legs in kitschy **Coombs** (p. 153) or **Cathedral Grove** (p. 154), through which you'll pass. Rain or shine, Tofino and the Long Beach section of the **Pacific Rim National Park** (p. 158) make the journey worthwhile. Hiking through these rainforests is stunning. Many trails are easy walks; some are strenuous hikes. Whale-watching, surfing, and wildlife-viewing are first rate; and sea-kayaking around the usually calm waters of **Clayoquot Sound** (p. 159) is easy and rewarding.

Day 5: Ucluelet/Broken Group Island

Located within a 20-minute drive south of Tofino, Ucluelet is less touristy, some might even say a little rougher. It is home base to the impressive **Wild Pacific Trail** (p. 161) with easy-to-navigate **boardwalks** through forested terrain and solidly packed pathways that follow the coast. Ucluelet is nearest to the **Broken Group Islands** (p. 165), and you'll find several boat charters and kayaking outfitters in the marina that run tours across the Pacific Ocean swells directly into this oasis of exceptionally calm waters.

Day 6: Qualicum/Parksville

Surrounded by seven major **golf courses** (p. 147), all within a few minutes' drive of one another, this is tee-off central. For those not fond of the links, there's **Rathtrevor Beach** (p. 146), where you can beachcomb for sand dollars, or take time out to relax in British Columbia's largest spa at **Tigh-Na-Mara Resort** (p. 151).

Day 7: Return to Victoria

The leisurely drive back to Victoria is a chance to catch some of the attractions you missed on the way up. Stop for lunch at one of the wineries (p. 124) and pick up some specialty vintages to take home.

AN ADVENTURE-TRAVEL WEEK

If you start your itinerary in Nanaimo, all sorts of extreme (and soft) adventure options present themselves beyond what you find in Victoria's environs. This adventure itinerary is geared to take in the best eco-activity in the different regions while showcasing the wild side of Vancouver Island.

Day 1: Spelunking and Rappelling

From Nanaimo, take Highway 19 north to Parksville and Qualicum Beach, keeping your eyes open for the turnoff to **Horne Lake Caves Provincial Park** (p. 148). Pitch your tent here or in nearby Englishman's River and take the afternoon to explore the fossil-filled caverns at **Horne Lake Caves** (p. 148). Tours range from family excursions to extreme adventures.

Day 2: Hiking and Mountaineering

Continue north and, just before Campbell River, take the turnoff to **Strathcona Provincial Park** (p. 181). Strathcona was British Columbia's first provincial park, and it includes Elkhorn Mountain, Golden Hinde, and trail access to Mount Washington (p. 180). Whether you're a neophyte or an experienced adventurer, you'll find plenty of challenges, from rock climbing to wilderness hikes through meadow-filled mountain back-country.

Day 3: Fishing

Campbell River is nicknamed the Salmon Capital of the World and is where eco-activist and fishing expert Roderick Haig Brown cast his rod. Fishing die-hards may want to go for the great Tyee—a Chinook salmon in excess of 14kg

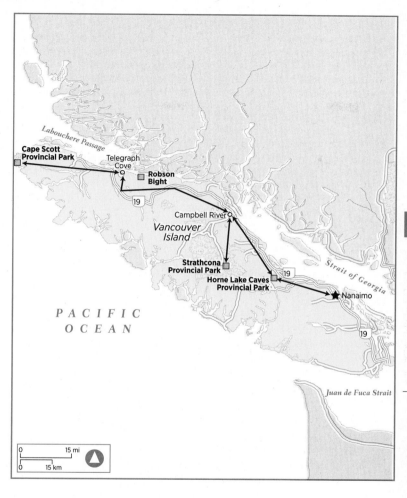

(31 lb.) (p. 188) or follow in Haig Brown's footsteps to fly-fish the fast-moving waters of Campbell River.

Day 4: Sea-Kayaking in Whale Waters

The road north leads up **Telegraph Cove** (p. 204), one of the remaining communities built on stilts over the water. Spend the afternoon sea-kayaking near **Robson Bight** (p. 205), a unique ecological reserve for whales; sightings are almost guaranteed. Continue on to Port Hardy for the ferries north, which travel via the scenic Inside Passage to the most northerly of BC's coastal islands, the Queen Charlotte Islands—land of Haida Gwai (see "Cruising the Queen Charlotte Strait," p. 191).

Days 5 & 6: Extreme Hiking

Cape Scott Provincial Park (p. 209) lies at the end of the road, literally. Its extreme wilderness takes you from relatively easy trails through always-damp rainforest to much harder muddy bogs, craggy shorelines, and naturally wild beaches. You need to be self-sufficient to make it through to the very tip of Vancouver Island, and have a plan to keep at least one pair of socks dry.

Day 7: Return to Nanaimo

Allow 6 hours for the drive back from Cape Scott to Nanaimo; the distance is approximately 450km (280 miles). You'll need a four-wheel-drive vehicle if you plan to take any detours to communities such as **Zeballos** (p. 203), or else the gravel road will turn a 40-minute trip into a 2-hour crawl. If this itinerary has you yearning for more, consider taking a day cruise aboard *UChuck III* (p. 197) out of Gold River.

4

VICTORIA

Whoever said Victoria was for the newly wed and nearly dead needs to take a second look. Although it certainly has its fair share of the blue-rinse brigade, Victoria is a romantic place and, in the past decade, has evolved into a thriving city. Described by painter Emily Carr as "more English than England," Victoria's charm is moving beyond its quaint facade. Sure, there are still plenty of double-decker buses, heritage brick buildings covered with clambering vines, English-style taverns, and ever-blooming gardens, but there's also a definite zip in the air as the city's staid and sedentary pleasures give way to hipper places to shop and dine, and more active pursuits to enjoy.

In fact, Victoria is now nicknamed the "recreational capital" of British Columbia, and its range of activities reads like an exhaustive shopping list: year-round golf, whale-watching, fishing, cycling, hiking, and much more. Victoria is located around one of Canada's prettiest harbors, and the water is always busy with ships, kayaks, and so many floatplanes—sometimes as many as 120 takeoffs and landings a day—that the harbor is actually certified as the first "water aerodrome" in North America. Accommodations are first-class, many attractions are worthy of a repeat visit, shopping is varied, and restaurants are cosmopolitan and always busy. The flip side of Victoria's growth, and its balmy climate, is a marked increase in panhandlers.

You'll want to spend at least 2 days here, just to get a taste of what Victoria is becoming. It's also the ideal base from which to explore the rest of Vancouver Island. Extending more than 450km (280 miles) from Victoria to the northwest tip of Cape Scott, the island offers some of the most dramatic stretches of coastal wilderness in the Pacific Northwest. (See chapters 6, 7, and 8 for coverage of the rest of Vancouver Island.)

ESSENTIALS
Getting There
BY PLANE   Most visitors arrive via a connecting flight from either **Vancouver International Airport** (© 604/207-7077; www.yvr.ca) or

Seatac International Airport in Seattle (☎ 206/787-5388; www.portseattle. org). Airlines flying into the rapidly expanding **Victoria International Airport** (☎ 250/953-7500; www.victoriaairport.com) include **Air Canada** (☎ 888/247-2262; www.aircanada.com), **Horizon Air** (☎ 800/547-9308; www.alaskaair. com), and **WestJet** (☎ 888/937-8538; www.westjet.com). The Victoria International Airport is near the BC Ferries terminal in Sidney, 26km (16 miles) north of Victoria off Highway 17. Highway 17 heads south to Victoria, becoming Douglas Street as you enter downtown.

Airport bus service, operated by **AKAL Airport** (☎ 877/386-2525 or 250/386-2526; www.victoriaairporter.com), takes about 45 minutes to get into town. Buses leave from the airport daily every 30 minutes, from 4:30am to midnight. The adult fare is C$18 one-way. Drop-offs and pickups are made at most Victoria area hotels. **Yellow Cabs** (☎ 800/808-6881 or 250/381-2222), and **Blue Bird Cabs** (☎ 800/665-7055 or 250/382-2222) make airport runs. It costs about C$50 one-way, plus tip.

Several car-rental firms have desks at the Victoria International Airport, including **Avis** (☎ 800/879-2847 or 250/656-6033; www.avis.com), **Budget** (☎ 800/668-9833 or 250/953-5300; www.budgetvictoria.com), **Hertz** (☎ 800/654-3131 or 250/656-2312; www.hertz.com), and **National (Tilden)** (☎ 800/227-7368 or 250/656-2541; www.nationalcar.com). Car reservations are recommended from June to September and during peak travel times on holiday weekends.

Vintage Car Rentals (☎ 250/588-1122) are among of the neatest vehicle rentals around. The 1920s era Mercedes SSK100, Bugatti, and 1937 Jaguar certainly look the part, but these kit-car look-alikes are, understandably, more reliable. Rentals are geared to scenic day trips—a treat for meandering the Cowichan Valley or Saanich Peninsula. A 2-hour rental is C$99; an 8-hour rental is C$199.

BY TRAIN **VIA Rail** trains arrive at Victoria's **VIA Rail Station** (450 Pandora Ave., near the Johnson St. Bridge; ☎ 888/842-7245; www.viarail.com).

BY BUS The **Victoria Bus Depot** is at 700 Douglas St. (behind the Fairmont Empress Hotel). **Pacific Coach Lines** (☎ 800/661-1725 within North America or 250/385-4411 in Victoria; www.pacificcoach.com) offers daily service to and from Vancouver, and it includes the ferry trip across the Georgia Strait between Tsawwassen and Sidney. **Greyhound Canada** (☎ 800/661-8747, or 250/385-4411 in Victoria; www.greyhound.ca) provides daily service up island to Nanaimo, Port Alberni, Campbell River, and Port Hardy.

BY FERRY **BC Ferries** offers crossings from the mainland to various points on Vancouver Island (☎ 888/BCFERRY [888/223-3779] outside the Victoria dialing area, or 250/386-3431; www.bcferries.com). **The Victoria Express** (☎ 800/633-1589; www.victoriaexpress.com) operates a seasonal passenger-only ferry service between Port Angeles and Victoria, as does **Clipper Vacations** (☎ 800/888-2535; www.victoriaclipper.com) between Seattle and Victoria Harbour. From the San Juan Islands, you can catch a **Washington State** passenger/car ferry (☎ 800/843-3779; www.wsdot.wa.gov/ferries) into Sidney, south of Victoria. **BlackBall Ferry Line** (☎ 360/457-4491 in Washington or 250/386-2202 on Vancouver Island; www. cohoferry.com) provides passenger and car service from Port Angeles into Victoria Harbour. See "Getting There," in chapter 3, for more information.

Visitor Information

The **Tourism Victoria Visitor Information Centre** (812 Wharf St.; ✆ **250/953-2033;** www.tourismvictoria.com) is an excellent resource for brochures, ideas for itineraries, and maps. Tourism Victoria also operates a **reservations hotline** (✆ **800/663-3883**) for last-minute bookings at hotels, inns, and B&Bs. The center is open daily September through April 9am to 5pm, May and June 8:30am to 6:30pm, and July and August 9am to 9pm. Take bus no. 1, 27, or 28 to Douglas and Courtney streets.

City Layout

Victoria was settled around the Inner Harbour in the mid-1800s and grew out from there. Because of the *curvy* shoreline, the grid system of streets doesn't kick in immediately, but there are three main **north-south arteries** that will get you almost anywhere you may want to reach in Victoria.

Government Street leads from the Inner Harbour to downtown (Wharf St. merges with Government St. in front of the Fairmont Empress Hotel); **Douglas Street** runs behind the Fairmont Empress, parallel to Government Street. It is the city's main business thoroughfare, as well as the highway north to Nanaimo and beyond. It's also the Trans-Canada Highway, Highway 1, Mile Zero is at the corner of Douglas Street and Dallas Road. **Blanshard Street,** which runs parallel to Government and Douglas streets, becomes Highway 17, the route to the Saanich Peninsula, Butchart Gardens, and the ferry terminals to Vancouver and the San Juan islands.

Three major east-west streets of note are **Johnson Street,** in Old Town/Downtown—the Johnson Street Bridge divides the Upper Harbour and the Inner Harbour. **Belleville Street** runs in front of the Parliament Buildings, along the Inner Harbour's southern edge up to Fisherman's Wharf. It then loops around to become **Dallas Road,** which follows the water's edge towards Oak Bay.

When you're looking for an address, be aware that the suite number precedes the building number, which generally speaking, goes up in increments of 100 per block as you travel north and east. Addresses for all east-west downtown streets (Fort, Yates, Johnson, and so on) start at 500 at Wharf Street. This means all buildings between Wharf and Government streets fall between 500 and 599; the next block, between Government and Douglas streets, are numbers 600 through 699, and so on. Detailed maps of downtown and farther afield are available for free at the Tourism Victoria Visitor Info Centre. Invariably, hotels have maps they will mark up with a highlighter pen, showing you the quickest, easiest, and most interesting routes.

Victoria's Neighborhoods in Brief

Victoria central is so compact that it's hard to draw definitive lines dividing the three major neighborhoods. Suffice it to say that the nearer you are to the water, the more expensive the hotel room, so unless you're absolutely hooked on having a view, save yourself a few dollars by heading a block or two inland.

INNER HARBOR

For most visitors, this is where it's at, and it's what those glossy tourism brochures depict in their Victoria sell. Framed by the Parliament Buildings on one side and the Fairmont Empress on another, the Inner Harbor is where to find cabs, horse-drawn carriage rides, double-decker tour buses, ferries, floatplanes, whale-watching outfitters, and a host of other tourist services. Attractions such as the **BC Royal Museum** and **Undersea Gardens** are here, alongside some of the city's most expensive hotels. There's an easy waterside stroll that takes you around the harbor perimeter; in summer it fills up with artist-vendors selling photographs, Native carvings, and inexpensive jewelry. It's touristy and expensive, but also picturesque.

DOWNTOWN & OLD TOWN

Head away from the water, and within 2 to 3 blocks, you're in Victoria's social and commercial centers. Because the two neighborhoods blend together, Victorians usually refer to them together. **Old Town** tends to include Bastion and Market squares—the areas that grew up around the original Fort Victoria at View and Government streets. **Downtown** tends to include everything east of Wharf Street, and is where you'll find the bulk of the city's shopping, banking, restaurants, bars, and hotels. Staying here may save you a few dollars, but it can be noisy, especially when the pubs and nightclubs let out.

CHINATOWN

The size of this area belies its history. Although only 2 square blocks, Victoria's Chinatown is the oldest in North America. The historic alleyways and buildings make for an intriguing visit, especially **Fan Tan Alley,** Canada's narrowest commercial street. Just over a meter (3¼ ft.) wide, this narrow alleyway cuts a divide between brick buildings that once housed gambling joints and opium dens, but has given way to curiosity and souvenir shops.

JAMES BAY, OAK BAY, ROSS BAY, FERNWOOD & ROCKLAND

Largely residential, these peaceful and postcard-pretty neighborhoods boast some large turn-of-the-20th-century manor homes and gardens—some are distinctive B&Bs—as well as newer homes. **Oak Bay,** in particular, has retained a quintessential, quieter English ambience and offers excellent beaches, golf courses, and tea houses. Although away from Victoria central, the property taxes are hefty enough here to warrant higher-than-expected room rates. An address in neighboring **Rockland,** too, has cache, likely because it is home to the official residence of British Columbia's Lieutenant Governor. All these neighborhoods are easiest to reach by car.

BEAR MOUNTAIN

A little farther out, Bear Mountain is a still-developing neighborhood that has turned a rural mountain into a resort hamlet much akin to Whistler in style and setting. Its central focus is year-round golf, which is attracting a mix of investment rental-pool condos; golf-keener retirees; and, at the base of the development, young families.

GETTING AROUND
By Public Transportation

The **Victoria Regional Transit System** (BC Transit; © **250/382-6161;** www. bctransit.com) operates approximately 40 bus routes throughout **Greater Victoria** and the outer suburbs of **Sooke** and **Sidney.** Regular service on the main routes runs Monday to Friday from 6am to midnight. Call for schedules on the weekends. Consult the **"Victoria Rider's Guide"** for schedules and routes, available at the **Tourism Victoria Visitor Information Centre** (see "Visitor Information," above). The guide outlines transit routes for many of the city's neighborhoods, landmarks, and attractions. Popular routes include no. 2 (Oak Bay), no. 11 (Downtown, James Bay, Beacon Hill Park), no. 14 (Craigflower, University of Victoria), no. 23 (Art Gallery of Victoria), no. 61 (Sooke), no. 70 (Sidney, Swartz Bay), and no. 75 (Butchart Gardens). This route includes a pickup at the Sidney ferry terminal and is handy for those arriving from the mainland without a vehicle.

Fares are no longer based on the number of geographic zones a passenger crosses; they are a flat fare to travel from Sidney to Sooke: C$2.55 adults, C$1.65 seniors and children to grade 7, free for children 5 and under. Transfers are valid for travel in one direction with no stopovers. A **DayPass**—which costs C$7.75 adults, C$5.50 seniors and children—is available at the Tourism Victoria Visitor Information Centre, at convenience stores, and at outlets displaying the FareDealer symbol. See "Specialized Travel Resources," in chapter 3.

By Car

If you must bring your car (exploring downtown is really best done on foot), make sure your hotel has parking. Parking spaces around the city center are at a premium. (Hotels that have parking are identified in "Where to Stay.") For out-of-town activities, car-rental agencies include **Avis,** at 1001 Douglas St. (© **800/879-2847** or 250/386-8468; www.avis.com); **Budget,** at 757 Douglas St. (© **800/268-8900** or 250/953-5300; www.budgetvictoria.com); **Hertz Canada,** at 2634 Douglas St. (© **800/263-0600** or 250/385-4440; www.hertz.com); and **National (Tilden),** at 767 Douglas St. (© **800/387-4747** or 250/386-1213; www.nationalcar.com). Renting a car averages C$60 per day but may be less with various discounts.

By Taxi

Yellow Cabs (© 800/808-6881 or 250/381-2222) and **Blue Bird Cabs** (© **800/655-7055** or 250/382-2222) are good bets. But do call ahead—very few stop for flag-downs, especially when it's raining. Rides around the downtown area cost C$7 to C$10, plus a 10% to 15% tip.

By Ferry

Once you're downtown, scooting across the harbor in one of the tiny, 12-passenger ferries operated by **Victoria Harbour Ferry** (© **250/708-0201;** www.victoria harbourferry.com) is fun—and expedient—in getting from one part of the city to another. The squat, cartoon-style boats have big wraparound windows that allow everyone a view. Ferry connections to the Fairmont Empress, the Coast Harbourside Hotel, and the Delta Victoria Ocean Pointe Resort run May through October daily every 15 minutes from 9am to 9pm. From November to April, the ferries run only on sunny weekends from 11am to 5pm. When the weather is "iffy," call the ferry office to check whether the ferries are running that day. The cost per hop is C$5 adults, C$2.50 children 12 years and under. See "Organized Tours," later in this chapter, for other ways to enjoy a ferry ride.

[Fast FACTS] VICTORIA

American Express

There is no Victoria office. To report lost or stolen traveler's checks, call © **800/221-7282.**

Business Hours

Banks in Victoria are open Monday to Thursday from 10am to 3pm, Friday from 10am to 6pm. **Stores** are open Monday to Saturday from 10am to 6pm. Many stores are also open on Sunday in summers. Last call at the city's bars and cocktail lounges is 2am.

Royal British
Columbia Museum **46**
Victoria Bug Zoo **39**
WildPlay Elements Park **6**

RESTAURANTS ◆
Aura **35**
Azuma Sushi **27**
Baan Thai **17**
Barb's Place **52**
Black Olive **22**
Blue Crab Bar & Grill **51**
Bon Rouge Bistro &
Boulangerie **40**
Brasserie L'Ecole **23**
Cafe Brio **16**
Camille's **30**
Foo Asian Street Food **19**
Il Terrazzo Ristorante **33**
James Bay Tea Room &
Restaurant **61**
Lucy's in the Square **8**
The Mark **59**
Pagliacci's **28**
Pescatore's **42**
Pink Bicycle **18**
Pizzeria Prima Strada **65**
rebar Modern Food **31**
Red Fish/Blue Fish **36**
Restaurant Matisse **25**
Santiago's **56**
Smoken Bones
Cookshack **5**
Stage **9**
Superior Restaurant **50**

James Bay Inn **62**
Magnolia Hotel & Spa **38**
Oak Bay Guest House **10**
Ocean Island
Backpackers Inn **20**
Oswego Hotel **57**
Prior House B&B Inn **13**
Queen Victoria Hotel **45**
Royal Scott
Suite Hotel **58**
Spinnaker's
Guest House **34**
Swans Hotel **24**
Victoria Marriott
Inner Harbour **43**
Villa Marco Polo **12**
Westin Bear Mountain
Golf Resort & Spa **4**

ATTRACTIONS ●
Abkhazi Garden **11**
All Fun Recreation Park **2**
Art Gallery of
Greater Victoria **15**
Beacon Hill Park **63**
Centre of the Universe **3**
Craigdarroch Castle **14**
Finnerty Garden **7**
Hatley Park & Museum **1**
Maritime Museum of
British Columbia **29**
Miniature World **37**
Pacific Undersea
Gardens **48**
Parliament Buildings **47**

ACCOMMODATIONS ■
Abigail's Hotel **44**
Admiral Inn **49**
Albion Manor **53**
Andersen House B&B **55**
Bedford Regency **26**
Dashwood Manor **64**
Delta Victoria Ocean
Pointe Resort & Spa **32**
Fairmont Empress **41**
The Gatsby Mansion **54**
Hotel Grand Pacific **60**
Hotel Rialto **21**
Inn at Laurel Point **35**

Currency Exchange

The best rates of exchange are at bank ATMs. Try the **Royal Bank** (1079 Douglas St.; ✆ **250/356-4500**), in the heart of downtown. **Calforex Foreign Currency Services** (606 Humboldt St. (✆ **250/380-3711**) is open 7 days a week. **Custom House Currency Exchange** ((✆ **250/389-6007**) is also open daily and has locations at 815 Wharf St. and the Bay Centre.

Dentists

Most major hotels have a dentist on call. You can also visit the **Cresta Dental Centre** (28–3170 Tillicum Rd., at Burnside St., in Tillicum Mall; ✆ **250/384-7711**). Open Monday to Friday from 8am to 9pm, Saturday from 9am to 5pm, and Sunday from 11am to 5pm. Call ahead for an appointment.

Doctors

Hotels usually have a doctor on call or are able to refer you to one. Clinics include the **Downtown Medical Clinic** (622 Courtney St.; ✆ **250/380-2210**), open Monday to Friday 8:30am to 5:30pm; and the **James Bay Treatment Centre** (100–230 Menzies St.; ✆ **250/388-9934**), open Monday to Friday from 9am to 6pm, Saturday 10am to 4pm. Call for an appointment.

Drugstores

Pick up your allergy medication or refill your prescription at **Shoppers Drug Mart** (1222 Douglas St.; ✆ **250/381-4321**). Open Monday to Friday from 7am to 8pm, Saturday from 9am to 7pm, and Sunday from 9am to 6pm. **Rexall Drug Store** (649 Fort St.; ✆ **250/384-1195**) is open Monday to Saturday from 9am to 6pm, and Sunday and holidays from noon to 4pm.

Emergencies

Dial ✆ **911** for police, fire, ambulance, and poison control.

Hospitals

Local hospitals include the **Royal Jubilee Hospital** (1900 Fort St.; ✆ **250/370-8000**, or 250/370-8212 for emergencies); and **Victoria General Hospital** (1 Hospital Way; ✆ **250/727-4212**, or 250/727-4181 for emergencies).

Hotlines

Emergency numbers include **Royal Canadian Mounted Police** ((✆ **250/380-6261**), **Crime Stoppers** ((✆ **250/386-8477**), **Emotional Crisis Centre** ((✆ **250/386-6323**), **Sexual Assault Centre** ((✆ **250/383-3232**), and **Poison Control Centre** ((✆ **800/567-8911**).

Internet Access

Nearly all hotels have either Wi-Fi or high-speed access in a public lounge or in guest bedrooms. The Greater Victoria Public Library (735 Broughton St.; ✆ **250/382-7241**) has a dozen terminals and is open Monday, Wednesday, Friday, and Saturday 9am to 6pm, Tuesday and Thursday 9am to 9pm. Or try James Bay Coffee & Books (143 Menzies St.; ✆ **250/386-4700**); it's just around the corner from the Parliament Buildings.

Police

Dial ✆ **911** for emergencies. For non-emergencies, the **Victoria City Police** can be reached at ✆ **250/995-7654.**

Post Office

The main **Canada Post office** is at 714 Yates St. ((✆ **250/953-1352**). The **Oak Bay post office** is at 1625 Fort St. ((✆ **250/595-2552**). There are also postal outlets in **Shoppers Drug Mart** (see "Drugstores," above).

Safety

Crime rates are quite low in Victoria, but transients panhandle throughout the downtown and Old Town areas. Lock items in the glove compartment or trunk when you park your car, and avoid dark alleys and uninhabited areas.

Weather

For local weather updates, call ✆ **250/363-6717** and follow the prompts. Or check www.theweather network.com.

WHERE TO STAY

Victoria has a wide choice of fine accommodations, and all are in, or within walking distance of, the **Inner Harbour** and **downtown core.** These are the pricier neighborhoods, especially those in sight of the water in the height of summer. Generally speaking, the quality of both service and amenities is also high, or at least, is priced accordingly. It's always worth asking about special rates and other discounts, and speaking with the hotel directly instead of a central reservations system (in the case of the big chains), since they're more apt to give you a preferred rate. Victoria relies heavily on visitors from the U.S. and does well to keep its tourist product fresh. Because the city's small by international standards, hospitality still feels genuine. Like in many cities, though, parking is an issue, so if you can get free parking, grab it, or you'll find your reasonable room rate suddenly inflated by $10 or even $28 per night. Thankfully, this is a walking destination, so the best advice is to leave your car at home, even if you decide to stay in a neighboring neighborhood. Further afield in Sooke, Sidney, and Brentwood Bay, there are some truly spectacular options, and transit connections make them convenient, too (see chapter 6 for where to stay).

Inner Harbour & Nearby

VERY EXPENSIVE

Delta Victoria Ocean Pointe Resort and Spa ★   Huge rooms, great bathrooms, and deluxe bedding are all part of the relatively clutter-free decor, which highlights the gleaming woods and the soft, natural colors throughout. Located on the north side of the Inner Harbour, many of the guest rooms have floor-to-ceiling windows that view the Legislative Buildings and the Fairmont Empress. For a few dollars more, you get Signature perks of breakfast, evening hors d'oeuvres, and turn-down service. All rooms come with the usual toiletries, down duvets, and cuddly robes. The European-style spa rivals the Fairmont's Willow Stream for top spa billing, and is a destination in itself. The hotel's sports and fitness facilities are also extensive, including racquet courts and a large, glass-walled indoor pool that feels like swimming outdoors. **Lure Seafood Restaurant and Lounge** (✆ **250/360-5873**), boasts the best dining-room views in the city, not to mention serving quality dishes. It's an especially romantic spot when night falls, and you can savor the very pretty night lights of the city's harbor front.

45 Songhees Rd., Victoria, BC V9A 6T3. ✆ **800/667-4677** or 250/360-2999. www.deltahotels.com. 250 units. Apr to mid-Oct C$129–C$399 double, C$439–C$799 suite; mid-Oct to Mar C$119–C$319 double, C$329–C$629 suite. Additional adult C$30. Children 18 & under stay free in parent's room. AE, DC, DISC, MC, V. Valet parking C$15. Pets accepted (C$35 per stay). **Amenities:** Restaurant; bar; babysitting; health club; ozonated indoor swimming pool; room service; spa; 2 night-lit outdoor tennis courts; 1 indoor racquetball & squash court. *In room:* A/C, TV/DVD player, hair dryer, minibar, Wi-Fi.

Fairmont Empress ★★   It's an ivy-adorned harbor-side landmark, and staying here is the quintessential Victoria experience. Ongoing renovations maintain the old girl's elegance, but even Fairmont's magic couldn't make many of the 1908-era rooms any larger, so this still means small rooms (billed as "cozy"), narrow corridors, and a disparity of views that might just as easily include the unsightly rooftops of the hotel's working areas as the harbor. If you're slightly claustrophobic, don't even think about these. They're a lot of money for what you get, too. That said, guest rooms, as well as studio-, one-, and two-bedroom suites, are all superb, and Fairmont Gold are superb-plus, offering extra-large beds and windows that let the light pour in, as well as extras such as TVs in the bathrooms and iPod docks. Gold guests have private check-in, their own concierge, and a private lounge with an honor bar, complimentary hors d'oeuvres (often enough for a light supper), and breakfast. The **Willow Stream Spa** (✆ **250/995-4650**), still ranks as the city's finest spa retreats, and some of the services are priced accordingly. Dining choices include the Bengal Lounge (its ceiling fans and tall palms are very colonial-India), the Empress Dining Room, and Kipling's. The famous afternoon tea is served year-round in the Main Tea Lobby, spilling into surrounding areas as the number of tea drinkers dictates. Call ✆ **250/389-2727** for all dining reservations.

721 Government St., Victoria, BC V8W 1W5. ✆ **800/441-1414** or 250/384-8111. www.fairmont.com/empress. 477 units. July–Sept C$249–C$800 double, C$429–C$1,509 suite, C$399–C$1,500 Fairmont Gold; Oct–June C$199–C$479 double, C$229–C$1,269 suite, C$299–C$1,269 Fairmont Gold. Children 11 & under stay free in parent's room. Packages available. AE, DC, DISC, MC, V. Underground valet parking C$29. Bus: 5. Small pets accepted (C$25). **Amenities:** 2 restaurants; bar/lounge; tearoom; babysitting; health club; large heated indoor pool; room service; spa. *In room:* A/C, TV w/pay movies, hair dryer, minibar, iPod dock, Wi-Fi.

Hotel Grand Pacific ★★ The "grandness" begins as you approach the hotel beneath a canopy of trees—beside ducks paddling in waterfall-fed pools. Located next to the Parliament Buildings, the Grand Pacific sits right on the waterfront. Guest rooms are more sizeable and elegantly contemporary than those in the other waterfront hotels, and because of the wide range of accommodations, from standard rooms facing the Olympic Mountains and smallish bathrooms to multi-room harbor-view suites with fireplaces and lavishly large bathrooms, you might be able to afford top-notch luxury here for less than what's offered elsewhere. The hotel has a quality spa; the city's most extensive fitness facilities (with a huge ozonated indoor pool); and dining options that include the Mark (see "Where to Dine," later in this chapter), geared to high-end, romantic encounters. On weekends, a sophisticated dim sum is served in the Pacific Restaurant, paired with an extensive loose leaf tea menu.

463 Belleville St., Victoria, BC V8V 1X3. ✆ **800/663-7550** or 250/386-0450. www.hotelgrandpacific.com. 304 units. Mid-May to Sept C$199–C$389 double, from C$249 suite; Oct to mid-May C$139–C$269 double, from C$189 suite. Children 17 & under stay free in parent's room. AE, DC, DISC, MC, V. Parking C$15. Bus: 30 to Superior & Oswego sts., 27, or 28. **Amenities:** 2 restaurants; lounge; babysitting; health club; indoor ozone-filtered lap pool; room service; spa; squash court. *In room:* A/C, TV w/pay movies, hair dryer, minibar.

EXPENSIVE

Andersen House B&B ★ This small 1891 house, with its high ceilings, stained-glass windows, and ornate Queen Anne–style fireplaces, is filled with furnishings that echo the old British Empire, only to be spiced up with splashes of Art Deco paintings. The combination is very lively. Every room has a private entrance and is unique. The sun-drenched Casablanca Room has French doors and a window seat overlooking the Parliament Buildings; the Captain's Apartment comes with a claw-foot tub and an extra bedroom; and the ground level Garden Studio, the most secluded and least expensive of the three rooms, has a hot tub. Rates include a splendid breakfast.

301 Kingston St., Victoria, BC V8V 1V5. ✆ **250/388-4565.** www.andersenhouse.com. 3 units. June–Sept C$235–C$265 double; Oct–May C$135–C$195 double. Rates include full breakfast. MC, V. Free off-street parking. Bus: 30 to Superior & Oswego sts. Children 11 & under not accepted. **Amenities:** Jacuzzi. *In room:* TV/DVD player, hair dryer, Wi-Fi.

The Gatsby Mansion   Overlooking the Inner Harbour, just across from where the Seattle–Port Angeles ferry docks, this heritage complex comprises three buildings, each trapped in a time warp, with antique furniture, Italian stained glass, velvet tapestries, frescoed ceilings, and meandering hallways. The main Gatsby Mansion (ca. 1897) exudes a Queen Anne style, the Judges House (ca. 1877) incorporates Italianate architecture, and the Middle House (ca. 1872) was the site's original cottage. Whatever the building, staying here is like staying in a museum, and if you're drawn to the eccentric, this place will appeal. Each guest room has a different configuration, so you might get a square room or one with corner nooks, or even a 1.5m (5-ft.) corridor into a sitting area. Bathrooms are small and functional. All beds feature the comforts of down duvets and fine linens. Breakfast, lunch, dinner, and a gracious high tea are served beneath twinkling chandeliers in what were once the front parlor, drawing room, and dining rooms. *Tip:* If you want space, forgo the harbor view and opt for a room at the back. The **Ramada Huntingdon Hotel & Suites** (✆ **800/663-7557** or 250/381-3456) next door has the same owners. The hotel is less ornate but its large rooms, pullout beds, and in-room fridges make it a value option for the budget-conscious.

309 Belleville St., Victoria, BC V8V 1X2. ✆ **800/563-9656** or 250/388-9191. www.bellevillepark.com. 20 units. Mid-May to Sept C$99–C$299 double; Oct to mid-May C$79–C$299 double. Rates include full breakfast. Packages available. AE, MC, V. Free parking. Bus: 5 to Belleville & Government sts., 27, 28, or 30. **Amenities:** Restaurant; lounge. *In room:* TV w/pay movies, Wi-Fi.

Inn at Laurel Point ★   One of the Inner Harbour's first modern hotels, the Inn at Laurel Point received a recent makeover, updating its initial simple Japanese-style design with West Coast–style slate, fresh earth-toned furnishings, and lots of windows facing the waterfront. Japanese visitors love the place. It also boasts being BC's only carbon-neutral hotel. There are two wings, and all guest rooms have balconies with views; the scene, harbor or inland, helps determine the price you'll pay. Rooms in the south wing are more spacious and have an Asian theme, including shoji-style sliding doors, down duvets, and plenty of Asian art. The exquisite Japanese Garden features a large reflecting pond and a waterfall that cascades over a whopping 21,300 kilograms (46,958 lb.) of rock. The **Aura Restaurant** is the most significant change; a veritable parade of food and views (see "Where to Dine," later in this chapter). *Tip:* The inn is on the waterfront pathway that links Fisherman's Wharf, BlackBall Ferry, the Parliament Buildings, and the Royal BC Museum.

680 Montreal St., Victoria, BC V8V 1Z8. ✆ **800/663-7667** or 250/386-8721. www.laurelpoint.com. 200 units (135 double, 65 suites). June to mid-Oct C$199 double, C$309 suite; mid-Oct to May C$119 double, C$189 suite. Additional adult C$25. Children 18 & under stay free in parent's room. Packages available. AE, DC, MC, V. Parking C$18. Small pets accepted (C$50). **Amenities:** Restaurant; babysitting; small heated pool; room service. *In room:* A/C, TV w/pay movies, hair dryer, iPod dock, Wi-Fi.

Oswego Hotel   From the outside, Victoria's first purpose-built hotel looks like a swish apartment complex catering to the W-hotel crowd. Offering a mix of studio rooms and one- and two-bedroom suites, units boast enormous windows; chocolate-colored and crisp-white designer furnishings; full kitchens with snazzy slate floors; granite countertops; and instead of the obligatory coffeemaker, look for a French coffee press. Bath amenities, too, incorporate an extra touch: a laminated menu of different bath recipes, which are delivered as silk sachets filled with special ingredients and, perhaps, a tea light. Time for Two (C$12) includes dried hibiscus and rose petals; the Detox (C$12) is an Ayurvedic blend of cleansing herbs. Once bathed and relaxed, you'll find the queen beds to be comfortable, and extra sofa beds will accommodate partners with insomnia.

877 Oswego St., Victoria, BC V8V 5C1. ℂ **877/7-OSWEGO** (877/767-9346) or 250/294-7500. www.oswego victoria.com. 90 units. C$179–C$269 studio; C$229–C$329 1-bedroom suite; C$329–C$449 2-bedroom suite. Additional adult C$25. Children 18 & under stay free in parent's room. AE, DC, MC, V. Parking C$10. Pets accepted (C$25). **Amenities:** Restaurant; lounge. *In room:* HD satellite TV, hair dryer, Wi-Fi.

MODERATE

Albion Manor ★   Recent renovations have worked miracles, transforming this 1892 heritage house into an art-inspired home. The artist-owners have a background in staging international expos, so decor incorporates whimsical sculptures (sometimes edgy and always theatrical), Victorian-era antiques, and well-traveled pieces from Morocco to Papua New Guinea for an eclectic, one-of-a-kind ambiance. Nearly every item has a story. Guest rooms, beds, and lounges are exceptionally comfortable, with intriguing items that each have a story. The grand bed in room 6 once belonged to the Governor of Wisconsin; the 1870s bed in room 7 is from Brittany, France, and the imposing, elaborately carved four-poster in room 8 is from 1750s England. Some rooms have a private entrance, verandah, or Jacuzzi tub. Delicious breakfasts are served, family style, in the formal dining room.

224 Superior St., Victoria, BC V8V 1T3. ℂ **877/389-0012.** www.albionmanor.com. 8 units. June–Sept C$159–C$199 double; Oct to mid-Mar C$109–C$149 double; mid-Mar to May C$119–C$159 double. MC, V. Free parking. Pets accepted (C$30). **Amenities:** 2 lounges. *In room:* TV/DVD player, hair dryer, iPod dock, Wi-Fi.

James Bay Inn ⚑   There aren't many budget rooms around the Inner Harbour, but this is one of them. Granted, the 1907 manor has a faded quality about it, and rooms are on the small side and very simply furnished, but at least you can say you slept in the same house where Emily Carr, one of Canada's most beloved painters, once lived. The real bargain is the renovated heritage cottage next door. The four suites may be small, but they come with full-size kitchens and somewhat better furnishings. High-season rates here are C$241 with two free parking spaces. A third building nearby sleeps eight and runs at C$197 to C$231 per night. *Tip:* All guests receive 15% off meals at the on-premises restaurant and pub.

270 Government St., Victoria, BC V8V 2L2. ℂ **800/836-2649** or 250/384-7151. www.jamesbayinn. bc.ca. 45 units. July–Oct C$125–C$215 double; Nov–June C$69–C$159 double. Additional adult C$15. Children 16 & under stay free in parent's room. AE, MC, V. Free parking. Bus: 5 or 30 to Niagara St. **Amenities:** Restaurant; bar. *In room:* TV, hair dryer, Wi-Fi.

Queen Victoria Inn 🏨   The only hotel to be surrounded by parks, this dear old lady has sat on this corner for 40 years, yet seems to fly beneath the radar in most guidebooks and brochures. The Queen does a hefty trade in tours but really deserves a second look by those in-the-know. It's unpretentiously comfortable, with a nice restaurant and inviting hotel lobby. Rooms provide all the comforts of home without frills, unless you get into the suites, where Italian marble creeps into the bathroom (as it does along some of the narrow corridors). The marble baths in the Penthouse suites are enormous. The Italian touches speak to the inn's Italian family ownership, which in the bedrooms means colorful Mediterranean prints brightening up the walls. All rooms have balconies, and some have kitchens cleverly hidden behind sliding walls; some can be joined to create multi-room suites. If you're going to pay for parking, it's a steal here.

655 Douglas St., Victoria, BC V8V 2P9. © **800/663-7007** or 250/386-1312. www.qvhotel.com. 146 units. May–Sept C$205–C$230 double, C$300–C$650 suite; Oct–Apr C$112–C$125 double, C$165–C$375 suite. Additional adult C$25. Children 14 & under stay free in parent's room. AE, MC, V. Parking C$4. **Amenities:** Restaurant; lounge; fitness center; Jacuzzi; indoor pool; sauna. *In room:* TV, fridge (on request), hair dryer, kitchen (in some units; C$20 fee), Wi-Fi.

The Royal Scot Suite Hotel ★ 🗡️ ☺ Situated a block from the Inner Harbour, this suite hotel provides excellent value if you're not hooked on a waterfront view. Converted from an apartment building, guest rooms are large with lots of cupboard space. Studios include a living/dining area and kitchen; one-bedroom suites have separate bedrooms with king-size, queen-size, or twin beds. Kitchens are fully equipped, and living areas come with sofa beds. This is an ideal home base for families; weary parents in need of a few zzz's will love having their offspring scoot off to the children's games room or the indoor pool. **Jonathan's Restaurant** (© **250/383-5103**), has a summer patio. There are nine room types, ranging from guest rooms to two-bedroom corner suites, so you're bound to find something that fits. If you didn't bring your car, the Royal Scot operates a complimentary guest shuttle to downtown. *Tip:* Internet specials can offer up to 40% savings, even in high season.

425 Quebec St., Victoria, BC V8V 1W7. © **800/663-7515** or 250/388-5463. www.royalscot.com. 176 units. C$155–C$249 double; C$185–C$419 suite. Weekly, monthly & off-season discounts available. Children 11 & under stay free in parent's room. AE, DC, MC, V. Parking C$10. Bus: 30. **Amenities:** Restaurant; babysitting; small heated indoor pool; hydrotherapy pool; room service; sauna. *In room:* TV, hair dryer, Wi-Fi.

Downtown & Old Town

EXPENSIVE

Abigail's Hotel ★★ Tucked into a quiet residential cul-de-sac, only 3 blocks from downtown Victoria and the Inner Harbour, this European-style Tudor inn is about as chintzy and romantic as it can get. Guest rooms are resplendently decorated with antiques, wood-burning fireplaces, two-person Jacuzzis, fresh-cut flowers, and welcoming treats such as truffles and fruit. The six Coach House suites have extravagant touches such as four-poster beds, custom-made furniture, and Italian marble bathrooms with Jacuzzi tubs. Since the chef has cooked for the Queen, breakfast is fit for royalty—literally—and will be brought to your bedside on request. The small Pearl Spa offers a full range of quality spa services. Abigail's is geared to adults; children are discouraged.

906 McClure St., Victoria, BC V8V 3E7. © **800/561-6565** or 250/388-5363. www.abigailshotel.com. 23 units. May–June, & Sept to mid-Oct C$219–C$379 double; July–Aug C$249–C$409 double; mid-Oct to late Apr C$189–C$259 double. Rates include full breakfast & evening hors d'oeuvres. Spa, honeymoon & wine tour packages available. AE, MC, V. Free parking. Some pets accepted (C$25). Bus: 1. **Amenities:** Spa. *In room:* TV/DVD player, hair dryer, Wi-Fi.

The Magnolia Hotel & Spa ★★ With its central downtown location, this stylishly European boutique hotel offers lots of finishing touches to make you feel immediately welcome: a huge bowl of apples, a large arrangement of fresh flowers, and crisp daily newspapers. The hotel's personalized butler service adds to this attentiveness with an array of complimentary amenities, though sadly, not a real-McCoy butler. Guest rooms are bright, with floor-to-ceiling windows, custom-designed furniture, two-poster beds, and oversize desks. Executive Diamond suites have gas fireplaces. Of special note is the excellent **Aveda concept spa**

(www.spamagnolia.com), which recently expanded into new, ground-floor premises, and the hotel's **Prime Steakhouse & Lounge** (𝄞 **250/386-2010** reservations), a first class steak and seafood restaurant.

623 Courtney St., Victoria, BC V8W 1B8. 𝄞 **877/624-6654** or 250/381-0999. www.magnoliahotel.com. 64 units. July–Sept C$209–C$349 double; May & June C$189–C$229 double; Oct–Apr C$165–C$189 double. Rates include continental breakfast. Additional adult C$30. Children 11 & under stay free in parent's room. AE, DC, DISC, MC, V. Valet parking C$15. Bus: 5. Small pets accepted (C$60). **Amenities:** Restaurant; access to nearby health club; room service; spa. *In room:* A/C, TV w/pay movies, fridge, hair dryer, minibar, iPod dock, Wi-Fi.

Victoria Marriott Inner Harbour   Its modern and urban ambience may seem more geared to the business executive than a casual visitor, the enthusiastic staff will give you a warm welcome. Earning the honor of Lodging Top Operations from Marriott International in 2008, this Marriot's customer service really goes beyond lip service. Rooms have all the usual Marriott amenities, including a concierge level that offers a pleasant lounge with complimentary hors d'oeuvres in the evening and a continental breakfast. Rooms even have windows that open, which for many is a breath of fresh air. The hotel's location is central, and although set behind the Empress, from the upper-floor guest rooms, the views stretch to the Olympic Mountain Range in Washington State. Hotel amenities include a cozy bar and a full-size indoor pool. The **Fire & Water Fish and Chop House** serves high-quality seafood and steaks—the prime rib is especially noteworthy.

728 Humboldt St., Victoria, BC V8W 3Z5. 𝄞 **877/333-8338** or 250/480-3800. www.victoriamarriott. com. 236 units. C$100–C$300 double. AE, DC, MC, V. Valet parking C$20; self-parking C$16. **Amenities:** Restaurant; lounge; fitness center; hot tub; indoor pool; room service; sauna. *In room:* A/C, TV, fridge, hair dryer, minibar, Wi-Fi.

MODERATE & INEXPENSIVE

Admiral Inn 🗡 ☺   The harbor views here will more than make up for the small, motel-like rooms and bathrooms. Besides, they are comfortable and immaculately clean, and available at rates that attract couples, families, seniors, and others in search of a multimillion-dollar vista without the expense. Larger rooms have fridges, microwaves, pullout sofa beds, and balconies; the suites have full kitchens. The inn is a family-run operation, so service is empathetic and includes extras like free bicycles, cots, and cribs; free local calls; and lots of friendly advice on what to see and do. Parking is free, and that's a bonus anywhere near the city's core.

257 Belleville St., Victoria, BC V8V 1X1. 𝄞 **888/823-6472** or 250/388-6267. www.admiralinnhotel.com. 33 units. May & June C$129–C$179 double; July to mid-Oct C$149–C$229 double; mid-Oct to Apr C$99–C$139 double. Rates include continental breakfast. Additional adult C$10. Children 11 & under stay free in parent's room. AE, DC, MC, V. Free parking. Bus: 5 to Belleville & Government sts. Pets allowed (C$15). **Amenities:** Complimentary bikes. *In room:* A/C, TV, fridge, hair dryer, kitchen (in some units), Wi-Fi.

The Bedford Regency 🎁   Located on the main commercial drag (the entrance gives the impression that you're entering a shopping mall), the Bedford is one of Victoria's oldest hotels. Although tasteful renovations have brought it up to modern standards, its heritage gives way to an idiosyncratic guest room layout. Some are so tiny that the foot of the bed is just inches from the pedestal sink. Some have a fireplace "around the corner" beside a reading chair, while others might have two queen-size beds facing each other because the room is long and narrow. Bathrooms are small and very Art Deco. All rooms are elegantly comfortable with down duvets and quality toiletries, and the 12 Superior rooms have Jacuzzis and fireplaces. Window boxes mask the busy street scene below, which in summer can be a bit noisy until midnight. On the mezzanine level, a rather vacuous lounge keeps morphing from one concept to the other; the latest is as a GLBT venue called **The Ledge** (see p. 104). **The Garrick's Head Pub,** however, remains tried and true. *Tip:* If your travel plans are firm, check out the hotel's nonrefundable Internet rates at 35% savings.

1140 Government St., Victoria, BC V8W 1Y2. $©$ **800/665-6500** or 250/384-6835. www.bedfordregency. com. 40 units. June to mid-Oct C$149–C$200 double; mid-Oct to May C$89–C$169 double. AE, MC, V. Parking C$10. Bus: 5 to Douglas & Johnson sts. **Amenities:** Restaurant; pub; lounge. *In room:* TV, fridge, Wi-Fi.

Hotel Rialto 🎁 Like a phoenix from the ashes, the Rialto has risen out of a has-been hotel to become the city's hippest new boutique hotel. Named after the famous Rialto Bridge in Venice, the hotel's overall decor speaks to the new owner's Italian heritage. The widespread use of marble throughout the lobby and dining areas are typical of northern Italy, though most of this marble is quarried locally. Guest rooms are modern with dark wood furnishings, granite countertops, an in-room wine bar, flat-screen plasma TVs, and superior queen or king-size beds. The lower lobby displays the building's history, including some oriental antiques. **Veneto Tapas Lounge** ($©$ **250/383-7310**) has shot to the top of the "in" list for local trendies and after-work gatherings.

653 Pandora Ave., Victoria, BC V8W 1N8. $©$ **800/332-9981.** www.hotelrialto.ca. 39 units. July & Aug C$159–C$219 double; Sept-Mar C$119–C$C$189 double; Apr–June C$129–C$199 double. Additional adult C$25. Children 11 & under stay free in parent's room. AE, MC, V. Parking C$10. **Amenities:** Restaurant; bar. *In room:* TV w/pay movies, DVD player, fridge, hair dryer, iPod dock, Wi-Fi.

Ocean Island Backpackers Inn 🎁 This historic, four-level youth hostel–cum–apartment building attracts all age groups and families. Dorm accommodations sleep four to six people, and you can find co-ed as well as women-only rooms. If you're a twosome, the rates are reasonable enough that it's worth booking a whole dorm to yourself. Special family rooms are more hotel-like and have a private bathroom, multiple beds, and a fridge. This is not a place for shrinking violets. The lounges, bar, and dining room are magnets for lively and multilingual conversations with fellow travelers. In addition, Ocean Island operates a 1907 character house in the James Bay area that contains three self-contained, self-catering suites.

791 Pandora Ave., Victoria, BC V8W 1N9. $©$ **888/888-4180,** 866/888-4180, or 250/385-1788. www. oceanisland.com. 80 units. C$20–C$28 dorm bed; C$28–C$84 private room; C$99–C$160 family room. AE, MC, V. **Amenities:** Lounge; kitchen. *In room:* No phone, Wi-Fi.

Spinnaker's Guest House Located right on the waterfront, at the entrance to Victoria Harbour, Spinnakers is best known by locals for its brewpub (see "Suds Up!," later in this chapter). It can get a bit noisy around closing, but the guesthouse operation is an alternative to central lodgings, provided you don't mind a 15-minute walk to downtown or a 5-minute ferry ride. The complex includes two completely renovated circa-1880 buildings, the Heritage House and the Garden Suites, which are more like self-contained studio apartments; and the Bungalow has a large private backyard with pear trees. All rooms feature queen-size beds, soft earth-toned West Coast–style furnishings, and in-room Jacuzzis (except for shower-only room no. 4), and some have wood-burning fireplaces. Room no. 9 is one of the nicest; it has a vaulted ceiling close to 4.3m (14 ft.) high, a fireplace, a sitting room, a full kitchen, and a south-facing private sun deck.

308 Catherine St., Victoria, BC V9A 3S3. ✆ **877/838-2739** or 250/384-2739. www.spinnakers.com. 11 units. July to mid-Oct C$179–C$279 double; mid-Oct to June C$149–C$209 double. Rates include continental breakfast. AE, DC, MC, V. Free parking. Bus: 24 to Catherine St. **Amenities:** Brewpub. *In room:* TV, hair dryer, kitchen (in some units), Wi-Fi.

Swans Hotel ★★   The charming Swans offers a warm welcome in an intimately comfortable modern-day tavern. But it's more than a bed-and-beer experience. One of Victoria's best-loved heritage restorations, this 1913 warehouse now provides guests with 30 distinctive—and really roomy—suites. Most of the open concept studios and one- and two-bedroom suites are two-story lofts with 3.3m (11-ft.) exposed-beam ceilings and nifty layouts that have many, if not most, of the comforts of home. The studios have king beds; the rest have queen-size. Accommodating up to six adults, they feature fully equipped kitchens, separate living and dining areas, and private patios. If you want to go for the gusto, there's even a three-level, 279-sq.-m (3,003-sq.-ft.) penthouse with its own Roy Henry Vickers totem pole. Speaking of which, the hotel has one of Canada's largest private art collections, but you only get to see what's in the lobby since many pieces are in guest rooms. The **Wild Saffron Bistro & Wine Bar** is open daily. Other facilities include **Swans Pub** and **Buckerfields' Brewery** (see p. 102), which offers tours by appointment.

506 Pandora Ave., Victoria, BC V8W 1N6. ✆ **800/668-7926** or 250/361-3310. www.swanshotel.com. 30 suites. Mid-June to Sept C$199 studio, C$289–C$359 suite; Oct to mid-June C$179–C$189 studio, C$219–C$259 suite. Rates include continental breakfast. Weekly & monthly rates available. Additional adult C$35. Up to 2 children 12 & under stay free in parent's room. AE, DC, MC, V. Parking C$9. Bus: 23 or 24 to Pandora Ave. **Amenities:** Restaurant; wine bar; brewpub; babysitting; access to nearby health club; room service. *In room:* TV, fridge, hair dryer, kitchen, Wi-Fi.

Victoria Neighborhoods
EXPENSIVE

Dashwood Manor   Overlooking the bluff of the Pacific Ocean at the edge of Beacon Hill Park, just a 20 minute walk to downtown, this heritage inn has a West Coast exterior and a British colonial interior. Every guest room has an ocean view and comfortable sitting areas, fireplaces, and in some rooms, double chromo-therapy tubs—the ones with changeable colored lights. The breakfast room feels like those of a traditional (very nice) seaside guest house circa 1950s with six individual tables; the breakfast itself is certainly more elaborate. Expect extra home-baked muffins for the road or for walking along the coastline that weaves past your door. *Tip:* Indigo blue irises put on a show-stopping display each spring.

1 Cook St., Victoria, BC V8V 3W6. ✆ **800/667-5517**. www.dashwoodmanor.com. 10 units. C$169–C$239 double. MC, V. Free parking. Children 11 & under not accepted. **Amenities:** Lounge. *In room:* TV/DVD player, hair dryer, Wi-Fi.

Prior House B&B Inn   Out in the quiet and pretty Rockland neighborhood, this former English governor's manor and gardens are among the most picturesque in Victoria. Everything here takes you back to an earlier time: oak-paneled rooms with wood-burning fireplaces, stained-glass windows, hardwood floors, and a blend of antique and replica Edwardian furnishings. Every guest room is comfortable, with custom-made goose-down duvets and bathrooms fashioned in marble and sporting air-jetted tubs for two. Although the Lieutenant Governor's Royal Suite is the inn's pièce de résistance, with its 1880 king-size canopied bed, crystal chandeliers, and spa-style bathroom with gilded walls, the less ostentatious Windsor Penthouse Suite is just as much of a private sanctuary. The Hobbit Garden Studios are more simply decorated but no less appealing, with private patios into the well-tended garden. Attention to detail is what this inn is all about; you can even choose to have breakfast served to you in bed.

620 St. Charles St., Victoria, BC V8S 3N7. ✆ **877/924-3300** or 250/592-8847. www.priorhouse.com. 6 units. Mid-June to mid-Sept C$219–C$299 double; mid-Sept to mid-Oct & May to mid-June C$189–C$279 double; mid-Oct to Apr C$99–C$229 double. Rates include breakfast & afternoon tea. MC, V. Free parking. **Amenities:** Lounge. *In room:* TV/CD/DVD player, hair dryer, Wi-Fi.

Villa Marco Polo ★★★   Just down the road from the Lieutenant Governor's residence, everything about this Italian Renaissance mansion is true to its well-traveled namesake. First are the gardens, with their ornamental statues, reflection pool, and fountains. Then there are the public lounges, filled with antiques collected from all over the world—the Chinese cabinet in the lounge, the handmade books in the library, the Italian crystal chandelier in the dining room, to mention a few. Each of the four bedrooms is thematically decorated, with plush European linens fitted to king-size beds. The Silk Road suite has vaulted ceilings and hand-painted Tuscan murals; the Persian Suite is decorated with Persian fabrics and antiques; the Zanzibar suite has French doors onto a Juliette balcony; and the most eye-catching, the Alexandria Suite, is adorned with carved Turkish wooden shutters. The top of the house has been converted into a tiny loft spa and yoga/meditation area. Breakfast is a feast for the senses. Freshly baked goods may include buttermilk 10-grain muffins or caramelized pineapple pecan cakes, while entrees run from hot lemon lavender soufflés to baked eggs Florentine with a Persian pepper hollandaise.

1524 Shasta Place, Victoria, BC V8S 1X9. ✆ **877/601-1524** or 250/370-1524. www.villamarcopolo.com. 4 units. Mid-June to mid-Sept C$145–C$295 double; mid-Sept to mid-Oct & mid-Apr to mid-Jun C$125–C$265 double; mid-Oct to mid-Apr C$105–C$225 double. Rates include breakfast, afternoon tea & hors d'oeuvres. 2-night minimum July & August. AE, MC, V. Free parking. **Amenities:** Lounge; spa. *In room:* TV/CD/DVD player, hair dryer, iPod dock.

Westin Bear Mountain Golf Resort & Spa   Canada's first and only 36-hole Nicklaus-designed championship golf courses are the focal point of this new master-planned resort and residential community. The mountain-lodge style resort also includes five restaurants that range from fine dining to a sushi bar (the Cellar has a 12,500-wine bottle collection), Sante Spa, with a whole bunch of therapeutic and pampering treatments, and a state-of-the-art health club. Guest rooms have an earth-toned, natural decor with sitting areas, fireplaces, bathrooms with slate tile floors, well-stocked kitchenettes, and either a balcony or terrace overlooking the fairways and Mount Finlayson. If you're not a golfer, there are plenty of trails to hike and bike. Be aware of an optional, daily C$15 resort fee that includes amenities such as parking and Wi-Fi.

1999 Country Club Way, Victoria, BC V9B 6R9. ✆ **888/533-BEAR** (888/533-2327) or 250/391-7160. www.bearmountain.ca. 156 units. June–Sept C$229–C$459 double; Oct–May C$159–C$389 double. Additional adult C$30. AE, MC, V. Resort fee (C$15) includes parking, Wi-Fi, fitness club access, golf bag valet & storage. **Amenities:** 5 restaurants; lounge; pub; 2 golf courses; health club; saltwater pool; spa; mountain-bike rentals. *In room:* TV w/movies, DVD player (in suites), fridge, hair dryer, Wi-Fi.

MODERATE & INEXPENSIVE

Oak Bay Guest House 🍴   While a nearby resort still undergoes its from-the-ground-up redevelopment, this is the only place to stay in residential Oak Bay, and

Ponder This

Oak Bay is the Palm Tree Capital of Canada, with 2,669 palm trees in the municipality.

it exudes old England. New owners have considerable plans for modernizing, but until those take hold, you can still step inside the 1912 Tudor-style inn and enjoy the incoherency of an older building trying to make good in the 21st century. Stairs creak, corridors are narrow, and rooms are odd shapes because each has had an en suite added as plumbing could dictate. But that's the charm of the place—and the value. It's clean, comfortable, offers the basics, and is run by a staff who really makes you feel welcome.

1052 Newport Ave., Victoria, BC V8S 5E3.© **800/575-3812** or 250/598-3812. www.oakbayguesthouse. com. 11 units. May to mid-Oct C$89–C$179 double; mid-Oct to Apr C$79–C$149 double. Rates include breakfast. MC, V. Free parking. **Amenities:** TV lounge. *In room:* Hair dryer, no phone, Wi-Fi.

WHERE TO DINE

Purporting to have the second-highest number of restaurants per capita in North America (behind San Francisco), Victoria offers something for every taste and budget, and refreshingly, you don't always have to pay through the nose to get quality. And that includes one or two holes-in-the-wall. What you will pay for is the restaurant's proximity to a waterfront view. Most of the best restaurants are either in or within walking distance of downtown hotels, so you don't have to worry about who'll be the designated driver. While tapas and small plates continue to be hot sellers, check out rivals in charcuterie selections; at the lavish end of the scale are multi-course tasting menus, complete with wine pairings.

Vancouver Island is hugely influenced by the 100-Mile Diet and Slow Food movement, which takes full advantage of the island's extraordinary number of micro-climates where fresh produce, fisheries, farms, and vineyards thrive. The collaboration between chefs is creating a very sustainable restaurant and agri-tourism economy, all of which is best showcased in locally inspired menus. An Ocean Wise logo identifies restaurateurs (and/or their dishes) that use sustainable harvest. Although there's still a tendency for Victorians to eat early (restaurants are packed 7–9pm), many trendier restaurants accept late-night reservations.

Inner Harbour & Nearby

EXPENSIVE

Aura Restaurant ★ REGIONAL   With a chef who is in training to represent Canada at the 2012 World Culinary Olympics, you know the food's going to be above average. Regional cuisine, artisan wines, and such dishes as Dungeness and snow crab quesadilla for lunch, or a sour cherry glazed duck breast served with cauliflower ricotta gnocchi for dinner, are earning major kudos from local foodies. Every item has a recommended wine pairing, so it's a real opportunity to educate and titillate the palate. The restaurant's contemporary style includes floor-to-ceiling windows, from which you can take in breathtaking harbor views.

In the Inn at Laurel Point, 680 Montreal St.© **250/414-6739.** www.aurarestaurant.ca. Reservations recommended. Main courses lunch C$12–C$18, dinner C$26–C$31. AE, DC, DISC, MC, V. Daily 7am–9pm.

Blue Crab Bar & Grill ★★ SEAFOOD   This is the best seafood spot in the city, with killer views of the harbor to boot, so naturally, it's always busy and has a tendency to get noisy. Blue Crab's seafood specials, featured on their signature blackboards, are what keep this restaurant at the top. Dishes are unpredictable inventions, such as blue crab fish pot, grilled salmon with crispy yucca-root spaetzles, or smoked Alaskan black cod poached in coconut milk with a hint of red curry. For a real treat, the platters for two include sampler morsels from several menu items. There's also a good selection of landlubber dishes for those whose tastes run away from the sea. The wine list is excellent, particularly when it comes to BC and California wines. It consistently wins awards, as do its chefs, who in 2008 garnered several accolades at Salon Culinaire at Hotelympia in London, England.

In the Coast Hotel, 146 Kingston St. ℂ **250/480-1999.** www.bluecrab.ca. Reservations required. Main courses lunch C$8–C$25, dinner C$20–C$26. AE, DC, MC, V. Daily 6:30am–10pm. Nibbles available until 1am.

The Mark ★★ CONTINENTAL   The Mark has no view, preferring to create an intimate dining experience within the confines of a discreet, wood-paneled room, but it's perfect for memorable and romantic encounters—it seats only 26 diners. The upscale menu matches the high-end wine list with dishes such as long pepper–rubbed ahi tuna with cardamom-scented white bean and endive marmalade, and a truffle infused fallow venison loin. The six-course apple-tasting menu celebrates the Gulf Islands' apple heritage, which today produces more that 300 varieties. There's apple linguine, apple caviar, apples and oysters, and a mouth-watering frangipane Gala-apple pie with Tugwell honey cream and vanilla-bean gelato. Waiters are well informed on dishes, and the service has gracious finesse (extra butter arrives quietly almost before you realize it's running out), without staff hovering.

In the Hotel Grand Pacific, 450 Quebec St. ℂ **250/380-4487.** www.themark.ca. Reservations recommended. Main courses C$30–C$43; six-course tasting menu C$70, add C$40 with wine pairings. AE, DC, DISC, MC, V. Daily 5–9:30pm.

Pescatore's Seafood & Grill SEAFOOD   Frequently ranked among Victoria's best seafood restaurants, this spot's artsy decor, good service, and extensive seasonal menu create a great dining alternative to the Blue Crab, even though it hasn't got the view. The daily fresh sheet usually features at least 10 items, and whether you go for oysters at the raw bar (open in the evenings only), crab, clams, salmon, or halibut, you won't be disappointed. Try the 1-1-1 soup taster in your selection: Pescatore's three chowders—the slightly spiced prawn bisque is a standout. There are also non-fish entrees—pastas, steak, and lamb. A late-night tapas-style menu is offered after 10pm, and weekends include live-jazz brunches.

614 Humboldt St. ℂ **250/385-4512.** www.pescatores.com. Reservations recommended. Main courses lunch C$12–C$16, dinner C$25–C$35. AE, DC, MC, V. Mon–Fri 11:30am–11pm; Sat & Sun 11am–midnight.

MODERATE & INEXPENSIVE

Barb's Place FISH AND CHIPS   Absolutely no frills here; this floating restaurant at Fisherman's Wharf serves fish and chips at their very tastiest, although it's received such rave reviews that the eatery is on the verge of being overrated. After all, this is only fish and chips, and it's served in newspaper pouches, not on bone china. Get your cod, oysters, or halibut grilled, steamed, or deep-fried any way you like it. Barb serves it all up with hand-hewn chips. Douse your chippies in salt and vinegar, the way they do in England, and enjoy the feast at picnic tables while watching the boats, seagulls, and other harbor-side activities.

Erie St., Fisherman's Wharf (at the entrance to the Inner Harbour). ⓒ **250/384-6515.** www.barbs place.ca. Reservations not accepted. Main courses C$10–C$20. AE, MC, V. Mar–Oct daily 11am–sunset. Closed Nov–Feb.

The James Bay Tea Room & Restaurant PUB FARE   When these folks tried to dump the traditional British fare from the menu, it caused such an uproar that home-style bangers and mash, Welsh rarebit on toast, and roast beef with Yorkshire pudding have returned with zeal. It's one of the few places that serves kippers for breakfast, which lasts all day, alongside burgers, soups, salads, and even low-carb, Atkins-friendly items. Then there's high tea, which starts in earnest mid-morning, and represents better value than most. The decor includes Tiffany lampshades, brass knickknacks, and sepia-tinted family portraits. Tables are crowded with locals, and the atmosphere is lively, with English-accented chatter. Tarot card readings are offered on Saturday afternoons.

332 Menzies St. (behind the Parliament Buildings). ⓒ **250/382-8282.** www.jamesbaytearoomand restaurant.com. Reservations recommended. Main courses breakfast & lunch C$6–C$10, high tea & dinner C$16–C$29. AE, MC, V. Mon–Fri 7am–5pm; Sat & Sun 8am–5pm.

Red Fish/Blue Fish ★ FISH AND CHIPS   Move over Barb's (above) as the prima donna of take-out fish eats, enter one of the most innovative concepts around: a 6.1×3m (20×9¾-ft.) gourmand's fish-and-chips cafe out of a repurposed ship's container, much like the metal freight boxes you see rolling down the highway atop 18-wheelers. This one was used to ship a Hummer and now has a rooftop garden (which also acts as roof insulation) and a conscientious green program that includes composting and recycling potato starch. It also uses only Ocean Wise seafood, some caught by the owners themselves. Here, you get wild Pacific halibut, salmon, or cod coated with a light tempura batter; twice-fried, hand-cut potatoes, some slathered in curry; grill-seared tuna; fish tacones (taco-cones); and mushy edamame, a quirky twist on mushy peas. Because tables are forbidden on the dock, the cafe provides stools for waterside dining, year-round.

1006 Wharf St. (on the pier below). ⓒ **250/298-6877.** www.redfish-bluefish.com. Main courses C$10–C$17. MC, V. Daily 11:30am–7pm.

Santiago's LATIN AMERICAN   The colorful strings of lights make the place look like a Mexican fiesta and speak to the upbeat personality of this cheery cafe. The menu is a creative mix of tasty dishes from Malaysia, Spain, and South America, so you get tapas dishes alongside items like Pollo Naranja (chicken with oranges) and a spicy paella that brims with mussels, shrimp, sausage, chicken, and artichoke hearts. Meals come with tortilla chips and salsa, sour cream, and guacamole, and the service is friendly and fast.

660 Oswego St. ⓒ **250/388-7376.** Reservations not accepted. Main courses C$10–C$20. MC, V. Daily 8am–9pm.

Superior Restaurant ★ ▓ REGIONAL   Everything here is designed to evoke the senses and share, from its nightly, live entertainment and small plates of regional cuisine to a lovely garden patio shaded by trees and an interior of surrealist art. The building dates back to 1912 and once housed wayward sailors. Graze on dishes of bruschetta, charcuterie, pate, or a grilled Caesar salad while enjoying everything from jazz to classical to R&B. On Friday and Saturday nights, non-diners can expect a cover charge after 7:30pm; on other nights, a bucket is passed, New Orleans–style.

106 Superior St. © **250/380-9515.** Reservations recommended. Main courses C$10–C$16. MC, V. Tues-Sun 11am–3pm & 5–11pm. Closed Mon.

Downtown & Old Town
EXPENSIVE

Black Olive CONTINENTAL   With 30 years in the restaurant biz, owner Paul Psyllakis has created an elegant dining room that exudes a Mediterranean warmth. The menu has a West-Coast base, with olive-oriented undertones, as in the salmon with artichokes and black olive pesto, and a savory bread pudding that uses olive bread, leeks, Portobello mushrooms, artichokes, and Greek cheese. Grandma's bread pudding never tasted like this! A selection of non-olive dishes gives the menu broad interest: There's an excellent roasted vegetable dish in phyllo pastry; Greek-style beef tenderloin medallions, pan-seared with a mushroom and red wine sauce; as well as a fish of the day that you pick from an iced, central display. Usually there's everything from lobster to colossal shrimp to yellow-fin tuna. Paul's extra virgin olive oil is made from his own olives in Crete, Greece. The restaurant's more casual off-shoot, **Penelope's Café,** next door, offers up a tasty, all-day brunch from 11am.

739 Pandora St. © **250/384-6060.** www.theblackolive.ca. Reservations recommended. Main courses lunch C$10–C$16, dinner C$18–C$34. AE, DC, MC, V. Daily noon–2pm & 5–10pm.

Bon Rouge Bistro & Boulangerie FRENCH   Housed in a 1920s building, this place is just like one you might find off the Champs Elysees. Traditional items include a tasty *coq au vin* and light, fluffy crepes stuffed with savory mixes. The daily plate du jour is a good bet, especially the fish-on-Friday number. Keep an eye open for a succulent cast-iron skillet–seared stuffed pork chop full of wild mushrooms, green beans amandine, and Marsala sauce, and the traditional Sunday roast, usually herbed lamb. There's a C$29 prix fixe menu offered Sunday through Thursday. The curbside patios add to the Parisian facade.

611 Courtney St. (bakery at 850 Gordon St.). © **250/220-8008.** Reservations not accepted. Main courses lunch C$10–C$19, dinner C$15–C$36. MC, V. Daily 11:30am–10:30pm.

Brasserie L'Ecole FRENCH   A local favorite, this simple French bistro never fails to please. Food rarely incorporates heavy, creamy sauces, and this lighter approach makes for a delicious *boeuf a la bourguignonne,* frites with parmesan, garlic, parsley, and truffle oil that are positively addictive, and steaks done to French perfection. Remember, though, that asking for medium-rare in France is pretty blue by North American standards, and that's what you'll get here. The extensive wine list features mostly French wines, listed on chalkboards "brasserie" style. *L'ecole* is French for school—the building once housed a Chinese school.

1715 Government St. © **250/475-6260.** www.lecole.ca. Reservations recommended. Main courses C$21–$29. AE, MC, V. Tues-Sat 5:30–11pm.

Cafe Brio ★ REGIONAL   This award-winning bistro-style restaurant serves delicious Tuscan-inspired West-Coast fare (and decor), likely because its two chefs, one Canadian and one Italian, blend their styles into the ever-changing menu that's based on whatever organic produce they purchased that day. The result is a creative mix of natural flavors zinging with just the right amount of added spices. In winter, expect substantial items such as venison shank and confit of duck. In summer, items are lighter: a charcuterie menu featuring local salami, lomo, pâtés, and terrines, and served with homemade mustards and pickles; and seared scallops topped with crisp potato rösti. Service is top-notch, and the wine list is exceptional, with more than 300 wines by the bottle and 30 by the glass or half-liter. Tip: The entire menu is available in half portions.

944 Fort St.© **250/383-0009.** www.cafe-brio.com. Reservations recommended. Main courses C$16–C$36. AE, MC, V. Daily 5:30–10:30pm.

Camille's ★ PACIFIC NORTHWEST The restaurant's owner was one of the founders of the Vancouver Island Farm Co-Operative, so, true to form, the ever-changing menu is seasonal and packed with locally sourced ingredients. This might mean tender fiddleheads in spring, and wild salmon and blackberry desserts in the autumn. Canadian bison, wild boar, and caribou might also be on the menu, alongside pheasant, quail, and partridge. Everything has an unexpected touch, such as prawn bisque with ginger and lemon, or fennel cakes in a champagne sauce. Camille's is a very romantic spot with cliché, crisp white linens, exposed-brick walls, stained-glass lamps, soft jazz, and candlelight. As with many Victoria restaurants, the five-course tasting menu (C$90) includes a bit of everything; add C$30 for wine pairings.

45 Bastion Sq. © **250/381-3433.** www.camillesrestaurant.com. Reservations recommended. Main courses C$26–C$37. AE, MC, V. Tues–Sat 5:30–10pm.

Il Terrazzo Ristorante ITALIAN While some locals deem the place overrated, others have voted Il Terrazzo Victoria's best Italian restaurant year in, year out. The restaurant's three talented chefs create specialties of their homeland that include wood-oven–roasted pizzas, fresh grilled seafood, and a wide variety of homemade pastas, as well as steaks, *osso bucco*, and other mostly northern-Italian specialties. An excellent choice is the *misto di carn alle griglia*—char-grilled skewers of marinated lamb, chicken, and pork tenderloin served over white bean, tomato, and arugula *ragu* with red onion marmalade. Set in a converted heritage building, the restaurant's atmosphere is warmly romantic and features a flower-filled heated courtyard, surrounded by brick fireplaces and lit by wrought-iron candelabras. Inside, exposed brick walls, wooden beams, and intimate nooks and crannies are a delight.

555 Johnson St., Waddington Alley (off Johnson St., at Wharf St.).© **250/361-0028.** www.ilterrazzo. com. Reservations recommended. Main courses lunch C$9–C$23, dinner C$15–C$28. AE, MC, V. Mon–Fri 11:30am–3pm; daily 5–10pm.

Restaurant Matisse FRENCH Wrought-iron gates give way to an Edith Piaf–esque ambience, filled with soft lights and a profusion of fresh flowers. This award-winning 40-seat restaurant has been noted for its service, elegance, and quality, and justifiably so. Savor fresh bread, filet bordelaise, slow roasted duck, a masterful Coquilles St. Jacques a la Perigord (a classic scallop dish with black truffle–scented potato topped with Gruyere cheese, baked in a rich Mornay sauce), and a feathery-light crème brûlée. Menu items are always fresh and innovative, presenting new recipes and ideas garnered during annual pilgrimages to France. The four-course chef's sampler prix-fixe dinners are C$52; add C$30 for wine pairings.

512 Yates St. (at Wharf St.). © **250/480-0883.** www.restaurantmatisse.com. Reservations recommended. Main courses C$26–C$34. AE, MC, V. Wed–Sun 5:30–10pm.

BEST breakfasts

Great breakfast places are growing exponentially, so here are four top choices:

- Blue Fox Café (919 Fort St.; *250/380-1683*): A small, always jam-packed cafe that oozes expectation and serves mountain-high pancake stacks, eight varieties of eggs Benny, and homemade granola. Get there early to avoid long lineups.

- Molé (554 Pandora Ave.; *250/385-6653*): A hangout for artists and other characters who gravitate towards its bohemian atmosphere, Molé prepares sage-roasted yam omelet, Portobello-stuffed avocado, and curry tofu scramble. On Friday and Saturday nights only, the restaurant keeps the doors open beyond the usual 4pm closing for dinner and musical jam sessions.

- Cabin 18 (607 Pandora Ave.; *250/590-1500*): Although equally bohemian, Cabin 18 has a more rambling, artsy charm with enough space to find a seat, be it at a table, on a scruffy couch, or at the (no alcohol is served) bar. Staff is uber-friendly, and the food is down-to-earth scrumptious.

- Willie's Bakery & Café (537 Johnson St.; *250/381-8414*): BC's oldest bakery is famous for light banana waffles and ultra tasty bacon-and-maple sausages—something to do with a special double-glaze Dijon. Maneuver past the line-ups and aromatic hot-from-the-oven baked goods to the adjoining brick patio for the best seats.

MODERATE & INEXPENSIVE

Azuma Sushi SUSHI   This modern, busy, and bright restaurant has the best-value sushi in town. Rumor has it that at his previous restaurant, Azuma's chef developed quite the following for his special rice sauce, the secret of which he has brought with him. The seafood is top quality (not an imitation crab in sight), and the *unagi nigiri* and spicy tuna sashimi are especially good. The daily two-for-one bento boxes are a real bargain for hungry appetites.

615 Yates St. (btw. Broad & Government Sts.). *250/382-8768.* Reservations recommended. Main courses C$10–C$20. Daily 11am–10pm.

Baan Thai THAI   Unconventional art from Thailand creates an elegant restaurant where food and spices are taken seriously. The Singha beer and many ingredients are imported directly from Thailand. The menu has a variety of classic dishes, pad Thais, stir-fries, curries, and burning-hot (count the peppers) garlic prawns. The green curry with eggplants, bamboo shoots, and sweet basil leaves in coconut milk is especially good. Most items can be adapted to accommodate vegetarians, and dishes can be made as hot or as mild as you prefer. Portions are on the small side, however, so if you're sharing, order an extra item.

1117 Blanshard St. *250/383-0050.* www.baanthaivictoria.ca. Main courses C$12–C$18. Mon–Sat 11:30am–10pm; Sun 5–10pm.

Foo Asian Street Food ★★ 🏠 ASIAN   Superlative Asian food served in a take-away box off a street corner just about sums up one of Victoria's hottest concepts. By avoiding fine-dining overheads such as linens and wait staff, the restaurant devotes its creativity and effort into a menu inspired by the multiple food carts found around various regions in Asia: Thai red coconut curry, Indian butter chicken, Vietnamese Ginger caramel chicken, as well as a fabulous green papaya salad, prawn and pork lettuce cups, crispy pakoras and *paneer* cheese dumplings. Pull up a chair, sit at the bar to watch the chefs create their magic, or join others on the patio, sitting around a repurposed university lab table, complete with student etchings. Inside seats about 8; outside about 12; most orders, however, are take out.

769 Yates St. ✆ **250/383-3111.** www.foofood.ca. Main courses C$9–$12. Mon–Fri 11:30am–10pm; Sat & Sun 5–9:30pm.

Pagliacci's ITALIAN   Opened in 1979 by expatriate New Yorker Howie Siegal, Pagliacci's is not your ordinary Italian restaurant. Named after the Italian word for *clown,* it's elbow-to-elbow most nights, and tables are quite close together. This is not the place for private tête-à-têtes or for connoisseurs in search of exquisite Italian cuisine. Pagliacci's is just fun. You can mix and match selections from the menu in true *When Harry Met Sally* style, especially when items have such an imaginative Hollywood take that you'll want to experiment: take Popeye's Salad (with spinach, naturally) or the Mae West Veal Medallions as examples. You'll also find more traditional menu items such as veal parmigiana and almost two dozen a la carte freshly made pastas, including wheat-less alternatives. And if all this isn't entertainment enough, there's live jazz Sunday through Wednesday. The likes of Diana Krall and Etta James have played Pagliacci's.

 bargain MEALS

These tiny and inexpensive Asian eateries aren't much on decor (wear your jeans), but they're big on flavor and small in price. **My Thai Café** (1020 Cook St.; ✆ **250/472-7574**) doesn't offer a huge variety on the menu, but what there is, is excellent home-cooked Thai food. The beef salad is tasty. The Vietnamese noodle soups at **Pho Vy** (772 Fort St.; ✆ **250/385-5516**) are spiced and hearty. **Wah Lai Yuen** (560 Fisgard St.; ✆ **250/381-5355**) offers an authentic Chinatown dining experience. If you can put up with the sometimes-offhand service, the humongous servings make this a real deal. **Posh** (1063 Fort St.; ✆ **250/382-7074**) is a cook-your-own sukiyaki—a kind of Japanese fondue, which arrives with a ton of vegetables and extras. Two can eat for less than C$20. Carnivores can't go wrong with **Pig** (800 Yates St.; ✆ **250/381-4677**), a take-out diner in the Atrium Building that dishes up some of the best pulled-pork and beef-brisket sandwiches in town—basted, seasoned, marinated to tasty perfection, with trimmings such as pickle on a stick.

And for gamblers? Order the C$10 Mahoney at **Floyd's Diner** (866 Yates St.; ✆ **250/382-5114**), and let the kitchen cook up whatever it wants. After eating, flip a coin, and if you win, the meal is free. If you lose, you pay double.

1011 Broad St. © **250/386-1662.** Reservations not accepted. Main courses lunch C$7–C$12, dinner C$12–C$25. AE, MC, V. Mon–Thurs 11:30am–11pm; Fri & Sat 11:30am–midnight; Sun 11am–11pm.

The Pink Bicycle REGIONAL   Victoria's only specialized gourmet burger joint means that everything is handmade and as locally sourced as possible. Highlights include a blue-cheese organic lamb burger infused with rosemary pesto and sweet apricots, a barbeque bison cheeseburger, and a seared ahi tuna burger topped with a ginger sesame slaw and wasabi aioli. There are plenty of veggie options, too, such as the Moroccan burger of spiced garbanzo beans and dates, finished with mintro sauce (a blend of mint, cilantro, and yoghurt). The Blue Buck beer-battered onions rings are to die for.

1008 Blanshard St. © **250/384-1008.** www.pinkbicycleburger.com. Main courses C$12–C$15. MC, V. Mon 11:30am–2:30pm; Tues–Sat 11:30am–8:30pm.

rebar Modern Food ★ ☺ VEGETARIAN   This bright and busy basement restaurant is likely the best vegetarian cafe on the west coast. The juice bar alone boasts more than 80 varieties of deliciously healthful smoothies, shakes, wheatgrass drinks, and power tonics. The stress-busting Soul Change—a blend of carrot, apple, celery, ginger, and Siberian ginseng—is a winner. The menu is geared to vegetarian and vegan diners (though not exclusively), featuring international cuisine, from Thai curries and pastas to hummus and fresh shrimp quesadillas. The homemade muesli is dynamite, and the Cascadia Bakery produces everything from decadent vegan Belgian chocolate fudge cake to hand-shaped whole-grain specialty breads. The small wine list offers predominately BC wines, and even when it's really busy (which is most of the time), the service remains fast and friendly.

50 Bastion Sq. (downstairs). © **250/361-9223.** www.rebarmodernfood.com. Reservations not accepted. Main courses C$8–C$16. AE, MC, V. Mon–Thurs 8:30am–9pm; Fri & Sat 8:30am–10pm; Sun 8:30am–3:30pm. Reduced hours in winter.

Victoria Neighborhoods
MODERATE & INEXPENSIVE

Lucy's in the Square REGIONAL   Sharing the square with the Belfry Theatre in Fernwood, it's nigh impossible to get into this tiny restaurant without at least a week's notice, unless it's post the 8pm curtain. Menus change almost daily according to what's fresh locally, so you might come across a Cowichan chicken confit; a thick-cut roasted pork chop with rosemary-cured kale; or braised ling cod with clams, leeks, and bacon potatoes. Lunches have an excellent salad selection and sandwiches such as warm bacon and pear brie; brunches are equally simple and delicious events. Tuesdays are pizza nights; flatbreads, really, with unusual toppings.

1296 Gladstone Ave. © **778/430-5829.** www.lucysinthesquare.com. Reservations recommended. Main courses C$10–C$22. MC, V. Tues–Fri 11:30am–2pm, Sat & Sun 10am–2pm; Tues–Sat 5–11pm.

Pizzeria Prima Strada ★★ PIZZA   Here's a pizza parlor that will change your perception of pizzas, as the pizzas here are that good. The secret is in delivering Neapolitan, wood-fired oven pies as they are enjoyed in the old country: simple toppings on wafer thin, melt-in-your-mouth crusts. There are plenty of choices, but to test for the best, always go for the *margherita*, with Italian plum tomatoes, fresh herbs, and mozzarella. With an oven temperature that fires up to 900 degrees, every pizza is cooked to fragrant perfection in only 3 minutes. The atmosphere is a far cry

THE tea EXPERIENCE

When the Duchess of Bedford complained about a "sinking feeling" in the late afternoon, she invented afternoon tea to keep her going until dinner. Today, however, tea has come to mean everything from a genteel cup of Earl Grey to a full-blown meal in itself with scones with whipped cream, savory crust-less sandwiches, sweet tartlets, and home-baked biscuits. Among the top choices are:

- The Fairmont Empress (721 Government St.; *C* **250/389-2727**): Serves its famed epicurean feast in the Tea Lobby and elsewhere as the throngs of tea-takers dictate. It's expensive (C$44–$C55 per person in high season) and, quite frankly, overrated, although the inflated price does include a keepsake of nicely packaged Empress tea.

- The Blethering Place Tearoom (2250 Oak Bay Ave., Oak Bay; *C* **250/598-1413**): Slightly less pretentious and has the art of tea down pat. Tea menus start at C$20 and are what a quintessential Victorian teahouse is all about.

- White Heather Tea Room (1885 Oak Bay Ave., Oak Bay; *C* **250/595-8020**): A local favorite just down the road from the Blethering Place Tearoom. Small, bright, and exceptionally friendly, the Big Muckle Giant Tea for Two (C$40) is the grand slam of all teas. Smaller options are available.

- Point Ellice House (2616 Pleasant St.; *C* **250/380-6506**): Where Victoria's social elite gathered in early 1900s. Take a 5-minute ferry ride across the Inner Harbour and enjoy tea (summer only) near the water on carefully mowed lawns. The cost of C$23 per person includes a half-hour tour of the mansion and gardens.

- Murchie's Tea and Coffee (1110 Government St.; *C* **250-383-3112**): Has purveyed tea since 1894 and offers one of the best selections of teas in the city, plus good coffee and everything from snacks to full-blown sandwiches and salads (C$5–C$14).

- Dutch Bakery (718 Fort St.; *C* **250/385-1012**): Where to go for a quick pick-me-up, as well as a one-of-a-kind baked treat and European-style sugared confection. This is a fourth-generation Victoria institution that still feels a part of the '50s era. Try the dollar, a sponge roll and marzipan.

- The Butchart Gardens Dining Room (800 Benvenuto Ave.; *C* **250/652-4422**): Although farther afield, taking tea here is worth the drive, although you can only enjoy the experience if you've also paid for admission to the gardens. A full tea is C$27.

- Silk Road Tea (1624 Government St.; *C* **250/704-2688**): For something entirely differently, tea tasting here is like sampling flights of wine. A 30-minute revelation of exotic infusions from all over the world is C$10 per person. Silk Road also pairs its teas to the Hotel Grand Pacific's weekend dim sums for some inspired combinations.

from take-out pizzeria. You can almost taste Italia in the warm and convivial atmosphere. Wines are the best of Italy and BC. PPS has a smaller, second location nearer the downtown core at 2960 Bridge St. (© **250/590-4380**), a rewarding detour off the Galloping Goose Trail.

230 Cook St. © **250/590-8595.** www.pizzeri-aprimastrada.com. Main courses C$11–C$15. MC, V. Daily 11:30am–9:30pm.

Smoken Bones Cookshack ★★★

CAJUN/CREOLE Chef/owner Ken Hueston is high up in the food chain of the island's Chefs Collaborative. This box-like restaurant lies in a small strip mall and positively pulsates with activity every minute it's open. Here's why: The southern BBQ and Cajun-Creole–influenced dishes are phenomenal, the result of natural wood-smoking techniques that see pork ribs spending hours in the smoker. The restaurant goes through about 20,000kg (44,092 lb.) of pork ribs a month! Because the island would soon be pig-less with this kind of ongoing volume, Hueston buys about 20% of his products from the mainland. But for everything else—for the spicy Gumbo, fresh-baked cornbread, braised collard greens, and butter-fried cabbage—it's backyard shopping. The portions are generous, so it's a real find for families, with lots of opportunity for sharing plates and eat-all-you-can buffets to satiate hearty appetites.

101-721 Station St. © **250/391-6328.** www.smokenbones.ca. Reservations recommended. Main courses C$12–C$18. MC, V. Mon–Sat 11:30am–9pm; Sun noon–9pm.

Stage REGIONAL Best described as a small-plates wine bistro, Stage sits just down from the Belfry Theatre in Fernwood, which means its 50 seats fill up fast pre- and post-shows. The bar is made from a salvaged bowling lane, and the wood floors, open kitchen, and exposed brick walls create a cool vibe that gets very noisy with chatter. If you enjoy sharing platefuls of intriguing flavors with friends, Stage is a winner. Selections are themed to charcuterie, vegetarian, fish, meat, and dessert. If you're tasting wines alongside—bottles average C$45, and many are served in 89mL to 149mL (3- to 5-oz.) pours—the organic wood-fired breads and cheese trays are phenomenal. Recommendations include the garlic *langos*, walnut-arugula pesto, grilled zucchini and blue cheese, and the chicken curry with grilled corn naan and house chutney. Stage owners also operate **Paprika Bistro** (2524 Estevan Ave., © **250/592-7424**), a French-Hungarian restaurant in Oak Bay.

1307 Gladstone Ave. © **250/388-4222.** Reservations recommended. Plates C$12. MC, V. Daily 5pm–midnight (4:30pm–midnight during Belfry matinees).

EXPLORING VICTORIA

If you're staying anywhere near the downtown core, trade the car for a good pair of walking shoes because virtually everything in this chapter is doable on foot. Besides, walking is by far the best way to appreciate some of Victoria's diverse architecture: heritage residences, refurbished turn-of-the-century warehouses, and assorted show-pieces. Start with the attractions around the Inner Harbour and fan out from there for a refreshing walk through Beacon Hill Park, or head in the opposite direction for great shopping. The waterfront is also the departing point for most of the city's tours, whether you're off to Butchart Gardens (see chapter 6), or up for whale-watching or a kayaking excursion. Attractions that are out of Victoria Central, such as Craigdarroch Castle, Abkazi Garden, and Hatley Park, are only a 10-minute cab ride away. **Tip:** If you're planning to do a lot of sightseeing, invest C$20 in a **City Passport** (© 604/694-2489; www.citypassports.com), a pocket-size book packed with visitor information and discounts on attractions of up to 50% at over 30 Victoria attractions.

The Top Attractions

Art Gallery of Greater Victoria

Located near Craigdarroch Castle, the AGGV, as it's often called, exhibits more than 15,000 pieces of art, drawn mainly from Asia, Europe, and North America. Permanent collections include a life-size dollhouse and a Shinto shrine that is part of Canada's most extensive Japanese art collection. Most compelling is the Emily Carr exhibit, which integrates her visual and written work alongside images from the BC provincial archives, together creating an in-depth portrait of this pre-eminent Victoria artist. The Gallery organizes an annual *en plein air* every summer, an outdoor painting event for local artists.

1040 Moss St.© **250/384-4101.** www.aggv.bc.ca. Admission C$12 adults, C$10 students & seniors. Fri–Wed 10am–5pm; Thurs 10am–9pm. Bus: 11, 14, or 22.

Craigdarroch Castle ★★

If you've got it, flaunt it. That's what coal baron Robert Dunsmuir (the wealthiest and most influential man in British Columbia back in the 1880s) decided to do. More than a home, this Highland-style castle rises 87 stairs through five floors of Victorian opulence—and there's not an elevator to be had! Children might think it's like something out of Disneyland. The nonprofit society that runs Craigdarroch does so with diligent care; the stained glass, Persian carpets, and intricate woodwork are treasures to behold. Visitors receive a self-guided tour booklet, and volunteers love sharing sidebars of Dunsmuir's family history. Head to the top for a view of Victoria, the Strait of Juan de Fuca, and the Olympic Mountains. Allow about an hour to tour the castle.

1050 Joan Crescent (off Fort St.).© **250/592-5323.** www.craigdarrochcastle.com. Admission C$14 adults, C$13 seniors, C$78 students, C$5 children 6–12, free for children 5 & under. Mid-June to after Labor Day daily 9am–7pm; Sept to mid-June daily 10am–4:30pm. Take Fort St. out of downtown just past Pandora Ave. & turn right on Joan Crescent. Bus: 11 or 14.

Maritime Museum of British Columbia

Located in a former Victoria courthouse, this museum celebrates British Columbia's seafaring history in film and exhibits, from whalers and grand ocean liners to military conflict and 20th-century explorers. Highlights include a replica of the HMS *Temeraire*, constructed entirely of beef and chicken bones by French naval prisoners captured during the Napoleonic Wars. Check out the heritage courtroom renovated by Francis Rattenbury and one of Victoria's most ornate elevators. Plan to stay 1½ hours—longer, if you have salt in your veins; the museum maintains a registry of heritage vessels and a wealth of information for maritime buffs. The gift shop has an excellent selection of nautical paraphernalia. Kids' programs include a sleepover in this purportedly haunted place!

EMINENT victorian: FRANCIS MAWSON RATTENBURY

As one of Victoria's most famous people, **Francis Mawson Rattenbury** ("Ratz," as he was known) not only left his architectural mark on the city (including the Parliament Buildings and the Empress Hotel), but also was among Victoria's most controversial residents. In 1892, at 25 years of age, he arrived here from England, having won a competition to design the Parliament Buildings. It was an impressive start to an illustrious career, during which he only ever sought the largest commissions and boldest opportunities. These included branches for the Bank of Montreal, the Vancouver Hotel, and provincial courthouses in Nanaimo, Nelson, and Vancouver.

Rattenbury's reputation, however, suffered when, in his mid-50s, he left his wife Florrie and appeared publicly with his mistress, Alma Packenham—a beautiful woman 30 years his junior and already twice married. After divorcing Florrie, Rattenbury married Alma, and in 1930, when they realized they had become social pariahs, they left for England. But the age differences began to tell, and increasingly, Rattenbury took solace in the whiskey bottle.

In 1934, when 17-year-old George Stoner was hired as their chauffeur, Alma quickly seduced the young man and installed him in the spare bedroom as her lover-in-residence. But, driven wild at the prospect of being discovered, Stoner came upon a dozing Rattenbury in the living room and clubbed him to death. Both Alma and Stoner were charged with murder, and after a sensational trial, Alma was acquitted and Stoner sentenced to hang. Alma, however, was unable to face Stoner's execution, and within 4 days, she committed suicide by stabbing herself through the heart. Stoner was later released from prison.

28 Bastion Sq. ✆ **250/385-4222.** www.mmbc.bc.ca. Admission C$12 adults, C$10 seniors & students, C$5 children 6–11, free for children 5 & under; C$25 families. Daily 9:30am–4:30pm. Bus: 5 to View St.

Miniature World ☺ If you ever wondered what Gulliver felt like in the land of the Lilliputians, this little world reveals all. Children and the young at heart will love the more than 80 miniature displays (many of them in motion) of solar systems, battle scenes, fancy 18th-century dress balls, a three-ring circus, and dozens of scenes from beloved fairy tales. A big favorite is the Great Canadian Railway, one of the world's largest model railways, although close contenders are the world's smallest operational sawmill and two of the world's largest dollhouses. Allow an hour.

649 Humboldt St. ✆ **250/385-9731.** www.miniatureworld.com. Admission C$13 adults, C$10 children 12–17, C$8 children 3–11, free for children 2 & under. Mid-June to Labor Day daily 9am–9pm; after Labor Day to mid-June daily 9am–5pm. Bus: 5, 27, 28, 30, or 31.

Pacific Undersea Gardens ☺ The stark exterior looks out of place in Victoria's Inner Harbour, but descend the sloping stairway and you're in another world—below the waterline. From a glass-enclosed sunken vessel, you get to experience the harbor's marine life, which swims all around you in natural aquariums. All manner of fish—from brilliant red snapper to stonefish and octopi—swim through the kelp forest. Divers descend every hour to show the audience some of the harder-to-see creatures, like starfish tucked in rocks, wolf eels, and sharks. The observatory also cares for injured and orphaned seals, many of which prefer to stay in the area after their release. Buy a bag of herring in the gift shop and feed them a feast. Plan to stay about an hour, although feeding the seals is so captivating you may want to hang around.

490 Belleville St.© **250/382-5717.** www.pacificunderseagardens.com. Admission C$10 adults, C$9 seniors, C$8 children 12–17, C$6 children 5–11, free for children 4 & under. June–Sept daily 9am–8pm; Oct–May daily 10am–5pm. Bus: 5, 27, 28, or 30.

Parliament Buildings   By night, this architectural gem is lit by more than 3,300 lights so that it looks more like the Hogwarts School for Wizards than the provincial Parliament Buildings. Designed by then-25-year-old Francis Rattenbury, one of the most sought-after architects of the day, the buildings were constructed between 1893 and 1898 at a cost of nearly C$1 million. The interior is equally mystical, filled with mosaics, marble, woodwork, and stained glass. If the Legislature is sitting, head up to the visitor's gallery. There's not a lot of room there, but it's fun to watch politicians in action. British Columbia is known for its eccentric politics, and Question Period, in the early afternoon, can be very entertaining. The "been there, done that" crowd could do this in 20 minutes; guided tours (summer only) last about 40 minutes and leave every half-hour from the central lobby; they include dialogue with interpretive actors along the way.

501 Belleville St.© **250/387-3046.** www.victoriabc.ca/victoria/parliamentbuildings.htm. Free admission. Daily 9am–5pm. Bus: 5, 27, 28, or 30.

Royal British Columbia Museum ★★★ ☺   As one of the best regional museums in the world, a visit to this museum is worthy of at least a half-day. The dioramas are so lifelike you'll feel as if you're stepping back in time—whether it's coming face-to-tusk with a wooly mammoth, tracking through a BC forest or to the edge of a glacier, or meandering down the cobblestone streets of a pioneer town. Feel the train rattle the timbers of the old train station each time it passes or enjoy old Charlie Chaplin movies in the movie theater. Just like an IKEA store, the museum has a route that doesn't bypass a thing, so start at the top in the Modern History Gallery (items from the early 1900s through to the power '80s highlight the lifestyles of each decade), and work your way down through the second-floor Natural History Gallery and the First Peoples Gallery, with its totems, Native longhouses, and artifacts. Once in a while, John Lennon's famous 1968 psychedelic Rolls Royce escapes its basement storage and it's displayed in the lobby. The museum also has an IMAX theater, showing an ever-changing variety of large-screen movies (© **250/953-IMAX** [250/953-4629] or 250/953-4629; www.imaxvictoria.com). Behind-the-scenes tours are a new addition to the summer schedule. Thunderbird Park, beside the museum, houses a cedar longhouse, where Native carvers work on new totem poles. *Note:* Admission rates are sometimes higher during special exhibitions.

675 Belleville St. © **250/356-7226.** www.royalbcmuseum.bc.ca. Admission C$15 adults; C$9.50 seniors, students & children 6–18; free for children 5 & under; C$40 families. Museum-IMAX combination & IMAX-only tickets available. Daily 9am–5pm. Bus: 5, 28, or 30.

Victoria Bug Zoo ★★ ☺   In the heart of downtown Victoria, enter an amazing world of international insects: walking sticks, praying mantises, tarantulas, and scorpions, to name a few. Although all the creepy-crawlies are behind glass, an entomologist (bug scientist) is on hand to answer questions and show you how to handle some of the multi-legged creatures, which include a 400-leg millipede that stretches the length of your forearm. Even if you're spider-wary, this is a fascinating place. Kids will want to spend a couple of hours here.

631 Courtney St. ℂ **250/384-2847.** www.bugzoo.bc.ca. Admission C$9 adults, C$8 seniors, C$7 students, C$6 children 3–16, free for children 2 & under; C$25 annual family pass. Daily 11am–5pm. Any downtown bus.

Parks & Gardens

Victoria is famed for its garden landscapes and for its abundance of flowers. Even if there's not a horticultural bone in your body, you really can't help but appreciate the efforts that have earned the city such acclaim. Look overhead, and chances are that there'll be an overstuffed hanging basket trailing with colorful blooms. And in most of the residential neighborhoods, private homeowners take special pride in their gardens.

Among the most spectacular examples are the **Gardens at Government House** (1401 Rockland Ave.; ℂ 250/387-2080; www.ltgov.bc.ca/gardens), the official (and private) residence of British Columbia's Lieutenant Governor. The formal gardens are free to wander from dawn to dusk, and for rose lovers in particular, they're well worth the visit. Guided tours run May through September (C$35 for groups of five or fewer) and include areas not normally open to the public.

Nearby **Abkhazi Garden** (1964 Fairfield Rd.; ℂ 250/598-8096; www. conservancy.bc.ca—click through to heritage tabs) is a dramatic, half-hectare (1¼-acre) jewel of a garden created by Prince and Princess Nicholas Abkhazi in the 1940s. Amid the woodland, rocky slopes, and rhododendrons is a quaint tearoom and gift shop. The gardens are open March to October daily 11am to 5pm. Another once-private residence is **Hatley Park & Museum** (2005 Sooke Rd.; ℂ 250/391-2666; www.hatleygardens.com). A National Historic Site, the museum boasts one of the few Edwardian estates in Canada, complete with Italian, Rose, and Japanese gardens. There are hundreds of heritage trees, including 250-year-old Douglas firs, an ecologically important salt marsh estuary, and a series of natural springs. Admission is C$9 adults, with discounts for seniors and students. Children 12 and under are free; admission is half-price October through April. In summer, castle tours are offered daily for an additional C$6.

Next door, **Royal Roads University** (ℂ 250/391-2511) features extensive floral gardens, which are open to the public, free of charge. The University of Victoria, too, has gardens that are free to wander: **Finnerty Gardens** (3800 Finnerty Rd.; ℂ 250/721-7606) contain one of Canada's best collections of rhododendrons, many of which were started from seed from famous plant explorers. There are over

---

On the Garden Trail

Although many of Vancouver Island's best gardens are in this guide, green-thumb enthusiasts can follow their hearts with a **Garden Trail Map** (available at any visitor center or at www.vancouverislandgardentrail.com) to explore smaller gems, including **St.** **Ann's Academy** downtown Victoria, the **Horticulture Centre of the Pacific** at **Glendale Botanical Gardens** in central Saanich, and **Organic Fair Garden** in Cobble Hill. Glendale is the site for Talking Organic, an annual festival on sustainable living (www.organicislands.ca).

Fisherman's Wharf, near the Inn at Laurel Point, is a delightful 15-minute walk along the waterfront from the Inner Harbour, at the end of which you'll find a picturesque flotilla of working fishing boats, houseboats, yachts, and other sailing vessels. Here's where to buy fish right off the boats—shrimp, halibut, crab, and whatever is the catch of the day. The other waterfront is **the pier** just below Wharf Street on the far side of the sea wall—look for the bubblegum-pink building—where seaplanes, kayak outfitters, and whale watchers stake their base camps. People-watch from either wharf and wager with locals on which one offers the best fish and chips.

500 different varieties, as well as 1,600 trees, shrubs, companion plants, and ornamentals. The gardens cover 2.6 hectares (6½ acres) so allow an hour to tour. They are open daily from dawn to dusk, and admission is free. The entrance to the gardens is near the University Chapel, on the southwest edge of the campus. Proceed around the Ring Road to parking lot 6.

If you're staying put around the downtown core, a walk through **Beacon Hill Park** is a must. Gifted to the city by the Hudson's Bay Company in 1882, today, it stretches from just behind the Royal BC Museum to Dallas Road. Without doubt, it's the top park in Victoria—an oasis of indigenous Garry oaks, floral gardens, windswept heath, ponds, and totem poles. There's also a children's farm (see "Especially for Kids," later in this chapter), an aviary, tennis courts, a lawn-bowling green, a putting green, playgrounds, and picnic areas. En route, drop by tiny **Thunderbird Park** (at the corner of Bellevue and Douglas sts., beside the Royal BC Museum). It has several totem poles, and in summer, there's an outdoor studio for experienced carvers to create new poles. Adjacent to the park lies **Helmcken House,** the oldest house still on its original site in British Columbia.

Outdoor Activities

Vancouver Island, and even urban Victoria, is garnering quite a reputation for its range of outdoor activities. Hiking and biking are big pastimes for both residents and visitors, and there is an excess of whale-watching companies. And farther afield, activities include scuba diving (**Ogden Point Dive Centre,** 199 Dallas Rd.; ✆ 888/701-1177 or 250/380-9119; www.divevictoria.com) and birding (**Victoria Natural History Society; ✆ 250/479-6622;** www.vicnhs.bc.ca).

BIKING Cycling is such a popular mode of transportation that Victoria has been nicknamed Canada's Cycling Capital. Consequently, bike paths abound, thanks largely to the Greater Victoria Cycling Coalition, a growing and influential lobby group. There's a scenic **Marine Drive bike path** that takes you around the peninsula and over to Oak Bay. The Inner Harbour also has a bike lane alongside the pedestrian pathway. The city's jewel, however, is the 60km (37-mile) **Galloping Goose Trail** (✆ 250/478-3344; www.gallopinggoosetrail.com for maps and information). This terrific rail-to-trail conversion starts in Victoria at the south end of the Selkirk Trestle, at the foot of Alston Street in Victoria West, and travels the back roads through urban, rural, and semi-wilderness landscapes. There are access points along the entire trail route with many parking areas. It is named after a gawky and noisy 1920s gasoline-powered passenger car that operated on the abandoned CNR line between Victoria and Sooke.

Great Pacific Adventures (811 Wharf St.; ℂ **877/733-6722** or 250/386-2277; www.greatpacificadventures.com) rents bikes from C$8 per hour or C$35 per day (call ahead in winter), as does **Cycle BC,** with two locations—at 686 Humboldt St. for bikes and 950 Wharf St. for scooters and motorcycles (ℂ **250/380-2453;** www.cyclebc.ca). Twenty-one-speed bicycles are C$7 per hour; off-road bikes start at C$12 per hour. Honda Scooters are C$16 per hour for a single seater (C$69/day) and C$19 per hour for a double seater (C$79/day); and for the hard-core biker in us all, a Harley Davidson Road King rents for C$58 per hour, C$225 per day. **Eco Scooters** (ℂ **250/588-1122;** www.ecoscooterentals.ca), on the wharf below the Visitor Information Centre, rents bio-fuel scooters (C$49 for 2 hours), and electric scooters (C$39 for 2 hours). Longer rentals are available, though 2 hours should suffice to follow a see-it-all downtown route. A driver's license isn't required for the electric ride.

CANOEING & KAYAKING   **Ocean River Sports** (1824 Store St.; ℂ **800/909-4233** or 250/381-4233; www.oceanriver.com), on the waterfront, caters to novice and experienced paddlers alike, with rentals, equipment, dry-storage camping gear, and a number of guided tours. Beginners should opt for the 2½-hour "Explorer" around Victoria Harbour (C$125). More adventuresome kayakers can go for the multi-day, bring-your-own-tent adventure to explore the Gulf Islands (C$635, including meals). Rentals are C$25 for 2 hours, C$50 for an 8-hour day. *Tip:* Because of Ocean River's waterfront location, absolute beginners can rent a kayak for a try-out paddle in the harbor's protected waters. The sunset tour is a special treat.

Victoria Kayak Tours (950 Wharf St.; ℂ **250/216-5646;** www.victoriakayak. com) does 2½-hour naturalist tours to Seal Island (C$59) and a 6-hour excursion to the Strait of Juan de Fuca (C$125).

FISHING   Saltwater fishing is very popular here, and guides will show you the current hot spots. **Adam's Fishing Charters** (ℂ **250/370-2326;** www.adamsfishing charters.com), **Beasleys Fishing Charters** (ℂ **866/259-1111** or 250/381-8000; www.beasleysfishingcharters.com), and **Foghorn Fishing Charters** (ℂ **250/658-1848;** www.foghorncharters.com) are good starting points. Rates start at C$95 an hour, for a minimum of 5 hours. Full-day charters are around C$800.

To fish, you need a **saltwater fishing license,** available at Adam's (see above) and the **Marine Adventure Centre** (950 Wharf St., ℂ **250/995-2211**). For nonresidents, a 1-day license costs C$13, a 3-day license C$25, and a 5-day license C$35. Fees are reduced for BC and Canada residents. If you're interested in taking the wheel yourself, **Great Pacific Adventures** (811 Wharf St.; ℂ **877/733-6722** or 250/386-2277; www.greatpacificadventures.com) rents watercraft, including 4.9m (16-ft.) powerboats at C$50 an hour.

For fly-fishing, **Robinson's Outdoor Store** (1307 Broad St.; ℂ **888/317-0033** or 250/385-3429; www.robinsonsoutdoors.com) is an excellent resource for information and all outdoor gear, including specialty flies for area waters, rods, reels, and resource books. They also sell **freshwater fishing licenses.** For nonresidents, a 1-day license is C$20 and an 8-day is C$50, with lower fees for BC and Canada residents.

GOLF   Victoria has an enviable number of good courses. The fees are reasonable, the scenery is spectacular, and most courses are open year-round. Co-designed by

Jack Nicklaus and his son Steve, the Mountain Course, which lies in the foothills of Mount Finlayson atop **Bear Mountain Golf Resort** (1999 Country Club Way; © **888/533-BEAR** [888/533-2327] or 250/744-2327; www.bearmountain.ca) is a hot favorite, so book well in advance to avoid disappointment. It's Canada's only 36 holes of Nicklaus-designed golf. Rates are C$150 Monday through Thursday and C$145 Friday through Sunday. Rates include a GPS-equipped cart.

The **Olympic View Golf Club** (643 Latoria Rd.; © **800/I-GOLFBC** [800/445-5322] or 250/474-3671; www.golfbc.com), is one of the top 35 golf courses in Canada, with two waterfalls and 12 lakes sharing space with the greens. The 6,414-yard course is par 72, and green fees range from C$45 in the winter season to C$80 on a summer weekend. The **Cedar Hill Municipal Golf Course,** at 1400 Derby Rd. (© **250/475-7151;** www.golfcedarhill.com), is a more modest 18-hole public course located only 3.5km (2¼ miles) from downtown Victoria. Daytime fees are C$45; twilight, junior, and winter fees are C$30. Tee-off times are first come, first served.

The **Cordova Bay Golf Course,** at 5333 Cordova Bay Rd. (© **250/658-4444;** www.cordovabaygolf.com), is midway between the Victoria International Airport and downtown Victoria—about a 20-minute drive from either location. It's par 72; expect some tight fairways and 66 sand traps. May to September, daytime green fees Friday to Sunday are C$89, and Monday to Thursday are C$69, when booked 7 days in advance. Tee times within 7 days are for members only. From October to April, green fees range from C$49 weekdays to C$62 weekends (including Fri).

The website **www.vancouverisland.com/golf** lists golf courses around the island, including Arbutus Ridge at Cobble Hill and Glen Meadows Golf & Country Club in Sidney. If you're tight for time, call the **Last Minute Golf Hotline** at © **604/878-1833** for substantial discounts and short-notice tee times at courses in and around Victoria. Book online at www.lastminutegolfbc.com.

SAILING & BOATING   Sailors have often remarked that the Juan de Fuca Strait is some of the best and prettiest sailing areas in the world. **Blackfish Sailing Adventures** (© **250/216-2389;** www.blackfishal.com) leaves Oak Bay Marina for 3-hour and full-day excursions aboard an 11m (35-ft.) Beneteau "oceanus" sloop. You can participate, learn to crew, or just relax. Binoculars are provided. Blackfish organizes sails around Vancouver Island, which are available to do in legs or in its entirety. It also operates the 45-foot *Aquitania,* which is modeled after an early 1900 cedar-strip Edwardian launch and motors out of Victoria's Fisherman's Wharf to Fort Rodd Hill and Fisgard Lighthouse (p. 114). **Tall Ship Adventures** (© **877/788-4263** or 250/885-2311) is an even more romantic option, where you can hop aboard the 17m-tall (55-ft.) ship *Thane.* It's a 1978 vessel modeled after Joshua Slocum's *Spray,* the first vessel to circumnavigate the world single-handedly, in 1895. Departures are from the Inner Harbour; 3-hour trips are C$69 per person. If jetting around in a 4.9m (16-ft.) Double Eagle with a 50HP Honda is more your style, hourly rentals (C$50/hr.) are available through **Island Boat Rentals** (450 Swift St.; © **250/995-1211** or 250/995-1661; www.greatpacificadventures.com).

WHALE-WATCHING   Orcas (killer whales), harbor seals, sea lions, porpoises, and gray whales ply these waters year-round, so whale-watching outfitters abound. Competition keeps prices in line—expect to pay about C$95 to C$115 for a 2- to 3-hour excursion—so the real choice is between riding the waves in a zippy 12-person Zodiac or in a larger, more leisurely craft. Some reputable outfits include **Orca Spirit**

Adventures (© **250/383-8411;** www.orcaspirit.com), which departs from the Coast Harbourside Hotel dock; **Seafun Safaris Whale Watching** (950 Wharf St.; © **877/360-1233** or 250/360-1200; www.seafun.com); and **Prince of Whales** (812 Wharf St.; © **888/383-4884** or 250/383-4884; www.princeofwhales.com), which also offers Victoria/Vancouver one-way trips and circle runs with stopovers at Butchart Gardens and the Gulf Islands. Prince of Whales has also teamed up with Adrena Line (p. 113) for adventure whale-watch and zipline packages.

Organized Tours

AIR TOURS Hyack Air (© **250/384-2499**) offers floatplane adventures from Victoria Harbour. A 30-minute sky-view orientation of the city ranges from C$99 to C$125 per person, depending on the number of passengers. You can also fly around and above the Gulf Islands, Tofino, and Butchart Gardens. The latter includes admission.

BUS TOURS Grayline of Victoria (© **800/663-8390** or 250/388-6539; www.graylinewest.com) conducts tours of the city and, notably, of **Butchart Gardens.** The 1½-hour **Grand City Tour** costs C$29 for adults, C$18 for children 2 to 11. It runs as a hop-on/hop-off loop aboard colorful trolleys and double-decker buses, as do its competitors. Tickets are valid for 48 hours, so you can make the most of visiting attractions en route. In July and August, daily tours depart every 30 minutes from 9:30am to 4:30pm. In spring and fall, tours depart hourly, and in winter, there are only three departures a day. Call ahead for exact times. Grayline also offers seasonal tours, such as Ghost Tours and Murder Mysteries.

FERRY TOURS Departing from various stops around the Inner Harbour, **Victoria Harbour Ferries** (© **250/708-0201;** www.victoriaharbourferry.com) offers 45- and 55-minute tours of the harbor. See shipyards, wildlife, marinas, fishing boats, and floating homes from the water. Tours cost C$22 adults, C$20 seniors, and C$12 children 12 and under. For March, April, and October, they operate daily every 15 minutes from 10am to 5pm. From May through September, they run daily from 9am to 9pm. If you want to stop for food or a stroll, you can get a token that's good for reboarding at any time during the same day.

SPECIALTY TOURS In the mood for something a little different? Climb into one of the bicycle-rickshaws operated by **Kabuki Kabs** (526 Discovery St.; © **250/385-4243;** www.kabukikabs.com). They hold up to four people, operate seasonally, and run just like regular taxis; you can flag one down or (usually) find them parked in front of the Fairmont Empress. Rates run about C$1 per minute for a two-person cab and C$1.75 per minute for a four-person cab. A typical 30-minute tour (you can set your own itinerary) runs about C$30 to C$60.

Tallyho Horse Drawn Tours (© **866/383-5067** or 250/383-5067; www.tallyhotours.com) has conducted horse-drawn carriage and wagon tours in Victoria since 1903. Wagons hold up to 20 strangers and, as such, are by far the most affordable of the horse-drawn tours you'll find at C$15 adults, C$12 seniors, and C$7 children for a 45-minute roll around the city. In summer, tours depart daily every half-hour from 9am to dusk. By far the most romantic are the turn-of-the-20th-century two-person carriage tours, offered by several horse 'n buggy outfits. Competition keeps prices on par with one another, from a short-and-sweet 15-minute harbor tour for C$50 to a 45-minute ride through Beacon Hill Park at C$130 or a 100-minute Romance tour for

The **Old Cemetery Society of Victoria's** (© 250/598-8870; www.oldcem.bc.ca) Sunday-only cemetery tours have become so popular that the group now has a full summer program. Guides take you through Ross Bay Cemetery, as well as the Old Burying Ground of Pioneer Square Cemetery (the evening Lantern Tour is quite eerie). Visit the graves and hear Victoria's history through the lives of Emily Carr, Gold Rush prospectors, and others. Meet at 1:45pm in front of Starbucks at Fairfield Plaza (1516 Fairfield Rd.). Tours are C$5. No reservations needed.

C$240. All Tallyho and carriage rides start at the corner of Belleville and Menzies streets (across from the Royal London Wax Museum).

To get a bird's-eye view of Victoria, **Harbour Air Seaplanes** (950 Wharf St.; © 800/665-0212 or 250/384-2215; www.harbour-air.com) provides 30-minute sky-tours of Victoria's panorama for C$99, as well as a romantic Fly 'n' Dine tour that combines a flight to Butchart Gardens, garden admission and dinner, and a limo ride back into town. The cost is C$239 per person.

You can also take a limousine-only tour with **Heritage Tours and Daimler Limousine Service** (713 Bexhill Rd.; © 250/474-4332) around Victoria; rates start at C$90 per hour. Stretch limos for 8 to 10 people are also available; hourly rates are C$90 to C$100.

WALKING TOURS   Victoria is such a marvelous walking city that guided walks proliferate. Sure, there are themed, self-guided walks (maps are available at the Visitor Information Centre and at www.victoria.ca/tours), but to get the most out of what you're seeing, nothing beats hearing the history, gossip, and anecdotes that tour guides can offer. **Discover the Past** (© 250/384-6698; www.discoverthepast.com) is the leader of the pack, offering walks conducted by historian and entertaining storyteller John Adams. Ninety-minute tours run year-round from the Visitor Information Centre at Government and Wharf streets, and they cover eight themes or areas, from ghostly walks in Old Town to historical walks around Chinatown; starting points may vary. Tours run June through September and cost C$15, cash only.

Walkabouts Historical Tours (© 250/592-9255; www.walkabouts.ca) is the only company that tours the Fairmont Empress. Dressed in turn-of-the-20th-century clothes, guides are exceptionally well informed about this historical hotel (which is said to be haunted). Their knowledge adds a whole new dimension to enjoying high tea there later. The 90-minute, C$10 tour departs daily at 10am sharp; meet at the Fairmont Empress store located next to the Tea Lobby (on the Belleville St. end of the hotel).

Victoria Bobby Walking Tours (© 250/995-0233; www.walkvictoria.com) offers a variety of walks around the city neighborhoods; they depart from the Visitor Information Centre May through mid-September daily at 11am. Your guide is an English ex-bobby either wearing that distinguishing helmet or brandishing an umbrella; bring along C$15.

Travel with Taste (© 250/385-1527; www.travelwithtaste.com) hosts a deliciously appetizing Urban Culinary Walking Tour around central downtown, during which you can literally forage your way through hand-crafted chocolates, smoked meats, pâtés, teas, baked treats, and wine. Four-hour tours cost C$89 per person, operate seasonally, and begin at 11am near the gates of Chinatown. This is a must for foodies and for those wanting to get the low-down on the hottest eateries in town. Winery tours can also be arranged.

Another culinary tour to consider is with **Heidi Fink** (www.chefheidifink.com), an accomplished chef who takes the confusion out of the bewildering array of unfamiliar foodstuffs for sale in Chinatown. Two-hour tours run Sunday afternoons and cost C$50. Advance reservations are required for both these culinary capers.

ESPECIALLY FOR KIDS

There's no doubt that Victoria caters well to getaway travelers, whether looking for romance or simply a quality urban destination. But families with children of all ages also find much to enjoy here. There are the obvious city attractions such as the touchy-feely, creepy-crawly **Victoria Bug Zoo** (p. 85) that's bound to be a sure-fire hit; the watery kingdom of **Pacific Undersea Gardens** (p. 84); and the diminutive displays at **Miniature World** (p. 84). Then there's the very unstuffy **Royal BC Museum** (p. 85), which really does have something for all ages, especially when combined with a visit to the **IMAX** theater.

For youngsters, the **Beacon Hill Children's Farm** (Circle Dr., Beacon Hill Park; ✆ **250/381-2532**) is a well-established petting zoo with rabbits, goats, and other barnyard animals, which makes for a super outing, especially when coupled with some kite flying on Beacon Hill or picnicking at the wading pool and playground nearby.

Outside of the downtown core, remember to check out the **Butterfly Gardens** (p. 108); the new **Rose Carousel** in Butchart Gardens' Children's Pavilion (p. 107); **Fort Rodd Hill & Fisgard Lighthouse** (p. 114); the amazing **Shaw Ocean Discovery Centre** (p. 108) in Sidney; and nearby **Mineral World & Scratch Patch** (9891 Seaport Place, Sidney; ✆ **250/655-4367**; www.mineralworld.ca), an indoor/outdoor arena containing two gold-panning pools, a pond filled with tropical shells, and mounds of semi-precious gemstones. Admission to Mineral World is free, though if you're stone-digging, you must buy a collector's bag for C$6 to C$15; anything you find, you can keep. The Patch is open daily September to June 9am to 6pm, with extended hours to 9pm in July and August.

For more kid-friendly suggestions, take a look at *The Kids' Guide to Victoria,* which details more than 50 places to go and things to do around Vancouver Island. You can get this guide by contacting Tourism Victoria (✆ **250/953-2033;** www.tourismvictoria.com).

All Fun Recreation Park   The park has two go-kart tracks, mini-golf, and batting cages, all priced separately, so it can get expensive. For example, the cost of go-karting is C$13 per 6-minute session; mini-golf is C$6 per adult, C$4 per child; and swinging at 25 baseballs will set you back C$4. Save a few dollars and get a C$20 pass that includes a go-kart ride, 18 holes of mini-golf, and 50 balls in the batting cage.

2207 Millstream Rd.✆ **250/474-1961.** www.allfun.bc.ca. Admission C$4–C$20; C$6 observers (including access to an 80-person hot tub & beach volleyball courts). Mid-June to Labor Day daily 11am–7pm.

Centre of the Universe   The larger of the two telescopes trained to the heavens was once the largest in the world, so you know that the stargazing is good—depending on the cloud cover. Nighttime vigils for the public are offered somewhat sporadically (especially in winter), as they're scheduled between bookings by professional astronomers. The daytime 75-minute tour of the aging observatory is still a fun excursion from the downtown core.

5071 West Saanich Rd. © **250/363-8262.** www.cu.hia.nrc.gc.ca. Admission 3–7pm C$9 adults, C$8 seniors & students, C$5 children 5-12 years; 7–11pm C$12 adults, C$9 seniors & students, C$7 children 5-12 years. Tues–Sat 3–11pm.

WildPlay Elements Park   Located 20-minutes north of downtown, near Bear Mountain, this park offers high-flying adventure through a progressively more challenging tree-to-tree obstacle course. The course includes ziplines, bridges, scramble nets, and swing logs, many of which are 18m (59 ft.) above ground through a forest of Douglas firs. Children must be 7 years and older, and some restrictions apply to those 13 years and under. Sunset rides are especially popular.

1767 Island Hwy. © **888/856-7275** or 250/590-7529. www.wildplay.com. Admission C$40 full course; C$20 kids course. Daily 9am–5pm; call ahead for special 7pm sunset rides.

SHOPPING

Great Shopping Areas

Victoria has dozens of specialty shops that make browsing a real pleasure. Nearly all are within walking distance of one another. Stores are generally open Monday through Saturday from 10am to 6pm; some are open on Sundays from noon to 5pm.

The first shopping foray for most visitors is to head up the brick-paved **Government Street promenade,** about 5 blocks north from the Inner Harbour. Many of the stores are housed in handsome heritage buildings, and stepping inside is like stepping back a century. You'll find various specialty shops here, including ones featuring First Nations art. But be warned: Amid the jewels is a surplus of souvenir shops, each waist-deep in bottles of maple syrup and Taiwanese knickknacks.

The largest shopping area runs north-south along Douglas Street and east-west along several cross streets, in particular Yates Street—the focal point of many restaurants and bars, too. It's where to find banks, camera suppliers, music stores, and other outlets. The multi-level **Bay Centre** (© **250/952-5690;** www.thebaycentre. ca) anchors this city core and is where to shop for top-name fashions and mainstream goods. **The Bay** itself is also a popular department store; it got its start over 330 years ago as a series of trading posts across the country and is the oldest corporation in North America. Aside from designer labels and general housewares, you can still buy their famous red-, green-, and yellow-striped point blanket, an item that was once traded for beaver pelts.

Just off Government Street, adjacent to the Bay Centre, are intriguing shopping streets: **Trounce Alley,** Victoria's former red-light district now transformed into a chic area, complete with 125-year-old gaslights, and nearby **Broad Street,** a small and bustling strip packed with gift shops, galleries, and specialty stores. The area in and around Johnson Street has been dubbed **LoJo** (short for Lower Johnson) with more owner-operated, hip 'n happening outlets; most are geared to the younger crowd. Farther north,

Old Town/Market Square is a fascinating blend of turn-of-the-20th-century buildings and shops, reminiscent of San Francisco's Garibaldi Square, but quainter, and with live performances in summer. Nearby, Victoria's **Chinatown** is so tiny, you might miss it. Search out **Fan Tan Alley**. It's Canada's thinnest commercial street, just over a meter (3¼ ft.) wide at either end, yet crammed with oddball paraphernalia and a maze of doors leading to small courtyards—and even more doors leading to more back alleys, stairs, and living quarters. When the police used to raid gambling clubs, participants could easily escape through the myriad passageways. **Dragon Alley** is another alley weaving through what used to be tenement buildings in the 1880s, when 16,000 Chinese lived here, and is now home to a Thai spa, a dog boutique, and sex shop.

At the edge of Chinatown, adjacent to City Hall, is an up-and-coming area, which tourism officials are marketing as the city's new **Designer District**. Frankly, it's a bit of a stretch, but if you search, you will find one or two edgy housewares outlets such as **Urban Barn** (520 Herald St., ✆ 250/360-9067), and **Chintz** (1720 Store St., ✆ 250/381-2404), home decor studios, and specialty stores like Miroirs (1824 Government St., ✆ 250/351-3382), which sells mirrors of every shape, size, and design. **Humboldt Street,** behind the Convention Centre, is also trying to establish itself as the Humboldt Valley shopping destination, primarily for galleries, arts, and crafts. Again, it's early days, but the concept is gaining traction. If antiquing is your thing, make your way to **Fort Street,** fondly known as Antique Row, on the eastern edge of the downtown core. Items with hefty price tags are right alongside stores selling bric-a-brac, and you can find **Kilshaw's Auctioneers** (1115 Fort St., ✆ 250/384-6441), where an unexpected bargain might be on the chopping block. If you follow a "shop local" philosophy, look out for a *We Are Local* brochure, which features local, independent retailers of all genres (www.modernurbanguides.com).

Shopping A to Z

ANTIQUES & COLLECTIBLES

Renowned for its high-quality British collectibles, Antique Row is a 3-block stretch along Fort Street between Blanshard and Cook streets. Unfortunately, it's beginning to wane as a destination. Demand isn't what it was, and several long-time dealers are retiring. Nevertheless, it's still the best place to find the finest in estate jewelry, silverware, heritage china, and furniture, especially at the two auction houses, **Lunds** (926 Fort St.; ✆ 250/386-3308) and **Kilshaws** (1115 Fort St.; ✆ 250/384-6441).

In addition to those listed below, check out **Charles Baird** (1044A Fort St.; ✆ 250/384-8809) for antique furniture, **Britannia & Co.** (839 Fort St.; ✆ 250/480-1954) for porcelain figurines, and **Romanoff & Co.** (837–839 Fort St.; ✆ 250/480-1543) for its impressive collection of coins and silverware. For the recreational antiquer looking for a bargain, the **Old Vogue Shop** (1034 Fort St.; ✆ 250/380-7751) is a generalist shop with a hodgepodge of items and styles.

Classic Silverware   A gorgeous shop that specializes in discontinued sterling silver and silver-plated flatware and tea service sets, it also maintains a registry for missing and discontinued china. 826 Fort St.✆ 250/383-6860.

David Robinson Antiques   Come here for high-quality period furniture, silver, Oriental rugs, paintings, and other fine antiques. 1023 Fort St.✆ 250/384-6425.

Faith Grant's Connoisseur Shop   Housed in an 1862 heritage building, this store has a labyrinth of rooms filled with high-end household furnishings. 1156 Fort St. ✆ 250/383-0121. www.faithgrantantiques.com.

Vanity Fair Antique & Collectibles Mall   With more than 40 dealers of crystal, glassware, furniture, and jewelry all under one roof, this mall offers everything from a mortgage to other more affordable items that might even leave change in your pocket. 1044 Fort St. ✆ **250/380-7274.** www.vanityfairantiques.com.

ART/CONTEMPORARY

Fran Willis Gallery   With its 5m-high (16-ft.) ceilings and high, arched windows, Victoria's oldest and largest contemporary gallery is certainly one of the nicest display spaces in the city for established and emerging Western Canadian artists. 1619 Store St. ✆ **250/381-3422.** www.franwillis.com.

Jade   Mined along the Coast Range of North America, this jade is renowned for being the brightest, hardest, greenest, and most translucent nephrite jade ever found. This gallery has sculptural pieces, as well as jewelry. 911 Government St. ✆ **250/384-5233.** www.jademine.com.

The West End Gallery   This open, airy gallery encompasses the works of over 100 Canadian artists. Its specialty is paintings, sculpture, and art glass. 1203 Broad St. ✆ **250/388-0009.** www.westendgalleryltd.com.

Winchester Galleries   Offering a diversity of Canadian art, both historical and contemporary, Winchester Galleries features names that include the Group of Seven, Jack Shadbolt, Mary Pratt, and Toni Onley. Two almost-adjoining galleries are helping to anchor Humboldt Valley, the city's newest shopping district. A smaller gallery is in Oak Bay Village, at 2260 Oak Bay Ave. 796 Humboldt St. ✆ **250/382-7750.** www.winchestergalleriesltd.com.

ART/NATIVE

Alcheringa Gallery   Recognized for its museum-quality (and expensive) aboriginal work from all over the world, this gallery offers pieces that have a West Coast and Australasia influence. 665 Fort St. ✆ **250/383-8224.** www.alcheringa-gallery.com.

Eagle Feather Gallery   This gallery carries one of the finest First Nations collections of authentic jewelry, arts, and crafts, all exclusively created by First Nations artists. A percentage of all profits is donated to First Nations' youth programs. 904 Gordon St. ✆ **250/388-4330.** www.eaglefeathergallery.com.

Hills Native Art   One of the most respected stores for established BC First Nations artists, this is the place to find traditional pieces, such as wooden masks, drums, and talking sticks, alongside items for the less-serious collector, such as dream catchers and souvenir totem poles. 1008 Government St. ✆ **250/385-3911.** www.hillsnativeart.com.

BOOKS

Chapters Downtown   The mother ship of all local Chapters bookstores, this location has three floors of book titles, DVDs, and stationery. In addition to the usual bargain tables on the main floor, there are some good deals on kids' books in the basement. 1212 Douglas St. ✆ **250/380-9009. www.chapters.indigo.ca.**

Chronicles of Crime   Every one of the more than 25,000 new and used book titles is spy-related, criminal, and mysterious. 1067 Fort St. ✆ **250/721-2665.**

Munro's   Described as Canada's most magnificent (architecturally speaking) bookstore, the range of titles within the 1909 former bank building should satisfy most bookies, as will the remainder tables' discounts. 1108 Government St. ✆ **250/382-2464.** www.munrobooks.com.

Russell Books As Canada's largest used book store, this longtime family business houses discounted new, used, antiquarian, and out-of-print titles on two floors. 734 Fort St.© **250/361-4447.** www.russellbooks.com.

Shepherd Books If you've ever watched the movie *You've Got Mail,* then you'll understand the dilemma of a small, independent bookstore trying to make its way, seemingly on sheer passion for the written word alone. This is one such store, specializing in quality new and second-hand books. Some are rare finds, such as a first edition of *The Little Prince,* by Antoine de Saint-Exupéry. 826 Fort St.© **250/383-3981.** www.shepherdbooks.ca.

CRAFTS

Cowichan Trading Company Best known for its authentic Cowichan sweaters and handmade moccasins, this store also sells a slew of junky T-shirts, giftware, and souvenirs. 1328 Government St.© **250/383-0321.** www.cowichantrading.com.

Sidestreet Studio Also located in Oak Bay Village (2250 Oak Bay Ave.), this second outlet is in the new Humboldt Valley shopping district. Everything here is Canadian, handcrafted, and one-of-a-kind—jewelry, pottery, wood turnings, glass, and textiles. Prices are more affordable than large, established galleries. 729 Humboldt St.© **250/590-4644.** www.sidestreetstudio.com.

Starfish Glass Works A former bank building now serves as a gallery-cum-workshop. Watch from the mezzanine level as award-winning artists transform molten glass into ingenious works of art. ***Note:*** Glass is blown during afternoons only, and not at all on Mondays or Tuesdays. 630 Yates St.© **250/388-7827.**

FASHION/WOMEN

Although The Bay Centre holds court for many mainstream retailers such as La Senza, Guess?, and Jacob, specialty stores are best for that more memorable purchase.

Freedom Kilts When the Edinburgh Tartan Shop downsized to a boutique nook inside a larger store for outdoor wear, Freedom Kilts picked up the gauntlet and is plaid-happy with tartans, custom-made kilts, and accessories. 1919 Fernwood Rd. © **250/386-KILT (250/386-5458).** www.freedomkilts.com.

Hughes Clothing Look for names such as Eileen Fisher (U.S.), Nougat (London), Xandres (Belgium), and J. Lindeberg (Sweden). 564 Yates St.© **250/381-4405.** www.hughesclothing.com.

She She Bags The most discriminating of bag fetishists will be satiated here, with all manner of offbeat and jewel-studded bags. Most of the whimsical designs are for the bold at heart, with the occasional classic design thrown in for good measure. Trendsetting locals consider its sister store, **She She Shoes** (616 Trounce Alley; © **250/383-1883**), among the most drool-worthy foot coverings in Victoria. 616 View St.© **250/388-0613.**

Smoking Lily This tiny, home-based 4-sq.-m (43-sq.-ft.) store—one of the smallest in the world—is like a test-run showcase for new ideas in women's clothing and accessories. Consequently, there's always something new and innovative on hand. 569A Johnson St.© **250/382-5459.** www.smokinglily.com.

FASHION/MEN

Outlooks for Men Victoria's most fashion-forward menswear store will appeal to the younger demographic. Cutting-edge labels include Hugo Boss, Orange Label, Z Zegna, Melting Pot, and Horst. 554 Yates St.© **250/384-2848.** www.outlooksformen.ca.

W&J Wilson   The Wilson family has operated this clothing store since 1862. Although the store certainly doesn't carry fashions from that era, they do lean toward sensible casuals for men, largely from England, Scotland, and Ireland. 1221 Government St. ✆ **250/383-7177.** www.wandjwilson.com.

GREEN SHOPPING

The Good Planet Store   Shop with a conscience in this eco-aware store, in which everything—from bedroom and bathroom items to kitchen utensils, baby wear, and body-care products—is about as earth-friendly as it can get. Wind-up and solar gadgets share shelf space with gear for your pet. 764 Fort St. ✆ **250/477-0146.** www.goodplanet.com.

Not Just Pretty   This sweatshop-free store carries organic, natural-fiber fashions (cotton, wool, and silk), where the production emphasis is on sustaining communities. Items range from T-shirts and skirts to dresses, jackets, cashmere sweaters, scarves, and hats. 1036 Fort St. ✆ **250/414-0414.** www.notjustpretty.com.

Shift Natural Fashion   Its focus is on unique, contemporary, and cutting-edge natural, sustainable, and ethically made clothing and accessories, as well as body-care products. Most items are made locally, using local materials. 547 Johnson St. ✆ **250/383-7441.** www.shiftfashion.ca.

JEWELRY

Artina's   Featuring the silver and goldsmithing work of more than 20 Canadian and First Nations artists, most necklaces, rings, pendants, and bracelets have a refreshingly modern take on traditional designs, whether aboriginal motifs or simply a stylized heron. 1002 Government St. ✆ **250/386-7000.** www.artinas.com.

Jade Tree   Here's where to find jewelry made from British Columbia jade. Mined in northern Vancouver Island, the jade is crafted and polished for a variety of items, including necklaces, bracelets, pendants, and small ornaments. 606 Humboldt St. ✆ **250/388-4326.**

The Patch   This is the island's largest purveyor of body jewelry—for your nose, navel, nipple, and ears. Many of the studs, baubles, and rings are quite funky. 719 Yates St. ✆ **250/384-7070.**

Shi Studio   Chinese silk brocades, often using traditional dynastic patterns, is fused into pendants, belt buckles, brooches, cuffs, and earrings. This is a working studio, so it's best to call ahead. 420-620 View St. ✆ **250/995-2714.** www.shistudio.com.

Violette Veldor   If you love accessories, check out this store's eclectic mélange of jewelry. Find designs from local talent and international names such as Alex & Chloe and Sugar Lime. 1223 Government St. ✆ **250/388-7752.** www.violetteboutique.com.

MARKETS

Market Square   This eclectic little shopping and restaurant complex is made up of former warehouse and shipping offices from the 1800s. Shops here sell everything from used cameras, second-hand books, and designer dog-biscuits to teddy bears and condoms. The central courtyard comes into its own in the summer, with live performances and casual patio dining. 560 Johnson St. ✆ **250/386-5534.** www.marketsquare.ca.

SPECIALTY GIFTS/SOUVENIRS

As in all touristy destinations, souvenir stores that sell T-shirts and tacky memorabilia are a dime a dozen in Victoria. For ideas that say "Victoria" in a different way, try these suggestions.

English Sweet Shop If Sharp's toffee bonbons, lemon sherbets, licorice allsorts, and pear drops mean something to you, then this is a must-visit. The shop celebrated its 100th anniversary in 2010 and still serves candies by weight, from oversized glass jars. 738 Yates St.🕐 **250/382-3325.** www.englishsweets.com.

Irish Linen Stores A fixture in this 1884 Victoria Italianate heritage building since 1917, this store sells fine Irish damask towels, linens, laces, and sweaters. 1019 Government St.🕐 **250/383-6812.** www.irishlinenvictoria.com.

Plenty Epicurean Pantry Shelves and corners are stacked with an eclectic range of foodstuffs from all over the world, as well as plenty of local products from Victoria. The store mantra is organic, fair trade, ethnic, and artisan. 1034 Fort St. 🕐 **250/380-7654.** www.epicureanpantry.ca.

Rogers' Chocolates A Victoria institution for more than a hundred years, Rogers' offers cream-filled specialty chocolates that have been enjoyed by royalty and others. The store is enchanting, filled with Tiffany glass, ornamental tile-work, and old-fashioned, highly polished wooden counters. Old man Rogers (who, ironically, hated milk chocolate) is said to haunt the place. 913 Government St.🕐 **250/384-7021.** www.rogerschocolates.com.

Satin Moon Quilt Shop Here, you can browse creative, handmade, and locally designed quilts and accessories made from all manner of traditional, First Nations, and Asian-inspired fabrics. Custom orders are shipped worldwide. 1689 Government St. 🕐 **250/383-4023.** www.satin-moon.com.

Silk Road Aromatherapy & Tea Company This pleasing tea emporium in the heart of Chinatown features loose-leaf and exclusive blended teas, equipage, and even tea-based aromatherapy products. There's a tea-tasting bar offering a host of intriguing flavors, as well as a small basement spa offering green-tea facials and the like. 1624 Government St.🕐 **250/704-2688.** www.silkroadtea.com.

Simply the Best Small in size it may be, but the price tags and range of goods are quite the opposite. Simply the Best boasts more than 10,000 items, many of which sport the world's most exclusive brand names in clothing, housewares, and office and dining accessories. 1008 Broad St.🕐 **250/386-6661.**

Tuscan Kitchen The glorious colors of Tuscany will draw you into the store; the hand-painted Italian majolica platters, dishes, and fashionable cookware will have

---

💬 A Bit about BC Jade

Jade actually refers to two distinct gemstones, nephrite and jadeite. Nephrite, the original jade, is an amphibole and the toughest natural material due to its felted interlocking fibers. Jadeite is a pyroxene, a much younger mineral with a more crystalline structure so is usually dyed and chemically altered to enhance its texture, clarity, and depth of translucency. Since many green stones are misrepresented as jade, be sure to buy from a reputable dealer. BC's jade is a quality nephrite, highly valued by the Inuit and other northern nations. The Chinese, too, revered jade as the Stone of Heaven, believing it to possess sacred qualities that had the power to channel spirits and vital chi energy. So prized was jade that it is said that a Chinese emperor once traded five cities for a small jade carving that fit into his hand.

spas IN VICTORIA

Whether nestled in the rainforest, perched on craggy shores, or presented as urban getaways of serenity, spas are plentiful on Vancouver Island. Some of the best ones are in and around Victoria.

Sapphire Day Spa Although small, this spa feels fresh and spacious with its clean and contemporary look. It is the only spa in Victoria offering quality Ayurvedic treatments (alongside European services). It even has a Swedana herbal cedar steam chest, one of the hallmarks of quality Ayurveda services. 714 View St. ✆ 250/385-6676. www.sapphiredayspa.com.

The Spa at Delta Victoria A luxurious, European-style sanctuary, this spa includes a complete fitness facility, pool, and sauna. It's consistently rated one of the city's best spas. Ocean Pointe Resort, 45 Songhees Rd. ✆ 800/575-8882 or 250/360-5858. www.thespa deltavictoria.com.

Willow Stream Spa Chic, expensive, and a true spa oasis, all treatments include time in the sauna, steam room, and Hungarian mineral pool, so you can turn a pedicure into a spa getaway. 721 Government St. ✆ 866/854-7444 or 250-995-4650. www.willowstream.com.
Essence of Life Spa A 30-minute drive from Victoria, this oceanfront spa and aroma garden pulls out the stops on a wide range of European services, especially the couples massage. Brentwood Bay Lodge, 849 Verdier Ave.

✆ 888/544-2079 or 250/544-2079. www.brentwoodbaylodge.com/spa.

Spa Magnolia Veteran spa-goers know the name Aveda, and this Aveda concept spa does the name proud. Its move to lovely new digs on the ground floor of the Magnolia Hotel now makes the spa one of the heavier hitters in town. 623 Courtney St. ✆ 250/920-7721. www.spamagnolia.com.

Le Spa Sereine Located in a three-level character building, this independent, urban day spa is a local favorite. Refinement services are separated from the relaxing stuff so the scents of (toxic) hair colors don't ruin the aromas of massage oils. 1144 Government St. ✆ 866/388-4419. www.lespasereine.ca.

Sante Spa Although run by Canada's premier MediSpa outfit, Sante Spa does not offer medical esthetics. However, the spa's traditional spa treatments have healthful qualities and an indigenous twist, using locally harvested seaweed and Canadian glacial clay. The mountaintop location is pretty spectacular. Bear Mountain, 1999 Country Club Way. ✆ 888/533-2327 or 250/391-7160. www.santespa.com.

Frilly Lilly The setup is whimsical, girly, and only about hands, feet, and waxing services that are the best in town. Started in Calgary, this dessert-inspired chain has taken its "frills" to as far north as Anchorage and as far south as Hong Kong. 811 Fort St. ✆ 250/590-4400. www.frillylilly.ca.

you stay a while; the offer to ship worldwide will seal the deal. 653 View St. ✆ **250/386-8191.** www.thetuscankitchen.com.

The Wine Barrel You'll find the largest selection of BC VQA (Vintner Quality Alliance) wines in the province here. Walls are stacked with more than 300 varieties, including ice wines and limited editions, as well as an enormous selection of wine accessories. 644 Broughton St. ✆ **250/388-0606.** www.thewinebarrel.com.

VICTORIA AFTER DARK

As vibrant as Victoria is by day, once the hour hand passes 10pm, city activity just seems to fade into the darkness. Granted, the pubs and the Yates Street area remain pretty busy, especially on weekends, but all in all, when the theaters, concert venues, and movie houses close up shop, so does downtown.

Monday magazine (**www.mondaymag.com**) covers everything going on in town, from nightclubs and the performing arts to films and poetry readings. You name it, *Monday's* got it. You can also call the **Community Arts Council of Greater Victoria's** events hotline at ℂ **250/381-ARTS** (250/381-2787). Tickets and schedules are also available at the **Tourism Victoria Travel Visitor Information Centre** (812 Wharf St.; ℂ **250/953-2033**).

The Performing Arts

Although Victoria is a primary tourist destination, visitors aren't the mainstay of the city's performing arts. Consequently, there's still a community feel to the audiences and venues, many of which are shared among the professional groups.

VENUES The **Royal Theatre** (805 Broughton St.; ℂ **250/361-0800;** www.rmts.bc.ca) dates from the early 1900s. Renovated in the 1970s, it hosts concerts (including the Victoria Symphony), dance recitals, and touring plays, as well as performances by Pacific Opera Victoria. The **McPherson Playhouse** (3 Centennial Sq.; ℂ **250/361-0800**; www.rmts.bc.ca) was built in 1914 as the first Pantages Vaudeville Theatre. It hosts smaller stage plays and performances by the Victoria Operatic Society. The Royal and the McPherson share a box office at the **McPherson Playhouse** (ℂ **888/717-6121** or 250/386-6121; www.rmts.bc.ca). Box-office hours are Monday to Saturday from 9:30am to 5:30pm, and on performance days for the 2 hours prior to show time. Take bus no. 6 to Pandora and Government streets.

CLASSICAL MUSIC The **Victoria Symphony Orchestra** (846 Broughton St.; ℂ **250/385-6515;** www.victoriasymphony.bc.ca) kicks off its season in August with **Symphony Splash,** a free concert performed on a barge in the Inner Harbour. The regular season begins in September and runs through May at the Royal Theatre or the University Farquhar Auditorium. Tickets average C$60 for adults, depending on the series, with discounts for seniors and students. Watch for special concerts at Butchart Gardens and Beacon Hill Park.

DANCE Dance recitals and full-scale performances by local and international dance troupes such as **Danceworks** and the **Scottish Dance Society** are scheduled throughout the year. To find out who's performing while you're in town, call **Tourism Victoria** (ℂ **250/953-2033**) or contact the **Community Arts Council of Greater Victoria** (1001 Douglas St.; ℂ **250/381-ARTS** [250/381-2787] or 250/381-2787; www.cacgv.ca).

OPERA The **Pacific Opera Victoria** (1316B Government St.; ℂ **250/385-0222,** or ℂ 250/382-1641 for box office; www.pov.bc.ca) presents productions during the months of October, February, and April. Tickets are available at the McPherson Playhouse and Pacific Opera box offices (ℂ **250/386-6121**). The **Victoria Operatic Society** (798 Fairview Rd.; ℂ **250/381-1021;** www.vos.bc.ca) stages old-time musicals and other popular fare year-round at the McPherson Playhouse. They may not be to the standard of Carnegie Hall, but they make for a good evening out.

THEATER   The nationally acclaimed **Belfry Theatre Society** (1291 Gladstone St.; © **250/385-6815;** www.belfry.bc.ca; bus no. 22 to Fernwood St.) stages contemporary productions in an intimate church-turned-playhouse space. Works are generally of Canadian origin and are often interspersed with visiting productions, such as *The Syringa Tree* and *Spelling B.* The **Intrepid Theatre Company** (301-1205 Broad St.; © **250/383-2663;** www.intrepidtheatre.com) runs two theater festivals annually. In late April and early May, it's the **Uno Festival of Solo Performance,** a unique event of strictly one-person performances with tickets at C$18 adults, C$16 seniors and students. Multi-show passes are also offered. From late August to early September, Intrepid stages the **Victoria Fringe Festival** (© **250/383-2691** for box office), an amazingly eclectic selection of alternative theater. More than 50 performances from all over the world are staged in six venues around the city, including the Victoria Conservatory of Music, St. Andrew's School, and the Downtown Community Activities Centre. Compared to mainstream theater, festival tickets are cheap (the artists set their own ticket prices to a maximum of C$12), performances are about an hour, and content is unpredictable.

Theatre Inconnu (© **250/360-0234;** www.islandnet.com/~tinconnu) is Victoria's longest surviving alternative theater company, with more than 20 seasons under its belt. It produces Victoria's annual **Shakespearean Festival,** which takes place in the historic St. Ann's Academy, at 835 Humboldt St., in July and August. Ticket prices (C$15) reflect the groups' semi-professional status, but don't be deterred: Plays are of an exceptionally high caliber. Every year, Theatre Inconnu also stages a two-man adaptation of Charles Dickens's *A Christmas Carol.* The **Langham Court Theatre** (805 Langham Court; © **250/384-2142;** www.langhamcourttheatre.bc.ca) performs works produced by the **Victoria Theatre Guild,** a local amateur society dedicated to presenting a wide range of dramatic and comedic works that are surprisingly good. Tickets are a bargain at C$18. Take bus no. 14 or 11 from downtown to Fort and Moss streets.

The Bar & Pub Scene

There are few places outside of England that do pubs as well as Victoria does, even though some of them verge on lounge status. Here are the best drinking places; pick according to your mood. Some, like the Bengal Lounge, are classy and elegant; others, like the Sticky Wicket, are as you would find in the old country. Most are hybrids.

Bard and Banker   A repurposed bank building (circa 1862) sets rather a grand stage for this enormous, bi-level space that includes a patio, a lounge, and a restaurant. With over 30 different draught beers, an inordinate amount of wines by the glass (a nifty techno-cellar makes sure open wine bottles are well preserved), a high-end pub menu, and live entertainment every night, "the Bard" is nearly always busy. 1022 Government St. © **250-953-9993.**

The Bengal Lounge ★   This lounge salutes Queen Victoria's role as the Empress of India with a colonial elegance that includes huge leather coaches, oversize palms, ceiling fans, and a lengthy cocktail list. It's the chic place to go, especially for the live jazz on Friday and Saturday nights. This is where to try BC's only handcrafted gin, the product of Winchester Cellars in Saanich. Fairmont Empress Hotel, 721 Government St. © **250/384-8111.**

Big Bad John's   Without doubt, this is the rowdiest spot in town. Despite a decor that includes an ever-increasing collection of bras hanging from the ceiling and a

SUDS up!

Victorians take their locally brewed hops seriously, so naturally, brewpubs hold a special status in the hearts and taste buds of many a self-professed beer lover. Top spots to sip these artisan brews include:

Harbour Canoe Club Be prepared for a crowd here; it's always busy, especially with the after-work crowd, many of whom will stay on for dinner. The atmospheric heritage brick-and-beam building has an on-site micro-brewery that produces some excellent brews; the six-small-glass taster option is the best deal in town at C$11 a fleet. 450 Swift St. ✆ 250/361-1940.

Spinnakers Brewpub ★ It all started here, and from the get-go, this brewpub remains one of the best. Though the view across Victoria Harbour almost makes it reason enough to come here, its brewed-on-premises ales, lagers, and stouts are the big draw. There's even an on-site bakery selling beer breads. The pub fare is good, too. 308 Catherine St. ✆ 250/386-2739.

Swans Butterfield Brewpub If there's a live band scheduled for the weekend, the place gets very busy and noisy. It occupies the ground floor of a heritage warehouse, above which is one of Victoria's most unique inns (see "Where to Stay," earlier in this chapter). Against the decor of old brickwork and beams is an ever-changing display of First Nations art. The signature British-style ales and German and Canadian beers are brewed on site. 506 Pandora Ave. ✆ 250/361-3310.

floor inches deep in discarded peanut shells, it's a clean-cut place where half the fun is letting it all hang out. Strathcona Hotel, 919 Douglas St. ✆ **250/383-7137.**

Darcy's Wharf Street Pub This large, bright, waterfront watering hole is where you'll find the lively younger crowd enjoying fine brews and pool tables. Live bands play occasionally on the weekends. 1127 Wharf St. ✆ **250/380-1322.** www.darcyspub.ca.

The Reef Strictly speaking, The Reef is a restaurant, though as the evening progresses, its upbeat Caribbean tone gives it the feel of a reggae hangout with a mix of martinis, rum punches, and DJ and live music. 533 Yates St. ✆ **250/388-5375.** www.thereefrestaurant.com.

Sips Artisan Bistro Tasting is Sips *raison d'etre,* especially when they're serving limited edition wines from Vancouver Island, the Okanagan, or elsewhere in the province. Customized flights of 59mL (2-oz.) pourings average C$3.50 per pour. All sips, plus handcrafted ales and lagers, are included on the menu, paired with a rotating selection of plates such as artisan cheeses, charcuterie, smoked meats, and other locally sourced foods. Sips is part of the Spinnakers Brew Pub organization. 425 Simcoe St., ✆ **250/590-3519.** www.spinnakers.com.

Soprano's Karaoke & Sports Bar Don't come for the food, come to let your hair down and have a silly, fun time. With almost 5,000 titles to choose from, the song library is inexhaustible. Then there are the 23 sports screens and two oversized beauties, which flip visuals between sports events and crooning singer. If there's an event at nearby Save on Foods Memorial Centre, the place is at crush-capacity pre- and post-event. 730 Caledonia St. ✆ **250/382-5853.** www.sopranoskaraoke.com.

The Sticky Wicket Reminiscent of a turn-of-the-20th-century Irish pub, this is as close as you can get to a traditional pub (including its pub grub). Most of its stained glass windows, dark wood interior furnishings, and long teak bar were shipped over from Ireland. Less Irish is the Strath's resident meandering magician who does sleight of hand tricks at your table, picking up tips along the way. It's a whole other world to Big Bad John's in the basement and the volleyball sands of the rooftop patio. Strathcona Hotel, 919 Douglas St. © **250/383-7137.**

Suze Lounge & Restaurant   One of *the* places for martinis and Sinatra-flavored schmoozing. Aim for a seat at the 7.6m (25-ft.) mahogany bar. 515 Yates St. © **250/383-2829.**

Union Pacific After Dark   By day, the Union Pacific is a coffee house in Dragon Alley, Chinatown. By night, it becomes a bohemian spot to chill over its selection of wines, nibble tasty morsels off a charcuterie plate, and listen to live music, usually on Wednesday nights. 537 Herald St. © **250/380-0005.** www.unionpacificafterdark.com.

The Club Scene
DANCE CLUBS & LIVE MUSIC

New venues come and go with regularity (at time of writing, the Strathcona Hotel was set to open a new upscale grill and late night lounge), so what's listed below are the tried-and-trues—those clubs that have found a winning formula. Most places are open Monday through Saturday until 2am and Sunday until midnight. Drinks are C$4 to C$9; some clubs have covers (usually weekends only) ranging from C$3 to C$7.

Hermann's Jazz Club   Although not chic, for 25 years, Hermann's has delivered Victoria's best live jazz and Dixieland. Martinis are named after famous musicians such as Duke Ellington and Ella Fitzgerald. The club's usually open Wednesday through Sunday (call ahead to check), and if you play jazz and bring your instrument, there'll likely be an opportunity to jam. 753 View St. © **250/388-9166.** www.hermannsjazz.com.

The Lucky Bar   This is probably one of Victoria's hottest nightspots. It doesn't get into gear until after 9pm. Hence, drinks in the long, darkly lit lounge are a natural follow-through to an earlier meal next door at **Luciano's** (515 Yates St., © **250/388-5824**), or you can go just for the martinis and music, which is a mix of DJ-spun and live bands. 517 Yates St. © **250/382-5825.** www.luckybar.ca.

Touch Lounge   This location has undergone various incarnations, but whatever its name, it always ends up being (for a time, anyways) the city's "hottest new lounge." Touch is no different, regardless of what the advertising says. There are three rooms, each with a different sound, light show, and ambiance for dancing, boozing, and schmoozing. The place is geared to the under-30s crowd; you'll want to dress to impress and express. The DJs spin mainly Top 40, retro, hip-hop, funk, and R&B. 751 View St. © **250/384-2582.** www.touchlounge.ca.

Gay & Lesbian Bars

The gay scene is so small in Victoria that most gay-friendly bars have relaxed any gays-only policies in order to keep their doors open. Most gays entertain at home and have established a by-invitation network to these behind-private-doors gatherings. One resource that might put you in contact with some of the private parties held in people's homes is www.gayvictoria.ca.

   Hush (1325 Government St.; © **250/385-0566;** www.hushnightclub.ca) is one of the few clubs that has stayed the course, although the crowd is becoming increasingly straight. Loud music (usually live) and electronica pack the place on weekends. With techno, progressive, drum-'n'-bass, and trance, the experience is more like a rave. Hush is open Wednesday to Sunday; entrance/ticket prices range between C$10-C$25 depending on the entertainment. **Paparazzi Night Club** (642 Johnson St.; © **250/388-0505**; www.paparazzinightclub.com) is Victoria's only true gay and lesbian nightclub. It has a full menu and a lounge that's large enough to host drag shows. Enjoy an offbeat selection of techno, disco, and hip-hop music, or sing a little karaoke—there are thick binders full of song titles. Prism is open Monday to Friday 3pm to 2am, and 1pm to 2am on the weekend. There's a C$5 cover charge on Fridays and Saturdays after 9pm. At press time, the **Bedford Regency Hotel** (1140 Government St., © **250/384-6835**), had turned its mezzanine into a hip GLBT venue called **The Ledge**. This space has seen many incarnations—it's a large and comfortable room—so perhaps this one will stick.

For hotter, get-down-to-it action, head into the alley entrance to **Steam Works** (582 Johnson St.; © **250/383-6623;** www.steamworksvictoria.com), which opens nightly from 7pm to 9am. If you indulge in fetishes, kink, and themed gatherings, check out **Sagacity** (sagacitygroup.net), which holds monthly socials for like-minded individuals.

SOUTHERN VANCOUVER ISLAND

Exploring Southern Vancouver Island is a relaxing change of pace from visiting downtown Victoria. The entire area can be reached within a day, so itineraries are easy to plan. Or you can stay in the city and simply make an afternoon of touring the countryside. Places like East Sooke Regional Park, with one of the most accessible and prettiest trails in Canada; Fort Rodd Hill & Fisgard Lighthouse National Historic Site; the picturesque seaside community of Sidney; and the world-famous Butchart Gardens are all within a 30-minute drive from Victoria. All are worthwhile destinations where you can spend a few hours, with or without the kids.

If you're an outdoor enthusiast who really wants to taste the island's wild west coast without traveling too far, the Juan de Fuca Trail delivers rainforest coast, wilderness beaches, and spectacular landscapes. It has earned the reputation of being the easier-to-hike cousin of the famed West Coast Trail. Unlike its arduous relative, the Juan de Fuca can be enjoyed in an afternoon (or multi-day) outing. Botanical Beach lies farther up the coast and is a beachcomber's paradise, with tidal pools and sandstone rock formations to explore.

Goldstream Provincial Park is another terrific outing, offering hikes for all abilities through well-maintained forested trails. One of the more challenging hikes is a direct ascent of Mount Finlayson, while an easier walk leads to an abandoned mine—Goldstream got its name during the 1860s gold rush, and if you arm yourself with a gold pan, the river still yields flecks of gold.

Agri-tourism is one of Vancouver Island's fastest growing movements, and nowhere is this better seen than in the Cowichan Valley, Canada's hottest new food and wine destination. Here's where driving through the back country really pays dividends with farms, orchards, artisan cheese factories, and plenty of vineyards to visit. Little wonder that Slow-Food fans have dubbed the area the New Provence and officially designated Cowichan Bay "Cittaslow"; North America's first certified "slow town." The valley deserves a day to do it justice.

If you're staying in Victoria but want to sample its urban wilderness or pastoral beauty, taking in any part of the southern part of Vancouver Island will do just that.

THE SAANICH PENINSULA

The Saanich Peninsula is the neck of land north of Victoria, through which nearly all island arrivals travel to get to the capitol city. Mostly residential, it's where to find sun-dappled country roads, cottage wineries, and picturesque bedroom communities that are obviously some of the most well-to-do on the island. At its heart lies Sidney, a bustling seaside village filled with scenic parks and gardens, waterfront restaurants, galleries, and more bookstores than any other community on Vancouver Island. It is small-town Canada gift-wrapped in beautiful scenery. Sidney is located 26km (16 miles) north of Victoria, and approximately 6km (3¾ miles) south of the BC Ferries terminal in Swartz Bay. Washington State ferries, arriving from Anacortes, dock at Sidney.

Essentials

GETTING THERE

BY CAR AND FERRY   If you're driving out of Victoria, head north on **Blanshard Street,** which becomes **Highway 17,** or take BC Transit bus no. 70, 72, or 75 from downtown Victoria. If you're driving from Swartz Bay (BC Ferries terminal), Sidney is a 6km (3¾-mile) drive south on **Highway 17. BC Ferries** (© **888/223-3779** or 250/386-3431; www.bcferries.com) runs a passenger- and car-ferry service between Swartz Bay and **Tsawwassen,** on the mainland.

June through August, crossings are every hour on the hour, from 7am to 11pm. September through May, crossings are every other hour. Additional ferries are often scheduled during holiday periods. One-way fare is C$14 adults, C$7 children 5 to 11, and C$47 for a standard-size vehicle. BC seniors travel free Monday through Thursday, except on holidays.

BY FERRY   The **Washington State Ferry** terminal is located in Sidney, at 2499 Ocean Ave. (© **888-808/7977** or 206/464-7977; www.wsdot.wa.gov/ferries). Ferries sail once a day, mid-morning, between Sidney and Anacortes. Crossing time is 3 hours. Summer vehicle reservations are highly recommended and must be made by 5:30pm the day prior to travel. One-way passenger fares during the high season (May to early Oct) are C$16 adults, C$13 students 6 to 18 years, C$8 seniors, and C$55 for a standard-size vehicle. Fares are lower in the off season (Oct 2 to May 2).

GETTING AROUND

Although buses run between the ferry terminal, Sidney, Victoria, and beyond, a car (or bicycle for the physically fit) is by far the best way to see the region, which really showcases itself along the back roads.

If you have the extra time and the ferry schedules don't cooperate, **Island Camping** (© **250/656-4826;** www.islandcamping.ca) operates an 11-passenger water taxi service out of Sidney to your Gulf Island of choice. The service is great for day trips, touring, or transport to a "base-camp" beach for kayaking. Trips cost C$140 per hour, generally split among the number of passengers.

For a point of reference, Pender Island is a half-hour boat ride from Sidney. **Eco-Cruising Tours & Transport** (② **250/655-5211;** www.ecocruising.com) is licensed to provide a shuttle service to the Gulf Islands National Marine Park Reserve. It also offers eco-cruises from Sidney's waterfront, Canoe Cove Marina near the BC Ferry Terminal, and Brentwood Bay Marina. Ask about The Butchart Gardens fireworks by water-limo.

VISITOR INFORMATION

The **Sidney Chamber of Commerce** operates two visitor information centers on the Saanich Peninsula. One is located at 10382 Pat Bay Hwy. (② **250/656-0525;** www.peninsulachamber.ca). It is open year-round Monday through Friday from 8:30am to 5:30pm. The other information center is located in Sidney, opposite the Washington State Ferry terminal, at A-2295 Ocean Ave. (② **250/656-3260**). The center is open April through October 15 Monday through Saturday from 10:30am to 12:30pm, to coincide with ferry arrivals. It's closed October 16 through March.

The Top Attractions

British Columbia Aviation Museum You'll want to dig out your bomber jacket for a visit to this hangar on the edge of the Victoria International Airport. It's a working museum that illustrates the province's aviation history. Volunteers restore vintage aircraft to add to the collection, which already has several reconditioned vintage airplanes, helicopters, and kit planes. Most are in working order. Look for a 1930s Bush Plane; an A26 World War II Bomber; a Gibson Twin (built in Victoria in 1911); a replica of the Chanute Glider, built in 1897; a Bell 47 Helicopter (best known as the busy MedEvac-type chopper in *M.A.S.H.*), and more. This may not stack up to the great aviation museums in Europe, but for aviation nuts or for a family looking to wile away an hour or two, it's an enjoyable attraction.

1910 Norseman Rd. ② **250/655-3300.** www.bcam.net. Admission C$7 adults, C$5 seniors & students, free for children 11 & under (must be accompanied by an adult). June-Sept daily 10am–4pm; Oct-May daily 11am–3pm. Closed Dec 25. Take the airport turnoff from Hwy. 17; the museum is on your right as you approach the airport. Bus: 70 (Airport Bus).

Butchart Gardens ★★★ Converted from an exhausted limestone quarry back in 1904, Butchart Gardens is an impressive place: 20 hectares (49 acres) of gardens, and not a blade of grass out of place! Just shows what having 50 gardeners can do. Every flower is grown to be a perfect match to the others in height, color, and tone, including the 300,000 bulbs that bloom in spring. On summer evenings, the gardens are illuminated with soft colored lights. Musical entertainment is provided June through September on Monday through Saturday evenings. Kids will love the new Rose Carousel, the fireworks every Saturday night through July and August, and the gi-normous displays of Christmas lights in December. An excellent lunch, dinner, and afternoon tea are offered in the **Dining Room Restaurant** (② **250/652-8222** for reservations; more casual fare is served in the **Blue Poppy Restaurant.** The gift shop sells seeds for some of the plants on display. If you're not traveling by car, your best bet is to take a Grayline Tour (see "Organized Tours," in chapter 5) that includes admission (C$56) or a combination Garden-Grand City Tour (C$76).

Grayline Shuttle runs an hourly, summer-only shuttle (C$19 round-trip) between the gardens and downtown Victoria. Call for exact times (② **250/388-6539**). *Tip:* Plan your visit for post-3pm to avoid the more intense crowds.

800 Benvenuto Ave., Brentwood Bay. ℃ **866/652-4422** or 250/652-4422, or 250/652-8222 for dining reservations. www.butchartgardens.com. Admission C$28 adults, C$14 children 13–17, C$3 children 5–12, free for children 4 & under. Rates lower in winter. Daily 9am–sundown (call for seasonal closing time). Bus: 75. Take Blanshard St. (Hwy. 17) north toward the ferry terminal in Saanich, then turn left on Keating Crossroads, which leads directly to the gardens.

Shaw Discovery Centre ★★ ☺

The elevator ride "down" into the ocean is pure showmanship but sets the stage for the Centre's vibrant undersea world of exhibits. More than 80 tons of seawater teems with thousands of fish, invertebrates, rarely seen plankton, algae, backlit jellies, and marine plant life that represent the Salish Sea. The whole place is designed as a seafloor-to-seashore adventure, complete with a high-tech classroom full of microscopes, live Internet links to undersea sites, and specimens to study. There's a lot of interactivity with both educators and displays, as well as plenty of hands-on/hands-wet touching pools. The Sea of Promises wall is smothered with pledges written on blue-sticky notes, mainly from school children promising an activity that will contribute to the health of our oceans. Whether it's to "become an ocean scientist," "cycle to school every day in all weathers," or "loving sea life till I'm old and grey," all are inspirational. Allow yourself at least 2 hours at this must-see center for young and old alike.

9811 Seaport Place, Sidney. ℃ **250/665-7511.** www.oceandiscovery.ca. Admission C$12 adults, C$6 children 6–17; free for children 5 & under. Daily 10am–4:30pm. Closed Dec 25. Bus: 70 from downtown or Swartz Bay. Take Hwy. 17 to Sidney, turning right down Beacon Ave., to Seaport Place.

Sidney Historical Museum

If you're an ambler who loves funky detours, this attraction is bound to delight. Tucked away in the basement of the 1939 post office building, the tiny museum is lovingly tended by volunteers and includes a surprisingly varied range of monthly exhibits, from toys and quilts to model railways and radio-controlled boats. It also has a number of historical photographs and artifacts portraying the early lives of Coast Salish, European, and Asian local peoples. A half-hour visit will probably suffice unless you hit upon an exhibit of personal interest and get talking to one of the knowledgeable, and enthusiastic, curators.

2423 Beacon Ave., Sidney. ℃ **250/655-6355.** www.sidneymuseum.ca. Free admission (suggested donation C$2 adults, C$5 groups). Daily 10am–4pm. Closed Dec 25. Bus: 70 from downtown or Swartz Bay. Take Hwy. 17 to Sidney, then turn right on Beacon Ave. to 4th St.

Victoria Butterfly Gardens ★★ ☺

Hundreds of exotic species of butterflies flutter through this lush tropical greenhouse, from the tiny Central American Julia to the Southeast Asian Giant Atlas Moth (its wingspan is nearly a foot). Pick up an identification chart before you enter so you can put names to the various flying wonders around you. Then wander freely through the gardens. Along the way, you'll encounter naturalists happy to explain butterfly biology, who pepper their speech with slightly bizarre factoids, such as "Butterflies taste with their feet" and "If a human baby grew at the same rate as some caterpillars, it would weigh 8 tons in only 2 weeks." Hmm. Food for thought. Between November and February, you need a reservation to see the gardens. Combine a visit here with the Butchart Gardens nearby (see listing above) for a full day's excursion.

1461 Benvenuto Ave., Brentwood Bay. ℃ **877/722-0272** or 250/652-3822. www.butterflygardens. com. Admission C$13 adults, C$12 seniors & students, C$6.50 children 5–12, free for children 4 & under; 10% discount for families. Mar–May & Oct daily 9:30am–4:00pm; June–Sept daily 9am–5:30pm. Closed Nov–Feb. Bus 75.

Sidney's summer evening **arts market** is one of the region's best kept secrets. Every Thursday from 5:30 to 8:30pm, 4 blocks of Beacon Avenue become a pedestrian-only walkway filled with kiosks selling everything from pottery and herbs to local jam, photography, macramé, paintings, and textiles. Several artisans from the Gulf Islands are here, as are many families enjoying supper-on-the-go from one of the food stalls. Check out the Terralicious stand, a phenomenal gardening and cooking school based in the peninsula that's really making a name for itself. The market runs June through August.

Parks & Beaches

Located off Highway 17 in Saanich, **Elk Lake/Beaver Lake Park** is a lovely place to spend an afternoon. The park's big draw is a 240-hectare (593-acre) freshwater lake rimmed by four beaches, with plenty of play areas and picnic tables. The lake provides for all sorts of aquatic recreation and is a particularly good place for beginner windsurfers. It is also home to the University of Victoria Rowing Club and the site of the annual international boat races, one of the five top rowing events in the world. Nearer to Victoria, off Cordova Bay Road, is **Mount Douglas Park,** a 10-hectare (25-acre) park in its natural state. The park is located 8km (5 miles) northeast of Victoria at the north end of Shelbourne Street. Another 1.5km (1 mile) up Churchill Drive brings you to the summit parking lot and to several great viewpoints of the surrounding area. There are several **easy hiking trails** to the mountaintop. These include the **Irvine Trail** off Cordova Bay Road and the **Merriman Trail** (it has an easy start but takes a little scrambling near the top). Both trails are well signposted from the road.

The lower park can be accessed near the intersection of Ash and Cordova Bay roads. A trail to the beach leads down from a large parking lot. There's also a playground and picnic area. For a fairly level, easy walk, look for the **Norn Trail,** which roughly parallels Cordova Bay Road and takes you through some very tall Douglas firs.

Where to Stay

Brentwood Bay Lodge & Spa ★★   Service matches the excellent facilities at Brentwood, the region's only five-star oceanfront resort, which in 2010 Expedia rated on its *Insider Select* list. The entire place is a showcase for West Coast style with picture windows, natural finishes, and beamed, high-gabled ceilings. Each of the 33 suites has a balcony or patio view of the inlet, forested peaks, and marina; gas fireplaces; hand-crafted furnishings; and local art. The rooms' spa-like bathrooms feature hard-to-resist double-jetted tubs, and shuttered windows let you sit in the tub and bask in the views. This is only outdone by the **Essence of Life** spa itself (✆ **250/544-5111**)—a lavish affair. There's **SeaGrille** (✆ **250/544-5100**), a fine-dining restaurant that offers an ever-changing menu of primarily local seafood and regional game; a sushi-sake bar; and a marine pub that serves distinctive craft beers, upscale comfort foods and delicious brick-oven pizzas. Live entertainment, from jazz to classical guitar, runs Wednesday to Friday nights. Six oceanfront, two-bedroom villas opened in late 2010, each one including a 12m (39-ft.) boat slip. Rates were not available at press time. The hotel is a licensed PADI dive center and has an eco-marine center with kayak rentals and charters.

849 Verdier Ave. (on Brentwood Bay), Victoria, BC V8M 1C5. ☎ **888/544-2079** or 250/544-2079. www.brentwoodbaylodge.com. 39 units. Mid-June to mid-Oct C$329–C$349 double, C$549 suite; mid-Oct to mid-June C$189–C$299 double, C$389–C$499 suite. AE, MC, V. Free parking. Take Pat Bay Hwy. north to Keating Crossroads, turn left (west) to Saanich Rd., then turn right (south) to Verdier Ave. **Amenities:** Restaurant; pub; cafe; Jacuzzi; heated outdoor pool; room service; spa; 40-slip marina. *In room:* A/C, TV/DVD player, fridge, iPod dock, Wi-Fi.

The Sidney Pier Hotel & Spa You can't beat its downtown waterfront location, with views of Mt. Baker in Washington State. That's why you should spend the extra dollars for a room on the ocean side, not facing the town, especially if you indulge in one of the few promenade one-bedroom suites. These have a "wow" factor. All rooms, however, feel limitless, with expansive windows, fashionable furnishings (including "sink-into" swivel chairs, as well as touches like heated towel racks), and waste bins divided into four recyclable options. **Haven Spa** (☎ **250/655-9797**), **Haro's** restaurant (see "Where to Dine," below), and the coffee shop are all worth visiting—especially the latter, which has a loyal following who come for its frothy coffees and home-baked scones. Many bring their dogs, since they've befriended the hotel's ambassador walker, Dave, a spoiled black Labrador. Book whale-watching excursions here with **Emerald Sea Adventures** (☎ **250/893-6722**), and **Sea-Quest Adventures** (☎ **250/655-9256**).

9805 Seaport Place, Sidney, BC V8L 4X3. ☎ **866/659-9445** or 250/655-9445. www.sidneypier.com. 55 units. Mid-June to late Sept C$179–C$229 double, C$259–C$489 suite; Oct–Mar C$139–C$189 double, C$219–C$449 suite; Apr to mid-June C$159–C$209 double, C$239–C$469 suite. Additional adult C$25. AE, DC, MC, V. Parking C$5. Pets accepted (C$30 one time charge plus C$15/night). **Amenities:** 2 restaurants; lounge; airport shuttle; concierge; spa. *In room:* A/C, TV/DVD player, fridge, hair dryer, Wi-Fi.

Where to Dine

Deep Cove Chalet FRENCH A local favorite for special occasions, this charming 1914 chalet was originally the terminus building of the British Columbia Electric Railway. Perched on a grassy bank overlooking a beautiful inlet, the restaurant offers top-notch service; a superb menu that emphasizes local seafood, lamb, and game; and a cellar that boasts some 18,000 bottles in its reserve, some dating from 1902. It even has its own fledgling vineyard. If you're looking for a classic fine-dining experience, the chalet is a delight, especially on a sunny day. The a la carte menu selections can add up to be pricey (duck bouillon *en croute* is C$25); four-course prix-fixe dinners, though, won't break the bank and feature items such as roast venison, Dungeness crab, and curried scallops.

11190 Chalet Drive Rd., Sidney. ☎ **250/656-3541.** Reservations recommended for Sunday brunch & dinner. Main courses brunch C$30, lunch C$23, dinner C$26–C$38; prix-fixe dinner C$58–C$75. AE, MC, V. Wed–Sun noon–2:30pm; Tues–Sun 5:30–9:30pm.

Dish Cookhouse & Diner 🍴 DINER It's a bit out of the way, but for breakfasts, this modern take on an old-fashioned diner is hard to beat. The decor may not win you over, but the twist given to traditional favorites (as in a smoked turkey, ham, and asparagus Bennie; or coconut oat-encrusted French toast) definitely will. The skillets are outstanding, especially the corned beef hash and sausages; the chefs are real meat-smiths who cure, smoke, stuff, and invent, all on-site. Breakfast evolves into lunch after 11am on weekdays but runs all day on the weekends.

2031 Malaview Ave., Sidney. ☎ **250/655-5295.** Main courses C$9–C$15. MC, V. Mon–Fri 7:30am–3:30pm; Sat & Sun 9am–2pm.

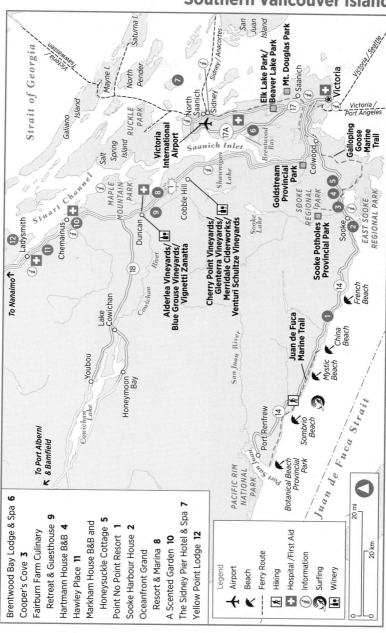

Strait of Georgia

Victoria / Tsawwassen

Mayne I.

North Pender

Saturna I.

Galiano Island

Salt Spring Island

Stuart Channel

RUCKLE PARK

Ladysmith

Chemainus

To Nanaimo

To Port Alberni & Bamfield

Youbou

Lake Cowichan

Cowichan Lake

Honeymoon Bay

Cowichan River

MAPLE MOUNTAIN PARK

Duncan

Cobble Hill

Alderlea Vineyards/ Blue Grouse Vineyards/ Vignetti Zanatta

Cherry Point Vineyards/ Glenterra Vineyards/ Merridale Ciderworks/ Venturi Schultze Vineyards

Saanich Inlet

Shawnigan Lake

Sooke Lake

SOOKE REGIONAL PARK

Goldstream Provincial Park

Sooke Potholes Provincial Park

Sooke

EAST SOOKE REGIONAL PARK

Galloping Goose Marine Trail

Colwood

Brentwood Bay

Brentwood Bay

North Saanich

Sidney / Anacortes

San Juan Island

Sidney

North Saanich

Elk Lake Park/ Beaver Lake Park

Mt. Douglas Park

Victoria

17

Victoria / Port Angeles

Victoria / Seattle

Victoria International Airport

17A

18

San Juan River

French Beach

China Beach

Mystic Beach

Juan de Fuca Marine Trail

14

Port Renfrew

Port San Juan

Sombrio Beach

Botanical Beach Provincial Park

PACIFIC RIM NATIONAL PARK

Juan de Fuca Strait

Brentwood Bay Lodge & Spa **6**
Cooper's Cove **3**
Fairburn Farm Culinary
  Retreat & Guesthouse **9**
Hartmann House B&B **4**
Hawley Place **11**
Markham House B&B and
  Honeysuckle Cottage **5**
Point No Point Resort **1**
Sooke Harbour House **2**
Oceanfront Grand
  Resort & Marina **8**
A Scented Garden **10**
The Sidney Pier Hotel & Spa **7**
Yellow Point Lodge **12**

Legend
✈ Airport
⚓ Beach
--- Ferry Route
🏃 Hiking
✚ Hospital /First Aid
ⓘ Information
🌊 Surfing
🍷 Winery

20 mi

20 km

111

Cider by the Sea

Sea Cider's beautiful setting by the sea (2487 Mt. St. Michael Rd., Saanichton; *©* 250/544-4824; www.seacider.ca) is the stuff of novels and worth the winding drive to get there. Part of the peninsula wine lands, with a half-dozen estate wineries, this vibrant, sprawling apple orchard grows more than 50 varieties of apples and is a great place for a pre-ferry stopover and a casual date. Cider tastings are well paired with charcuterie plates; the most fun is its long flight of nine generous samples, ideal for sharing. En route there, watch for roadside stalls with honesty boxes, selling everything from help-yourself manure to ducks' eggs and fields of pick-all-you-can tulips.

Dockside Grill PACIFIC NORTHWEST You can't dine nearer to the water than this—perched on the pier, virtually on top of Van Isle Marina, though easily missed from the road since all you'll see is a parking lot. View windows give the room a contemporary ambience, although in summer, the heated and covered patio is the favored spot. The menu focuses on local and seasonal items: The Shellfish Steamer pots are a must for zest-loving palettes, as is the Cowichan Valley chicken cooked with minted quinoa, lemon yogurt, and braised bison shortribs. The artisan cheeses and homemade breads, tapas selections, desserts, and ice cream are all delicious. If you're not up to a full meal, at least treat yourself to the latter. There's often live music on Sunday and Monday evenings.

2320 Harbour Rd., Sidney.*©* **250/656-0828.** Main courses lunch C$14, dinner C$18–C$26. AE, MC, V. Daily 11:30am–11pm; kitchen closes at 9pm

Fish On 5th FISH AND CHIPS The little blue heritage house dishes up some of the best fish and chips, including an award-winning clam chowder. The burger selection alone comes as grilled halibut, fried oysters, and salmon, with a nod to carnivores with chicken, and veggie selections such as falafel and walnut burgers. Ask for portions in traditional newspaper, and it's C$10 extra. The atmosphere is convivial and the fishy formula so successful that owners duplicated the concept on Pender Island (p. 233) to equal accolades. Their newest venture is Beacon & Eggs, a diner-bistro hybrid located in a shopping mall just off Beacon Avenue.

9812 5th St., Sidney.*©* **250/656-4022.** www.fishon5th.com. Main courses C$8–C$15. MC, V. Daily 11am–8pm.

Haro's PACIFIC NORTHWEST It's the only upbeat, au courant bistro in Sidney with floor-to-ceiling water views which, in the evening, create a very romantic buzz. The quality of service and food is excellent with menu items that include casual plates such as grilled albacore tuna melt and a modernization of classics like pizza and pasta. For lunch, fish tacos are delicious—a glorious mix of halibut, mango salsa, guacamole, and house slaw. In the evening, Haro's becomes even more of a happening place, serving an extensive share-plates menu of hazelnut-crusted pork tenderloin; grilled, marinated tofu; and the restaurant's signature Malaysian curry. Live jazz and blues plays most nights.

Sidney Pier Hotel, 9805 Seaport Place, Sidney.*©* **250/655-9445.** www.sidneypier.com. Main courses C$12–C$32. AE, MC, V. Daily 7am–11pm.

THE SOOKE REGION

To the west of Victoria lies Southern Vancouver Island's wild side. Within a couple hours' drive of the city, you are met with windswept beaches and trails through old-growth forest. Whether you're an urbanite looking for a spectacular afternoon side trip, a soft adventurer, or a hardy hiker, this drive along **Highway 14,** toward Port Renfrew, delivers. The trip from Victoria to Port Renfrew is 107km (66 miles), but the twisting, scenic road is slow; allow a good 2 hours just for travel time and a full day if you really want to enjoy the ride. Better still, make the tranquility of Sooke your home base. Just 32km (20 miles) out of Victoria, you're on the edge of outdoor-adventure country. Sooke is one of those wish-you-were-here coastal towns. Its name is derived from the first inhabitants of the region, the T'sou-ke band. The "e" in both T'sou-ke and Sooke is silent, just like the morning mist that lingers over the harbor.

Essentials

GETTING THERE

BY CAR   Driving from Victoria, take **Douglas Street** north and follow the signs to **Highway 1,** toward Sooke. Take the **Highway 14 (Island Hwy.) exit** at **Colwood,** and you're on your way. Highway 14 follows the coast all the way through Sooke and along to Port Renfrew. Remember to get gas in Sooke; it's the last gas station before Port Renfrew. Sooke is a 32km (20-mile) drive west from Victoria; Port Renfrew is 74km (46 miles) west of Sooke.

BY BUS   Board at the Western Exchange on Highway 14 (Island Hwy.) at Colwood (about 20 min. out of Victoria). Take **bus no. 50** (get a transfer), then **bus no. 61** to Sooke. Depending on traffic, the trip can take up to an hour from Victoria, and because of the transfers, it might be a frustrating journey, especially as once you're in Sooke, you'll be tempted to explore farther along the coast.

VISITOR INFORMATION

Head to the **Sooke Region Museum Visitors and Information Centre** (2070 Phillips Rd., right off Sooke Rd./Hwy. 14; © **866/888-4748** or 250/642-6351). It's open July through August daily from 9am to 5pm. It keeps the same 9am to 5pm hours from October to May, but it's closed Mondays. The staff here is knowledgeable and very enthusiastic, with all kinds of ideas for places to stay and things to do, particularly when it comes to both soft- and rugged-adventure activities. There are options for self-guided explorations or escorted tours. The center is wheelchair accessible.

The Top Attractions

Adrenaline Zip Adventures   One of the region's most exhilarating eco-experiences is zipping between the treetops covering some 40 hectares (99 acres) of rainforest. Riding the wires is a great family excursion, albeit at 46m (151 ft.) off the ground. Lines run between 40 and 305m (131–1,001 ft.) in length, and getting to the staging platforms is fun, too, via a 10-minute ATV ride and across two suspension bridges. The company provides a shuttle service to and from Victoria (C$10 per person, round-trip), and it has partnered with **Sooke Coastal Explorations** (© 250/642-2343; www.sookewhalewatching.com) for whale-watching and **Rush Adventures** (© **250/642-2159;** www.rush-adventures.com) for ocean-kayaking adventures, whereby you earn a 10% to 15% discount if you experience all three activities in the same season. Dutch courage can be absorbed at the nearby **17-Mile House Pub** (5126 Sooke Rd., ⓒ **250/642-5942**), though you would be better advised to hold off any alcohol until post-zip.

5128 Sooke Rd. (next to the 17-Mile Pub). ⓒ **866/947-9145** or 250/642-1933. www.adrenalinezip.com. Admission C$75 adults, C$65 children 5–17. Apr to late Oct Mon–Fri 9am–6pm, Sat & Sun 9am–7pm.

Fort Rodd Hill & Fisgard Lighthouse National Historic Site ☺ The Fisgard Lighthouse is the oldest lighthouse on Canada's west coast. From its vantage point atop a volcanic outcrop, it has guided ships toward Victoria's sheltered harbor since 1873. Although the beacon has long been automated, the site has been restored to its original appearance, and the lighthouse, which you can climb, houses some displays that show how keepers lived some 100 years ago. The surrounding park is filled with old military installations: camouflaged searchlights; underground armories; and guns dating from the 1890s, which, in more than half a century, have never fired a shot in anger. Canada has designated it a National Historic Site. Plan to pass an hour or so here; longer if you're tossing a Frisbee, picnicking, or beachcombing.

603 Fort Rodd Hill Rd. ⓒ **250/478-5849.** www.fortroddhill.com. Admission C$4 adults, C$3.50 seniors, C$2 children 6–16, free for children 5 & under; C$10 families. Mar–Oct daily 10am–5:30pm, Nov–Feb daily 9am–4:30pm. Follow Hwy. 1 out of Victoria, taking the Colwood exit (exit 10) onto Hwy. 1A. Continue for 2km (1¼ mile), turn left at the 3rd traffic light onto Ocean Blvd & follow the signs to the site.

Sooke Region Museum Fittingly, the museum is housed in Moss Cottage (built in 1870), Sooke's oldest building and somewhat of a museum piece itself. Sharing space with the Visitor Information Centre (see "Essentials," above), the museum houses a charming, compact collection of diorama exhibits and pioneer memorabilia. On summer weekends, an interpretive guide in the character of "Aunt Tilly," the original owner of Moss Cottage, will chat with visitors while bustling about doing her household chores. A 30-minute stop here is well worth the extra time while you're picking up information on the area.

2070 Phillips Rd. (right off Sooke Rd./Hwy. 14). ⓒ **866/888-4748** or 250/642-6351. Free admission (suggested donation C$2). July & Aug daily 9am–5pm; Sept–June Tues–Sun 9am–5pm.

Hiking Trails

Whether you like to cycle, hike, horseback ride, or just stroll, the **Galloping Goose, Lochside,** and **Peninsula trails** are the places to be. Laid out like a green ribbon from Sidney and the Saanich Peninsula to Sooke, their 100km (62 miles) of pathways link the region's parks to form a chain of green spaces. Named for the gawky and noisy gas rail car that carried passengers between Victoria and Sooke in the 1920s, the popular **Galloping Goose Trail** follows the abandoned rail beds and trestles of that railway legacy. **Leechtown,** once the site of a gold-mining community, marks the westernmost reach and terminus of "the Goose," as it's affectionately called. For more information on the Galloping Goose and Peninsula trails, many of which make for easy half-day outings, contact the **Capital Region District Parks** at ⓒ **250/478-3344.**

Stretching 47km (29 miles) along the near-wilderness coastline from **China Beach** to **Botanical Beach** is the **Juan de Fuca Marine Trail**. A neighbor to the famed (and very strenuous) West Coast Trail (see below), the less demanding Juan de Fuca Marine Trail offers similar scenic beauty yet can be completed as a comfortable, albeit strenuous, 4- or 5-day trek (or as several 1-day hikes from different trail heads). It isn't easy going, though—you'll be hiking through muddy trails, over fallen trees, across suspension bridges, and along wilderness beaches. If you're not up to the full distance, each of the four main trail heads at China Beach, Sombrio Beach, Parkinson Creek, and Botanical Beach offers parking lots that allow day hikes and smaller family hikes down to the beach. If you're more interested in the 4- or 5-day trek, you can start at either **Botanical Beach** or **China Beach.** Because this is a wilderness trail, conditions are always changing, so check the trail-head information centers for updates. Be sure to wear proper footwear and appropriate clothing. Campsites are regularly spaced along the trail. A great online resource is www.vancouverislandoutdoors.com. The site has maps, photos, safety pointers, and camping information for the Juan de Fuca Marine Trail. **Note:** As you hike, watch for orange balls that mark exits from the beach to the trail. Be aware, however, that beaches may be cut off from the trail during high tides and storms.

Of all the trails on Vancouver Island, the **West Coast Trail** is the most famous. It is known as one of the most extreme, rigorous, and beautiful trails in the world. With its easternmost trail head just outside of Port Renfrew, the West Coast Trail is virtually the town's only raison d'être. Now a part of **Pacific Rim National Park,** the trail originally was constructed for the rescue of mariners shipwrecked along the rugged west coast, appropriately referred to as the "graveyard of the Pacific." Running approximately 75km (47 miles) north between Port Renfrew and Bamfield, it takes an average of 5 to 7 days to complete and is a challenge for even the most experienced hikers. For more information about the West Coast Trail, check out www.westcoasttrailbc.com. See chapter 7 for more on the West Coast Trail and Pacific Rim National Park.

Parks & Beaches

Goldstream Provincial Park is a favorite escape for Victoria residents and visitors alike. Picnic beneath 600-year-old red cedars (the best spot is near the parking lot), or hike through beautiful rainforest. Watch out for old mine shafts where, in the late 1800s, prospectors mined for gold (hence the park's name); or try panning for gold yourself in the river. All you need is a 31 or 38cm (12- or 15-in.) steel pan, and a whole lot of patience. You can take several easy loop hikes that explore a range of ecosystems: deep forests of Douglas fir, dry upland ridges with arbutus and Garry oak, and a salt marsh estuary at the head of Saanich Inlet. Favorite hikes include the 419m (1,375-ft.) climb up the Mount Finlayson Trail. Although only a 1km (.6-mile) ascent, the hike is very steep and rigorous enough that you should allow 3 hours for the round trip. The Upper Goldstream Trail is much easier, and although approximately the same distance, most hikers complete the return in half the time. This trail takes you through some of the oldest and biggest Douglas firs in the park, and at the end, you're rewarded with waterfalls. It's a good choice for kids, but not those in strollers.

From mid-October through November, thousands come to Goldstream Provincial Park to watch salmon spawn, while in December and January, they come for the Bald Eagle Count (see "Calendar of Events," in chapter 3). Many areas of the park are wheelchair accessible. For information on Goldstream Provincial Park and all other provincial parks on the South Island, contact BC Parks (www.env.gov.bc.ca/bcparks). The park's **Freeman King Visitor Centre** (✆ **250/478-9414;** www.naturehouse. ca) is open daily from 9am to 4:30pm and offers a nature house and year-round guided walks, as well as programs geared to children. Interested in camping in the park? Choose from among 173 sites. Reserve through **Discover Camping** (✆ **800/689-9025** or 604/689-9025; www.discovercamping.ca).

In Sooke, **Sooke Potholes Provincial Park** features an unusual rock formation over which the Sooke River flows onto a series of ledges and waist-deep swimming holes, and from there into rock pools below. In summer, the chilly waters are just warm enough to attract a swarm of swimmers. The park has picnic facilities, while easy hiking trails are firm under foot. A network of over 50km (31 miles) of trails can be found in **East Sooke Regional Park,** lacing through the park's 1,421 hectares (3,511 acres) to beaches, secluded coves, forested areas, petroglyphs, and an abandoned copper mine. In the heart of the park, stumps of Douglas fir and red cedar, some measuring 2 to 3m (6½–10 ft.) in diameter, hold clues to the era when loggers felled their riches with the springboard, axe, and crosscut saw. One of these trails, the **East Sooke Coast Trail,** is considered a premier day hike. Though it covers only 10km (6.2 miles), the trail is rough, winding, and a challenging 6- to 8-hour trip. You can access East Sooke Regional Park at **Aylard Farm,** off Becher Bay Road (popular with picnickers and those looking for easy excursions); at **Anderson Cove** (for hikers heading to Babbington Hill and Mount Maguire); or at **Pike Road,** off East Sooke Road, an old logging road that winds through forest to meadow and beach. Information posted at these trail heads will help you choose a trail suitable to your hiking ability. Many trails are wheelchair accessible. As you wind your way west along Highway 14 (also known as the West Coast Rd.) toward Port Renfrew, you'll pass a series of beaches—many of which are worth pulling over to explore. Some are more accessible than others, and trails often link one stretch of sand to another (but sometimes only at low tide). *Note:* If you park your car, remove all valuables. Thefts are common; rental cars are favored targets.

The first beach you'll come to, ironically, is called **Second Beach,** a small sand-and-cobblestone beach, subject to strong storm and tidal action. At low tide, it's possible to walk along the beach to **Jordan River,** a popular wintertime surfing and windsurfing area, or to **China Beach,** where fine sand makes an ideal spot for picnicking, building sandcastles, wading, and relaxing. There's a hidden waterfall at the west end of the beach. From the parking lot, follow the wide gravel trail through lush forest to the beach itself. The trail is easy to navigate and therefore suitable for children, as well as older travelers. It takes about 20 minutes one-way; watch for some steep sections. China Beach is the southern terminus of the Juan de Fuca Marine Trail. Camp overnight in your vehicle (it's allowed) or at one of the beach campsites.

Getting to **Mystic Beach** involves a fairly strenuous, 2km (1.2-mile) hike along a steep rainforest trail, which can take up to 45 minutes to complete. But you'll be rewarded by a sandy beach surrounded by sandstone cliffs, shallow waves, and a waterfall. If you can manage it, the trip is worth making. Beachfront campsites are available, but pit toilets are the only amenity. Bring your own water, or if you take water from the streams, remember to purify it. Farther along is **French Beach,** a sand and gravel beach that's a hot spot from which to watch for passing **gray whales.** Picnic tables and an adventure playground are located on an open, grassy area between the parking lot and beach, making this a good family destination. Sixty-nine campsites are right on the beach. The winds, breakers, and rollers of the Pacific Ocean make **Sombrio Beach** a favorite spot for surfers. An old logging road winds down from Highway 14 to a large parking lot. From there, it's an easy 10-minute walk to the beach. Sombrio Beach is another entry route to the Juan de Fuca Marine Trail. Overnight camping in your vehicle is allowed, and there are a number of beach sites. But the real treasure is **Botanical Beach Provincial Park,** about 4km (2½ miles) south of Port Renfrew. A terrific place for kids, it's one of the richest intertidal zones on North America's west coast and a magnet for avid poolies, who gather to enjoy the ocean's bounty. Over the millennia, tidal action has carved out spectacular pits and pools that have filled with purple sea urchins, gooseneck barnacles, fiery red blood stars, and other marine flora and fauna. Check local tide tables: A low tide of 1m (3¾ ft.) or less is best for viewing. In spring and fall, watch for passing gray whales. Camping is prohibited at this park.

For information about camping at any of these beaches, and to reserve campsites, contact **Discover Camping** (*©* **800/689-9025** or 604/689-9025; www.discover camping.ca).

Port Renfrew

Port Renfrew is a sleepy fishing village quite literally at the end of the road (Hwy. 14), and unless you're heading to the West Coast Trail (see "Hiking Trails," above, and chapter 7), there aren't a whole lot of reasons to stay. Most accommodations are geared to hikers and include a complete range of camping facilities for both tents and RVs. You might want to try the **Port Renfrew Recreational RV Retreat** (6574 Baird Rd.; *©* **250/647-0058**). Thirty-three full RV hookups are C$35 each per night; six tent sites are C$20 each per night. **Port Renfrew Resorts** (17310 Parkinson Rd.; *©* **250/ 647-5541;** www.portrenfrewresorts.com), beside the community wharf at the end of Parkinson Road, is a bit more upscale, with 11 well-appointed waterfront cabins and four motel-style studio rooms, starting at C$240 (25% less in low season). It also runs the 22-room **West Coast Trail Motel** (17285 Parkinson Rd.; *©* **250/647-5541;** www.westcoasttrailmotel.com); rooms here cost C$130. If you're tackling the West Coast Trail (see p. 164), book accommodation early.

Where to Stay

Coopers Cove 🏨 This guest house is a real find for foodies. The owner, Angelo Prosperi-Porta, is an ex–Olympiad chef, and his culinary school and interactive dinners are legendary. They've even been featured on the *Oprah Winfrey Show.* Few places let you muse over dinner preparations—with an option to participate—as an elaborate, multi-course dinner is created before your very eyes. Guest rooms are tasteful, with downy, soft duvets on comfortable king- and queen-size beds; warm pine furniture; and touches like homemade truffles on your pillow to sweeten the night. All rooms have water views and a fireplace. You don't have to love food to enjoy your stay, but the culinary packages are where this inn excels. Suffice it to say, breakfast is the mother of all meals, with home-baked croissant, bread, yogurt, cheese, and edible flower garnishes.

5301 Sooke Rd., Sooke, BC V0S 1N0. *©* **877/642-5727** or 250/642-5727. www.cooperscove.com. 4 units. C$175–C$225 double. Culinary packages available. AE, MC, V. **Amenities:** Lounge; hot tub. *In room:* Fridge, hair dryer, Wi-Fi.

Hartmann House B&B ★ Hartmann House is at its best in spring: shrouded by wisteria and surrounded by hydrangeas, peonies, rhododendrons, azaleas, and other flowering plants. The stunning, and very private, English country garden–style setting has graced the pages of *Better Homes & Gardens, Country Garden,* and *Sunset* magazines. Inside is just as welcoming. The cedar finish throughout the home adds warmth and character, and is accented by a roaring fire and overstuffed rattan couches. These elements extend into the two private, self-contained and spacious suites, each with its own entrance, private veranda, and oversize whirlpool tub. You can expect complimentary chilled wine waiting for you upon arrival, alongside Belgian chocolates and a fruit-and-cheese plate. Breakfast is delivered to your door through a butler's pantry. A truly one-of-a-kind romantic retreat.

5262 Sooke Rd., Sooke, BC V0S 1N0. ℰ **250/642-3761.** www.hartmannhouse.bc.ca. 2 units. May–Oct C$195–C$225 suite; Nov–Apr C$175–C$195 suite. Rates include full breakfast. V. **Amenities:** Lounge. *In room:* TV/DVD player, fridge, hair dryer, Wi-Fi.

Markham House B&B and Honeysuckle Cottage ★★
Nestled into a 4-hectare (10-acre) hillside, this Tudor-style home is bordered by towering firs and flowering perennials. A golf tee and bocce ball court are set up on the lawns, and intriguing pathways lead to mossy bluff lookouts. Guests enjoy afternoon tea on the veranda or in the old English–style living room filled with antiques. Each guest room has all the trimmings necessary for cocooning: featherbeds, duvets, and comfortable sofas, as well as luxurious bathrobes and double Jacuzzis. There's a separate 56-sq.-m (603-sq.-ft.) cottage tucked away in the woods that has its own private deck, outdoor Jacuzzi, woodstove, full kitchen, and barbecue. It's the ultimate "we want to be alone" couple's getaway.

1853 Connie Rd., Victoria, BC V9C 4C2. ℰ **888/256-6888** or 250-642-7542. www.markhamhouse.com. 4 units. C$120–C$195 double; C$250 cottage. Additional adult C$25. Special packages & off-season discounts available. AE, DC, MC, V. **Amenities:** Lounge; hot tub. *In room:* TV/DVD player, hair dryer, Wi-Fi.

Point No Point Resort
It's the definitive getaway—a private cabin, the ocean as your front yard, and 16 hectares (40 acres) of wilderness "out the back." Since this waterfront resort has been in business more than 50 years, the size and relative quality of the cabins vary, depending on when they were built. Some are large enough for families; others are cozy romantic retreats. All have wood-burning fireplaces, full kitchens, private bathrooms, stunning ocean views, and a strip of private beach, which includes a beach house and fire pit. Lunch and traditional tea are served daily in a central teahouse overlooking the Juan de Fuca Strait. Bring a flashlight and ask for a cabin away from the generators, which can hum all night. Dinner is served Wednesday through Sunday. Portions are on the large side (share if you have a small appetite) and include items such as grilled salmon; braised chicken with chanterelles; seafood linguine; and crepes over-stuffed with pork, caramelized onions, and gorgonzola. Every table has a set of binoculars to watch eagles and other wildlife.

1505 West Coast Hwy. (Hwy. 14), Sooke, BC V0S 1N0. ℰ **250/646-2020.** www.pointnopointresort.com. 25 cabins. C$180–C$270 cabin. 2-night minimum stay on weekends; 3-night minimum stay July & Aug, holiday weekends & Christmas holidays. AE, MC, V. Free parking. Small pets accepted (C$10). **Amenities:** Restaurant. *In room:* Kitchen, Wi-Fi.

Sooke Harbour House ★★★
Poised on the end of a sand spit, this little inn has an understated elegance with a friendly, yet completely unobtrusive, staff. An eclectic blend of antiques, original art, and whimsical crafts is showcased throughout the inn and comprises one of the largest public art collections on Vancouver Island. Each of the 28 guest rooms is decorated in a unique way, though they all express a Northwest theme. All have wood-burning fireplaces, exquisite views, and all but one have sundecks. Many have Jacuzzis and showers with beautiful stained-glass doors. Speaking of showers, or rather rain, rooms are well equipped with umbrellas, rubber boots, and rain jackets. If the sun is shining, take time to wander the gardens, a trove of edible wildflowers, herbs, and display blooms. And take note: This Inn was eco-conscious before it was in vogue and offers many green initiatives, including substantial water reclamation and composting programs. There's even a

"green" turf parking lot. The experience wouldn't be complete without enjoying a meal at the **Sooke Harbour House** restaurant, which is the best in the region (see "Where to Dine," below). If you're not a guest at the hotel, dining here often means making a reservation weeks in advance, especially in summer. The **Sea-renity Spa** offers an excellent range of massage and aesthetic services, including seaweed treatments using Outer Coast Sooke seaweed spa products.

1528 Whiffen Spit Rd., Sooke, BC V0S 1N0. ☎ **800/889-9688** or 250/642-3421. www.sookeharbour house.com. 28 units. July & Aug C$399–C$589 double; Sept–June C$309–C$459 double. Rates include breakfast & picnic lunch. Children 12 & under stay free in parent's room. DC, MC, V. Free parking. Take Island Hwy. to the Sooke-Colwood turnoff (junction Hwy. 24), continue on Hwy. 14 to Sooke, turn left onto Whiffen Spit Rd. Pets accepted (C$20). **Amenities:** Restaurant; babysitting; room service; spa. *In room:* Hair dryer, Wi-Fi.

Where to Dine

Markus' Wharfside Restaurant ★ PACIFIC NORTHWEST   This small restaurant has such a loyal, local following that the menu changes weekly, not only to keep them coming back, but to take advantage of the freshest, most seasonal ingredients available. And return they do, whether it's for freshly-caught seafood such as sautéed spot prawns with a white wine, lemon, and garlic butter sauce; an oven-roasted chicken; or a flat iron steak, grilled to perfection. Try the risotto—always different and oh-so-tasty. When it comes time for dessert, opt for the Trio, thus providing you tastes of whatever three signature dishes are on the hot list; hope that one is the melt-in-your-mouth *panna cotta*. The co-owner is a sommelier, ensuring the wine list is kept up to snuff.

1831 Maple Ave., Sooke. ☎ **250/642-3596.** www.markuswharfsiderestaurant.com. Main courses C$14–C$32. MC, V. Tues–Sat 5:30–10:00pm.

Mom's Cafe 🏠 DINER   Tucked away by the community hall in downtown Sooke, Mom's Cafe is the quintessential 1950s diner, complete with juke boxes at the booths and its fair share of bric-a-brac (you just know Mom never throws anything away). It serves up excellent home cooking and is considered one of the top 10 diners in British Columbia. Mom's is always packed with locals and visitors alike. Mom's homemade dessert pies are absolute musts.

2036 Shields Rd., Sooke. ☎ **250/642-3314.** Main courses C$8–$C15. MC, V. Sun–Thurs 8am–8pm; Fri & Sat 8am–9pm. Drive into Sooke on Hwy. 14; take the first right after the traffic light at Murray Rd.

Six Mile Pub PUB FARE   You'll find a good variety of brews on tap and tasty food seasoned with fresh herbs from the pub's own garden—burgers, as well as some higher-end dishes such as braised lamb shank, and beef tenderloin. The Six Mile Pub is one of several franchised "mile" pubs you'll find along Highway 1A, all of them, to some degree, incorporating a mock-Tudor, oak-beamed, fireside ambience of yesteryear. The pubs were once mile-measured stops for stagecoaches that traveled up-island from Victoria. This one has a particularly rich history. Dating back to 1855, it was the hub for provincial bootleggers during Prohibition. Since Victoria continued the ban on booze until the early 1950s, "mile houses," as they were known, were the only places Victorians could get a tot outside of the city.

494 Island Hwy., Victoria. ☎ **250/478-3121.** www.sixmilepub.com. Main courses C$7–C$28. MC, V. Sun–Thurs 11am–midnight; Fri & Sat 11am–1am. Follow Hwy. 14 to Six Mile Rd.

FINE fermentation

Tugwell Creek Honey Farm & Meadery (8750 West Coast Rd.; ✆ **250/642-1956;** www.tugwellcreekfarm.com) uses its 150 hives and the oldest art of fermentation to create all manner of honey products, including several varieties of honey wine, better known as mead. Once enjoyed by royalty and peasants alike, mead was purported to bestow the drinker with courage, wisdom, and strength—perhaps that's why Tugwell retails almost 3,000 bottles a year. You can test that theory: The Meadery's tasting room and shop are open during the summer every Wednesday through Sunday afternoon and on weekends October to April, except when it closes in January.

Sooke Harbour House ★★★ REGIONAL   The cuisine has seduced thousands of palates, and the restaurant's award-winning wine cellar is regarded as one of the best on the West Coast. Chef Edward Tuson's imaginative menu focuses on local seafood and organically grown produce, much of it harvested from the over 200 herbs, greens, flowers, and vegetables grown on the premises. Their culinary transformation creates predominately seafood dishes such as creamy broccoli soup with smoked sablefish and daylily oil, or yellow split pea–crusted lingcod with a carrot-and-mint emulsion. Even the sorbets are a cornucopia of flavors served together: green apple and mint; yellow plum and Anjou pear black currant. The food is so good here that you should probably opt for the multi-course gastronomic adventure tasting menu. These are C$120; add C$80 or more if you choose the wine pairings. The four-course set menu is an excellent value at C$75 and includes a vegetarian option. Dinner is by reservation only, at least 3 days in advance (but you'd be better off calling 3 weeks in advance in the summer). Breakfast and lunch are served for hotel guests only.

In Sooke Harbour House, 1528 Whiffen Spit Rd., Sooke.✆ **250/642-3421.** Reservations required. Main courses C$35; prix-fixe menu C$47–C$75. DC, MC, V. mid June–mid Sept daily 5–9:30pm; mid Sept–mid June Thurs–Mon 5–9:30pm. Take Island Hwy. to the Sooke-Colwood turnoff (junction w/Hwy. 24), continue on Hwy. 14 to Sooke & turn left onto Whiffen Spit Rd.

Stick in the Mud CAFE   Eighty percent of coffee in North America is sold before 10am, which is why this hole-in-the-wall opens early and closes mid-afternoon. If you've made an early start out of Victoria, this is the place to catch up on a breakfast of fresh-baked goodies and a quality caffeine boost. Baristas here live and breathe their passion for the bean, refusing to serve any dark roasts, any coffees roasted more than a week ago, and certainly no drips. If you're serious about your coffee, meet a connoisseur. Just get there early.

6715 Eustace Rd.✆ **250/642-5635.** Main courses C$5. MC, V. Mon–Fri 6am–3:30pm; Sat & Sun 8am–4pm.

EN ROUTE TO NANAIMO: THE COWICHAN VALLEY

This blood pressure–lowering trip north along Vancouver Island's east coast to Nanaimo can take you from 1½ hours to all day, depending on how many stops you make. The **Cowichan Valley** is an ideal side trip if you're staying in Victoria and a wonderful meander through rich, rolling countryside. The more direct route is along the Trans-Canada Highway (Hwy. 1), over the mountain hump of the **Malahat,** and down through the Cowichan Valley. The Quw'utsun' people call the valley the Warm Land, and with good reason: Here, you'll find many small, family-owned farms and orchards selling homemade products such as jams, candles, and soaps. You can also visit estate **vineyards** featuring award-winning wines, as well as potters' studios, craft stores, and galleries. Many artisans work out of their homes, and other than the annual open-house tour (usually the second week of July), they may not work regular hours. Pick up a map from the Victoria or Duncan visitor information center or download it from www.visions arttour.ca, and then either take your chances or phone ahead for appointments.

One detour of interest is the city of **Duncan,** nicknamed **"City of Totem Poles"** for its impressive collection of, you guessed it, totem poles! This part of the world is famed for its residents' carving skills, yet most historic totem poles are in museums or stand in abandoned villages reclaimed by nature. In the 1980s, the mayor of Duncan commissioned local First Nations artists to carve new totem poles, and today, the city showcases one of the world's largest collections of modern totem carving. If you're just driving through Duncan, catching sight of them can be a bit hit-or-miss, however, as many are on side streets. The best suggestion is to follow the **yellow shoeprints** on the pavement or take a free **walking tour**

totem POLES

Representing history and tradition, and full of symbolism, totem poles are some of the most fascinating examples of aboriginal art. In the Pacific Northwest, they are carved from mature cedar trees with skills that have been handed down from one generation to the next. In the past, a totem was created for a specific purpose: to tell a story, to honor a deceased elder, or to record a link to the Great Spirit—elements that were, and still are, so much a part of aboriginal culture. Most important, a totem is the emblem of tribal unity; through its imagery, a totem conveys a tribe's ancestry, prestige, and accomplishments. Contrary to popular belief, totem figures were not gods, and they were never used to ward off evil spirits.

Symbols are called crests and nearly always reflect a link between humanity and nature (usually an animal). For example, some Northwest Coast families claim as a crest the Thunderbird, who descended from the sky to take off his animal clothing and become their human ancestor.

Today, both Native and non-native people carve totem poles, which are a source of pride and tradition for the people in the Pacific Northwest.

Some common totem symbols include:

- **Bear:** Strength, teaching, motherhood
- **Eagle:** Powerful leadership and prestige
- **Frog:** New life, communicator
- **Hummingbird:** Love, beauty, a spirit messenger
- **Killer Whale:** Traveler and guardian
- **Otter:** Trusting, inquisitive, a loyal friend
- **Owl:** Wisdom
- **Raven:** Knowledge, bringer of the light
- **Salmon:** Dependable, a good provider
- **Sun:** Healing energy; guardian of the day

Enraptured with Raptors

Pacific Northwest Raptors (1877 Herd Rd., Duncan; ✆ 250/746-0372) is a rehabilitative home to a stunning array of eagles, hawks, owls, vultures, and other raptors. It's the only facility of its kind in the Pacific Northwest and operates a visitors center from mid-March until the end of October, where you can observe, learn about, and even handle birds of prey. If you prefer to see birds in the wild, head for Somenos Marsh, right next to the BC Forest Discovery Centre (see p. 123), for some of the best bird-watching in the area.

that starts at the **Cowichan Valley Museum,** in the VIA Rail station, at Station Street and Caan Avenue. Call ✆ 250/715-1700 for information. You can also check in at the **Duncan-Cowichan Visitor Information Centre** (381A Trans-Canada Hwy., ✆ 888/303-3337 or 250/746-4636).

Another worthwhile detour is the town of **Chemainus.** When the building of the Trans-Canada Highway bypassed Chemainus and the local lumber mill slowed to a virtual standstill, the town turned its declining fortunes around by painting the exteriors of its quaint buildings. Today, more than 300,000 visitors stop each year to see the more than 40 murals and 13 sculptures, particularly in July and August each year, when more are added. Check out www.muraltown.com for details.

Try to find Isabel Askew, one of the town's founders who is played by an actor dressed in 1800s attire. Her historical walking tour (www.chemainuswalkingtours.com) shares the challenges of settling the region as a young widow of eight children. Tours start from the Visitor Centre Wednesday through Saturday at 10am, 12:30, and 2pm.

If you do stop in or near Chemainus, stay in one of the heritage B&Bs (see "Where to Stay," below). Spend the evening at the **Chemainus Theatre** (9737 Chemainus Rd.; ✆ 800/565-7738; www.chemainustheatrefestival.ca). Year-round, this troupe offers professional live theater in the town's most eye-catching building, a late-19th-century opera house. Past shows have included quality productions of *The Miracle Worker, South Pacific, My Fair Lady,* and *Guys & Dolls.* Every December, there's a seasonal family show. Tickets range from C$15 for the preview to C$40; C$48 to C$64 for the dinner- or brunch-theater package. The **Visitor Information Centre** is housed in an old railroad car at 9796 Willow St. (✆ 250/246-3944). If you're still in the mood for detours, drop by **Ladysmith,** named by *Harrowsmith Country* magazine as one of Canada's 10 prettiest towns. The Visitor Information Centre is at 411 First Ave. (✆ 250/ 245-2112).

Essentials

GETTING THERE

BY CAR   Take Douglas Street north out of Victoria, which becomes Highway 1 (the Trans-Canada Hwy.). From there, it's about 111km (69 miles) to Nanaimo.

BY BUS   **Laidlaw Coach Lines** operates between Victoria and Nanaimo, with various stops along the way. Schedules and reservations are handled by **Greyhound Canada** (✆ 800/661-8747; www.greyhound.ca). There are five departures a day from Victoria, from 7:30am to 7pm. Fares to Nanaimo are C$26 nonrefundable/C$30 refundable for adults, C$12 nonrefundable/C$14 refundable for seniors, and C$9.50

nonrefundable/C$11 refundable for children 5 to 11. The trip between Victoria and Nanaimo takes 2 to 2½ hours.

BY TRAIN **The Malahat,** run by VIA Rail (© **888/842-7245;** www.viarail.com), operates a daily service between Victoria and Courtenay. One-day sightseeing trips from Victoria include stops in Chemainus, Duncan, and Nanaimo. Trains depart from Victoria's VIA Rail station, at 450 Pandora Ave. One-way fares to Chemainus and Duncan are C$22, to Nanaimo C$30, and to Courtenay C$59, with discounts for buying online, as well as for children, students, and senior travelers. Seniors should check into promotions that allow them to buy one ticket and travel with a companion for free. Travel time between Victoria and Courtenay is about 4¼ hours.

VISITOR INFORMATION

Obtain maps and information at the **Tourism Victoria Information Centre** (812 Wharf St., © **250/953-2033;** www.tourismvictoria.com). The center is open May and June daily from 9am to 8pm, July and August daily from 9am to 9pm, and September through April daily from 9am to 5pm. You can also contact **Tourism Vancouver Island** (501-65 Front St., Nanaimo, © **250/754-3500;** www.vancouverisland.travel). The center is open year-round Monday through Friday from 8:30am to 5pm.

The Top Attractions

BC Forest Museum Park/BC Forest Discovery Centre ☺
An affiliate of the Royal BC Museum, this is a fabulous learning and nature experience for the entire family. Focusing on forestry practices and preservation, the museum features an exhibit on the history of logging, a miniature town, a logging camp, a sawmill, a fire-watching tower, and a ranger station. Don't miss the 20-minute ride on a full-size steam train; it's included in the ticket price and is a lot of fun. Expect to stay for 1½ hours, allowing an additional half-hour for the train.

2892 Drinkwater Rd., Duncan. © **250/715-1113.** www.bcforestmuseum.com. Admission C$14 adults, C$12 seniors & students, C$9 children 5–12, free for children 4 & under; C$50 families. Apr–Oct daily 10am–4:30pm. Closed Nov–Mar. Take Hwy. 1 past Duncan, watching for the double-span bridge over the Cowichan River. The center is approximately 3km (1¾ miles) past the bridge, off the highway to the right, after the fourth set of traffic lights at Beverley St.

Quw'utsun' Cultural Centre ★★
The Cowichan were the original inhabitants of the valley that now bears their name. Their culture and way of life are creatively illustrated at the Cowichan Native Village. Storytelling, dancing, and traditional feasting are some of the activities here. Go on a guided walking tour of the village, which includes several modern longhouse structures; talk to carvers as they work, or enjoy the excellent multimedia theater presentation that retells the Cowichan myth and history. A visit takes about an hour, though you might want to stop longer to try some authentic native cuisine in the **Riverwalk Café** (© **250/746-4370**), including a designed-to-share, Salish Afternoon Tea (C$24) for two. The art gallery is the best place in the valley to buy the famous bulky, durable Cowichan sweaters, knitted with bold motifs from hand-spun raw wool.

200 Cowichan Way, Cowichan. © **877/746-8119** or 250/746-8119. www.quwutsun.ca. Admission C$13 adults, C$10 seniors & students, C$6 children 12 & under; C$35 families. Mon–Sat 10am–4pm. Take Hwy. 1 past Duncan, cross the double-span bridge over the Cowichan River & take Cowichan Rd. E. en route to Duncan Mall.

6 Meandering among the Wineries

The wine scene in British Columbia just keeps getting better in quality and variety, and although the vineyards on Vin-couver Island are young compared to those found in the province's interior, they are beginning to produce some excellent vintages. As you make your way north through the Cowichan Valley toward Nanaimo, consider a stop at any one of the vineyards that dot the route northward from Victoria. Touring is as easy as following the burgundy-and-white Wine Route signs.

The first pocket of wineries along the route is in Cobble Hill, south of Duncan. **Cherry Point Vineyards** (840 Cherry Point Rd., R.R. 3, Cobble Hill; © **250/743-1272**; www.cherrypointvineyards.com) is one of the most prominent in the Cowichan Valley, with national awards to prove it. Cherry Point's California-like vines produce some of the finest Gewürztraminer in the country, and its Solerra blackberry dessert wine is equally sought after. Try it with locally made Shawnigan Lake chocolates—yes, chocolate and wine pairings are all the rage. The tasting room is a Swiss-style chalet (open year round), which opens up into a quaint bistro and patio where lunches and Spanish tapas are served April to December.

Many of the other Cowichan-area wineries are much smaller than Cherry Point, and some choose not to host formal tours. Still, visitors are welcome to drop by, and it's not uncommon to meet an owner working in the vineyard as you roll up a dusty driveway. In fact, the locals often refer to vineyards as "farms" to illustrate their working nature—tractors, manure heaps, and all. As small as it is, **Glenterra Vineyards** (3897 Cobble Hill Rd., Cobble Hill; © **250/743-2330**) produces award-winning wines. Their Vivace is exclusively from their own estate-grown grapes. Also, try their Pinot Gris and Meritage. Glenterra has a tasting room and casual eatery, Thistles, that features daily lunch specials of tapas, soups, sandwiches, and good homemade desserts.

Merridale Ciderworks (1230 Merridale Rd., R.R. 1, Cobble Hill; © **800/998-9908** or 250/743-4293; www.merridalecider.com) is dedicated to cider and wine apples. Chat with the cider-makers, tour the apple mills, presses, and fermentation casks, and feel free to wander the orchards around where you'll see fairy figurines going about their business. Kids love them. Visit in April, and you'll see the orchard in magnificent bloom; turn up in October through November to watch the fragrant press. In 2008, it released its first cases of fruit brandies; a calvados-style brandy from cider apples made its debut in 2010. The bistro, La Pommeraie, offers authentic country-style cooking and a virtual showcase of artisan pizzas, breads, and fruit pies from its brick-oven bakery, Flour Water Salt. It is open daily for lunch. **Venturi-Schulze Vineyards** (4235 Trans-Canada Hwy., R.R. 1, Cobble Hill; © **250/743-5630**; www.venturischulze.com) is the smallest winery in the Cowichan Valley, and it's truly a family affair, centered on the 100-year-old farmhouse. The winery, built partially underground, paved the way to convert the old winery into a vinegary. All wines and vinegars are grown, produced, and bottled on the property.

Another group of wineries worth visiting is found near Duncan. **Averill Creek** (6552 North Rd., Duncan; © **250/709-9986**) is a relative newcomer. Its tasting room opened in 2010, and while some oenophiles think their wines still need to mature, the Prevost has already earned awards, and the Pinot Gris is the choice du jour in many fine restaurants. **Alderlea Vineyards** (1751 Stamps Rd., R.R. 1, Duncan; © **250/746-7122**) is located on a picturesque 4-hectare (10-acre) site. Creating wines from grapes grown only in their own vineyard, Alderlea produces an excellent Bacchus, Pinot Gris,

Gourmet Safaris

Grand Wine Tours (📞 250/881-1000; www.grandwinetours.com) operates out of Victoria, with a deluxe limo tour to four wineries, including a three-course lunch with pairings. **Island Gourmet Trails** (📞 250/650-1956; www.island gourmettrails.ca) provides half-day and full-day options into the Comox Valley with itineraries that might include a cooking lesson, a visit to an oyster farm, or a meander through an organic berry patch. Prices range from C$125 to C$550. **Travel with Taste** (📞 250/385-1527; www.travelwithtaste.com) also offers a variety of culinary adventures to working farms, cheese-makers, a hand-crafted organic gin distillery, and wineries, along with a tasty lunch (C$195 adults in Cowichan Valley; C$225 adults on Saanich Peninsula). Their customized multi-day tours are more akin to gastronomic safaris. See chapter 5 for information on Victoria's only Urban Culinary Walking Tour.

Hearth (a port-style dessert wine), Pinot Auxerrois, and Angelique blend. **Blue Grouse Vineyards** (4365 Blue Grouse Rd., Duncan; 📞 250/743-3834; www.bluegrouse vineyards.com) is one of the founding estate wineries on Vancouver Island and is renowned for its exclusive premium wines. All are 100% estate-grown and produced on what are purported to be the warmest 4 hectares (10 acres) in the valley. Because of this, the Pinot Gris has a slightly pinkish tone and, along with their Ortega, Pinot Noir, and exclusive Black Muscat, is an award-winner. Wine tastings are held in a comfortable European-style tasting room overlooking the valley. In summer, picnic tables under the arbor are perfect for a savory lunch. **Vignetti Zanatta** (5039 Marshall Rd., R.R. 3, Duncan; 📞 250/748-2338; www.zanatta.ca) is one of the oldest vineyards on Vancouver Island. Wines here are made by an old-world Italian method using grapes grown only on the property. Try the Ortega, a dry, fruity white wine; or the Glenora Fantasia, a sparkling wine. The Pinot Grigio, Pinot Nero, and special Damasco are all commendable. Plan to stop for lunch or dinner at **Vinoteca** (see "Where to Dine," below), featuring many foods grown on the Zanatta 49-hectare (121-acre) farm. Touring maps are available at most visitor centers and from Wine Islands Vintners Association; www. wineislands.ca/vancouver-island.

Where to Stay

IN DUNCAN

Fairburn Farm Culinary Retreat & Guesthouse ★★ Ranked as one of the top 45 culinary vacations in the world by *Gourmet Magazine*, this one-of-a-kind inn offers guests an idealized farm experience—you can be coddled with comfort, exquisite food, and surroundings of a working farm, orchard, vineyard, and dairy. The farm's resident, and North America's only, herd of European River Water Buffalo produces yogurt, ice cream, and mozzarella. Built in the 1880s, the rambling but upgraded farmhouse has high ceilings, antique moldings, tiled fireplaces, and a broad, columned porch that overlooks 53 hectares (131 acres) of gardens and meadows, with mountain slopes visible in the distance. Each of the three large, year-round guest rooms is individually decorated with fine Italian linens and original art. Two have fireplaces. A fixed-up 1930s caretaker's cottage has created an additional two rooms in the summer; they're not as fancy, but if food is your motivation for being here, then these represent great savings. The two-bedroom cottage, too, is available only during the summer months. It includes a fully equipped kitchen and, with its simpler furnishings, is ideal for families. Fairburn's showcase kitchen is the source of its reputation and is where guests enjoy cooking lessons, bread-making demonstrations, and other culinary programs such as the participatory Saturday dinners. Food programs reflect seasonal cycles, so call ahead of your stay to check the schedule. Breakfast, which is included in the room rate, is a homemade farm-fresh feast.

3310 Jackson Rd., Duncan, BC V9L 6N7. 🕿/fax **250/746-4637**. www.fairburnfarm.bc.ca. 7 units. Nov–Mar C$130–C$155 double; Oct 1–15, Apr & May C$145–C$175 double; June–Sept C$120–C$199 double. Additional adult C$20. MC, V. Closed mid-Oct to mid-Nov. **Amenities:** Lounge. *In room:* Hair dryer, no phone, Wi-Fi.

IN CHEMAINUS

A Scented Garden   Staying here puts you within steps of the oceanfront, Old Town, and Chemainus Theatre. The renovated family home makes a comfortable B&B with a contemporary West Coast atmosphere. Rooms are appointed with country furnishings and decor, and include queen beds. The Island Thyme room features a double Jacuzzi, while the Mountainview room overlooks Mount Brenton. Breakfast is served in a common-area lounge where there's a shared fridge, coffee, and tea, although the crows-nest viewing loft (accessed via a ladder) is a treat to hang out in, as much for its harbor views as for it lofty privacy. Or grab a sunny spot in the garden which, true to its namesake, is filled with lavender, honeysuckle vines, and other scented flora.

9913 Maple St., Chemainus, BC V0R 1K1. 🕿 **877/244-9202** or 250/246-6796. www.ascentedgardenbb. com. 2 units. C$100–C$120 double. MC, V. **Amenities:** Lounge. *In room:* TV/DVD player, fridge, Wi-Fi.

IN LADYSMITH (NEAR CHEMAINUS)

Hawley Place   Finding such a grand building in the middle of such rural surrounds is rather incongruous, but if Victorian kitsch is your thing, you'll find this Victorian replica home a real charmer. The public lounge, appointed with period pieces and traditional Victoria-era furnishings, is well stocked with complimentary refreshments. The guest rooms are themed: one has a Raj-India feel, with a sleigh queen bed; one takes its cue from Africa (it has the largest en suite bathroom) while the China Rose is the king-sized-bed suite. All have sumptuous linens and amenities such as robes and slippers. Breakfasts rank highly since the chef has a culinary arts degree.

302 Hawley Place, Ladysmith, BC V9G 1X9. 🕿 **877/244-4431**. www.hawleyplacebandb.com. 3 units. C$125–C$140 double. MC, V. **Amenities:** Lounge. *In room:* TV/DVD player, hair dryer, Wi-Fi.

Yellow Point Lodge   Yellow Point Lodge began operating in the 1930s, and its blend of summer camp and luxury resort has remained a perennial favorite, especially with families. The main lodge has an enormous lobby, a huge fireplace, and a dining room with communal tables. Meals—good, home-style cooking such as prime rib and Yorkshire pudding, roast turkey and mashed potatoes, and a splendid seafood buffet on Friday nights—are included and served at set times. There are a number of comfortable hotel-like guest rooms in the lodge, all with ocean views. Away from the lodge, self-contained cabins range from rustic, barrack-style accommodations with shared bathrooms and beach cabins with no running water to luxurious one-, two-, and three-bedroom cottages; some are on the lodge's private beach, most are tucked in between the trees. The lodge is surrounded by 67 hectares

(166 acres) of private, mostly first-growth coastal rainforest, with over 2.4km (1½ miles) of waterfront facing the Gulf Islands.

3700 Yellow Point Rd., Ladysmith, BC V0R 2E0. © **250/245-7422.** Fax 250/245-7411. www.yellow pointlodge.com. 53 units. May to mid-Oct & winter weekends C$199–C$210 double, C$172–C$212 cabin, C$137 barrack; rates 10% lower mid-Oct to Apr weekdays. Rates include all meals. AE, MC, V. Children 13 & under not accepted. **Amenities:** Restaurant; bikes; Jacuzzi; sauna; 2 outdoor tennis courts. *In room:* Fridge (in some rooms), no phone.

IN COWICHAN BAY

Oceanfront Grand Resort & Marina   Every one- and two-bedroom suite faces the water, and all have been refurbished in the last few years. Out with drab and neutral; in with Italian marble floors, handcrafted furniture, up-to-date kitchens, and exceptionally comfortable king- and queen-size beds. Some rooms have fireplaces and views of the marina below. Oceanfront has a good steak and seafood restaurant that adds a sushi twist at the weekends. It also features wines from every single winery in the Cowichan Valley, as well as international labels. The marina provides kayak rentals and boat charters.

1681 Cowichan Bay Rd., Cowichan Bay, BC V0R 1N0. © **800/663-7898** or 250/715-1000. Fax 250/701-0126. www.thegrandresort.com. 57 units. Mid-Apr to Sept C$159–C$179 1-bedroom suite, C$219 2-bedroom suite; Oct to mid-Apr C$99–C$119 1-bedroom suite, C$139 2-bedroom suite. AE, MC, V. Free parking. **Amenities:** Restaurant; bar; gym; hot tub; heated indoor pool; boat rental. *In room:* TV/DVD player, fridge, hair dryer. Wi-Fi.

Where to Dine
OVER THE MALAHAT

Amuse Bistro ★★★ REGIONAL/FRENCH   Just over the Malahat en route to Shawnigan Lake lies a tiny destination restaurant set in what used to be a private home. You're greeted like a houseguest, welcomed into its open kitchen before heading upstairs into the living room that seats about 20. In summer, the heated, garden patio doubles capacity. The food is superlative and puts a French inspiration into local ingredients, with a different *amuse-bouche* offered at every meal. If that serves to awaken the palette, other dishes will do no less. Look for items like pan-seared medallions of farm-raised pork tenderloin with caramelized apples and pan juices, finished with organic black currants, purple heritage carrots, rainbow Swiss chard, golden beets, Russian blue potatoes, and Egyptian walking onions. The braised wild sockeye salmon is wonderfully flavored with Beaujolais, and the warm gingerbread gateau, dolloped with lemon preserve, is accompanied by a red wine–pocked pear and spiced ice cream. In addition to an a la carte menu, there are three-, four-, or five-course table d'hôte menus (C$36–C$59); add about C$30 for wine pairings.

753 Shawnigan-Mill Bay Rd., Shawnigan Lake. © **250/743-3667.** www.amusebistro.com. Reservations recommended. Main courses C$19–C$32. MC, V. Wed–Sun from 5pm.

IN COWICHAN BAY

Crow & Gate PUB FARE   This classic Tudor-style pub was built in 1972 yet looks like it was plucked out of Cornwall, with its stone-and-timbered walls, leaded-glass windows, and low-slung ceilings. Even the hand-painted sign is just like the old pub signs you still find in England. Surrounded by a working farm, this popular watering hole offers the best of British pub fare, including traditional

Ploughman's Lunch, roast beef and Yorkshire pudding, pasties, and shepherd's pie. There's a flower-laden patio in summer.

2313 Yellow Point Rd. ℂ **250/722-3731.** www.crowandgate.com. Reservations recommended for dinner. Main courses C$9–C$17. MC, V. Daily 11am–11pm.

Masthead Restaurant ★ REGIONAL   As one of the region's top destination restaurants, Masthead serves great food in an historical environment dating back to the 1800s, complemented with engaging views of a working harbor. The menu reflects the 100-Mile ethos, as in Queen Charlotte Coho salmon; Fanny Bay oysters; Cowichan Valley venison, chicken, and pork; and Salt Spring Island mussels. Most dishes, including house-made pastas, are prepared without too much filigree: Grilled tenderloin with béarnaise sauce has just a touch of bacon, and venison is simply flavored with sautéed mushrooms and a mustard demi-glaze. The fancy fixings, however, do come as side garnishes such as a potato croquette stuffed with figs, goat cheese, and a ginger puree. The three-course table d'hôte is good value for taste experiences and dollars spent. Masthead has dibs on select limited editions produced annually by some Cowichan Valley Estate wineries, so you can expect to discover hard-to-find labels here like Venturi Schulze's Millefiori and Pinot Noir. Some of these are so in demand that they must be ordered two harvests in advance.

1705 Cowichan Bay Rd., Cowichan Bay. ℂ **250/748-3714.** www.themastheadrestaurant.com. Reservations recommended. Main courses C$22–C$33; 3-course menu C$33. MC, V. Daily from 5pm.

Rock Cod Café FISH AND CHIPS   Perched above the water, this busy cafe overlooks busy fishing docks and serves the best fish and chips in the area. After all, when the fish is pulled straight off the boats and put right into the pan, what would

🅞 picnic SUPPLIES

There's no better place to pick up simple but delicious picnic supplies than Cowichan Bay's seaside village, especially if you're planning to spread a blanket at one of the wineries.

True Grain Bread (1725 Cowichan Bay Rd.; ℂ **250/746-7664;** www.truegrain. ca) bakes organic, handcrafted breads, croissants, cookies, pretzels, and rolls using heritage wheat, natural leavens, sea salt, alternative grains, and freshly stone-milled products. At **Hilary's Artisan Cheese & Deli** next door (Village Store, 1737 Cowichan Bay Rd.; ℂ **250/748-5992;** www.hilaryscheese.com), you'll find farm-fresh, aromatic *fromages,* as well as over 100 specialty cheeses, cold

cuts, and homemade deli items. And to see you on your way? The **Udder Guy's Old Fashioned Ice Cream** (1721 Cowichan Bay Rd.; ℂ **250/954-5555**) has the best flavors on the island. Ingredients are fresh, with no artificial additives. Strawberry Extreme is made with local berries and real coconut, shredded and roasted on site, that are sublime.

In addition to stopping for food, try to make time to wander through the village. There's a picturesque boardwalk along the marina-front where historic, clapboard buildings house a glass-blowing studio, clayworks, and the prestigious Arthur Vickers Gallery. His brother, Roy Vickers, has a gallery in Tofino.

you expect? Check out the specials board: It's crammed with value-priced items based on whatever those boats bring in, as well as burgers, salads, and pasta dishes. This is a great place for takeout, especially family packs, or simply to fuel up for a stroll around the harbor.

1759 Cowichan Bay Rd. ℂ **250/746-1550.** www.rockcodcafe.com. Main courses C$7–C$15. MC, V. Daily 11am–9pm.

AROUND DUNCAN

The Genoa Bay Café PACIFIC NORTHWEST   Genoa Bay, a 20-minute drive from Duncan, was named by Giovanni Baptiste Ordano in 1858. The bay reminded him of his home in Italy and still retains a picturesque charm. The weathered-looking, clapboard cafe is on the pier of a marina complex and is always busy with sea-faring folks and locals. Although the menu leans to seafood, exquisitely prepared, you'll find items such as BBQ ribs, slow-roasted in apple and sun-dried cranberry BBQ sauce, and a rack of lamb with pesto and mango chutney glaze—an absolute winner. In the fall and winter months, tapas dishes are offered—a clever way to monitor purchases and portion controls during the slower season. Any time of year, however, it's fish that really tops the charts—mouth-watering halibut and candied smoked salmon in white-wine cream sauce, calamari with roasted-red-pepper pesto dip, or sole and scallops with a mango Thai chili sauce. The island's daily newspaper rated the chocolate-pecan pie the best of the island, though the lemon tart with raspberry *coulis* is a strong contender.

5100 Genoa Bay Rd., Genoa Bay Marina, Genoa Bay. ℂ **800/572-6481** or 250/746-7621. www.genoa baycafe.com. Reservations recommended. Main courses C$13–C$29. MC, V. Thurs–Sun 11:30am–2:30pm; daily 5:30–10pm.

Vinoteca ★★ CONTINENTAL   A combination wine-tasting room and tapas bar, Vinoteca is set amid the family-owned and -operated Vignetti Zanatta vineyards (see "Meandering among the Wineries," earlier in this chapter). The 1903 farmhouse has been lovingly restored and is a restful place to dine or sip your afternoon away. The menu reflects the family's Italian heritage, incorporating food that is grown either on the farm or locally. A great place for a light meal, here you'll find items such as marinated vegetables, bruschetta, as well as a daily fresh pasta selection (the chicken confit cannelloni is very good), and more substantial dishes such as espresso-marinated duck breast. What makes the food outstanding are unexpected combinations: a salad of melon, smoked rout, arugula and capers, and shellfish poached in coconut milk and served with saffron rice. All are complemented by wines from their vineyards.

5039 Marshall Rd. (near Glenora, south of Duncan). ℂ **250/709-2279.** Reservations recommended for dinner. Main courses C$11–C$16. MC, V. Wed–Sun noon–4:30pm; closed Mon & Tues. Closed mid Oct–Mar. Take the Miller Rd. exit off Hwy. 1 to the stop sign. Turn left onto Miller Rd., right on Koksilah Rd. & left onto Miller Rd. again. Turn left on Glenora Rd.; the vineyards are at the junction of Glenora & Marshall rds.

CENTRAL VANCOUVER ISLAND

The central part of Vancouver Island showcases some of the best of British Columbia's natural attractions—it's a real haven for eco-adventurers. And it's so diverse that much of it is also geared to family fun. Nanaimo, the island's second-largest city and the gateway to the region, is the arrival point for visitors traveling by ferry from the mainland. Families usually head for the neighboring communities of Parksville and Qualicum Beach, where sandy beaches, warm water temperatures, tranquil lakes, and exceptional golf courses prevail. They are year-round vacation destinations and are increasingly attractive to active retirees; few can resist the more than 2,000 hours of sunshine the townships receive each year.

Things begin to change, however, as you head inland, cutting across the island to the west coast. Here lie the deep Douglas fir forests of **Cathedral Grove** and the mill town of **Port Alberni,** from which you can explore the region's protected inlets. And once you reach the west coast, well, the changes in scenery are dramatic. The shores are windswept and wild. Fishing villages like **Tofino** ("Tough City") and **Ucluelet** (Yew-*kloo*-let) are home base to kayakers, hikers, surfers, naturalists, and photographers, who flock to explore **Pacific Rim National Park,** the Broken Group Islands, and Clayoquot Sound. Here, you can discover some of the most pristine and accessible coastline in the province.

NANAIMO

With a population close to 80,000, Nanaimo is quickly shedding its industrial roots. Once the center of vast coal-mining operations, Nanaimo developed into rather a parochial community. This image is finally beginning to change. Although its suburban environs are pretty nondescript, a small downtown nucleus is smartening up into a hip and pedestrian-friendly area where old buildings such as a century-old fire hall–turned–restaurant are finding new leases on life. The city's fathers mean business: 21 of 58 heritage commercial buildings have received grants for renovations since 2001, and in spite of recessionary times, more than 500 newly developed condominium units hit the market in the last 2 years alone. Around the revamped harbor front, you'll find a number of galleries, intriguing shops, and quality restaurants to enjoy. The Port of Nanaimo Centre opened in 2008 and is now the home to the Nanaimo District Museum, an open-air community plaza, and a convention center. Other developments reflecting Nanaimo's increasing stature include its rapidly-growing university, plans for a C$22-million floating cruise-ship terminal, and plans to expand the airport so it can handle bigger jets. Add to this Nanaimo's designation in 2008 as a "Cultural Capital of Canada," and it all points to an up-and-coming city on the fast track to adulthood.

> ## Naming Nanaimo
>
> Pronounced "Na-*nye*-mo," the city's name originated when the first white settlers tried to adapt a Coast Salish world "Snu-Ney-Muxw" meaning "The Meeting Place," into English. It was originally called Colvilletown.

Essentials

GETTING THERE

BY CAR   Nanaimo is located right off the Trans-Canada Highway (Hwy. 1), 111km (69 miles) north of Victoria.

BY PLANE   The **Nanaimo Airport** (© 250/245-2157) is 18km (11 miles) from downtown Nanaimo. **Air Canada Jazz** (© 888/247-2262) operates flights daily between Nanaimo and Vancouver. There are also several harbor-to-harbor flights among Vancouver, Nanaimo, Victoria, and Seattle. These seaplane carriers include **West Coast Air** (© 800/347-2222 or 604/606-6888; www.westcoastair.com), **Harbour Air** (© 800/665-0212 or 250/714-0900; www.harbour-air.com), and **Kenmore Air** (© 866/435-9524 or 425/486-1257; www.kenmoreair.com).

BY BUS   Greyhound Canada (© 800/661-8747) runs buses from Victoria to Nanaimo, Tofino, and Port Hardy. One-way fares from Victoria to Nanaimo are C$26 nonrefundable/C$30 refundable for adults. Fares for seniors are C$12 nonrefundable/C$14 refundable, and for children 5 to 11 are C$9.50 nonrefundable/C$11 refundable. **Island Link Bus** (© 250/954-8257; www.islandlinkbus.com) runs a passenger express service between the BC Ferries' terminal and Vancouver, Victoria, and Comox airports, plus several island hubs, including Nanaimo. One-way fares are slightly less than Greyhound, but schedules may not be as convenient. **The Nanaimo Airporter** (© 888/758-2133; www.nanaimoairporter.com) provides a shuttle service to downtown and ferry terminals. An adult fare is C$23.

BY TRAIN   The **Malahat,** operated by VIA Rail (© 888/842-7245; www.viarail.com), has daily service between Victoria and Courtenay. One-day sightseeing trips from Victoria include stops in Chemainus, Duncan, and Nanaimo.

BY FERRY   BC Ferries (© 888/BCFERRY [888/223-3779], or 250/386-3431; www.bcferries.com) runs between **Horseshoe Bay** in West Vancouver and **Departure**

Bay in Nanaimo, as well as between **Tsawwassen** and **Duke Point,** also in Nanaimo. The latter is used primarily by trucks and commercial vehicles, but if you're traveling by car (Duke Point is 16km/10 miles south of Nanaimo and not served by public transit), it's a good alternative to the very busy Horseshoe Bay–Departure Bay routing. Fares for either route are C$14 adults and C$47 for a standard vehicle.

VISITOR INFORMATION

Tourism Nanaimo is located at Beban House (2290 Bowen Rd., Nanaimo; ℂ **800/ 663-7337** or 250/756-0106; www.tourismnanaimo.com). A summer-only information center operates at the Pioneer Waterfront Plaza near the Bastion. Tourism Vancouver Island is also based in Nanaimo, at 501-65 Front St., Nanaimo; (ℂ **250/ 754-3500;** www.vancouverisland.travel or www.helloBC.com/vi).

GETTING AROUND

BY CAR Be alert to street signs; Nanaimo's roads go off at angles and change names along the way. For example, Bastion Street becomes Fitzwilliam Street (once Nanaimo's red-light district), which becomes 3rd Street, which leads to the Parkway before becoming Jingle Pot Road, named for the time when miners walked the route to work, "jingling" their lunches in metal pails along the way. Street parking is ample, and most hotels have secured underground parking.

BY PUBLIC TRANSPORTATION **Nanaimo Regional Transit System** (ℂ **250/390-4531;** www.rdn.bc.ca) provides public transport through Nanaimo's suburbs, mainly residential areas and a couple of strip malls. From a visitor's standpoint, they're buses that go nowhere unless you're heading up to Parksville and Qualicum. Fares are C$2.25 for adults and C$2 for seniors and children. If, for some reason, you're out in the boonies where there are few official stops, you can flag one down.

BY TAXI For cab service, call **AC Taxi** (ℂ **800/753-1231** or 250/753-1231; www.actaxi.ca) or **Swiftsure Taxi** (ℂ **250/753-8911**). You would be lucky to find a taxi hanging around the bus station or a downtown hotel; better to call ahead.

Exploring Nanaimo

The best thing about Nanaimo is its **Pioneer Waterfront**—refurbished with multi-level walkways, banks of flowers, marina restaurants, and gift shops—some touristy, others worthwhile. On most summer days, the walkways have a mix of one-person stalls selling paintings, junk jewelry, and carvings; and come Friday, they're joined by local farm vendors selling fresh produce, homemade jams, and baked goods. The Harbourside Walkway actually extends all the way to Departure Bay, 4km (2½ miles) away, and is a popular route for joggers. The waterfront is anchored by the **Bastion,** Nanaimo's oldest building and the only remaining fort structure of its type in North America. Getting around the harbor waters is most fun aboard the stylized 12-passenger shuttles run by **Nanaimo Harbour Ferry** (ℂ **877/297-8526** or 250/729-8738; www.nanaimo harbourferry.com); the same folks run the shuttles around Victoria's harbor. Catch a ride from Fisherman's Market Pier for a 45-minute tour (C$22 adults; C$20 seniors and students; C$10 children 12 and under) or hop over to Newcastle Island (C$8).

The **Old City Quarter,** a mere 3-block area, continues to improve with some good restaurants, coffee houses, and specialty gift shops. Top stops are **Flying Fish Gift-ware** (180 Commercial St.; ℂ **250/754-2104**) for handmade crafts, housewares, and whimsical items; **Tea Leaf Emporium** (13B Commercial St.; ℂ **250/753-9957**);

Petroglyph Provincial Park ★

It's a wonder more travelers don't stop by. Estimated to be at least 1,000 years old, this park's petroglyphs are an overlooked treasure. Although similar sandstone carvings exists elsewhere on Vancouver Island, including nearby Gabriola, rarely are they found in such concentration and as easily accessible. Look for mythological creatures—sea wolves, in particular—and a variety of other symbolic designs resembling bird, human, and fish. For the artistically inclined, an interpretive display of concrete castings taken from the nearby petroglyphs is available to make coffee-table-size rubbings. The originals are just a short distance farther along the walkway on a hill that overlooks Nanaimo Harbour. The Nanaimo Snuneymuxw First Nation community believe that the petroglyphs were carved by Thochwan, who is present among the carvings, having himself been transformed into stone by a supernatural visitor. The park is located on the east side of the Trans-Canada Highway, 4km (2½ miles) south of Nanaimo. Visit www.bcparks.ca for information or contact **Tourism Nanaimo** (✆ **800/663-7337;** www.tourismnanaimo.com).

and the **Artisan's Studio** (70 Bastion St.; ✆ **250/753-6151**), a co-op gallery run by and featuring the work of local artists. **Hill's Native Art** (76 Bastion St.; ✆ **250/755-7873**) is a reputable place for First Nations art. Just be aware that the "new" historic district backs onto the older area that still sports a couple of seamy clubs.

The Top Attractions

The Nanaimo Bastion   The white, fortified tower was built by the Hudson's Bay Company in 1852 to protect its Nanaimo trading post. At that time, Haida Indians traveled down from the northerly Queen Charlotte Islands and mounted a series of raids. The Bastion's three floors house a hands-on exhibit that explores early life in Nanaimo: On the first floor is the Company's Clerk's Office, displaying coal-mining gear of the time; the Arsenal is on the second floor (in summer, the Bastion Guards recreate the firing of the noon cannon daily at 11:45am); and the third-floor Refuge, once used in times of danger, now has displays on blacksmithing, homemaking, and farming.

Bastion & Front St., on Pioneer Waterfront Plaza. ✆ **250/753-1821.** www.nanaimomuseum.ca. Admission C$2 adults. May–Sept daily 10am–4pm.

Nanaimo District Museum   It took a while for the exhibits to settle into their new home, and a couple are still evolving. Nonetheless, the displays here provide a good overview of the history of Nanaimo's hardworking waterfront, while a coal miner's tunnel touches upon the city's other founding industry. A First Nations Gallery adds another dimension to this region's makeup with its re-creation of a Salish Indian village (the Snuneymuxw—the "Nanaimo people"). The old miner's cottage and restored 1890s locomotive remains in the museum's original location in Piper's Park, accessed by climbing two steep flights of stairs. Make your own petroglyph rubbings for an unusual souvenir or find Snuneymuxw wooden carvings in the gift shop.

100 Museum Way, Port of Nanaimo Centre. ✆ **250/753-1821.** www.nanaimomuseum.ca. Admission C$2 adults, C$1.75 seniors, C75¢ children 6–12. Mid-May to Labor Day daily 10am–5pm; after Labor Day to mid-May Tues–Sat 10am–5pm.

Central Vancouver Island

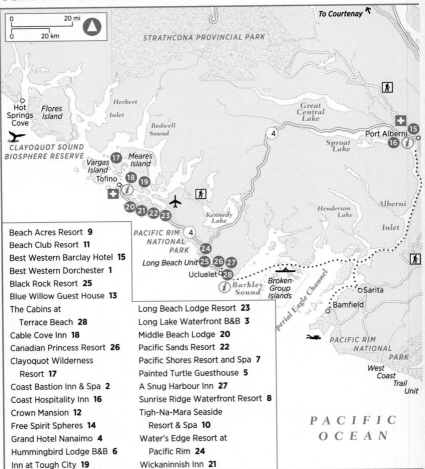

Beach Acres Resort **9**
Beach Club Resort **11**
Best Western Barclay Hotel **15**
Best Western Dorchester **1**
Black Rock Resort **25**
Blue Willow Guest House **13**
The Cabins at
   Terrace Beach **28**
Cable Cove Inn **18**
Canadian Princess Resort **26**
Clayoquot Wilderness
   Resort **17**
Coast Bastion Inn & Spa **2**
Coast Hospitality Inn **16**
Crown Mansion **12**
Free Spirit Spheres **14**
Grand Hotel Nanaimo **4**
Hummingbird Lodge B&B **6**
Inn at Tough City **19**

Long Beach Lodge Resort **23**
Long Lake Waterfront B&B **3**
Middle Beach Lodge **20**
Pacific Sands Resort **22**
Pacific Shores Resort and Spa **7**
Painted Turtle Guesthouse **5**
A Snug Harbour Inn **27**
Sunrise Ridge Waterfront Resort **8**
Tigh-Na-Mara Seaside
   Resort & Spa **10**
Water's Edge Resort at
   Pacific Rim **24**
Wickaninnish Inn **21**

Outdoor Activities

SCUBA DIVING   The Cousteau Society calls the waters around Nanaimo "the best temperate water diving in the world, second only to the Red Sea," so suffice it to say, scuba diving is big business here. Nicknamed the "Emerald Sea," its water is clear enough to see the likes of giant Pacific octopi, colorful sea anemones, and herds of marine mammals that appear to just "hang around" for entertainment. **Dodds Narrows,** between Vancouver Island and Mudge Island, is a hot diving spot. Other areas include **Snake Island Wall** (*Tip:* even if you're not a diver, you can snorkel with the seals on nearby Snake Island), **Gabriola Passage,** and the **largest artificial upright**

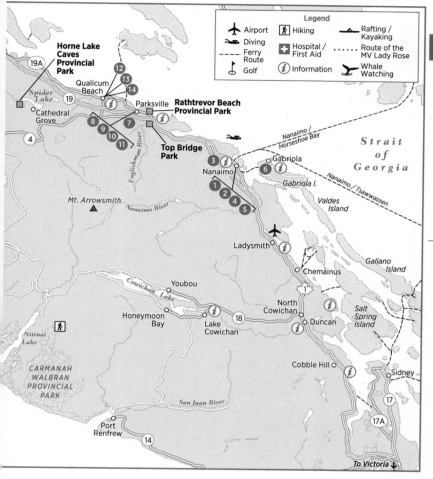

reef in the world. The reef is made up of a number of sunken wrecks, including the **HMCS *Saskatchewan*,** a 112m (366-ft.) Canadian Naval destroyer sunk in 1997, and the **HMCS *Cape Breton*.** In 2005, *Rivtow Lion,* a retired deep-sea rescue tug, was added to the reef. The *Rivtow* rests at a manageable depth of about 15m (49 ft.) right in Departure Bay, making it a interesting dive for those wanting to get a bit more comfortable before heading down deeper to the Cape Breton or Saskatchewan.

A good diving operator, which offers guided dives, equipment rentals, and instruction with fast, custom-dive boats, is **Divers Choice Charters** (1150-130 North Terminal Ave; © **866/716-8867;** www.divingbccanada.com). **Nanaimo Dive**

Outfitters (2205 Northfield Rd.; © **250/756-1863;** www.nanaimodiveoutfitters. ca) is also recommended. Prices are competitive, and range from C$50 to C$85 per dive, depending on equipment needs.

BUNGEE JUMPING & WILDPLAY PARK   Keeping your head above water delivers something quite different—if you've got the nerve, go for it. Set high over the Nanaimo River lies the "Only Legal Bridge Bungy Jump Site in North America." If free-falling 43m (141 ft.) at speeds of up to 140kmph (87 mph) doesn't appeal, watching the bungee brave-hearts is still a thrill. An on-site gift shop sells plenty of bungee paraphernalia, so you can always pretend you dared. Jumps are C$100 and include an I Did It! T-shirt. But that isn't all you'll find here. **Wild Play at the Bungy Zone** (© **888/716-7374;** www.wildplayparks.com) includes a high-elevation swing that cinches you up in a slingshot-like device (C$90) and a zipline ride across a wooded canyon at almost 100kmph (62 mph). The zip trips are a part of the aerial tree obstacle course called Monkido, which is set some 3 to 15m (9¾–49 ft.) high with suspended bridges, scramble nets, and swinging logs. There's a children's-only version of the course, and some courses have a minimum age of 12. Monkido prices range from C$25 to C$40. Bungy Zone is a great spot for teenagers who are looking for an adrenaline rush.

HIKING   One of Nanaimo's lesser-known trails is the 2km (1.2-mile) **Cable Bay Trail.** You hike through a serene forest to Cable Bay Bridge, where you can beach comb or observe migrating sea lions (Oct–Apr). The trail is an off-leash (dog-friendly) area. **Parkway Trail,** which runs alongside Highway 19, links Aulds Road to Chase River. The 20km (12-mile) paved and tree-lined span is best suited for long-distance cyclists and joggers. It leads to Buttertubs Marsh, Colliery Dam, Bowen Park, and the Harbourfront Walkway via the Millstone Trail. Because the **E&N Trail** is paved and level, it's a magnet not only for walkers, but for in-line skaters, bikers, and skateboarders, too. The 8km (5-mile) paved trail parallels the E&N Railway tracks and the old Island Highway 19A from Rosehill Avenue to Mostar Road and is the best option for "wheels." **Tracks Outdoor Adventures** (2130 Akenhead Rd.; © **250/754-8732;** www.tracksoutdooradventures.com) offers a variety of guided hiking excursions, from a heritage stroll through downtown Nanaimo to treks through rainforests, around Newcastle Island, and more.

KAYAKING   Nanaimo's sheltered waters make them ideal for kayakers, whether paddling over to Newcastle Island or taking a full day (even multi-day) excursion over to the Gulf Islands. **Adventuress Sea Kayaking** (3225 Uplands Dr.; © **866/955-6702** or 250/755-6702; www.adventuress.ca) runs several half-day and full-day excursions to the surrounding islands, starting at C$65 per person, including all gear. This outfitter also operates out of Parksville. **Wildheart Adventure Tours** (1560 Brebber Rd.; © **250/722-3683;** www.kayakbc.com) offers guided trips, including multi-day camping adventures starting at C$500.

Protection Island

This island is actually a part of the City of Nanaimo and sits like a protecting arm a kilometer (½ mile) offshore in Nanaimo Harbour. As close as it is, this tiny island, about 5km (3 miles) in circumference, is almost a place time forgot. With about 200 homes and a pirate theme that runs rampant (Capt. Morgan's Boulevard, Smugglers Lake, and Pirate Lane), it has no schools, churches, post office, stores, or other businesses, and virtually no cars. Island transportation is by foot, bike, or golf cart.

Tubs Ahoy!

For more than 40 years, daredevils have raced across the Georgia Strait in one- and two-man craft. In the early days, vessels were old claw-foot tubs fitted with engines. Often, they sank in the harbor—an event that these days could win the prestigious Silver Plunger Award. Today, contestants speed across the whitecaps in not only sleek-looking, individually designed, high-tech boats, but also wildly creative vessels that hark back to earlier times. The race is the highlight of the weeklong Marine Festival held in July, which includes a street fair, a parade, and a spirited atmosphere. For details, visit **www.bathtubbing.com**.

Ferries—actually converted lifeboats—make the 10-minute run from the mainland on the hour, from 7am to 10pm. Even the pub, the **Dinghy Dock** (Canada's only floating pub/restaurant; © **250/753-2373**), keeps ferry hours, with last call in time for mainlanders to catch the 10pm ferry home to Nanaimo. At low tide, hikers can wade across Pirate's Causeway to Newcastle Island.

Newcastle Island

Originally settled by the Coast Salish, then mined for coal and sandstone, and later a resort island for the Canadian Pacific Steamship Company, **Newcastle Island Marine Provincial Park** (© **250/754-7893;** www.newcastleisland.ca) has largely reverted to its natural state, though you can still see remnants of the 1850s coal mine, sandstone, and pulp stone quarries (the sandstone columns of the U.S. Mint in San Francisco were quarried and shaped here), and two Salish First Nations villages. Many visitors kayak over from the mainland; others make the 10-minute crossing with **Nanaimo Harbour Ferry** (© **250/729-8738;** www.nanaimoharbourferry.com), which runs trips daily on the hour in July and August from 10am to 9pm, until 5pm the rest of the year. The round-trip fare is C$9 adults, C$5 seniors and children; bikes and dogs are free. As a protected marine park, it has a network of hiking and cycling trails, and 18 year-round campsites (C$16 per night) with toilets, showers, fire pits, and wood.

Trail lengths vary, but if you're up to walking 2 to 4km (1.2–2.5 miles), the **Mallard Lake Trail,** the **Channel Trail,** and the **Shoreline Trail** are among the most rewarding. The Mallard Lake Trail takes you through the forested heart of the island to a freshwater lake; you can return via the Channel Trail that follows the shoreline across from the mainland and past an old sandstone quarry. The Shoreline Trail is on the opposite (ocean) side of the island overlooking Nanaimo, and winds itself up to Kanaka Bay Beach. If you've the energy, continue on to viewpoints at McKay Point and Giovando Lookout before hiking back past an old mine shaft and joining the Channel Trail back to the ferry docks. The entire perimeter hike is 7.5km (4.7 miles). There are interpretive signs along the way, as well as a visitor center, snack bar, and gift shop.

Where to Stay

Best Western Dorchester Hotel   This Best Western is not only a cut above most Best Westerns, it's the best value for the money in terms of services, quality, and central location in the Old City Quarter. The hotel stands on the site of the original Hudson's Bay Company trading post. Guest rooms may be on the small side, but they

Foodies' Fancy

Edible British Columbia (© **604/812-9660**; www.edible-britishcolumbia.com) hosts a series of 2- and 3-night kayaking getaways, where paddling and culinary adventure go hand-in-hand. Professional guides put a gourmet touch on every meal; accommodation choices include camping or intimate lodges. Prices start at C$750 per person, inclusive of transfers from the Nanaimo ferry terminal or seaplane landing to the launch site near Nanaimo.

are comfortably furnished, and if you opt for a harbor-view room, the vista is more than worth the C$10 extra you'll pay. Book via the Internet, and the savings can be substantial. Check out the stunning chandeliers in the lobby and the elaborate columns in the dining room—they came from the opera house that also once stood on this site.

70 Church St., Nanaimo, BC V9R 5H4. © **800/661-2449** or 250/754-6835. Fax 250/754-2638. www. dorchesternanaimo.com. 65 units. C$119–C$175 double. Additional adult C$10. Senior, Internet & seasonal discounts available. AE, DC, DISC, MC, V. Free parking. Pets accepted (C$20/day). **Amenities:** Restaurant; lounge. *In room:* TV w/movies, hair dryer, Wi-Fi.

Coast Bastion Inn & Spa   Overlooking the Strait of Georgia, right on the inner harbor, this hotel feels geared to the business traveler. It's taken a while, but finally the public areas were given a makeover to match the guest rooms. Drab and dull have been replaced with a ton of cool marble in the lobby, a slew of windows in the dining room, and snazzy furnishings throughout. The best feature, however, is still the waterfront views. Some suites have Jacuzzis with upgraded amenities and a lot more space, especially the corner units. **Pure Spa** (© **250/754-7889**; www.pure spananaimo.ca), rounds out the renovation package. Because the hotel is connected to the **Port Theatre** (125 Front St., © **250/754-8550** for ticket info), which hosts plays and musical concerts from Bruce Cockburn to London Symphony Quartets, theater packages are the best value in town.

11 Bastion St., Nanaimo, BC V9R 6E4. © **800/663-1144** or 250/753-6601.. www.coasthotels.com. 179 units. May–Sept C$135–C$205 double, C$195–C$265 suite; Oct–Apr C$125–C$165 double, C$185–C$225 suite. Additional adult C$10. Senior, AAA, off-season discounts & packages available. AE, DC, DISC, MC, V. Self-parking C$7.50; valet parking C$12. Pets accepted (C$10). **Amenities:** Restaurant; lounge; babysitting; health club; room service; spa. *In room:* A/C, TV w/pay movies, fridge, hair dryer, minibar, iPod dock, Wi-Fi.

Grand Hotel Nanaimo   This is Nanaimo's most luxurious full-service hotel, located within minutes of two malls, one of which is the biggest on Vancouver Island. The facilities are bright, modern, and even a shade pretentious for this up-and-coming town. The restaurant would do better if it weren't so focused on "fine dining"; while service staff are friendly, they are dressed in black suits and look ready to serve at a funeral or high-end New York hotel. That said, the afternoon high teas on the weekends are welcome respite after a shopping spree. Accommodations range from standard guest rooms to one-bedroom suites with jetted tubs. All have fireplaces, and many have balconies. There are 12 fully furnished two- and three-bedroom townhouses for long-term stays.

4898 Rutherford Rd., Nanaimo, BC V9T 4Z4. © **877/414-7263** or 250/758-3000. Fax 250/729-2808. www.thegrandhotelnanaimo.ca. 72 units. May–Sept C$149–C$209 double, Oct–Apr C$119–C$189 double; year-round C$229–C$350 suite. Additional adult C$15. Senior discounts available. AE, MC, V. Free gated/underground parking. **Amenities:** Restaurant; lounge; fitness center; indoor heated pool; room service. *In room:* A/C, TV, fridge, hair dryer, Wi-Fi.

Long Lake Waterfront B&B ★

All three suites here are beautifully decorated, well furnished, and have spectacular views of the lake, gracefully framed by a 700-year-old Douglas fir and a 250-year-old red cedar. The Arbutus Suite is the smallest with a queen-size bed, while the Madrona and Lakeside each have kings; the latter has its own entrance and kitchenette, and is more like a mini-apartment. Breakfasts don't disappoint. They are served in an atrium-lounge, overlooking the lake, and appear rather magically via a dumbwaiter that connects to the kitchen above. Guests can explore the lake beyond the views, as a kayak, a canoe, and a pedal boat are provided free of charge at the private dock.

240 Ferntree Place, Nanaimo, BC V9T 5M1. ✆ **877/758-5010** or 250/758-5010. www.lodgingnanaimo. com. 3 units. May to mid-Oct C$125–C$175 suite; mid-Oct to Apr C$100–C$125 suite. MC, V. Children 9 & under not accepted. **Amenities**: Lounge; hot tub. *In room:* TV/DVD player, fridge, Wi-Fi.

Painted Turtle Guesthouse ✦

A hybrid of an inn and a boutique hostel, a stay here is the best deal in town with a central location that's hard to beat. Guest rooms are simply furnished and spotlessly clean. All have queen beds; the family suites have additional bunk beds, and some rooms are set up hostel-style, four to a room. The share-bathroom ratio is about three rooms to one bathroom, and because there are separate lavatories, lineups aren't an issue. The Great Room is bright and inviting, with a large communal kitchen, an eating area, and sofas around a gas fireplace. It can get very social at night—with guitars, singing, or just meeting your fellow travelers who are a mix of backpackers, families on a budget, and active retirees.

121 Bastion St., Nanaimo, BC V9R 3A2. ✆ **866/309-4432** or 250/753-4432. www.paintedturtle.ca. 20 units. C$25 dorm bed; C$76–C$90 double. MC, V. **Amenities:** Lounge; kitchen. *In room:* No phone, Wi-Fi.

Where to Dine

Central Nanaimo has a surprising number of good dining spots, another indicator that this town is going places as it attracts more and more urban mainlanders. Tapas are still very "de rigueur" in Nanaimo, and ethnic fare is coming onto the scene beyond take-out burritos and chow mein. **Sukkho Thai** (123 Commercial St.; ✆ **591-8424**) and **Phoa Dong Vietnamese** (428 Fitzwilliam St.; ✆ **250/754-2523**) are good choices. More and more eateries are found on the waterfront and in converted heritage

---

CAMPING IN nanaimo

Running along the oceanfront, with a lovely swimming beach, **Living Forest Oceanside Campground & RV Park ★** (6 Maki Rd., Nanaimo, BC V9R 6N7; ✆ **250/755-1755**; www.livingforest. com) has 300 spacious sites spread over 21 forested hectares (52 acres). Each has a fire pit and picnic table. Overall facilities are so impressive that many bikers, hikers, families, tenters, and RVers stay a while. Oceanside is open year-round and has a cafe, store, adventure playground, kayak rentals, volleyball courts, laundry, hot showers, free Wi-Fi, a games room, and more. Rates go from C$26 for an unserviced forested tent site to C$41 for an oceanfront, full-hook-up RV lot.

buildings. One example, the **Lighthouse Bistro and Pub,** off Harbourside Walkway at 50 Anchor Way (*②* **250/754-3212**), serves up traditional burgers and grills alongside waterfront views of the seaplanes coming and going. There's also a converted fire hall that makes for an offbeat dining location. Unfortunately, restaurant tenants keep changing, but check it out because one day someone's cooking is going to fire this place up—all puns intended. For early risers, head for **Mon Petit Choux** (120 Commercial St.; *②* **250/753-6002**) for *tres bien petits dejeuners* (very good breakfasts).

Acme Rib & Seafood House ECLECTIC   Located on one of downtown Nanaimo's busiest corners, this triangular restaurant changed ownership (again). And although the menu has tamed its selection, the range is still pretty broad. House specialties include sushi and steaks, build your own burgers, and pulled-pork sliders. Since changing ownership, locals claim it has become inconsistent, but we saw no sign of it. The place is always busy, and the menu still turns out the unexpected: a Thai coconut bowl with wild Pacific salmon, Moroccan lamb skewers, and phyllo-crusted frazzled prawns. They also offer takeout.

14 Commercial St. *②* **250/753-0042**. www.acmefoodco.ca. Reservations recommended. Main courses C$8–C$23. MC, V. Daily 11am–midnight.

Diners Rendezvous ★ ECLECTIC   When the owners of Acme moved on to this venture, there was little doubt they would succeed in creating a new restaurant hot spot. Good food, reasonable prices, and live entertainment are, after all, a winning combination. Half the space is a quasi–martini lounge, complete with rendezvous-style banquettes, a dance floor, and a stage beneath a domed and twinkling sky; the other half is a contemporary bistro where the food really rules. Grilled items are the house signature and are given a tasty twist. There's a Malaysian risotto with seared ahi tuna and grilled pineapple served on a banana leaf, a warm artichoke hummus appetizer that's big enough to share, and a steak-and-seafood that really bursts with fired-up flavor. Portions are generous; take out leftovers are wrapped as aluminum foil swans.

4898 Rutherford Rd. *②* **877/414-7263** or 250/758-3000. www.dinersrendezvous.ca. Main courses C$9–C$18. MC, V. Daily 11am–10:30pm.

Fox & Hounds ★★ 🍴 PUB FARE   This is the best of merry old England. British food is served all day, and there's beer on draught and roast dinners every Sunday; they even stock English sodas such as Tango and Ribena. Easily recognized by the bright red phone booth at its entrance, this pub is located just 2 blocks up from the Old City Quarter and is worth the uphill climb. The decor is classic English pub, with a well-stocked bar, a chalkboard menu the size of a door, prolific oil paintings of the English countryside, and a fireplace mantle to cozy up to. Plates are heaped with hearty pub grub, all of which is excellent: The steak-and-kidney pie has good-sized mouthfuls of meat, and you can actually find a decent amount of kidneys. The chicken and vegetable pie is equally good, as is the cottage pie and oven-baked rice pudding. You don't have to be a Brit to appreciate this gem, though there are a fair number of English accents in the crowd.

247 Milton St. *②* **250/740-1000**. Main courses C$10–C$24. MC, V. Daily noon–10pm.

Le Café Francais FRENCH   Finding an authentic, family-run, French restaurant on the main drag of Old Town is a refreshing change from the omnipresent Pacific Northwest cuisine, and it's one that really celebrates French food. Menu items include superbly prepared escargot (done in various styles), *baquette* salads, and viand such as *coq au vin,* filet mignon with a cognac cream sauce, and a mouth-watering sole *beuniere*. None of the sauces are overbearing, and save for the snails, most ingredients are fresh from the farm. The decor is slightly homespun (gold lamé table cloths and walls decorated with the fleur-de-lis) but it adds to the restaurant's familial ambiance.

153 Commercial St. © **250/716-7866.** Main courses C$14–$27. MC, V. Tues–Sat 5–10pm

Mahle House PACIFIC NORTHWEST Built in 1904, Mahle (pronounced "Molly") House is a lovingly restored delight overlooking an enclosed English-style garden. This family-owned restaurant has been a local favorite for more than 20 years, and the menu changes weekly. Items may include marinated duck with peanut-crusted prawns and a coconut curry sauce, or free-range chicken stuffed with Dungeness crab and a lemongrass sauce. Everything comes from local suppliers, while the herbs come from the restaurant's own garden. Some evenings include wine tastings. You can come for "Tapas Thursdays"; "Adventurous Wednesdays," featuring a multi-course meal for C$40 (C$64 with wine); and a three-course Sunday dinner for C$35. The wine list is extensive and has been a Gold Medal winner in the Vancouver International Wine Festival.

2104 Hemer Rd., Cedar (10 min. south of Nanaimo). © **250/722-3621.** www.mahlehouse.ca. Reservations recommended. Main courses C$18–C$33. MC, V. Wed–Sun 5–10pm.

Red Martini Grill TAPAS A casual, jazz-style bistro that is a clever conversion of two side-by-side storefronts, where the more light-filled front room is geared for daytime dining (breakfast and lunch), and the moody back-room, aka "The Red Room," is for romantic trysts and live music. The tapas selection is comprehensive enough to suit every taste, with everything from chicken satay and coconut prawns to apricot- and date-stuffed pork tenderloin, all to be savored alongside imaginative martini mixes. There's jazz and blues Tuesday through Saturday (get there by 7:30pm to snag a booth) and an "all jammers welcome" night on Wednesday, which is about as fun and impromptu as music gets. Remember, Nanaimo is Diana Krall's hometown, so you know the area generates talent!

1075 Front St. © **250/753-5181.** www.redmartinigrill.ca. Tapas C$6–C$10; main courses C$12–C$23. AE, MC, V. Mon 11am–3pm; Tues–Fri 11am–midnight; Sat 4pm–midnight.

Wesley Street Restaurant ★ PACIFIC NORTHWEST A small, charming restaurant, dining progresses from a casual lunch of gourmet soups and sandwiches to a more sophisticated dinner menu that may offer roast quail with an exotic mushroom stuffing, a pumpkin seed–crusted rockfish with spot prawn risotto, or a carrot ginger soup sweetened with a dash of honey. The chef is more than willing to adapt menu items to accommodate allergies. Monday through Thursday, there's a three-course dinner for C$30 alongside an enormous wine list featuring many of the better BC labels. Dine inside or, in summer, opt for the flower-covered patio.

321 Wesley St. © **250/753-6057.** www.wesleycafe.com. Main courses lunch C$12–C$21, dinner C$25–C$31. AE, MC, V. Tues–Fri 11:30am–2:30pm; Tues–Sat 5:30–10pm.

Zougla While there's nothing extraordinary about this restaurant, it's a really safe bet for a nice meal. The decor is conservative, and the extensive menu is mainstream, with a nod to the Greek owner-chef. Some might argue the range is overly ambitious, but you can't go wrong with calamari, souvlaki, or the rack of lamb. And the daily sheets are always good value. For lunch, they include burgers, quesadillas, and Greek classics, such as an excellent moussaka. Dinner goes more upscale with steak and lobster, chicken topped with prawns and scallops, and a grilled halibut with a homemade Mediterranean-style sauce.

2021 Estevan Rd. ℭ **250/716-3233.** Reservations recommended. Main courses lunch C$9–C$21, dinner C$21–C$37. MC, V. Mon–Sat 11am–10:30pm; Sun 4–10pm.

GABRIOLA ISLAND

Although only a 20-minute ferry ride from Nanaimo Harbour, **Gabriola Island** (pop. 4,500) feels a world away from the bustle of Vancouver Island. Known as the "Queen of the Gulf Islands," Gabriola provides a little of everything: sandy beaches, kayaking, canoeing, restaurants, artisans' studios and galleries, petroglyphs, and tide pools.

Essentials

GETTING THERE

BC Ferries operates a vehicle and passenger ferry between Gabriola Island and Nanaimo, with crossings leaving almost every hour from 6am to 11pm. Sailing time is 20 minutes. Passage is C$9 adults, C$21 per vehicle, and C$2 per kayak. Bicycles are carried free of charge.

If you're getting to the island by your own boat, you can find moorage, services, and lodging at **Silva Bay Marina** (ℭ **250/247-8662;** www.silvabay.com) and **Pages Marina** (ℭ **250/247-8931;** www.pagesresort.com), where you can buy groceries, fishing licenses, and tackle, as well as rent bicycles, scooters, mopeds, kayaks, and diving gear.

GETTING AROUND

There is no public transit on the island, so most people bring their cars or bikes. If you do decide to come on foot but want to tour, call **Gabriola Taxi** (ℭ **250/247-0049**) or **Gabriola Tours** (ℭ **250/247-9795;** www.gabriolatours.com). Gabriola is an easy island to navigate with a main circular road, appropriately called South Road and North Road, depending on which side of the island you are on, that leads to a number of side trips. If time runs short, take some pastoral roads that cross the island's midsection. Like many of the Gulf Islands, but perhaps more so on Gabriola since its more northerly location has protected it from big-city influences, islanders regard hitchhiking as safe and dependable.

VISITOR INFORMATION

The Island has a first-rate Visitor Information Centre, located at **Folklore Village Centre** (🕾 **250/247-9332;** www.gabriolaisland.org), which is not "folksy" at all, but quite a swish shopping mall housed in the recycled Folklife Pavilion from Expo '86. For whatever reason, cellphone coverage is spotty, at best, on Gabriola.

Exploring the Area

Overall, Gabriola Island has a whimsical atmosphere, best seen when you start counting up the number of tongue-in-cheek wood creations and sculptures scattered all over the island. The artistic center of the island is at **Gabriola Artworks** (575 North Rd.; 🕾 **250/247-7412;** www.gabriolaartworks.com), a two-level, 279-sq.-m (3,003-sq.-ft.) gallery of work by local talent. You can also pick up a studio tour map and travel to various at-home galleries; open hours vary, so this self-drive meander might lead you down the odd garden path. Gabriola is also home to the **Silva Bay Shipyard School** (3200 Silva Bay Rd.; 🕾 **250/247-8809;** www.boatschool.com), Canada's only traditional wooden boat-building school. Visitors are welcome to view works-in-progress every Friday afternoon from 2 to 4pm.

The island's leading natural attraction is the **Malaspina Galleries,** an amazing series of sandstone formations carved by the surf into shapely caves and caverns. Most beaches are protected, providing excellent tidal pools and safe swimming; at **Drumbeg Park,** the sun heats the sandstone rocks enough to dry your towels. Scuba divers also use this area, as it provides shore-based access to nearby **Gabriola Passage.** Other recreational activities include biking and kayaking. Helpful charter contacts include **Silver Blue Charters** (🕾 **250/247-8807,** or 250/755-6150 for the boat phone; www.silverbluecharters.com) for sea-fishing excursions, **Jim's Kayaking** (🕾 **250/247-8335;** www.jimskayaking.com) for rentals and guided paddles, and **Gabriola Cycle & Kayak** (🕾 **250/247-9738;** www.gck.ca) for bike and kayak rentals.

Where to Stay & Dine

Hummingbird Lodge B&B ★★   This lodge is a gorgeously hand-built 465-sq.-m (5,005-sq.-ft.) home, made up of the cedar and alder trees from the area. Rooms are clean and comfortable, decorated with island art. High vaulted ceilings, floor-to-ceiling windows, and over 186 sq. m (2,002 sq. ft.) of open and covered decks help to bring the outdoors in. The sunroom fills with light and is home to a variety of instruments—a piano, guitars, and a banjo (as well as a comprehensive musical CD library)—to strike the right chord. The lodge is private and near to secluded, sandy Whalebone Beach.

R.R. 1 Site 55 C–54, Gabriola Island, BC V0R 1X0. 🕾 **877/551-9383** or 250/247-9300. www.hummingbird lodgebb.com. 3 units. Mid-June to mid-Sept C$129–C$149 double; mid-Sept to mid-Oct & mid-May to mid-June C$119–C$139 double; mid-Oct to mid-May C$99–C$119 double. MC, V. **Amenities:** Lounge; dining room; kitchenette; hot tub. In-room: Hair dryer, no phone, Wi-Fi.

Silva Bay Bar & Grill CASUAL   This is really the only show on the island. Located at the Silva Bay Marina, it's the best place to savor a sunset and to nibble your way through an extensive menu. Many dishes are designed for sharing over an on-tap ale. Primarily a pub-style restaurant, there's also a fully licensed area where families are welcome. Brunch is served every Sunday. In summer, tables extend along the dock overlooking the marina, and there's a BBQ deck for grills and salads.

A Marmot Moment

The Vancouver Island marmot is rarer than even the giant panda. It is found only on Vancouver Island, and its primary habitat, just outside of Nanaimo, is protected by a trust organization. In the mid-1980s, the population was estimated to be over 300 animals; today, the count is half that number, making them one of the rarest and most endangered mammals in the world.

3383 South Rd., in the Silva Bay Resort & Marina. ℂ **250/247-8662.** www.silvabay.com. Main courses C$10–C$22. MC, V. Mon-Sat 11:30am–9pm; Sun 11:30-8pm.

PARKSVILLE & QUALICUM BEACH

There was a time when Parksville and Qualicum Beach were sleepy seaside towns that swelled with family vacationers every summer. Now, that activity happens year-round. Oceanside, as the region is now called, is bursting with development for vacationers—with a whopping 35 resorts, hotels, and motels; nearly 30 B&Bs; and more than 30 vacation rentals—and for the waves of retirees making this golf Mecca their year-round home, not to mention young families finding an affordable alternative to expensive urban neighborhoods. In the past 2 decades, the area's population has nearly tripled and is expected to double again by 2016. The climate doesn't hurt, either. Mild temperatures and the island's lowest annual rainfall have earned it the moniker of Canada's Riviera.

As a consequence, much of Parksville's original park-like attributes have been overtaken by used car lots and motels that now line the highway through town, giving it a strip-mall-like air. It does redeem itself, however, with its expansive beaches—picked by *Better Homes & Gardens* as being among North America's most family-friendly—and waterfront resorts. Once through downtown Parksville, the Oceanside shoreline along Highway 19A opens up vistas to mountains and oceans, lush parks, formal gardens, and quaint shops and galleries. The Oceanside area extends beyond Parksville and Qualicum to include Horne Lake, Bowser, and Deep Bay, all sharing the same stretch of magnificent beach and among them offering activities such as swimming, nature hikes, golf, tennis, and spelunking.

Essentials

GETTING THERE

BY CAR   Parksville and Qualicum Beach are located 36km (22 miles) north of Nanaimo, off Highway 19.

BY BUS   Greyhound Canada (ℂ 800/661-8747) runs between Nanaimo and Parksville/Qualicum Beach along the Highway 1–Highway 19 corridor. One-way fares are C$13 nonrefundable/C$16 refundable for adults. Fares for seniors are 50% less than the adult fare; fares for children 5 to 11 are 25% less than for adults. **Island Link Bus** (ℂ 250/954-8257; www.islandlinkbus.com) also runs a passenger express service between BC Ferries' terminals and Vancouver, Victoria, and Comox airports to Parksville and Qualicum. One-way fares are slightly less than Greyhound, but schedules may not be as convenient.

BY TRAIN   VIA Rail's **Malahat** (✆ **888/842-7245;** www.viarail.com) stops in Parksville and Qualicum Beach on its daily trip from Victoria to Courtenay.

BY AIR   **KD Air** (✆ **800/665-4244,** 604/688-9957, or 250/752-5884; www.kdair.com) offers several daily flights from Vancouver to the Qualicum Beach Airport for C$250 round-trip, with discounts for seniors and children. **Orca Airways** (✆ **888/359-6722** or 604/270-6722; www.flyorcaair.com) also provides service between these two points.

VISITOR INFORMATION

The **Parksville Visitor Information Centre** is at 1275 East Island Hwy. (✆ **250/248-3613;** www.parksvillechamber.com). The **Qualicum Beach Visitor Information Centre** is at 2711 West Island Hwy. (✆ **250/752-9532;** www.qualicum.bc.ca). Another resource for Qualicum is available at www.visitparksvillequalicumbeach.com.

Exploring Parksville & Qualicum Beach

Of the two communities, Parksville is by far the more developed, both in terms of commercial businesses and in its destination resorts (see "Where to Stay," below), all of which have contributed to its Riviera reputation. Although Parksville is a heaven for fast-food junkies, it's being countered with a growing number of superior restaurants and specialty activities. For example, if you're a cheese aficionado, check out **Little Qualicum Cheeseworks** (403 Lowry's Rd., Parksville; ✆ **250/954-3931;** www.cheeseworks.ca). From June to September, there are guided tours and hayrides around the farm, as well as a small gift shop that's open year-round, where you can taste and purchase their artisan cheeses. Although based in Parksville, **Pacific Rainforest Adventure Tours** (215 Chestnut St.; ✆ **250/248-3667;** www.rainforestnaturehikes.com) provides easy walking half-day and full-day sightseeing and nature tours (suitable for seniors) to various destinations in the region, such as **Cathedral Grove; Pacific Rim National Park;** and **Green Mountain,** home to the endangered Vancouver Island marmot. This particular tour takes you by the Nanaimo River through a working forest and requires you to book a year in advance to receive a special permit.

Qualicum lies about 10 minutes north of Parksville, and although it overlooks the same stretch of beach, it is far more genteel. While here, follow the Art Walk to galleries and artisan studios, and browse the shops in the town center, which is actually set a few kilometers from the beach and has a garden-village ambience—perhaps because Qualicum residents are passionate gardeners, having earned their community the coveted Four Blooms Award in a province-wide annual Communities in Bloom competition. Take time to visit the **Old School House** (122 Fern Rd. W.; ✆ **250/752-6133;** www.theoldschoolhouse.org), which exhibits the works of potters, weavers, painters, and other local artists. It also holds frequent workshops, classes, and Sunday afternoon concerts, as well as jazz gatherings on Tuesday evenings.

The Top Attractions

Milner Gardens & Woodland ★★   Once the personal retreat of Queen Elizabeth and Prince Phillip, these princely gardens by the sea are now open to the public. After you've toured the Cotswolds-style house, put on your wellies and get set for a fabulous garden walk through a 4-hectare (10-acre) artist's garden within a 24-hectare (59-acre) old-growth Douglas-fir forest. It's a living laboratory of rare and unusual plants, combining avenues of rhododendrons (more than 500), indigenous plants, and rare and exotic species with towering Douglas firs. The ocean views are breathtaking, but then, you would expect nothing less for royals. Afternoon tea is served, but not included in the price of admission.

2179 W. Island Hwy., Qualicum Beach. © **250/752-6153.** www.milnergardens.org. Admission C$10 adults, C$6 students. May–Sept daily 10am–5pm; Apr & Oct Thurs–Sun 10am–5pm. Closed Nov–Mar.

Paradise Fun Park It's commercial and perhaps overrated, but if you're traveling with young children, it's one of the few places that is a one-stop-shop for activities. These include a miniature golf course with its full-rigged pirate galleon, a treasure cave and water mill, bumper-boat rides (equipped with water canons), and a games pavilion. Kids will want to make a day of it, and as a break from the beach, it serves its purpose. The park also features an RV park and motel.

375 W. Island Hwy., Parksville. © **250/248-6612.** www.paradisefunpark.net. Activities C$5–C$7, combination tickets C$12–$15. Mar to mid-Oct daily 9:30am–dusk. Closed mid Oct–Feb.

Tiger Lily Farm ☺ As a working farm, Tiger Lily is not a fancy place, so be prepared for dirt and mud. Visit with boots and hand-wipes because there are plenty of chicks to cuddle, goats to pet, and a barnyard to explore. Admission includes a free pony ride, as well as petting pigs, calves, turkeys, and gathering eggs. Kids will love the place. Go in the early spring to see the newborn lambs. The farm's location makes it a good stop when paired with a visit to Coombs (perhaps for lunch) or Englishman River Falls.

1692 Errington Rd., Errington. © **250/248-2408.** www.tigerlilyfarm.ca. Admission C$8 adults; C$30 families. Extra pony ride C$3. Mid-Mar to Oct daily 10am–4pm. Closed Nov–mid Mar.

Regional, Provincial & National Parks

Rathtrevor Beach Provincial Park ★★ is a family-oriented park that has nature displays; interpretive walks; and safe, sandy beaches. Contact the park (© **250/248-3198;** www.naturehouse.ca) for program information. For camping opportunities, the undulating sandstone formations on the beach, gentle tides, and forested sites make this one of the most popular areas in the province (see "Camping," below).

How Come Qualicum?

The name Qualicum comes from *squalli*, "chum salmon" in the language of the Pentlatch people who once fished here but were devastated by smallpox in the late 1700s.

Located approximately 5km (3 miles) up Englishman River from Rathtrevor Provincial Park, **Top Bridge** is designated "Mountain Bike Park" and, as one of only three in BC, is extremely popular with bikers from all over the world for its purpose-built trails deep in the forest. Nearby **Englishman River Falls Park** is one of the prettiest parks in the region, with camping, picnic areas, swimming, and easy hiking. There are two spectacular waterfalls in the midst of the forest; during the summer, a crystal-clear pool at the base of the lower falls turns into one of the best swimming holes in the area. Come fall, Englishman River fills with the return of spawning salmon, and throughout the year, the area serves as a protected estuary for more than 250 species of resident and migrating birds.

Just east of Parksville on Highway 4, the **Mt. Arrowsmith Regional Park** offers several moderate to difficult hiking trails from the **Cameron Lake** picnic area. The moderately easy hiking trail up to the 1,818m (5,965-ft.) summit follows, in part, an

TEEING up

There are seven golf courses in the Parksville–Qualicum Beach area and over a dozen within an hour's drive. All have a driving range, clubhouse, and pro shop. From April to October, green fees average C$70 for adults; from November to March, they average C$40 for adults. Twilight rates and discounts for children 18 and under are offered year-round. *Tip:* The greens can be deceptive, but as a general rule, they break toward the ocean.

The **Eaglecrest Golf Club** (2035 Island Hwy., Qualicum Beach; © **250/762-6311;** www.eaglecrestgolfclub.ca) is an 18-hole, par-71 course with an emphasis on shot-making and accuracy.

Fairwinds, just east of Parksville at 3730 Fairwinds Dr., Nanoose Bay (© **888/781-2777** or 250/468-7666; www.fairwinds.bc.ca), is a challenging 18-hole, par-71 course with ocean views and lots of trees.

Pheasant Glen Golf Resort (1025 Qualicum Rd., Qualicum Beach; © **877/407-4653** or 250/752-8786; www.pheasantglen.com) has a 6,628-yard,

par-72 championship-length links-style course; holes 16, 17, and 18 are reputed to be three of the toughest finishing holes in BC.

The long-established **Qualicum Beach Memorial** (469 Memorial Ave., Qualicum Beach; © **250/752-6312;** www.golfqualicum.ca), has 9 holes, stunning ocean views, a pro shop, and a restaurant.

Morningstar Golf Club (525 Lowry's Rd., Parksville; © **800/567-1320** or 250/248-2244; www.morningstar.com) is an 18-hole, par-72 championship course with seaside links and fairways running in and out of the woods.

Arrowsmith Golf and Country Club (2250 Fowler Rd., north of Qualicum Beach; © **250/752-9727;** www.golfarrowsmith.com) is a family-oriented course with 18 holes and a par-61 rating.

Brigadoon Golf Course (359 Martindale Rd., Parksville; © **250/954-0644;** www.brigadoongolfcourse.com is a 9-hole newcomer to the region's burgeoning golf scene. The 1,513-yard, par-3 layout is good for all ages and playing abilities, at fees starting as low as C$15.

old logging railway. The climb passes through a series of climatic zones, each with different vegetation and forest cover. The view from the slopes and high alpine meadows of Mount Arrowsmith overlooks the entire Strait of Georgia. Allow 6 to 7 hours for the round-trip. Or try the well-maintained trails up and down either side of the Little Qualicum River. They involve some stairs and uneven ground, but are good for sure-footed explorers of all ages. For something completely different, consider kayaking out from the Parksville-Qualicum shores to **Jedediah Marine Park,** located between Lasqueti Island and Texada Island in the Sabine Channel of the Strait of Georgia. Accessible only by boat, this recently created park was originally homesteaded in the late 1800s. The island is now inhabited by wild goats and sheep. The island has no amenities, but the settlers' cabins and outbuildings are maintained in their original condition so visitors can see how people lived on the coast before roads and electricity.

If you prefer to stay on land, **Spider Lake Park** is a smaller day-use park on the lake located just off the Horne Lake Road. Stocked with small-mouthed bass and trout, the lake has excellent fishing and a warm, safe, sandy beach to launch kayaks and canoes. No motorized watercraft are allowed, so it attracts swimmers, as well as anglers. Many visitors bypass Spider Lake, however, in favor of Horne Lake Regional

Park that sits at the west end of Horne Lake, adjacent to Horne Lake Caves Provincial Park (see below). This 105-hectare (259-acre) regional park includes about 3km (1¾ miles) of lakefront and another 2km (1¼ miles) of riverfront along the Qualicum River. Offering both wooded (C$20/day) and lakefront (C$24/day) campsites, it's an excellent base for family camping with day-use picnicking and swimming, canoeing, rock climbing, and spelunking activities, as well as evening and day nature programs. Call ✆ **250/927-0053** for camping reservations.

Note: To reach the Horne Lake area from Highway 19, take the Horne Lake Road exit (exit 75) and follow the signs. It's about a 13km (8-mile) drive on a mainly gravel road, which can get deeply rutted after a rainfall. Also, logging trucks use this road 7 days a week, so drive carefully—there are some narrow blind corners.

HORNE LAKE CAVES PROVINCIAL PARK ★★★

This is one of Vancouver Island's best outdoor-adventure destinations. Nestled in the mountains of the Beaufort Range, beside a lakeside park with camping and canoeing, Horne Lake Caves attracts spelunkers for half- or full-day adventures. Getting to the park is a bit of an adventure in itself. Take the **Horne Lake exit** off **Highway 19** (the Island Hwy.) or **Highway 19A,** and follow the signs for 12km (7½ miles). Drive with your headlights on and watch out for logging trucks.

Two caves are open year-round for self-guided tours, although you must bring at least two sources of light, and helmets are recommended. In summer, you can rent these from the **park office.** The park also offers a number of guided tours, catering to everything from easygoing family fun to extreme experiences. The 1½-hour **Family Cavern Tour** is the easiest of these tours and the most popular. It starts with a short uphill hike through the forest to the cave entrance, which leads to beautiful crystal formations and ancient fossils. This tour costs C$21 adults, C$17 children 11 and under. The 3-hour **Spelunking Adventure** is a shade more challenging, involving some tight passages and lots of cave scrambling. It costs C$54 adults, C$45 children 8 to 11. (The minimum age for the Spelunking Adventure is 8 years old.) For real diehards, there's a 5-hour **Extreme Rappel** tour. It includes instruction in basic rock climbing and roping, which you'll need to rappel down a seven-story waterfall known as the "Rainbarrel." Sturdy footwear and warm clothing is a must, although previous climbing experience is not. The tour costs C$149 adults. Two-hour **Outdoor Rappel** clinics are available and strongly recommended for those without recent rappel experience. The clinic cost is C$40 adults. *Note:* You must be 15 years or older, and sign a liability-waiver form to participate in the more extreme tours. Although you might get lucky and find space on one of the many daily Family Cavern Tours, advance reservations are required for all tours, year-round. Call ✆ **250/248-7829** for reservations or visit www.hornelake.com. Check out the new Camping Holiday and Best of Adventure activity packages.

Camping

Located next to 2km (1¼ miles) of sandy shore, Rathtrevor Beach Provincial Park offers 200 forested tent and RV sites, with showers, firewood, a sani-station, and interpretive programs. Reservations are a must; beachfront sites are obviously the hot favorites, but all sites are really well maintained with a natural, surprisingly private, landscape. Most folks are just grateful to be in. There's a 1-week-stay limit and usually a lineup of tenters and RVs in front of the park gate as early as 8am, waiting for cancellations. The early birds are often successful in securing a spot. Alternative camping space is at Englishman River Falls Provincial Park (13km/8 miles from Rathtrevor) and Little Qualicum Falls Provincial Park (24km/15 miles from Rathtrevor). All these parks accept reservations. Rates are C$21 to C$30 per day. Contact Discover Camping (✆ **800/689-9025** for reservations; www.discovercamping.ca). Also, see "Horne Lake Caves Provincial Park," above.

Where to Stay

Beach Acres Resort ★ ☺ Reminiscent of the traditional family resorts of days gone by, this forested, waterfront property entices families to return summer after summer to catch up with old friends and to make new ones. Located on Parksville's Rathtrevor Beach, Beach Acres offers 9 hectares (22 acres) of family fun with a carefree, summer-camp atmosphere. Children's programs include everything from scavenger hunts to sandcastle contests, and there's a supervised indoor swimming pool. While the children have fun, Mom and Dad can relax in the Jacuzzi or challenge each other to a tennis match. Accommodations-wise, there are cottages in a forest setting with country-style furniture, one-and two-bedroom Tudor-style cottages on the beach, or ocean-view town houses that sleep up to six people. All have full kitchens and either gas or wood-burning fireplaces. The resort has a roster of rentals such as high chairs, playpens, and BBQs. Because it's so hyper-busy in summer, try booking the shoulder season (with kids); or low season for a romantic getaway.

25-1015 East Island Hwy., Parksville, BC V9P 2E4. ✆ **800/663-7309** or 250/248-3424. Fax 250/248-6145. www.beach-acres.com. 55 units. June–Sept & holidays C$169–C$415 cottage; Oct–May C$139–C$229 cottage. Midweek, weekly & monthly rates available. 2-night minimum stay July, Aug & holidays. AE, MC, V. **Amenities:** Jacuzzi, large heated indoor pool; sauna; 3 tennis courts. *In room:* TV, fridge, kitchen, Wi-Fi.

Beach Club Resort Walk into any oceanfront suite and be prepared for the "wow" factor, especially if the tide is out. Not only is its location is stunning but, lying on the former site of the once venerable Island Hall hotel, the resort has history too—the Island Hall was prestigious enough to have hosted Queen Elizabeth II as well as Mahesh Yogi, founder of the International Mediation Society. Today this upscale, classy, West Coast–style resort (i.e., lots of wood and windows) incorporates much of the Hall's memorabilia in the main areas, with a rustic decor that brings the outdoors to the inside. The carpets mimic sand, and the custom design drapes, furnishings, and local art have a very chic, beachy feel. Rooms are a mix of spacious studios, as well as one- and two-bedroom suites with full kitchens, laundry facilities, and fireplaces.

181 Beachside Drive, Parksville, BC V9P 2H5. ✆ **888/760-2008** or 250/947-2101. Fax 250/947-2122. www.beachclubbc.com. 149 units. July–Sept C$169–C$269 double; Oct–Feb C$109–C$229 double; Mar–June C$119–C$249 double. Additional adult C$20. Children 16 & under stay free in parent's room. AE, MC, V. Free parking. **Amenities:** Restaurant; bar; fitness center; indoor pool; room service; spa. *In room:* TV, DVD player, fridge, kitchen (some), Wi-Fi.

Blue Willow Guest House Clematis and climbing roses add an English charm to this beautiful B&B, which has replaced the twee lace and chintz-covered furniture of previous years with old-country comfort. Tasteful throw rugs, hardwood floors, leaded-glass windows, and tables piled with interesting books create such a homey ambiance that you feel compelled to scuffle around in socks. The small conservatory is the perfect spot for breakfast. The separate Garden Cottage is the best if you're traveling with children or another couple. It has two bedrooms that share a bathroom, as well as an alcove with a twin bed.

524 Quatna Rd., Qualicum Beach, BC V9K 1B4. ✆ **250/752-9052.** Fax 250/752-9039. www.blue willowguesthouse.com. 3 units. Mid-Apr to mid-Oct C$135–C$145 double; mid-Oct to mid-Apr C$120–C$130 double. Additional adult C$30–C$50. MC, V. **Amenities:** Lounge. *In room:* No phone, Wi-Fi.

Crown Mansion 🏨 In its heyday, this former private home entertained celebrities and royalty. Fully renovated to its original 1930s elegance, the mansion is now a boutique hotel with six large guest rooms. All are superbly furnished with hardwood floors, plush throws and linens, and a hint of Hollywood personality that adds an understated pizzazz. The dining room, where a complimentary continental breakfast is served; central lobby; and a library that's also outfitted as a card-room, are graced with antiques and magnificent fireplaces, one of which is carved with the original family crest. The complex overlooks the the heritage, Qualicum Memorial Golf Course and is adjacent to several forest walking trails.

292 Crescent Rd. E., Qualicum Beach, BC V9K 0A5. ✆ **250/752-5776.** www.crownmansion.com. 6 units. May–Sept C$145–C$195 double; Oct–Apr C$95–C$135 double. Additional adult C$20. MC, V. **Amenities:** Lounge. *In room:* TV/DVD player, iPod dock, Wi-Fi.

Free Spirit Spheres 🏨 Roosting among tree-branches in these one-of-a-kind spheres is this funky, original and surprisingly comfortable treetop inn. The design has been a labor of love as much as anything else, and chances are, once you've climbed the ladder up into these engineering marvels, you'll want an orb of your own in your own backyard. The spheres are compact and although best suited for singles, they are just about roomy enough for two people living cheek-to-cheek. Running water is via a portable canister; light is battery-operated; and pit and flush toilets, and showers are at land level. Feeling the sphere move gently in the wind is like the softness of a lullaby. Pets are welcome but not permitted in orbs which the owners pride in being an allergy free environment.

420 Horne Lake Rd., Qualicum Beach, BC V9K 1Z7. ✆ **250/757-9445.** www.freespiritspheres.com. 3 units. C$125–C$195 per orb; minimum 2 nights in summer. MC, V. Children not accepted. *In room:* No phone.

Pacific Shores Resort and Spa ☺ Adjacent to the Nature Trust Bird Sanctuary and part of the Englishman River Estuary, the resort is set on a landscaped 5.5 hectares (14 acres). There are 102 two-bedroom suites that become studios or one-bedroom suites on demand by opening up or shutting off connecting doors, thereby creating quite a mix of accommodations. Studio suites are like regular hotel rooms; when configured into one- and two-bedroom units, they offer full kitchens, fireplaces, washers/dryers, and all the home-away-from-home amenities you need. The resort is popular with families in summer since child-friendly spaces include a thermally heated outdoor pool, a picnic and BBQ area, and an outdoor playground. **The Aquaterre Spa** provides respite for harried adults; **The Landing West Coast Grill** (see "Where to Dine," below) is worth a visit. Because this complex is a part of the Avia West Vacation Group (✆ **866/986-2222;** www.aviawest.com), you may want to ignore some of the Internet discounts and make your reservations directly with the resort. The discounts often have strings attached, like having to listen to the sales pitch for a timeshare.

1600 Strouler Rd., Nanoose Bay, BC V9P 9B7. ✆ **866/986-2222** or 250/468-7121. Fax 250/468-2001. www.pacific-shores.com. 102 units. July & Aug C$110–C$145 double, C$260–C$345 1- & 2-bedroom suite, C$500 3-bedroom suite; Sept to mid-Oct & mid-Mar to June C$100–C$160 double, C$210–C$270 1- & 2-bedroom suite, C$425 3-bedroom suite; mid-Oct to mid-Mar C$80–C$120 double, C$145–$190 1- & 2-bedroom suite, C$360 3-bedroom suite. AE, MC, V. Free parking. **Amenities:** Restaurant; babysitting; health club; large indoor pool; spa; free kayaks & canoes; Wi-Fi. *In room:* TV/DVD player, fridge, kitchen, Wi-Fi (in some).

Sunrise Ridge Waterfront Resort   As a development that was caught short in the financial crunch, the landscaping isn't all that it could be. But get beyond initial impressions, and the studio, one-, and two-bedroom units are urban-chic with modish furnishings, soaker tubs, luxurious linens, and an abundance of hardwood floors, marble counters, and stainless-steel appliances. Kitchens are classy. Until the hole-in-the-ground is filled with a geothermal pool and a restaurant arrives—all part of the grand plan—the complex will appeal to sophisticated travelers looking for independent, long-term stays. The villas along the water are magnificent. Room rates reflect the resort's unfinished state, so they're a real deal when compared to comparable accommodations. A little negotiation might reap further savings, depending on how fast things move along.

1175 Resort Dr., Parksville, BC V9P 2E3. © **866/812-3224.** www.sunriseridge.ca. 65 units. C$129 double; C$225-C$265 1-2-bedroom suites; C$429 villa. Children 12 & under stay free in parent's room. AE, MC, V. **Amenities**: Lounge. *In room:* TV/DVD player, kitchen, iPod dock, Wi-Fi.

Tigh-Na-Mara Seaside Resort & Spa ★★ ☺   Romantic family getaways might sound like an oxymoron, but not at Tigh-Na-Mara, Gaelic for "the house by the sea." Established in the 1940s on an 11-hectare (27-acre) forested waterfront beach near Rathtrevor Beach Provincial Park, this time-honored resort just keeps getting better. Romantics gravitate here for the Grotto Spa; it's the largest spa in British Columbia and offers a mineral pool and exceptional spa services. Tigh-Na-Mara's range of accommodations means that guests can stay in intimate one- or two-bedroom log cottages in a forest setting, luxuriate in spa bungalows, or splurge on the ocean-view condominiums (many with Jacuzzis). All guest accommodations have fireplaces, and some have kitchen facilities. The three- and four-room cottages can sleep up to eight. Families rave about Tigh-Na-Mara's supervised child-friendly programs as much as for its stunning location. The resort include a newly-renovated lounge and a welcoming cedar-paneled **Cedar Restaurant** (with summer BBQs). For its spa clients, the **Treetops Tapas & Grill** is a huge draw.

1155 Resort Dr., Parksville, BC V9P 2E5. © **800/663-7373** or 250/248-2072. Fax 250/248-4140. www.tigh-na-mara.com. 192 units. July & Aug C$179-C$299 double, suite & bungalow; C$199-C$359 cottage. May, June & Sept C$159-C$259 double, suite & bungalow; C$189-C$309 cottage. Oct-Apr C$129-C$209 double, suite & bungalow; C$169-C$289 cottage. 3- to 7-night minimum stay July & Aug. Seasonal & spa packages available. AE, MC, V. Pets accepted Sept–May (C$30). **Amenities:** 3 restaurants; lounge; babysitting; mountain bike rentals; fitness center; Jacuzzi; heated indoor pool; sauna. *In room:* TV, fridge, kitchen, Wi-Fi.

Where to Dine

Beach House Cafe REGIONAL   Located right at the water's edge, the fully licensed Beach House Cafe is a local favorite, serving good food without a lot of frills. Its bistro-style atmosphere carries through from an easy soup-and-sandwich lunch to a casual, intimate dinner. Some lunch items are repeated at dinner, although in the evening, you'll be treated to house fortes, such as a bouillabaisse loaded with local seafood. Homemade pies, whether savory steak-and-mushroom or sweet rhubarb-and-strawberry, are a must. It's a tiny place that fills up quickly, so if you make reservations, be on time.

2775 W. Island Hwy., Qualicum Beach. © **250/752-9626.** www.beachhousecafe.ca. Reservations recommended on weekends. Main courses lunch C$6-C$13, dinner C$11-C$20. MC, V. Sept–June daily 11am-2:30pm & 5-8:30pm; July & Aug daily 11am-10pm.

Giovanni's Ristorante ITALIAN   It might be small, but for fine Italian dining, the homemade pastas and *vitello picatta* (veal in a white whine and lemon sauce) don't get much better. The white linen clothes, tableware, and intimate atmosphere add to the room's simple elegance. The menu isn't as extensive as some, but with such a strong focus on traditional dishes, whether lightly battered calamari, minestrone (which is hearty enough as a light lunch), or a rack of lamb in a gorgonzola cheese and brandy cream sauce, each is prepared to perfection. The wine list, too, isn't overwhelming and features some better Italian labels. The three-, four-, and five-course table d'hôte menus are always good value at C$30, C$40, and C$50, respectively.

180 2nd Ave. W., Qualicum Beach. © **250/752-6693.** www.giovannisqualicum.com. Reservations recommended. Main courses lunch C$10–C$16, dinner C$18–C$27. MC, V. Mon–Fri 11am–2pm; daily 5–10pm.

Kalvas EUROPEAN   Inside the rustic-looking log cabin is an intimate dining room that locals favor as a special-occasion restaurant. The menu focuses on seafood and traditional German dishes. Consequently, you can't go wrong with sole amandine, the salmon Oscar (poached, topped with shrimp and hollandaise sauce), and wiener schnitzel, which is just about as good as it gets. The menu also has a wide range of steaks and pastas, and an excellent oyster and live crab bar—the latter is simply steamed and served with drawn butter. Be sure to ask for the house-made spaetzles.

180 Molliet St., Parksville. © **250/248-6933.** Reservations recommended. Main courses C$12–C$60. MC, V. Daily 5–10pm.

The Landing West Coast Grill REGIONAL   With so many seaside resorts lining these expansive beaches, it's hard to know which ones, if any, have decent restaurants that are open to the public. This is one of them. Despite an outdoor heated patio, wine bar, and at-your-feet ocean views, it's the 23,000L (6,076-gal.) curvaceous saltwater aquarium wall that will really catch your eye. Food focuses on seafood that is refreshingly simple in its preparation: a tuna dish served with warm tomato vinaigrette, mushroom risotto and grilled halibut with cilantro salsa, as well as local produce such as dry-rubbed, slow-smoked port back ribs; wood-smoked chicken confit; and a good vegetarian selection.

At Pacific Shores, 1600 Stroulger Rd., Nanoose Bay. © **888/640-7799** or 250/468-2400. www.landing grill.com. Main courses lunch C$8–C$18, dinner C$17–C$37. AE, MC, V. Mon–Fri 11am–9pm; Sat & Sun 10am–10pm.

Shady Rest Waterfront Pub & Restaurant CANADIAN   There's been an eatery here since 1924, although today's look neither hints to its heritage nor detracts from the real show—the beachside vistas. With skylights and a wall of windows fronting the beach, this restaurant offers a view to every seat in the house, although in warmer weather, you'll probably prefer a spot on the deck. Open for breakfast, lunch, and dinner, its menu items are no-frill classics such as steak and prawns, fish and chips, stir fries, schnitzels, pasta, and pizzas. It does these well for lunch and dinner, but the evening menu's fancier items are a bit hit-or-miss. Ask your waitress to be honest about the specials to avoid disappointment. Weekend brunches are the winners with various Benedicts (the sauces can be a bit heavy-handed, so ask for these on the side), scrambles, and skillets.

3109 W. Island Hwy., Qualicum Beach. © **250/752-9111.** www.shadyrest.ca. Reservations recommended for dinner. Main courses C$10–C$25. MC, V. Mon–Fri 11am–9pm, Sat & Sun 8am–9pm; pub open Fri & Sat 11am–1am.

HEADING WEST: PORT ALBERNI & BAMFIELD

Jump into your vehicle, hit the accelerator, and begin a memorable voyage from the east to the west side of central Vancouver Island. The trip is about 200km (124 miles) and takes about 3 hours to drive. En route, you'll pass through **Coombs,** a farming community with a good selection of country crafts boutiques. The **Old Country Market ★** (2310 Alberni Hwy.; © 250/248-6272), complete with goats on the roof, is a Kodak moment and a chance to stretch your legs, buy a delicious ice cream, or pick up picnic supplies. There's also an absorbing emporium with teapots, marmalades, imported clothes, and baskets. The market has become such a landmark that an entire landscape has sprouted up in the environs, a haphazard collection of gift and souvenir stores, many of which might be fun to browse. If you can put up with the squawking, drop by the **World Parrot Refuge** (2116 Alberni Hwy.; © **250/248-5194** or 250/951-1166; www.worldparrotrefuge.org) and its sanctuary for more than 400 previously owned parrots. Admission is by donation. The **North Island Wildlife Recovery Association** (1240 Leffler Rd.; © **250/248-8534;** www.niwra.org) is another sanctuary and rehabilitation center in nearby Errington. Admission is C$8 adults.

As you near the west coast, you pass waterfalls beneath a canopy of rainforest. **Port Alberni** is another interesting detour for a quick lunch and a wander, but unless you're taking a trip on the MV *Frances Barkley* (see "Getting There," below) to Bamfield, there's no reason to stay overnight. **Bamfield,** on the other hand, is a diversion that's worth at least a day trip, if not an overnight stay. Reached only by boat (the logging road there is pretty hazardous and very long), this village is built on boardwalks, with lovely coves, homes, and B&Bs tucked into the surrounding inlets.

Essentials

GETTING THERE

BY CAR   From Nanaimo, take the Island Highway (Hwy. 19) 52km (32 miles) north toward Parksville. Just before you hit Parksville, take the turnoff for Highway 4, which leads west to Port Alberni and on to the coastal towns of Tofino and Ucluelet. It's a good idea to leave Nanaimo in the morning to avoid having the afternoon sun in your eyes as you drive west (and to return in the afternoon so that the sun is behind you as you head east). A secondary highway, Highway 4 is narrow in places, as well as winding, slippery, and mountainous. Night driving isn't recommended. If you plan to drive straight through to Tofino or Ucluelet, gas up in Nanaimo and again in Port Alberni. Gas stations are scarce along Highway 4.

BY BUS   **Greyhound Canada** (© **800/661-8747;** www.greyhound.ca) operates regular daily service between Victoria and Tofino-Ucluelet, departing at 8:30am and arriving in Tofino about 1:45pm. The bus stops in Nanaimo to pick up passengers arriving on the Vancouver ferry (the bus station is a 10-minute cab ride from the ferry docks). Fares from Victoria to Tofino are C$67 nonrefundable/C$75 refundable; from Nanaimo to Tofino are C$44 nonrefundable/C$50 refundable; and from Nanaimo to Port Alberni are C$24 nonrefundable/C$28 refundable. **The Tofino Bus Company** (© **866/986-3466;** www.tofinobus.com) also runs a daily service from Vancouver and Victoria to Tofino-Ucluelet. From Vancouver the one-way (hotel-to-hotel) adult fare is C$66 (including ferry crossing); from Victoria, C$64; from Nanaimo, C$42.

Nanaimo to Port Alberni is also C$22. Discounts of about 10% apply to seniors, youths 12 to 17 years, and international hostel members; children 2 to 11 are half price. The Vancouver route will incur a C$3 surcharge for weekend and holiday travel. **Island Link Bus** (C 250/954-8257; www.islandlinkbus.com) runs a passenger express service between BC Ferries' terminals and Vancouver, Victoria, and Comox airports, to Port Alberni at fares that are comparable to the above.

BY TRAIN VIA Rail's **Malahat** (C 888/842-7245; www.viarail.com) stops in Parksville and Qualicum Beach on its daily trip from Victoria to Courtenay.

BY AIR **KD Air** (C 800/665-4244, 604/688-9957, or 250/752-5884; www.kdair.com) offers several daily flights from Vancouver to Port Alberni via Qualicum Airport and then bus transportation, all for C$285 round-trip. One-way fares are C$175, with discounts for seniors and children.

BY FERRY Although a somewhat unconventional ferry, **Lady Rose Marine Services** (5425 Argyle St., C 800/663-7192 or 250/723-8313; www.ladyrosemarine.com) runs the MV *Frances Barkley*, a packet freighter from Port Alberni to different points on the island's west coast, including a trip to Ucluelet. Call for seasonal sailing times and costs.

VISITOR INFORMATION

For more information on Port Alberni, the Alberni Valley Chamber of Commerce runs a **Visitor Information Centre** at 2533 Port Alberni Hwy. (C 250/724-6535; www.avcoc.com).

Exploring the Area

Located midway between Parksville and Port Alberni in MacMillan Provincial Park is the world-renowned **Cathedral Grove.** If you've time, don't simply drive through; take an hour or two to follow the interpretive trail system through the 1,000-year-old forest of Douglas fir, western hemlock, grand fir, and western red cedar. The trees stand so tall you'll feel like you're standing inside of a cathedral; hence the name. This day park gives you a sense of what Vancouver Island and the West Coast looked like before the arrival of European settlers. To see where many trees like these end up, you need look no farther than Port Alberni.

Port Alberni is a hard-working little town of nearly 20,000. Along the waterfront, logs are milled into lumber, pulp, and paper. Smoke from the mills spews up into the low-lying clouds that cling to the surrounding mountains. On a dull day, the entire town is grey with nary a hint of the fabulous views that a sunny day brings. Port Alberni is currently trying to revitalize its rather industrial facade, and its self-professed nickname "Positive Port Alberni" is beginning to show dividends, with sprawling urban development rising up the hill from the water, including two Wal-Mart outlets. A fun way to see the region is to catch the breezy updrafts on a scenic flight offered by the **Vancouver Island Soaring Centre** (C 250/667-3591), which operates out of Port Alberni Regional Airport. Trips start at C$95; add C$50 if your stomach can take aerobatics.

If you need to break the drive to the coast, head down to the redeveloped **Harbour Quay** area at the foot of **Argyle Street,** and you'll find restaurants and gift shops amid the cackle of seagulls and the full-throated honk of ship's horns. There's a **Maritime Discovery Centre** (C 250/723-6164; www.alberniheritage.com) housed in a lighthouse replica at the end of the pier; it tells the story of Port Alberni's seafaring past. Alberni's land-based history is shown at the **Alberni Valley Museum** (4255 Wallace St.; © **250/723-6164;** www.alberniheritage.com), which displays local Nuu Chah Nulth art and pioneer artifacts. Admission to both museums is by donation. And, thanks to money the provincial government gave in 2008 to help celebrate British Columbia's 150th birthday, Port Alberni has created a Spirit Square as a venue for festivals, events, and people gathering. Garden enthusiasts can head for **Rollins Art Centre and Gardens** (3061 8th Ave.; © **250/724-3412;** www. portalberniarts.com), a combination fine-arts gallery and gardens, including a traditional Japanese garden that was a gift from Abashiri, Port Alberni's sister city.

Aviation fans might want to stop at the home of the two remaining **Martin Mars Water Bombers** (www.martinmars.com), the largest water-bombing plane in the world, headquartered at lovely **Sproat Lake** nearby.

In summer, you can head over to the restored Port Alberni **railway station** (built around 1912) and board an antique locomotive for the 35-minute ride up to the McLean Mill National Historic Site. Upon request, the train also makes a stop at the **Case and Warren Estate Winery** (6253 Drinkwater Rd.; © **250/724-4906**) for a tour and tasting. Originally used by the Esquimalt and Nanaimo (E&N) Railway to transport logs and lumber between the mills and the harbor, the fully restored steam train now carries passengers. It operates two rides a day, Thursday through Monday. Call © **250/723-6164** for fares, which include admission to the McLean Mill (see listing below) and schedules.

A truly unique way to experience the area is a day trip with **Lady Rose Marine Services** (© **800/663-7192** Apr–Sept or 250/723-8313; www.ladyrosemarine.com), which operates **MV _Frances Barkley_,** a packet freighter that transports supplies to some of British Columbia's far-flung coastal communities along Barkley Sound and the Alberni Inlet. Passengers observe life aboard a coastal freighter first-hand as it delivers all manner of cargo: from newspapers and groceries bound for general stores to equipment for logging camps—even laundry. For some residents scattered along this coast, the MV _Frances Barkley_ is their only link to civilization. The scenery, of course, is spectacular. Kayakers and canoeists en route to the **Broken Group Islands** take the MV _Frances Barkley_ to a base camp at Sechart. Hikers bound for the **West Coast Trail** and day trippers can catch a ride to **Bamfield,** a picturesque fishing village just north of the trail head (see "A Side Trip to Bamfield," below). In summer, there are also day trips through the Broken Groups Islands to Ucluelet. Wear sensible shoes and bring warm, windproof clothing because the decks are open and weather on the coastal waters can be temperamental. Basic food such as egg-and-bacon sandwiches is available on board in a tiny galley-restaurant. The freighters depart year-round on Tuesday, Thursday, and Saturday at 8am from **Harbour Quay**, returning to Port Alberni at about 5pm. From June through September, there are additional 8am sailings on Monday, Wednesday, and Friday to Ucluelet, via Sechart near the Broken Group Islands, returning to Port Alberni at about 7pm, as well as an extra sailing on Sunday to Bamfield, again via Sechart to drop off/pick up kayakers.

Adult fares to Bamfield are C$34 one-way, C$68 round-trip; to Ucluelet C$37 one-way, C$74 round-trip; and to Sechart C$34 one-way, C$68 round-trip. If you're staying in Ucluelet, the trip to Sechart is a fun excursion at C$50 round-trip. Fares are half-price for children 8 to 15. Children 7 and under ride free. Reservations are required.

Butterfly World and Gardens   It's not quite to the standard of Butterfly Gardens near Victoria, but it's still a worthwhile detour. Outside, the gardens are planted to attract wild native butterflies, while inside are more exotic varieties, as well as a display of creepy-crawly insects (a kid's dream) and an aviary of exotic birds, including multi-colored finches. An Orchid Garden featuring hundreds of orchids from around the world is the largest indoor exhibit of its kind in Canada. Thirty minutes should be sufficient for a visit, longer if you love orchids or have bug-crazy children in tow.

1080 Winchester Rd. ✆ **250/248-7026.** www.nature-world.com. Admission C$11 adults, C$10 seniors, C$6 students, C$5 children 4–12. Mid-Mar to mid-Sept daily 10am–5pm.

McLean Mill National Historic Site   Built in 1926, this is the only family-run steam-driven sawmill in Canada and retains the township qualities it once had. More than 30 buildings include an operational mill, bunkhouse accommodations for the 20-odd millworkers who once worked here, and a schoolhouse for the workers' children, as well as a steam donkey (an antiquated steam engine that powered winches), logging trucks, and lumber carriers. Although operational only in summer, it's a place where visitors are welcome to wander year-round. Located on Smith Road, off Beaver Creek Road, west of Port Alberni, the site is easiest to reach by train (see above). Allow 3½ hours for the entire experience—more if you're a hiker or mountain biker. (The Mill happens to be the hub for a network of trails for hikers and mountain bikers alike.) The best trail is the Log Train Trail, an easy-to-moderate 26km (16-mile) linear trail that travels alongside the historic site.

5633 Smith Rd. ✆ **250/723-1376.** www.alberniheritage.com. Mid-June to Labor Day Thurs–Mon 10:30am–5:15pm; train departs from E&N Station (3100 Kingsway) 10am & 2pm, from McLean Mill 1 & 5:15pm. Admission, including train, C$30 adults, C$22 seniors & youth (13-17), C$15 children 5-12 C$80 families (2 adults & 3 children). Sawmill only, C$10 adults, C$9.50 seniors & youth (13-17), C$5 children 5-12.

Where to Stay

There are a lot of seedy dives in Port Alberni, so if you're staying overnight here, most likely because you're catching an 8am sailing aboard MV *Frances Barkley,* you want to stick to tried-and-true hotels. These two recommendations are standard, each with downtown locations, which offer a comfortable night's rest.

Best Western Barclay Hotel   This is as close to the waterfront as you can get and within walking distance of all its activities. Guest rooms are on the small side, but pleasantly furnished with pleasing blue-toned fabrics and warm woods. Suites have fridges, microwaves, and coffeemakers. The **Stamps Cafe** serves casual fare. If you're looking for something more lively, there are no fewer than 24 TV screens in **Pastimes Sports Bar and Grill.** The steam train stops at the back of the hotel to pick up guests for the ride to McLean Mill.

4277 Stamp Ave., Port Alberni, BC V9Y 7X8. ✆ **800/563-6590** or 250/724-7171. Fax 250/724-9691. www.bestwesternbarclay.com. 86 units. May–Sept C$129–C$199 double; Oct–Apr C$99–C$179 double. Additional adult C$10. Children 17 & under stay free in parent's room. AE, DC, DISC, MC, V. Free parking. Pets accepted (C$10). **Amenities:** Restaurant; pub; sports bar; exercise room; Jacuzzi; small heated outdoor pool (May-Oct); sauna. *In room:* A/C, TV, hair dryer, Wi-Fi.

Coast Hospitality Inn   A cozy fireplace in the lobby welcomes guests to this mock Tudor–style inn that is set away from the waterfront, a few minutes' drive down the hill. There's an upbeat, executive feel to the chocolate-brown and beige decor, and services include all the standard amenities such as fair-size rooms, comfortable beds,

A side trip TO BAMFIELD ★★

With its flowing high street, **Bamfield** (☏ **250/728-3006;** www.bamfield chamber.com) is the Venice of Vancouver Island, and although this isolated community can be reached from Port Alberni via a 102km (63-mile) unpaved road, most people arrive by boat or floatplane (see "Exploring the Area," above). Bamfield's high street is lined with marine suppliers and quirky boardwalks that join weather-beaten houses, stores, and resorts. Crossing the street means hitching a ride with a local boat owner or hailing a water taxi. Day-trippers off the MV *Frances Barkley* have just enough time to roam the boardwalks before the return trip to Port Alberni. Until recently, many buildings crumbled from their owner's neglect. Thankfully, as new owners start to take over there is a movement afoot to restore the historic **Bamfield Inn,** at least, which for the longest time has been the community's only watering hole.

Outdoor enthusiasts tend to linger, using Bamfield as a base for fishing, diving, or kayaking. **Broken Island Adventures** (☏ **888/728-6200** or 250/728-3500; www.brokenislandadventures.com) offers customized diving excursions in Barkley Sound, kayak rentals, and kayak and wildlife-viewing tours. Check out the **Bamfield Marine Sciences Centre** (100 Pachena Rd.; ☏ **250/728-3301;** www.bms.bc.ca), a stellar local attraction

with programs and hands-on displays, as well as a smart presentation venue that in July hosts an annual music festival of some of the world's finest young musicians. There are scenic hiking trails to Brady's Beach, Cape Beale, Pachena Lighthouse, Keeha Beach, and Tapaltos Beach. Hikers heading for the West Coast Trail use Bamfield as a pit stop before or after a week in the rugged coastal wilderness (see "Pacific Rim National Park," later in this chapter). **The Boardwalk Bistro** at Bamfield Lodge (☏ **250/728-3419;** www.bamfieldlodge.com) is a good place for food, though if you prefer to eavesdrop on their harrowing stories of survival, kayakers and hikers tend to gather at the **Tides & Trails Café** (242 Frigate Rd.; ☏ **250/728-3464**) and the **Hawks Nest Pub** (226 Frigate Rd.; ☏ **250/728-3422**). If you just want to get away from it all, **Woods End Landing Cottages** (168 Wild Duck Rd., Bamfield, BC V0R 1B0; ☏ **877/828-3383** or 250/728-3383; www.woodsend.travel.bc.ca) offers comfort and character. **The Great Canadian Adventure Company** (☏ **888/285-1676;** www.adventures.ca) offers an easy hiking tour on remote Tapaltos Beach. It starts with a 2-hour drive along the logging road to Bamfield before you hit the trail for an hour's hike through rainforest to the beach, where you can enjoy a picnic lunch and some beachcombing.

and nothing-to-write-home-about bathroom toiletries. The Inn is as geared to business travelers as it is to families, an arrangement that co-exists since each travel group travels at different times—so when kids want to take a dip in the pool, it's usually not to the chagrin of the corporate guest. There's an on-site liquor store, and the hotel sells fishing licenses. The **Harvest Restaurant's** strong suit is in home-style cooking, while **Polly's Pub** serves a lighter menu and traditional pub fare.

3835 Redford St., Port Alberni, BC V9Y 3S2. ☏ **877/723-8111** or 250/723-8111. Fax 250/723-0088. www.hospitalityinnportalberni.com. 50 units. June–Sept C$119–C$149 double; Oct–May C$99–C$129 double. Additional adult C$10. Family, AAA, senior & seasonal discounts available. AE, DC, MC, V. Free parking. Pets accepted (C$10). **Amenities:** Restaurant; pub; babysitting; exercise room; hot tub; pool; room service. *In room:* A/C, TV, hair dryer, fridge, Wi-Fi.

TOFINO, UCLUELET & PACIFIC RIM NATIONAL PARK

The scenic drive through the center of Vancouver Island is only a taste of what's to come once you reach the wild coast of Western Canada. Here, the Pacific Ocean rollers crash against the shore, beaches stretch for miles, and the mist clings to the rainforest like cobwebs. Most of what you'll see is part of **Pacific Rim National Park.** In winter, you'll witness some of the best storms in the world—as dramatic and angry as a Turner landscape. In summer, families play alongside surfers, kayakers, and others enjoying this Valhalla for outdoor activities. **Tofino** has long been the commercial center of the region and as such, has many services to offer visitors, including a sushi restaurant and decent, albeit small, shops and galleries. Tofino is the gateway to **Clayoquot Sound,** North America's largest remaining expanse of low-elevation old-growth temperate rainforest and a UNESCO World Biosphere Reserve. It's a "living laboratory," where you'll find isolated resorts and cabins clinging to the edge of the wilderness and bears scavenging the shoreline for tasty delicacies, flipping rocks like flapjacks. Unfortunately, Tofino becomes so busy in summer that its popularity is eroding its charm.

For many, the town of **Ucluelet,** 42km (26 miles) away, is a quieter choice. It's a little rougher around the edges, but you can link up with the Wild Pacific Trail and find B&Bs that are truly away from the madding crowd—although judging from new developments such as Black Rock Resort, it's only a matter of time until eco-adventurers and urban escapees start to influence the wilderness here, too. Wherever you decide to stay, to get from A to B, you really do need a set of wheels, or strong legs, to explore the area fully. If driving, be careful. Black bear and deer are common, and at times, the roads can be windy and unexpectedly foggy.

Essentials

GETTING THERE

BY CAR From Port Alberni, continue west on Highway 4 for about 145km (90 miles) to a T-junction. Turn north to Tofino (34km/21 miles), or south to Ucluelet (8km/5 miles).

BY PLANE Orca Airways (© 888/359-6722; www.flyorcaair.com) flies year-round between Vancouver and Tofino; one-way fares are about C$199 adults, with discounts offered on advanced bookings. The airline also offers a Victoria–Tofino schedule during the summer months at C$225 each way. **Tofino Air** (© 866/486-3247 or 250/725-4454; www.tofinoair.ca) provides charters and scenic tours. For both carriers, discounts for seniors and children are 5% to 10% off listed price.

BY BUS Greyhound Canada (© 800/661-8747; www.greyhound.ca) operates regular daily service between Victoria and Tofino-Ucluelet, departing at 8:30am and arriving in Tofino about 2:30pm. The bus stops in Nanaimo and will drop off/pick up at Port Alberni. Fares from Port Alberni to Tofino are C$28 nonrefundable, C$32 refundable adults. **The Tofino Bus Company** (© 866/986-3466; www.tofinobus. com) also runs a daily service from Vancouver and Victoria to Tofino-Ucluelet (see p. 153). From Port Alberni to Tofino single adult fare is C$27, and to Ucluelet it's C$25. The Vancouver route adds a C$3 surcharge for weekend and holiday travel. The company also runs a shuttle service between the two towns for C$10 each way, which includes the Park. In summer, the bus makes four runs per day, which trails off to a once-a-day service October through March. **Island Link Bus** (© **250/954-8257;** www.islandlinkbus.com) runs a passenger express service between BC Ferries' terminals, and Vancouver, Victoria, and Comox airports to Tofino and Ucluelet.

VISITOR INFORMATION

The **Tofino–Long Beach Chamber of Commerce** is located at 1426 Pacific Rim Hwy. (© **250/725-3414;** www.tourismtofino.com); open hours are March through September daily 11am to 5pm. Another good resource is www.gotofino.com. The **Ucluelet Chamber of Commerce** is at the foot of Main Street (© **250/726-4641;** www.uclueletinfo.com or www.ucluelet.com) and is open July to September Monday through Friday 11am to 5pm. **The Pacific Rim Visitor Centre** (© **250/726-4600**), at the junction of Highway 4 and Pacific Rim Highway, is a good stop for an overall orientation to the area, plus a chance to use the washroom after the cross-island drive. Cellphone coverage is usually non-existent crossing the island, and from here on in, reception can still be a hit and miss connection.

Exploring Tofino

Picturesque Tofino, or "Tough City," is a magical combination of old-growth forests, white-sand beaches, and the ever-churning Pacific Ocean. It got its name from a Spanish hydrographer who had a reputation for fights and wild living. But don't let the name's origins scare you. For most of the year, Tofino is a sleepy community. In summer, however, the town explodes into a frenzy, as visitors flock to the Clayoquot Sound Biosphere Reserve and the harbor buzzes with boat charters, whale-watching companies, fishing boats, and seaplanes.

The small high street has a number of junk souvenir shops, as well as several galleries showcasing aboriginal art. If you've time for only one stop, make it Roy Henry Vickers's **Eagle Aerie Gallery** (350 Campbell St.; © **250/725-3235**). As the first First Nations artist with his own gallery in British Columbia, Vickers and his work both inspire and dominate. The carved wooden door makes an impressive

---

ABOUT clayoquot

Clayoquot Sound contains the largest remnant of ancient temperate rainforest in the world. With its fjord-like inlets, protected archipelagos, and shores, the rainforest has a complex ecosystem of intertidal zones, extensive mudflats, giant kelp and eelgrass beds, and strong tidal currents. The rich diversity of its habitat serves an equally diverse population of both marine and terrestrial species such as migrating whales and shorebirds, basking sharks, Dungeness crabs, various shellfish, wild salmon, herring, ground fish, otters and sea lions, black bears, Roosevelt elk, marbled murrelets, cougars, wolves, bald eagles, and red-legged frogs.

The Nuu-chah-nulth people have occupied Clayoquot Sound and much of the west coast of Vancouver Island for the past several millennia. Of the Nuu-chah-nulth Nation, the Ahousaht, Tla-o-qui-aht, and Hesquiaht tribes live in Clayoquot Sound. First Nations make up approximately 50% of the population, primarily residing in the communities of Hot Springs, Opitsaht, Esowista, and Marktosis.

entrance, and the entire gallery feels like a life-revering chapel. First Nations artists carved all woodwork within the gallery; a percentage of sales of certain works is given to First Peoples recovery programs. **The Tofino Botanical Gardens** (1084 Pacific Rim Hwy.; © **250/725-1220;** www.tbgf.org) is a 10-minute drive from downtown Tofino. Wander past garden sculptures on boardwalks and trails that take you through the rainforest to themed clearings, such as a kitchen garden and beds filled with native plants, medicinal herbs, and English and Japanese imports that were introduced to the region by early homesteaders. The gardens are an excellent resource for finding out more about the Clayoquot Sound biosphere. On-site, there's a hostel-style field station for up to 34 guests, mostly as shared accommodations, for those who want to immerse themselves in the eco-experience. Two private rooms are C$85 and C$120 per person; the rest are bunk beds at C$32 per bed, sharing four to a room.

Side Trips from Tofino

An hour's boat ride north of Tofino (even faster by seaplane), **Hot Springs Cove** is the only all-natural thermal hot springs on Vancouver Island. A well-maintained 2km (1¼-mile) boardwalk winds through lush rainforest to the sulfur-scented springs. Wisps of steam rise from water that is 122°F (50°C) at its source and cools as it cascades through a series of pools to the sea. It's a busy place in summer, so if you want to experience the tranquility of the place, get there before 10am.

Just 30 minutes north of Tofino, **Flores Island** is where to find the 32km (20-mile) **Ahousaht Wildside Heritage Trail,** an easy hike through rainforests and along beaches. Nearby **Meares Island,** a 15-minute water-taxi ride from Tofino, is worth seeing both for its beauty and its devastation from clear-cutting. It's the site of many a past tree-hugger-versus-logging-company conflict. **The Big Cedar Trail** is a 3km (1.9-mile) boardwalked path through the forest with a long staircase leading up to the Hanging Garden Tree, said to be 1,500 years old. On **Vargas Island,** the **Ahous Trail** (5km/3.1-mile return) is an old telegraph trail that bisects the island from one magnificent beach to another, taking you through salal, tussocky bog, and hummocks of peat. Many Tofino outfitters offer tours and boat transportation to the islands (see "Outdoor Activities," below, for some recommendations). **Tofino Water Taxi (© 877/726-5485;** www.tofinowatertaxi. com) will get you from point A to point B, including a return shuttle service to Meares Island Big Trees Trail (C$30) and Lone Cone Mountain (C$35), as well as the remote beaches of Vargas Island (C$35). A trip to the hot springs is C$99— go early to avoid the crowds.

The traffic that explores **Clayoquot Sound** rises every year in direct correlation to the rise in people's eco-awareness and desire to experience pristine wilderness before it vanishes forever. Even though this is a UNESCO-protected region, the evidence of logging and clear-cuts lurks behind many a corner, and the cynics believe that it's only a matter of time until lack of resources will demand another look at this designation. Until then, most of the outfitters in Tofino have the Sound on their list of activities, be it for hiking, fishing, kayaking, or boating. But be warned: The myriad islands that are landmarks to locals can easily blur into each other to the untrained eye, so exploring this region is best, and safest, with a guide. Check "Outdoor Activities," below, for ideas.

Exploring Ucluelet

Smaller and less sophisticated than Tofino, Ucluelet (Yew-*kloo*-let) is waking up to the unique magnetism of the surrounding area. It used to be that Ucluelet was Tofino's "ugly little stepsister," but that's changing quickly. This modest little village is working at becoming a year-round resort and tourist destination in its own right. New developments are not only sprucing up the downtown core and harbor—where you'll now find the masts of classic fishing boats bobbing alongside moneyed yachts—but they also promise to boost the town's population from 1,650 to nearly 4,000 over the next decade. Projects either underway or just completed include **Reef Point Cottages** (© **877/726-4425;** www.reefpointcottages.com); **Black Rock Oceanfront Resort** (see "Where to Stay," below); and the incomplete, C$600-million **Wyndansea** oceanfront golf and marina resort which, as one of the largest projects on Vancouver Island, is languishing in the wake of the recession.

The **Wild Pacific Trail** is reason alone to visit Ucluelet. If you're not hardy enough to take on the West Coast Trail, then this is a good bet. The 14km (8.7-mile) trail is being developed in phases and will eventually run along the outer coast to Long Beach at Florencia Bay. The first 2.5km (1.6 miles) is a loop that leads along the coastline from **Amphitrite Point** and its **lighthouse** overlooking Barkley Sound to the Broken Group Islands. In winter, storm-watchers come to this headland to see it pounded by 9m (30-ft.) waves, and in March, this is *the* place to gather to watch the annual migration of the gray whales. Boardwalks lead you through rainforest to bluffs high above the ocean, where trees, beaten back by the wind, grow at 90-degree angles. It's an easy path that gets you close to the fury of winter waves or the splendor of summer sunsets. Another section (6km/3.7 miles) has been completed from Big Beach Park to the bike path just outside of Ucluelet. It's a mix of boardwalks, stairs, and gravel paths that follows the edge of the forest. The final section will extend the trail to Halfmoon Bay in Pacific Rim National Park. From there, you'll be able to pick up the Willowbrae Trail, a 2.8km (1.7-mile) loop trail that traces a portion of the pioneer route linking Ucluelet and Tofino. Access to this hike begins from a small gravel lane marked Willowbrae Road, 2km (1¼ miles) south of the Ucluelet-Tofino junction.

Attractions

Ucluelet Mini Aquarium ★ 🎁 Housed in a converted container, this mini public aquarium is likely the world's smallest. Displays are gathered from the surrounding waters and put together with imagination, creativity, and an eye to encourage touching, stroking, ogling, and questioning of the ever-enthusiastic student marine biologists in attendance. The presentations are as captivating as they are informative; did you know an octopus has three hearts, or that a sea star can travel 3kmph (1¾ mph) on its 10,000 feet? It's the West Coast ocean under a microscope, all of which is returned to the sea in the fall. This is a winner for kids and will charm curious adults, too. Fund-raising plans are in the works to create a permanent (and therefore year-round) center complete with green roof, geo-thermal pumps, and beachside tidal gardens.

Main St. at Waterfront Promenade (near Whisky dock). © **604/987-6992.** www.ucluquetaquarium.org. Admission C$5 adults. May–Oct daily 10am–6pm.

Outdoor Activities

BIRDING

With the rapidly aging baby-boomer generation, less strenuous pursuits like bird-watching have garnered an enthusiastic following. **Just Birding** (© **250/725-2520**; www.justbirding.com) provides guided birding tours for novice and expert birders (sometimes called "twitchers"). Tours are year-round and range from early-bird, half-day excursions to shorebird walks, full-day paddles with eagles, and mountain birding. Rates vary depending on the tour, but they start at C$100. The annual Shorebird Festival, in late April, is a big draw.

BIKING

Biking along the flat stretch of paved road that connects Tofino, the Pacific Rim National Park Reserve, and Ucluelet, is an easy and scenic 42km (26-mile) ride. Rent bikes in Tofino at **Eco Everything**, 150 4th St., (© **250/725-2193**). In Ucluelet, from **Ukee Bikes**, 1559 Imperial Lane, (© **250/726-2453**). If you're a runner, check out the annual marathon at www.edgetoedgemarathon.com.

FISHING

Tofino and Ucluelet are at the heart of the region's commercial fishing industry, and you'll find a number of sport-fishing charters in both marinas. The main hooks are salmon, steelhead, rainbow trout, Dolly Varden char, halibut, snapper, and cod. **Jay's Clayoquot Ventures** (561 Campbell St.; © **888/534-7422** or 250/725-2700; www.tofinofishing.com) is an experienced and reputable company that organizes fishing charters throughout Clayoquot Sound—both deep-sea and freshwater excursions. Saltwater fly-fishing trips start at C$115 per hour for a 5-hour minimum and include equipment and flies. **Lance's Sportfishing Adventures** (120 4th St.; © **888/725-6125** or 250/725-2569; www.fishtofino.com) combines fishing trips aboard 7.3m (24-ft.) off-shore vessels with a visit to Hot Springs—the advantage being you'll enjoy the springs before the crowds. Rates are C$110 per hour for a 6-hour minimum and include all gear. This outfitter also packages overnight deals with **Weigh West Marine Resort** (www.weighwest.com). In Ucluelet, **Roanne Sea Adventures** (© **250/726-4494**; www.roanne.ca) or **Long Beach Charters** (© **877/726-2878**; www.longbeachcharters.com) are respected outfitters with competitive rates that average C$600 per 7-hour trip.

HIKING

Tlaook Cultural Adventures (© **877/942-2663** or 250/725-2656; www.tlaook.com) offer guided hikes and walks for a variety of fitness levels, including boat trips to nearby islands. Led by First Nations guides, trips include cultural teachings, history, storytelling, identification of rainforest "medicines," and tide pool exploration. Rates are C$50 per hour. A full program of guided beach and rainforest walks, land-based whale-watching tours, and storm-watching hikes are available through **Oceans Edge** (855 Barkley Crescent, Ucluelet; © **250/726-7099**; www.oceansedge.bc.ca). All excursions are 3 to 6 hours over moderate terrain, and prices vary according to activity; budget around the C$225 mark for a half-day tour. Book well in advance or just hope for cancellation when you arrive. Other star hikes include the 3.5km (2.2-mile) **Gold Mine Trail** near Florencia Bay, so called for its gold-mining heritage; the partially boardwalked **South Beach Trail** (about 1.5km/.9 mile); and the even shorter **Schooner Beach Trail**, both of which take you through rainforest before opening up onto sandy beaches.

KAYAKING

Kayaking through Clayoquot Sound is one of the most intimate ways to experience its history, serenity, and natural beauty. The trick is to find an outfitter who can enrich the experience beyond just a paddle. The owners of **Rainforest Kayak Adventures** (© 877/422-WILD [877/422-9453]; www.rainforestkayak.com) helped set the benchmark for sea-kayak instruction in BC more than 20 years ago and have been guiding the area for almost as long. These are the folks to see if you're looking to become a guide or instructor yourself (C$685 to C$1,1550 and up). The **Tofino Sea-Kayaking Company** (320 Main St.; © 800/863-4664 or 250/725-4222; www.tofino-kayaking.com) also offers guided tours, ranging from a 2½-hour paddle at C$60 to all-day excursions at C$135, as well as daily rentals (C$40 single and C$74 double). **Remote Passages** (© 800/666-9833; www.remotepassages.com) leads guided kayaking to Meares Island (2½ hours at C$64) and to Clayoquot (4 hours at C$79). If you're based in Ucluelet, **Majestic Ocean Kayaking** (1167 Helen Rd., Ucluelet; © 800/889-7644 or 250/726-2868; www.oceankayaking.com) might be more convenient. They have a range of ecotourism adventures to Barkley Sound, Pacific Rim National Park, and Deer Group Islands. Prices start at C$60 for a 3-hour paddle around Ucluelet Harbour to a full-day trip to Broken Group Islands (including cruiser transport there) at C$235 adults. All-inclusive, multi-day wilderness camping and overnight trips to Vargas Island and others around Clayoquot Sound start at C$250 per day adults. For a blended paddle of environment and authentic First Nations culture, travel with **Tla-ook Cultural Adventures** (© 877/942-2663 or 250/725-2656; www.tlaook.com), where Nuu-chah-nulth First Nations guides take you aboard stylized dugout canoes, sharing their deep-rooted cultural history of the area and weaving in stories of aboriginal folklore (C$55 for 2½ hours; C$74 for 4 hours).

SURFING

The heavy, constant rollers of the Pacific Ocean against wide expanses of beach have made this one of the world's hot spots for surfing. Whether beginner or experienced, you'll find outfitters to help you catch the wave, year-round. **Live to Surf** (1180 Pacific Rim Hwy.; © 250/725-4463; www.livetosurf.com) is Tofino's original surf shop and offers rentals of boards and wetsuits, as well as daily surf lessons through its Westside Surf School (© 250/725-2404). Two-hour lessons include all the gear (wetsuit, booties, gloves, and board) and cost C$100 adults, with longer lessons offered for experienced and ultra-fit surfers. **Pacific Surf School** (440 Campbell St.; © 888/777-9961 or 250/725-2155; www.pacificsurfschool.com) holds 3-hour lessons (C$79) and provides private tutoring (C$135); and **Surf Sister** (625 Campbell St.; © 877/724-SURF [7873] or 250/725-4456; www.surfsister.com) is, as the name suggests, geared to women, with its mother-daughter camps and yoga surf retreats (C$75 includes a surfboard and C$65 if you have your own board). **Inner Rhythm Surf Camp** (© 877/393-SURF [877/393-7873]; www.innerrhythm.ca) and **Relic Surf** (© 250/726-4421; www.relicsurfshop.com) are based in Ucluelet, and each offers 2-hour winter sessions at C$69 adults, 3-hour summer sessions at C$79.

WHALE-WATCHING

Operating out of Tofino and Ucluelet, **Jamie's Whaling Station** (606 Campbell St., Tofino; © 800/667-9913 or 250/725-3919; 168 Fraser Lane, Ucluelet; © 877/726-7444 or 250/726-7444; www.jamies.com) is a pioneer of the adventure business. It's

A Lot of Lions

More than 2,400 Stellers and California sea lions congregate in Barkley Sound.

been around since 1982 and has evolved a full roster of whale-watching, bear-watching, and other wildlife tours. Venture out in 12-passenger Zodiacs— C$79 adults, C$65 children 4-12 years—or in the comfort of a 65-foot vessel—C$99 adults, C$65 children 4-12 years—complete with snack bar, inside heated seating, and washrooms. A C$2 surcharge is added, contributing to local wildlife research and rescue programs, and the local bird hospital. *Note:* Jamie's also has a 35-foot cabin cruiser for the 1¼-hour boat ride up to Hot Springs Cove, where you can soak up the waters for a couple of hours before the return trip, either by boat or by seaplane. The boat has space for sea kayaks. **Ocean Outfitters** (368 Main St., Tofino; ✆ 877/906-2326 or 250/725-2866; www. oceanoutfitters.bc.ca) is another popular option, also featuring Zodiac and family-travel vessels. In Ucluelet, **Archipelago Cruises** (Whiskey Landing Wharf, ✆ 250/726-8289) operates a 16m (53-ft.) Canoe Cove motor yacht; come rain or shine, cruising on the yacht includes sights, as well as a glass of champagne.

Pacific Rim National Park ★★★

Designated a national park in 1970 to protect the significant coastal environment, Pacific Rim National Park presents outstanding examples of coastal rainforest, surf-swept beaches, marine life, and the cultural history of the area's settlement. Composed of three "units," or sections, the **West Coast Trail Unit,** the **Long Beach Unit,** and the **Broken Group Islands,** the park spans 130km (81 miles) of shoreline. You access each unit via a different route. The variety of activities and level of services offered in each unit varies. The Long Beach Unit is the most accessible—a good choice for families and visitors who want to take it a little easier, whereas the West Coast Trail Unit is for no-nonsense hikers with nothing but trekking in mind. Contact the **Pacific Rim National Park Reserve** (P.O. Box 280, Ucluelet, BC V0R 3A0; ✆ 250/726-3500; www.pc.gc.ca) for information.

WEST COAST TRAIL UNIT

The West Coast Trail is billed as one of the most grueling treks in North America. And when you see experienced backpackers stagger out of its wilderness, muddy, bedraggled, and exhausted, you might think even that is an understatement. This once-in-a-lifetime wilderness adventure attracts 8,000 hikers each year to do battle with the 77km (48-mile) trail between **Port Renfrew** and **Bamfield** along the southwestern coast of Vancouver Island, known as the "graveyard of the Pacific" because of the numerous shipwrecks along the coast. The trail was originally cleared at the start of the 20th century as a lifesaving rail for shipwrecked mariners. It was upgraded in the 1970s, but trekking it still requires much experience, stamina, and strength. At any point on the trail, you may need to balance yourself on a fallen log to cross a deep gully, negotiate steep slopes, climb and descend ladders 25m (82 ft.) at a time, or wade thigh-deep across a river. In fact, hell on the WCT corresponds directly to rain, which can drop 15 centimeters (6 in.) in just 12 hours, turning the trail to mud. More than 100 people are evacuated from the trail every year; one of the main reasons is hypothermia. Bring painkillers and guards for ankle sprains, and be prepared to take a *minimum* of 5 days to complete the trail end to end.

Tip: If you're not up to the entire challenge, consider taking on the far more accessible 11km (6.8-mile) oceanfront stretch at the trail head near Bamfield. You'll still need your wits (and survival gear) about you, but at least you'll be able to wear the West Coast Trail badge of honor—or part of it, anyway! For peace of mind, such as is possible on this trail, you may prefer to spend the extra money and go with an experienced outfitter such as **Sea to Sky Expeditions** (*©* **800/900-8735** or 604/594-7701; www.seatoskyexpeditions.com), which offers 9-day guides through the West Coast Trail, starting at C$1,599, and an 8-day hike exploring a part of the Clayoquot region where, from a remote clearing in the rainforest, Annie Rae-Arthur ran a nursery garden and shipped plants across Canada. She was nicknamed Cougar Annie for her handiness with a rifle in defending her lonely lifestyle from hungry cougars.

Booking Your Hike

The West Coast Trail is open to hikers from May 1 to September 30. You should reserve up to 3 months ahead, since only 52 hikers are allowed to enter the trail a day: 26 from Bamfield, 26 from Port Renfrew. To reserve, contact **Tourism British Columbia** (*©* **800/HELLOBC** [800/435-5622], 250/387-1642 for international callers, or 604/435-5622; www.hellobc.com). There is a nonrefundable booking fee of C$25 (per hiker) and a C$129 hiking fee, both payable at time of booking. You also need to register at the park office before you set out, and be at the trail head by noon or lose your spot. For more information on weather conditions and last-minute options only, call the park's offices (*©* **250/647-5434** for hikers departing from Port Renfrew or *©* **250/728-3234** for hikers departing from Bamfield). *Note:* In high season, you may have to wait for up to 3 days, but there are six standby slots per day, filled on a first-come, first-served basis. Wait-list openings are at each trail head—Gordon River at the south end and Pachena Bay at the north end.

BROKEN GROUP ISLANDS

Made up of more than 100 rocky islands and islets in **Barkley Sound,** the Broken Group Islands can be reached only by boat. Amidst this pristine archipelago, eagles, sea lions, and marine life abound, and tide pools and dozens of sandy cove beaches lure nature enthusiasts, photographers, and boating sightseers. Chartered boats, guided tours, and transport for campers and kayakers can be booked in Bamfield, Tofino, and Ucluelet, or, you can arrive via the MV *Frances Barkley* (see "Exploring the Area," in "Heading West: Port Alberni & Bamfield," earlier in this chapter).

Only experienced boaters, canoeists, and kayakers should consider an expedition to this unit. Waters are studded with reefs, and visibility is often obscured by heavy fog. The weather in the channels that separate the islands can also be extremely variable. The most popular islands include Turtle and Effingham islands, as well as those eight islands designated for camping: Gibralter, Hand, Turret, Dodd, Willis, Clark, Benson, and Gilbert islands. In July and August, you can expect to share these sites with many other campers, all seeking the authentic back-country wilderness experience. Other than pit toilets, there are no facilities. Bring your own water. Call the **Pacific Rim National Park** offices for details and reservations at *©* **877/737-3783** or visit www.pccamping.ca.

LONG BEACH UNIT

Located between Tofino and Ucluelet, the Long Beach Unit is the most accessible and most developed component of the park. Named for its 20km (12-mile) stretch of

The only place you can camp on Long Beach is the forested bluff at **Green Point** (℃ 877/737-3783; www.pccamping.ca), which has 20 walk-in campsites. Access down to the beach is quite steep. There's an indoor theater with nightly interpretive programs and a real sense of camaraderie among campers. This is a busy family spot in high season; if you're looking for quieter times, book in June or September. The campsite is open mid-March to mid-October; walk-in sites cost C$23. There are flush toilets, but no showers or hookups. Expect to be wait-listed for up to 2 days in July and August.

surf-swept sand, Long Beach offers outstanding beaches, surfing, and more. Open year-round, the area offers nine hiking trails, each between 1 and 3.5km long (.6–2.2 miles), and most of them are boardwalk-surfaced and wheelchair accessible. Star hikes include the 2.8-km (1.7-mile) round-trip **Willowbrae Trail,** just south of Tofino at the Ucluelet junction. It leads down some very steep stairs and ramps to either **Half Moon Bay** (the most romantic cove on the Long Beach stretch) or Florencia Bay. The partially boardwalked **South Beach Trail** (about a 1.5km/.9-mile round-trip) and the shorter **Schooner Beach Trail** both take you through rainforest before opening up onto sandy beaches. **Radar Hill,** formerly cellared for a radar installation during World War II, is the only elevated hike from which to see panoramas of Clayoquot Sound. It claims to be the wettest spot on Vancouver Island. *Note:* Storm action can wash trails out or render them temporarily inaccessible, so it's always best to check with the **Wickaninnish Beach & Interpretive Centre** (℃ 250/726-4212) at the south end of Long Beach. It has a marine interpretive center and provides information on park programs, activities, and events.

Where to Stay

IN TOFINO/CLAYOQUOT SOUND

Cable Cove Inn ★ You'll find an exotic Ayurvedic flair to this inn and the first Ayucare Spa Centre in North America, a prototype for others opening in Whistler; South Africa; and Holland. Ayurveda is an approach to health that has been practiced in India for 5,000 years. That said, Cable Cove is certainly no ashram, and you don't have to be a yogi to enjoy the inn's creature comforts. The seven suites, which feature comfortable queen-size beds, fireplaces, and decks with views, include beautiful Indian silks, rugs, and upscale linens. The spa treatments are exceptional, as is the private dining experience, both for the West Coast–style food and for its location overlooking the cove. Dinner for two people is C$150 (three courses) or C$175 (five courses). There's a shared TV lounge with a fully stocked kitchen and telephone. Laundry facilities are also available. Cable Cove is located within a 5-minute walk of downtown Tofino.

201 Main St. (P.O. Box 339), Tofino, BC V0R 2Z0. ℃ **800/663-6449** or 250/725-4236. Fax 250/725-2857. www.cablecoveinn.com. 7 units. Mid-June to Sept C$225–C$340 double; Mar to mid-June & Oct C$170–C$245 double; Nov–Feb C$150–C$225 double. Rates include breakfast. AE, MC, V. Children 15 and under not accepted. **Amenities:** Lounge; sauna; spa. *In room:* Hair dryer, no phone, Wi-Fi.

Clayoquot Wilderness Resort ★★★ "Glamping" (glamorous camping) was invented here, beneath canvas accommodations that are geared to tender-footed eco-adventurers and seekers of a one-of-a-kind experience. Reached either by floatplane or 25-minute boat ride out of Tofino, the resort's splendid isolation means at night, the darkness is blacker than ebony, the stars brighter than diamonds, and the silence deliciously deafening. Nestled on wooden platforms in the trees, the Rockefeller-style safari sites are all opulently furnished with antiques, handmade furniture, Persian rugs, four-poster beds topped with down duvets, and freestanding propane and wood stoves. The cuisine is spectacular, as is the wine list, from pancakes made with freshly picked blueberries to alder-smoked grilled salmon over wild greens, or four-peppercorn-crusted tenderloin medallions in the evening. Stays are sold only as all-inclusive, multi-night packages. Trails around the resort invite mountain biking and horseback riding. Other activities include a trip to Hot Springs Cove as well as kayaking, fishing, and wildlife-viewing excursions. Prices include a 3% sustainability fee, which also covers an environmental legacy program for habitat restoration and wildlife studies. Everything about this resort is as green as you will find, from innovative compostable plastics made from corn and potato to its own sustainable run-by-the-river hydropower generator. This is the place to visit if you're looking for cocktail-party bragging rights.

Bedwell River, Clayoquot Sound (P.O. Box 728,) Tofino, BC V0R 2Z0. (✆) **888/333-5405** or 250/725-2688. Fax 250/725-2689. www.wildretreat.com. 21 outpost tents. Mid-May to Sept C$4,750–C$11,000 3-, 4- & 7-night stays. Rates include 3 meals/day, plus transport to & from Tofino. AE, MC, V. Parking in Tofino. **Amenities:** Restaurant; lounge; bike rental; hot tubs; spa; kayak rentals; free canoes; Wi-Fi. *In room:* Hair dryer, no phone.

Inn at Tough City 🏨
Take a close look, and you'll see this inn for what it is—a recycled treasure, and one of the quirkiest small inns in downtown Tofino. Constructed with over 45,000 recycled bricks, refurbished hardwood floors, and original stained-glass windows from as far away as Scotland, the Inn at Tough City is a find. You've got to love the vintage collection of advertising signs and old tins. All guest rooms have their own color scheme, accented with stained glass and antique furniture. They also have decks or balconies with water views, though room nos. 3 and 6 have only peek-a-boo ones. The upstairs guest rooms have fireplaces. All have custom-made bed linens in soft, environment-friendly, unbleached cotton. The inn doesn't provide breakfast but does have the only authentic sushi restaurant in town (see "Where to Dine," later in this chapter).

350 Main St. (P.O. Box 8), Tofino, BC V0R 2Z0. (✆) **250/725-2021.** Fax 250/725-2088. www.toughcity. com. 8 units. July–Sept C$179–C$229 double; Oct, Nov & Mar–June C$109–C$179 double. Closed Dec–Feb. AE, MC, V. **Amenities:** Restaurant; lounge. *In room:* TV, hair dryer.

Long Beach Lodge Resort ★★
This upscale resort lies on the beach at Cox Bay, between Pacific Rim National Park and Clayoquot Sound. Set among towering trees and taking full advantage of the rugged coastline and sandy beach, the cedar-shingled lodge rivals the Wickaninnish Inn (reviewed below) for views and service that here rates two staff for every three guests. The welcoming Great Room—with its dramatic First Nations art, oversize granite fireplace, and deep armchairs—is an ideal spot to relax overlooking the bay and sample the chef's daily, fresh, and organic creations for lunch, dinner, or as shared plates of hors d'oeuvres. Accommodations include 41 beachfront lodge rooms with oversize beds, fireplaces, Jacuzzis or extra-deep-soaker bathtubs, and private balconies, as well as 20 two-bedroom cottages nestled in the rainforest. Surfers opt for the ground floor, beachfront rooms that

literally put the rollers on their doorstep. Rain gear is provided to guests who want to venture forth into the storms. Rates include a buffet breakfast.

1441 Pacific Rim Hwy., Tofino, BC V0R 2Z0. ✆ **877/844-7873** or 250/725-2442. www.longbeachlodge resort.com. 61 units. Mid-Oct to mid-Mar C$159–C$249 double, C$269 cottage, C$469 suite; mid-Mar to May C$189–C$289 double, C$319 cottage, C$469 suite; Jun to mid-Oct C$289–C$389 double, C$489 cottage, C$579 suite; year-round C$629 penthouse. Rates include continental breakfast buffet. Additional adult C$30. Children 6–15 C$15 extra. AE, MC, V. Pets accepted (C$50). **Amenities:** Restaurant; lounge; oceanfront health club. *In room:* Hair dryer.

Middle Beach Lodge   Set among tall hemlocks with a steep slope down to a private beach, the rustic ambience of Middle Beach makes it less pretentious than some of the area's other resorts. Perhaps it's because much of the complex was built with recycled lumber, so it has a weathered appeal. There are various accommodations styles, including standard lodge rooms, suites, and self-contained cabins, one of which can sleep six. Of the entire complex, only two cabins are geared for families. Rooms are priced accordingly to what they offer: Some have no phones and ocean views; others have balconies and fireplaces, and still others have full kitchens and Jacuzzis. Room no. 26 is the most romantic with its king-size bed, kitchenette, and oceanfront location. The high-beamed restaurant and lounge overlook the ocean, serving up a menu of tasty standards such as salmon, steak, and pasta. Although it's open daily for breakfast and dinner during high season, open hours are sporadic in the winter. Some cabins close in winter.

400 MacKenzie Beach Rd., (P.O. Box 100), Tofino, BC V0R 2Z0. ✆ **866/725-2900** or 250/725-2900. Fax 250/725-2901. www.middlebeach.com. 45 rooms, 19 cabins. Mid-June to Sept C$140–C$230 double, C$170–C$450 suite & cabin; Oct to mid-June C$110–C$170 double, C$160–C$335 suite & cabin. 2-night minimum stay. Surf, whale-watching & kayak packages available. AE, MC, V. **Amenities:** Restaurant; lounge; exercise room; Wi-Fi. *In room:* TV/VCR/DVD player (in suite & cabin), fridge, kitchenette, no phone.

Pacific Sands Resort ★   This resort nudges against Pacific Rim National Park; white-sand beaches, islands, and old-growth rainforests are at your doorstep. The sound of the surf, although sometimes tumultuous, sets a metronome-like tranquility for sleep. Accommodations range from one- and two-bedroom suites to oceanfront cottages, all with kitchens, fireplaces, balconies, and spectacular views. Some have Jacuzzis. The newer two- and three-bedroom villas have an open floor plan and West Coast decor, including heated slate floors and deeper soaker tubs. They're especially suited for families or couples traveling together. Complimentary rain gear lets guests ignore the weather and ocean spray, and get outside. A mini-store sells the basics so you can shop for quick solutions such as pizza, milk, and eggs.

1421 Pacific Rim Highway, Cox Bay, Tofino, BC V0R 2Z0. ✆ **800/565-2322** or 250/725-2322. Fax 250/725-3155. www.pacificsands.com. 77 units. July–Sept C$325–C$375 studios & cottages; C$355-$415 2-bedrooms; C$610-C$730 villas; Oct–Jun C$205–C$275 studios & cottages; C$270-C$330 2 bedrooms; C$420-475 villas. Seasonal discounts available. AE, MC, V. **Amenities:** Bike rental; Wi-Fi. *In room:* TV.

Wickaninnish Inn ★★★   Perched on a rocky promontory overlooking Chesterman Beach, between old-growth forest and the Pacific Ocean, this Relais & Châteaux inn continues to set and refresh the standard by which other fine hoteliers seem to judge themselves. It describes itself as rustically elegant, which translates into handmade driftwood furniture; local artwork in every room, alongside fireplaces, big-screen TVs, richly textured linens and furnishings, and en suite bathrooms with double soakers; and all with breathtaking views of the ocean. The corner suites have an additional wall of windows that seems to beckon the outside in. Adjacent to the original lodge is the **Wickaninnish on the Beach,** with even more luxurious two-level guest suites and a health club.

In summer, the sprawling sands of Chesterman Beach are littered with sandcastles, tidal pools, and sun worshippers. In winter, it's quite a different story. As thundering waves, howling winds, and sheets of rain lash up against the inn's cedar siding, storm-watching becomes an art. Every guest room provides grandstand views through triple-glazed, floor-to-ceiling windows. The result is a surreal feeling of being enveloped by a storm in virtual silence, especially when snuggled up in front of the fire. Rain gear is provided for those brave souls who want to take on the elements first-hand. The **Ancient Cedars Spa** will mellow your mood, especially since each treatment begins with an aromatic footbath; the private massage hut on the rocks rocks. Cuisine is another one of the inn's draws. Reservations at the **Pointe Restaurant** (see "Where to Dine," below) are sought after, so be sure to make them when you book your room.

Osprey Lane at Chesterman Beach (P.O. Box 250), Tofino, BC V0R 2Z0. ℭ **800/333-4604** or 250/725-3300. Fax 250/725-3110. www.wickinn.com. 75 units. June–Sept C$420–C$580 double, C$540–C$620

camping IN TOFINO & UCLUELET

Crystal Cove Beach Resort (Mackenzie Beach [P.O. Box 559], Tofino BC V0R 2Z0; ℭ **250/725-4213;** www.crystalcove beachresort.com) has 76 RV and tent campsites, all with fire pits and a picnic table. Flush toilets, free hot showers, and laundry facilities are in a clean, modern, Wi-Fi–wired building. Full and partial hookups, sewer and water outlets, and a sani-station are also available. There are also 34 private log cabins with full kitchens, wood-burning fireplaces; decks with barbecues; and some with private hot tubs. Open year round. Sites are C$55, serviced C$62 (high season) and cabins range from C$290 to C$410. Off-season rates are available.

Bella Pacifica (400 MacKenzie Beach [P.O. Box 413], Tofino, BC V0R 2Z0; ℭ **250/725-3400;** www.bellapacifica. com) is another sought-after, year-round campsite offering 170 private sites nestled amid the trees, including a separate area for motor homes, and all with picnic tables, hook-ups, and outlets. The showers are coin-operated, so bring a

supply of loonies. Book in October if you're hoping to secure one of the 18 virtually on-the-beach sites. Rates for these are C$48 in peak season, while the others range between C$38 and C$46, depending on site location. Rates drop by as much as 40% in winter.

Mussel Beach (ℭ **250/893-2267;** www. musselbeachcampground.com) is a first come, first served wilderness site with no facilities except for a magnificent stretch of sand-and-rock shoreline, tidal pools, and millions of mussels. Get there via a 20-minute drive off the main highway on 13km (8 miles) of mostly unpaved logging road. Rates are C$25 for a standard site, C$30 for a waterfront site, and C$45 for a secluded beachfront site.

For information on other campsites in the region, check out **www.camping. bc.ca**. Reservations can be made March to September at www.discovercamping. ca, or call ℭ **800/689-9025** or 604/689-9025.

suite; Oct–May C$340–C$440 double, C$460–C$975 suite. Rates may vary over holiday periods. Storm-watching, spa & other packages available. AE, MC, V. **Amenities:** Restaurant; bar; coffee lounge; health club; spa. *In room:* TV/DVD player, hair dryer, minibar, iPod dock, Wi-Fi.

IN UCLUELET

Black Rock Resort At last, Ucluelet can compete with Tofino with this distinctive resort that faces the dramatic onslaught of Pacific Ocean waves crashing over black, volcanic rocks. Unlike its Tofino counterparts, though, Black Rock sports a very dramatic and open design where black marble sides up to burnished silver trim and floor-to-ceiling windows. Its very contemporary feel is in direct contrast to ubiquitous West Coast stylings and is carried through into the appointments in the bedrooms and bathrooms of the doubles in the main building and the more privately situated suites set near the Wild Pacific Trail. Staff are helpful, but service can be a bit uneven. The onside Drift Spa is small but serviceable. The restaurant, however, is a must for its unobstructed views and good Pacific Northwest cuisine that won't break the bank.

596 Marine Dr., Ucluelet, BC V0R 3A0. ✆ **877/762-5011.** www.blackrockresort.com. 133 units. June–Sept C$265–C$345 double, C$359–C$419 1-bedroom suite, C$595–C$709 2-bedroom suite; Oct–May C$165–C$209 double, C$209–C$299 1-bedroom suite, C$305–C$629 2-bedroom suite. Additional adult C$25. Pets accepted (C$25). **Amenities:** Restaurant; lounge; hot tubs, plunge pool, room service; spa. *In room:* TV/DVD player, fridge, kitchen, iPod dock, Wi-Fi (main lodge rooms).

The Cabins at Terrace Beach Constructed to resemble a 1920s West Coast fishing village, the sheltered cedar cabins feel more like adult tree houses, or even high-end camping. Furnishings are country chic, and all units are equipped with a kitchenette, deck, and BBQ. Boardwalks weave through the 350-year-old evergreens that lead to beachfront cottages, and the relatively calm waters of Terrace Beach, adjacent to the Wild Pacific Trail (accessible via a staircase). There's direct access to hiking trails and the beach, which, because of the wave-less waters, is the place for young tots.

1090 Peninsula Rd. (P.O. Box 315), Ucluelet, BC V0R 3A0. ✆ **866/438-4373** or 250/726-2101. Fax 250/726-2100. www.thecabins.ca. July & Aug C$169–C$329 double; Sept–June C$119–C$179 double. Additional adult C$20. Children 5 & under stay free in parent's room. Pets accepted (C$20). *In room:* Satellite TV, kitchen, Wi-Fi.

Canadian Princess Resort This former hydrographic survey ship, moored in Ucluelet's central harbor and completely refurbished, sails to nowhere but offers no-nonsense, nautical-style accommodations. Small guest cabins, brightly decorated, offer basic bunk-style beds with washbasins; showers and bathroom facilities are shared. Standard, more comfortable onshore accommodations are also available. These guest rooms have two double beds and private bathrooms. Larger rooms sleep up to four in loft-style rooms. The vessel's dining and lounge areas are cozy and add to the seafaring atmosphere. Remember, this was once a working ship, which is a part of its charm and is probably why it seems to attract the fishing crowd. It's also a find for families traveling on a budget.

1943 Peninsula Rd., Ucluelet Harbour, Ucluelet, BC V0R 3A0. ✆ **800/663-7090** or 250/726-7771. Fax 250/726-7121. www.canadianprincess.com. 76 units. May to mid-Sept C$85–C$179 ship stateroom, C$145–C$345 on-shore double. Additional adult C$25. Salmon- & halibut-fishing packages available. AE, MC, V. Closed mid-Sept to Feb. **Amenities:** Restaurant; 2 lounges. *In room:* A/C, TV (in on-shore rooms), hair dryer.

A Snug Harbour Inn ★ Set on a 26m (85-ft.) cliff overlooking the pounding Pacific, A Snug Harbour Inn is a romantic oasis that takes the credit for at least

85 wedding engagements. Each guest room is decorated a little differently: One has an Atlantic nautical theme, a three-level Lighthouse Suite boasts the best views, and the Sawadee tops the list for snuggly comfort. One suite was built for wheelchair accessibility, including a walk-in shower; and another is pet friendly. All have fireplaces, down duvets over queen- or king-size beds, double-jet bathtubs, and private decks boasting vast ocean views. For a nominal extra charge, you can order up items such as roses, champagne, and other gifts to add to your stay. There's a powerful telescope in the Great Room, through which you can watch sea lions on the rocks below, or at night, with no light pollution, enjoy some unparalleled stargazing. Outside, there's a trail of 75 steps down to the pebbly beach, appropriately called "Stairway from the Stars." It's worth the descent, but it's a bit of a hike back up—take it in the morning to whet your appetite for a terrific breakfast.

460 Marine Dr. (P.O. Box 367), Ucluelet, BC V0R 3A0. © **888/936-5222** or 250/726-2686. Fax 250/726-2685. www.awesomeview.com. 6 units. June–Sept C$270–C$355 double; Oct & Mar–May C$215–C$280 double; Nov–Feb C$190–C$225 double. MC, V. Pets accepted. **Amenities:** Lounge; Jacuzzi. *In room:* TV/DVD player, hair dryer, Wi-Fi.

Water's Edge Resort at Pacific Rim ★   Overlooking the fishing boats, commercial trollers, and yachts moored in Ucluelet's inner harbor, everything here exudes a rustic, West Coast style, most notably the cathedral windows that seem to beckon the outdoors. The resort includes one- and two-bedroom self-catering suites, each solidly constructed and beautifully finished with a designer's eye for texture and detail. Furnishings include items such as leather La-Z-Boys in front of gas fireplaces, original artwork, kitchens with designer kitchenware, luxury linens, and all the amenities you would expect in a fine hotel. Some have two-person hot tubs on private decks. Sadly, at press time, there were no plans to resurrect the spa and restaurant of the resort's previous incarnation. Still, if you're looking for a romantic hideaway, Water's Edge still has that vibe.

1971 Harbour Dr., Ucluelet, BC V0R 3A0. © **888/899-2842** or 250/726-2672. www.aviawest.com. 32 units. July & Aug C$210 1-bedroom suite, C$260 2-bedroom suite; Sept–June C$150 1-bedroom suite, C$200 2-bedroom suite. AE, MC, V. **Amenities:** Lounge; bicycles; kayaks; surf boards. *In room:* TV/DVD player, fridge, hair dryer, kitchen, Wi-Fi.

Where to Dine
IN TOFINO/CLAYOQUOT SOUND

Pointe Restaurant ★★★ WEST COAST   If the 240-degree view of the Pacific Ocean pounding at your feet doesn't inspire, then the food and award-winning wine list certainly will. The menu is an imaginative showcase of fresh coastal food and seafood that's caught within a stone's throw of the inn. Chanterelles, boletus, angel wings, and pine mushrooms are brought in from neighboring forests. Gooseneck barnacles come off the rocks on the beach, and Indian Candy, made from salmon marinated and smoked for 6 days, comes from Tofino. Everything is exquisitely presented—an endive and berry salad with lavender, buttermilk, and wildflower honey is perfectly combined with tempura oysters, and the prosciutto-wrapped pork loin is especially tasty. A chef's four-course tasting menu showcases the best of the season for C$150 with wine pairings, C$80 without. And if the tempest outside is brewing over your meal, take note. The restaurant has surround-sound to make it feel as if you're eating in the eye of a storm. Be sure to book a table well in advance, or at least when you book your room, or you might be disappointed.

At Wickaninnish Inn, 500 Osprey Lane at Chesterman Beach. © **800/333-4604** or 250/725-3100. www.wickinn.com. Reservations required. Main courses C$34–C$49. AE, MC, V. Daily 8am–9:30pm.

The Schooner Restaurant PACIFIC NORTHWEST   Originally constructed as the hospital for the World War II RCAF Squadron Unit at Long Beach, it was towed to its present location when the war ended and has had various food incarnations, from coffee shop to crab shack, since. One of the former chefs, Morris, is even said to be its resident ghost. These days, however, the shack is the place for a romantic or special-occasion dinner. Menu items include such appetizers as tuna wontons and Panko-crusted prawns, and entrees include beef tenderloin, a baked chicken with cranberries, as well as a range of creatively prepared seafood, often with an ethnic touch, as in the Pacific Rim Seafood Hot Pot—halibut, prawns, and scallops sautéed in a spicy red Thai-inspired curry-coconut cream and served with lime-leaf-scented basmati rice. If fish is your thing, go for the gusto with the Captain's Plate for Two (C$57), a tasty sharing platter of six or seven different fish dishes.

331 Campbell St. © **250/725-3444.** Reservations recommended. Main courses C$20–C$36. MC, V. Daily 9am–3pm & 5–9:30pm.

Shelter ★ PACIFIC NORTHWEST   Polished wood dominates the decor of this cozy spot, which also features a large stone fireplace. Although there's meat on the menu, fish is the specialty here, which is done to perfection, whether seared alba-core tuna, steamed mussels with caramelized onion and roasted garlic, or the yellow Thai seafood curry served with sticky rice steamed black in a banana leaf. Don't leave without at least trying the bouillabaisse (tasters are by request). It's the signa-ture dish crammed with local fish, from sable and Chinook salmon to prawns, clams, and mussels that have simmered away in a fire-roasted tomato sauce. Fish aside, the Angus rib-eye with Panko onion rings is pretty darn good, as is the best vegetarian dish on the menu: a char-grilled vegetable ratatouille. Most wines are award-winning whites from BC vineyards; nearly all are available by the glass.

601 Campbell St. © **250/725-3353.** www.shelterrestaurant.com. Reservations recommended. Main courses lunch C$11–C$18, dinner C$13–C$32. MC, V. Daily 11am–10pm.

SoBo ECLECTIC   Chef-owner Lisa Ahier has a long pedigree of cooking at high-end lodges, but this is a far cry from froufrou cooking. SoBo is actually short for Sophisticated Bohemian, which describes the decor: lots of glass, high ceilings, a huge open kitchen, colorful art, and easy bistro-style dining. Because Ahier started in a tiny purple catering truck, many of her items then (and now) are hand-held eats such as "gringo" soft chicken tacos, crispy shrimp cakes, or a fish taco filled with local wild fish and topped with a fresh-fruit salsa. Items are priced tapas-style, so you can order one as a snack or three if you're starving. Now that she has the space, the menu is more expansive, and there's a deli counter for takeout with items like woodstone oven pizzas, oysters encrusted with cornmeal, and frozen fish chowder to heat up later.

311 Neill St. © **250/725-2341.** www.sobo.ca. Main courses C$9–C$28. MC, V. Mon & Tues 11am–5:30pm; Wed–Sun 11am–9pm.

Sushi Bar at Tough City ★ SUSHI   A hard-won reputation for authenticity has grown a small bar to the entire main floor of this popular B&B, and in warmer weather, customers spill onto the outdoor patio. The menu has all the traditional favorites: sushi rolls, tempura rolls, *nigiri,* and sashimi, as well as other Japanese dishes such as teriyaki salmon, chicken, and beef. If you're not a fan of sushi but love crab, the Dungeness crab dinner (C$34) is one of the best, in part because it's so simply prepared—steamed and served cold with melted garlic butter and a fresh Caesar salad. In July and August, the bar opens for lunch, as well as dinner.

350 Main St. ⓒ **250/725-2021.** www.toughcity.com. Main courses C$10–C$24. AE, MC, V. Year-round daily 5:30–9pm; July–Aug daily 11:30am–9pm.

IN UCLUELET

Norwoods Restaurant 🍴 BISTRO   It has all the stylings of a wine bar, but with the open kitchen dominating this tiny, upbeat bistro, you know that food is taken seriously. And because menu items are composed of small plates, diners can share and experiment with an eclectic mix of styles, food fusions, and surprising combinations. Look for local salmon seviche in a chili-and-lime marinade, with shaved fennel and orange salad, and chutney; traditional beef carpaccio; and local albacore tuna with a seaweed and ginger salad, wasabi, and avocado puree. Although the menu leans to seafood, larger plates include duck, lamb, and filet mignon. Most menu items offer wine pairing suggestions.

1714 Peninsula Rd. ⓒ **250/726-7001.** www.norwoods.ca. Main courses C$14–C$30. MC, V. Daily 6–11pm.

Matterson House CANADIAN   From the outside, this tiny 1931 cottage is very nondescript, yet once inside, you're in for a treat. By day, there are generous breakfasts and lunches of traditional favorites: burgers, pasta, salads, and homemade breads. By dusk, the menu turns to ocean and from-the-garden cuisine with filling standards such as prime rib, fancier items such as almond-crusted chicken with blackberry sauce, and excellent seafood dishes that include shrimp and scallop skewers and a tasty seafood chowder. The wine list features mostly BC labels, some of them special order. With only eight tables, plus an outside patio of another seven tables, reservations are recommended. While the food is consistently good, the service can be painfully slow. The restaurant opens year round, but in winter, call because hours are determined by staff availability and what's happening in town.

1682 Peninsula Rd. ⓒ **250/726-2200.** Main courses C$18–C$26. MC, V. Tues–Sun 9am–9pm (call ahead to confirm).

Ukee Dogs ★★ 🍴 CANADIAN   Operating out of a converted gas station and garage, there's a delicious informality about this cafe where tables are within spitting distance of the open kitchen. Everything's made from scratch, and chef-owner Stephanie Deering chats to you over her hot stove about your order. You want onions? How about some cilantro? She gave up a long and lucrative career in fine dining to set up shop away from the rat race, so you can be assured her no-frills dishes will please. The hearty bean chili and cheddar is so good that many of the fishermen have it for breakfast in addition to the various breakfast scramblers on offer. The vegetable curry pie is simmered in a creamy Madras sauce; and the hot dogs? Well, they're what made Ukee's a household name in these parts, so they're a have-to-have. Everything on the menu is under C$7, and each meat item has a vegetarian counterpart.

1576 Imperial Lane. ⓒ **250/726-2103.** Main courses C$2–C$7. Cash only. Fall–spring Mon–Fri 8:30am–3:30pm; summer Mon–Sat 8:30am–3:30pm. Closed Sun.

The Wickaninnish Restaurant CANADIAN   Not to be confused with the restaurant at the Wickaninnish Inn up the road, this dining room sits right on, and above, one of the prettiest parts of Long Beach. There isn't a better spot to savor the area's expansive sands, either inside from behind humongous windows or on a heated ocean-front sun deck. Menu items can sometimes be overly ambitious, so if a lofty description takes your fancy, probe your waiter for an honest assessment. Lunches cover excellent soups, sandwiches, crepes, and quiches; dinners include pasta, seafood, and standards such as New York strip steak. The crowd is a mix of upscale hikers and urban escapees (in other words, any gloriously muddy hiking boots were likely changed in the car). This is one of *the* most romantic spots to view a West Coast sunset. ***Note:*** There's a regular shuttle that runs from the Canadian Princess Resort to the restaurant; if you're driving, ask your waiter for a complimentary parking pass.

Wickaninnish Interpretive Centre, Long Beach. (✆ **250/726-7706.** www.wickaninnish.ca. Reservations recommended. Main courses C$19–C$44. AE, MC, V. Daily Mid-Mar to mid-Sept 11:30am–9:30pm. Closed mid-Sept to mid-Mar.

Food on the Run

Three takeouts to note include **The Wildside** (1180 Pacific Rim Hwy; ✆ **250/ 725-9453**), tucked in a small cluster of buildings just off the highway on the way to Tofino where surfers tend to congregate. Don't be put off by the shack-like appearance: The pulled-pork sandwich is yummy, and the fresh-from-the-ocean fish is served tempura-style. The complex is also home to **The Tofitian,** a computer cafe with free Wi-Fi and the area's finest espresso (Lavazza). And in Tofino itself, the **Breakers** (430 Campbell St.; ✆ **250/725-2558;** www. breakersdeli.com) doles out tasty picnic supplies (Salt Spring Island goat cheese, Natural Pastures Pacific pepper *verdelait,* and the like), as well as whole-wheat pizzas. All take-out products are biodegradable and compostable to put your eco-conscience at ease.

NORTHERN VANCOUVER ISLAND

The differences between the north part of the island and the south are profound. The farther north you drive, the wilder Vancouver Island becomes, and as urban sophistication falls to the wayside, you'll start to discover the diversity of the area. Fewer than 4% of the island's residents live in the northern region, with its vast forests of deep green, its crystal-clear rivers, and its inviting beaches. It's a paradise for eco-adventurers and nature photographers—a Mecca for anyone looking for Canadian wilderness.

Some communities, such as Kyoquot, are accessible only by chartered floatplane or boat, and to reach them, you travel through country that is quintessential West Coast Canada. Travel inland is also an adventure. While the main road twists up and around the island's spine of coastal mountains (the weather can change on a single S-bend), off-the-beaten-track destinations are often reached via logging roads. If you drive these routes, remember to use caution. Logging is still a primary industry in this part of the world; logging trucks are numerous and have the right of way.

Natural resources have long been the economic backbone of Vancouver Island, and as those resources continue to diminish, towns are looking to alternative investments. In **Courtenay-Comox,** the fastest-growing region on the island and home to the fish-happy **Campbell River,** resorts are springing up alongside entire retirement communities. Far-flung mining hamlets like **Zeballos,** which once made its fortune in gold, and **Holberg** are becoming bases for eco-adventurers, and picturesque places like **Telegraph Cove** are succumbing to 21st-century development. Despite these changes, you'll still come across communities, such as **Port McNeill** and **Port Hardy,** that are pretty rough-and-ready, as well as places like **Alert Bay,** whose isolation has protected its rich First Nations culture.

This diversity is the region's primary appeal. If you're a culture buff, stay in Victoria. If you're traveling with very young children, again, stay south—

unless you're heading for **Mount Washington** to ski or to **Miracle Beach,** one of the province's most popular provincial parks. But if you're hankering to experience nature with no boundaries, you won't get much better than North Vancouver Island.

COURTENAY & THE COMOX VALLEY

If you drive 62km (39 miles) north of Parksville–Qualicum Beach on Highway 19, you'll come upon Vancouver Island's other set of twin towns, Courtenay-Comox. Unlike their neighbors to the south, Courtenay and Comox are refreshingly un-touristy and so close together that you can hop from one to the other in a matter of minutes. Courtenay, with a population of 24,000, is a center of lumber milling on Vancouver Island and basks in a wide agricultural valley, while its sister community, Comox, with a population of 13,000, lies on the peninsula just east of Comox Harbour. Originally known as Port Augusta, it was once the only harbor from which supply ships could reach mid-island communities such as Gold River.

Today, the Comox Valley (pop. 64,000) is being discovered, almost gentrified, with its influx of families and retirees who are attracted to the region's rural ambience, its foodie ethos (everything for year-round eating lies within a 50km/31-mile radius), and its urban amenities. The First Nations once called this region K'Omoks, meaning "Land of Plenty," and for travelers—particularly outdoorsy types—it is certainly the gateway to plenty of wilderness adventure. The Beaufort Mountains, **Mount Washington Alpine Resort,** and **Strathcona Provincial Park** are within easy reach, and the promise of alpine lakes, glacial basins, and craggy peaks brings an abundant opportunity to view wildlife, as well as to hike, ski, kayak, and much more. If you've time, spend a day or two touring **Denman and Hornby islands,** a 10-minute ferry trip from Buckley Bay, just north of Fanny Bay, best known for its famous oysters.

Essentials

GETTING THERE

BY CAR   The driving distance from Victoria to Courtenay, due north along Highway 19, is 220km (137 miles). From Nanaimo, the distance is 113km (70 miles). From Parksville, it is 73km (45 miles). Highway 19 becomes Cliffe Avenue as it enters Courtenay.

BY PLANE   **Air Canada Jazz** (© 888/247-2262; www.flyjazz.ca) and **Pacific Coastal Airlines** (© 800/663-2872; www.pacificcoastal.com) operate daily flights from Victoria, Port Hardy, and Campbell River to the **Comox Valley Airport** (© 250/890-0829; www.comoxairport.com). **WestJet Airlines** (© 888/937-8538 or 800/538-5696; www.westjet.com) operates nonstop flights between Comox and both Calgary and Edmonton. Small aircraft and floatplanes can land at the **Courtenay Airpark** (© 250/334-8545). **Island Link Bus** (© 877/954-3556; www.islandlinkbus.com) provides an airport service to Nanaimo; reservations are required.

BY BUS   **Greyhound Canada** (© 800/661-8747; www.greyhound.ca) operates between Victoria and Port Hardy, with various stops along the way. The one-way fare from Victoria to Courtenay is C$42 adults. From Nanaimo to Courtenay, it's C$20 adults. Seniors receive about a 10% discount; fares for children 2 to 11 are approximately 25% less than for adults. The trip from Victoria to Courtenay takes 4½ hours; from Nanaimo, it's 2 hours. **Island Link Bus** (© 250/954-8257; www.islandlinkbus.com)

runs a passenger express service between BC Ferries' terminals, and Vancouver, Victoria, and Comox airports, and several island hubs. One-way fares are slightly less than Greyhound, but schedules may not be as convenient.

BY TRAIN   Courtenay is the termination point of the daily service offered by the **Malahat,** run by **VIA Rail** (© **888-842-7245;** www.viarail.ca), between Victoria and Courtenay.

BY FERRY   **BC Ferries** (© **888/223-3779;** www.bcferries.com) operates two daily crossings from **Powell River,** on the BC Sunshine Coast, to **Little River,** in Comox, a 10-minute drive from Courtenay. One-way fares are C$13 adults, C$6 children 5 to 11, C$40 for a standard-size vehicle. The crossing takes 1¼ hours.

VISITOR INFORMATION

The **Comox Valley Information Centre** is at 2040 Cliffe Ave., Courtenay (© **888/ 357-4471** or 250/334-3234; www.discovercomoxvalley.com). If you'd like to find out more about the Comox Valley beforehand, you can contact the **Tourism Association of Vancouver Island,** Suite 501, 65 Front St., Nanaimo (© **250/754-3500;** www.vancouverisland.travel or www.hellobc.com/vi).

GETTING AROUND

The **Comox Valley Transit System** (© **250/339-5453;** www.busonline.ca) operates local bus service in and between Courtenay, Comox, and Cumberland, a smaller community about 8km (5 miles) south of Courtenay. **United Cabs** (© **250/339-7955**) provides taxi service in these same communities.

Exploring the Area
COMOX

The tallest building in **Comox** belongs to the Logger's Union and bears testimony to the backbone of the region's economy. The center of town, however, belies that heritage. In summer, the area bustles with activity, shops, galleries, tea cafes, and restaurants, including a hole-in-the-wall sushi bar. And the Lorne Hotel, a hitherto rather forlorn institution since 1878, now has a happening pub. It's a lovely stroll along very pretty, and landscaped, **harbor-side promenade,** where fishing boats are so plentiful, you can often buy fish or prawns straight from the vessel.

The Filberg Lodge and Park ★★   Once a private residence, the estate was first cleared in 1929 and today covers some 3.6 hectares (9 acres) of wooded and landscaped gardens. The handsome stone-and-timbered lodge rests on piles driven into an old salt marsh and Native shell midden (a refuse heap), and exudes old-world craftsmanship inside and out. Examples include hand-milled beams, a yew-tree handrail on the staircase, and a stone fireplace featuring a Native petroglyph. Outside, the waterfront gardens are filled with rare and exotic trees, hundreds of rhododendrons, and numerous flower beds. There's even a four-figure totem pole. Filberg appeals to all ages; kids will enjoy the hands-on petting farm (open mid-June to mid-Aug). Take the morning or afternoon to explore Filberg; the teahouse serves lunch, as well as traditional afternoon tea with cucumber sandwiches, scones, and Devonshire cream, so either way, you need not go hungry. Over the first weekend of August, the park is the site of the 4-day Filberg Festival (© **250/334-9242;** www.filbergfestival.com), an outdoor art exhibition showcasing the work of more than 150 of British Columbia's top craftspeople.

Northern Vancouver Island

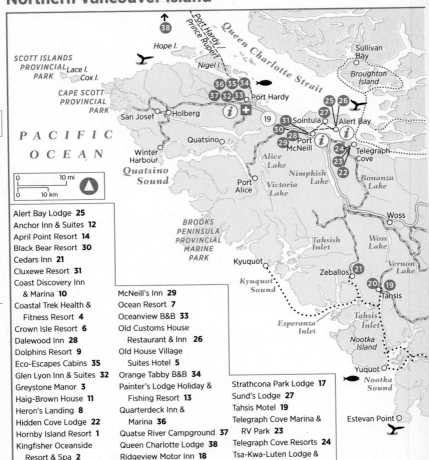

Alert Bay Lodge **25**
Anchor Inn & Suites **12**
April Point Resort **14**
Black Bear Resort **30**
Cedars Inn **21**
Cluxewe Resort **31**
Coast Discovery Inn
   & Marina **10**
Coastal Trek Health &
   Fitness Resort **4**
Crown Isle Resort **6**
Dalewood Inn **28**
Dolphins Resort **9**
Eco-Escapes Cabins **35**
Glen Lyon Inn & Suites **32**
Greystone Manor **3**
Haig-Brown House **11**
Heron's Landing **8**
Hidden Cove Lodge **22**
Hornby Island Resort **1**
Kingfisher Oceanside
   Resort & Spa **2**
Maquinna Resort **20**

McNeill's Inn **29**
Ocean Resort **7**
Oceanview B&B **33**
Old Customs House
   Restaurant & Inn **26**
Old House Village
   Suites Hotel **5**
Orange Tabby B&B **34**
Painter's Lodge Holiday &
   Fishing Resort **13**
Quarterdeck Inn &
   Marina **36**
Quatse River Campground **37**
Queen Charlotte Lodge **38**
Ridgeview Motor Inn **18**
Sonora Resort **16**

Strathcona Park Lodge **17**
Sund's Lodge **27**
Tahsis Motel **19**
Telegraph Cove Marina &
   RV Park **23**
Telegraph Cove Resorts **24**
Tsa-Kwa-Luten Lodge &
   RV Park **15**

61 Filberg Rd., Comox. ℂ **250/339-2715.** www.filberg.com. Admission by donation. May–Sept daily 8am–dusk; Oct–Apr daily 11am–3pm.

Kitty Coleman Woodland Gardens   Named after a First Nations woman who set up residence in the area in the late 1800s, the gardens are a loving creation of one man, Bryan Zimmerman, without the help of heavy equipment that might have destroyed the land. These spectacular, half-wild gardens must be seen to be believed—for the 3,000 rhododendrons alone! There are 9.7 hectares (24 acres) to explore, so bring along shoes with good treads; the bark-mulch trails can be slippery.

6183 Whittaker Rd. (just north of Seal Bay Park), Courtenay. ℂ **250/338-6901.** www.woodlandgardens. ca. Admission C$8 adults, C$3 children 5–12. Daily 9am–dusk.

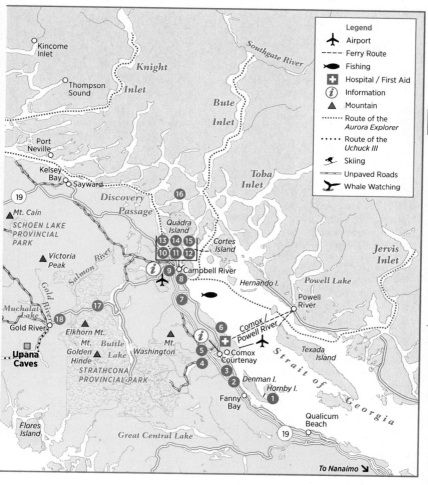

COURTENAY

Courtenay's sexiest claim to fame is that it's the hometown of Kim Cattrall, from the TV show *Sex and the City*. And let's not forget jazz performer Diana Krall, who also hails from here. But that's about it. Sure, Courtenay is a pleasant enough community, but it doesn't have a specific hub of activity, except for a few galleries and shops around 4th, 5th, and 6th streets, including the **Comox Valley Art Gallery** (580 Duncan St., at 6th St.; ✆ **250/338-6211**), opposite the library. There are more enclaves of local artists at the **Muir Gallery** (440 Anderton Ave.; ✆ **250/334-2983**) and at **Potter's Place** (180B 5th St.; ✆ **250/334-4613**).

The **Kingfisher Oceanside Resort & Spa, Old House Village Hotel & Spa,** and the **Crown Isle Resort** (see "Where to Stay," below) are doing their part to change all that, however. More than a place to stay, Crown Isle is an entire complex of expensive condominiums, restaurants, and lounges centered on an 18-hole links-style **championship golf course** that offers sweeping views of the Comox Glacier and Beaufort Mountains. The course is open year-round. From May to September, non-member green fees are C$90; from November to March, C$45; and in April and October, C$60. While you're there, do see the **Classic Car Museum,** featuring a collection of predominantly '50s and '60s Chevrolets and Fords, some of which were previously owned by the likes of Sylvester Stallone and Mary Hart.

The Courtenay & District Museum and Palaeontology Centre ★ ☺

Housed in the town's old post office, the center holds a collection of First Nations masks and basketry, pioneer artifacts, and a 12m (39-ft.) cast skeleton of an elasmosaur, a crocodile-like Cretaceous-era reptile. Half-day tours are offered year-round and run the gamut from exploring the paleontology lab to digging in the riverbed. A tropical sea once covered the Comox Valley, so there's a wealth of marine fossils to be found. To make the most of the experience, a tour is the way to go. The center also operates Capes Escape, a pretty, 1930s-style family home that's neat to rent for extended stays.

207 4th St. ℂ **250/334-3611.** www.courtenaymuseum.ca. Admission by donation. Tours C$25 adults, C$20 students & seniors, C$15 children 11 & under. May–Sept Mon–Sat 10am–5pm, Sun noon–4pm; Oct–Apr Tues–Sat 10am–5pm.

CUMBERLAND

Just 16km (10 miles) southwest of Courtenay, in the foothills of the Beaufort Mountains, the historic coal-mining town of **Cumberland** still stirs the imagination with pretty heritage homes, storefronts, and institutional buildings such as the rather imposing all-brick 1907 Customs & Post Office. Some buildings have found a new lease on life, which adds to the charm of this hamlet, with an Indian restaurant and **Riding Fool Hostel** (ℂ **888/313-FOOL** [888/313-3665]; www.ridingfool.com), a hostel geared to biking enthusiasts (Cumberland hosts an annual 12-hour bike-race relay on its hilly and winding trails). Founded by coal baron Robert Dunsmuir, and named after the famous English coal-mining district, Cumberland was once the second largest coal producer in North America. In 1912, one mine alone produced some 2,580 kilograms (5,688 lb.) of coal a day. Back then, the town's population was five times what it is today, made up of some 13,000 workers from around the world. Cumberland once claimed the largest Chinatown north of San Francisco. The mine was closed in 1966, but you can get a feel for Cumberland's story at the **Cumberland Museum & Archives** (2680 Dunsmuir Ave.; ℂ **250/336-2445;** www.cumberlandmuseum.ca).

MOUNT WASHINGTON ALPINE RESORT ★★

Drive north on Highway 19 and take exit 130 to the Mount Washington exit, about a 30-minute drive from Courtenay-Comox. Then, it's an ear-popping climb to the base of the resort. (The road is in excellent condition.) Mount Washington is hardly a resort in the upscale Whistler sense of the word, but it certainly caters to year-round activities. In summer, mountain bikers, alpine fly-fishing enthusiasts, and hikers adventure through the landscape. Many trails, such as those leading off the 2km (1.2-mile) **Paradise Meadows Loop Trail,** connect to Strathcona Provincial Park (see below). Take the scenic chairlift to the summit, and you'll find a number of easy bark-mulch, interpretive trails to explore. The scenic chairlift rides are C$15. Summer day passes are C$38 adults, C$34 students and C$25 children (6-12 years). Disc golf, mini-golf, and bungee trampoline are priced separately; all are under C$7.

In winter, skiing is the mountain's raison d'être. With a 505m (1,657-ft.) vertical rise and more than 60 groomed runs, most above 1,200m (3,937 ft.), Mount Washington's 647 hectares (1,600 acres) of riding terrain boast the deepest snowfall in Canada—that's an average of 11m (36 ft.). All of them are accessed by six lifts, a tubing lift, and two beginners' tows.

As for other winter sports, there's a 0-Zone **snow-tubing park,** a 250m (820-ft.) **luge run,** and 30km (19 miles) of track-set **Nordic trails** connecting to Strathcona Provincial Park. To avoid crowds and lift lineups, plan to go on a weekday—the mountain is remarkably quiet. This is something that can never be said about Whistler. From December to March, day passes for skiing are C$62 adults, C$50 seniors and children 13 to 18, C$32 children 6 to 12, and free for children 5 and under. The Alpine and Raven Lodges have restaurants, rentals, and some shops, and there's enough accommodations units—be they condos, chalets, lodges, or hotels—for 4,000 overnight visitors. For details on lift passes, snow-school programs, equipment, and condominium rentals, call the central information and reservations number (© 888/231-1499 or 250/338-1386) or log on to www.mountwashington.ca. Another resource is **Tourism Mount Washington** (© 250/338-0226; www.tourismmountwashington.com).

STRATHCONA PROVINCIAL PARK ★★★

Located almost in the center of Vancouver Island, Strathcona Provincial Park is a rugged wilderness of more than 250,000 hectares (617,763 acres). In the summer, it can be accessed via several moderately easy trails from Mount Washington Alpine Resort (see above) and, year-round, by driving to Campbell River on Highway 19 and taking the Highway 28 exit to Gold River.

Strathcona was British Columbia's first designated wilderness and recreation area (created in 1911) and is managed by the **Ministry of Environment, Lands, and Parks** (© 250/337-2400; www.env.gov.bc.ca/bcparks). The park brims with treasures: snow-capped mountain peaks, lakes set in amphitheaters of ice, valleys filled with pristine rainforest, and alpine meadows painted with heather, as well as rivers and waterfalls—including Canada's tallest waterfall, **Della Falls,** at 440m (1,444 ft.). Wildlife is plentiful, and because of Vancouver Island's separation from the mainland, there are no chipmunks, porcupines, coyotes, or grizzly bears, and species such as the Roosevelt elk, black-tailed deer, Vancouver Island marmot, and wolf here are slightly smaller than their mainland cousins. Birds are also numerous and include the chestnut-backed chickadee, red-breasted nuthatch, winter wren, ruffed grouse, and a limited number of unique Vancouver Island white-tailed ptarmigan.

But Strathcona's greatest treasures aren't exactly on display, so if you really want to explore this diverse park, you'll need to hike or backpack into the alpine wilderness. Getting to Della Falls, for example, requires a boat ride to reach the trail head and a multi-day hike that follows the old railway grade up the Drinkwater Valley.

In addition to Paradise Meadows (Mount Washington), **Forbidden Plateau** and **Buttle Lake** are good access points to the park, largely because they can be reached by car, and both have information centers. The Forbidden Plateau offers views to the horizon of glaciers, forests, and pastoral landscapes, and starting at the former ski lodge, a fairly steep 4.8km (3-mile) trail up Mount Becher. The views of the valley and the Strait of Georgia make the effort worthwhile. At Buttle Lake, you'll find camping facilities (for reservations, call Discover Camping, ☎ **800/689-9025**), a honey-hole for rainbow trout and Dolly Varden (a species of trout sometimes called bull trout or sea run dolly), and several trails. Three notable hikes are the easy 20-minute walk to Lady Falls, the 6.5km (4-mile) hike along Marble Meadows Trail, and the 3.2km (2-mile) Upper Myra Falls Trail through old-growth forests and past waterfalls.

Because of the diversity of this park, I suggest you check out the Strathcona Park Lodge (see "Where to Stay," below), if not to stay, at least to get the lowdown on their many programs, which are geared as much to wilderness neophytes as to experienced outdoor adventurers.

Where to Stay

Coastal Trek Health & Fitness Resort   Getting here takes faith, as the winding gravel road climbs high. Rest assured, though, the views from the top of Forbidden Plateau are worth the ascent. The resort feels like a hybrid of a contemporary home and a modern motel. Guest rooms are comfortable, though on the small side because they're not designed to be away-from-it-all personal retreats. That's left to the main area, with its magnificent post-and-beam construction, wall windows, a sunken great room with river-rock fireplace, and a huge cypress wood dining table. Hiking is the resort's forte—backpacks, hiking poles, and non-toxic water bottles are part of the in-room amenities, and hikes are tailored to your ability and health goals, alongside fitness assessments. The organic food puts to rest any notions of dull tofu and sprouts. Menus incorporate vegetables such as quinoa and Kohirabi, fruit-based butters, sugar substitutes, and a chocolate beet cake that tastes like its decadent relative. Stays are all inclusive and include meals, yoga classes, massages, a cooking class, daily guided hikes, and health-oriented evening programs.

8100 Forbidden Plateau Rd. (P.O. Box 3160), Courtenay, BC V9J 1L2. ☎ **250/897-8735**. Fax 866/860-8735. www.coastaltrekresort.com. 12 units. Apr–Oct C$1,595 for 3 days, C$2,995 for 7 days. Lower rates available Feb, Mar & for multi-week programs. MC, V. Free parking. Closed Nov–Jan. Children 16 & under not accepted. **Amenities:** Complimentary airport shuttle; hot tub; steam room; spa. *In room:* Hair dryer, no phone, free Wi-Fi.

Crown Isle Resort ★★★   A 72-par, Platinum-rated course, suitable for golfers at all levels, is the centerpiece of the development. But you don't have to be a member to play, and you don't have to be a golf nut to stay. The villas, which come in a variety of configurations, are lavish and are more like small town houses. Finishing touches include two-sided gas fireplaces with marble surrounds and deep soaker Jacuzzis, over which there's a starlit ceiling that twinkles from blue to yellow. Most have fully equipped kitchens; some have wet bars and separate dining areas. Another building offers equally sumptuous hotel-style rooms, though slightly set back from the fairway. All guests have access to the resort's fitness center in the clubhouse. There's a cozy pub, and if you're a steak connoisseur, the **Silverado Steak House** (see "Where to Dine," below) is a must.

399 Clubhouse Dr., Courtenay, BC V9N 9G3. ☎ **888/338-8439** or 250/703-5050. Fax 250/703-5051. www.crownisle.com. 90 units. May–Sept C$159 double, C$259-319 villa/loft; Oct & Apr C$129 double, C$199–C$219 villa/loft; Nov–Mar C$129 double, C$169–C$219 villa/loft. Additional adult C$25. Children 17 & under stay free in parent's room. Golf & ski packages available. AE, MC, V. Free parking. **Amenities:** 2 restaurants; pub; golf course; health club; room service. *In room:* TV/DVD player, hair dryer, Wi-Fi.

Greystone Manor   The name conjures up a *Wuthering Heights*–style grandeur, only instead of heather-covered moors, it offers up gorgeous gardens that are chock-full of

English perennials through which are winding grassy pathways down to the beach, and stunning vistas of the coastal mountains. Built in 1918, the heritage manor has a formal dining room where full breakfasts are served and a piano lounge where there are always refreshments. There are three comfortably furnished rooms which feel less stately than expected, two with queen beds and en-suite bathrooms, one with twin beds with a private bathroom across the hall. Although the manor was for sale a while back, recessionary times have seen it carry on. Still, you should probably check that's still the case before arriving at their door.

4014 Haas Rd., Courtenay, BC, V9N 9T4. *866/338-1422.* www.greystonemanorbb.com. 3 units. C$110 double. MC, V. Closed Dec & Jan. Children 12 & under not accepted. **Amenities:** Lounge. *In room:* Hair dryer, no phone, Wi-Fi.

Kingfisher Oceanside Resort & Spa ★★   Located 7km (4¼ miles) south of Courtenay, this adult-oriented destination resort is a winner. Bright and colorful rooms tend to be extra-large, and many come with balconies or patios overlooking the ocean. The even roomier beachfront suites come with kitchenettes and heated bathroom floors; you'll pay more, of course, but you can save dollars by cooking your own meals. Most people come for the impressive spa, which includes a heated outdoor pool with a shoulder-massaging waterfall, a cave steam-room and sauna, and spa services that range from thalassotherapy wraps, Reiki and reflexology to facials and drop-in yoga classes. A complimentary shuttle runs between the resort and downtown, to the Comox Valley Airport, and to Mount Washington Alpine Resort (see "Mount Washington Alpine Resort," above). The Kingfisher Oceanside Restaurant is one of the better places to dine in the area (see "Where to Dine," below).

4330 Island Hwy. S., Courtenay, BCV9N 9R9. *800/663-7929* or 250/338-1323. Fax 250/338-0058. www.kingfisherspa.com. 64 units. C$170 double; C$220–C$350 suite; C$455 deluxe suite. Additional adult C$25. Low-season discounts available; spa, ski & golf packages available. AE, DC, DISC, MC, V. **Amenities:** Restaurant; lounge; health club; room service; spa; unlit outdoor tennis court; canoe & kayak rentals. *In room:* TV/DVD player, hair dryer, Wi-Fi.

Old House Village Suites & Hotel ★   There's nothing old about this boutique hotel which exudes West Coast style with its timber frame, locally made furniture, stonework, windows, and natural hues. A recent addition now sees this complex spread over two buildings, which are anchoring the redevelopment along the shores of the Courtenay River. The studio, one-, and two-bedroom suites include a king-size bed and top-notch amenities such as a flat-screen HDTV, fireplace, and a queen-size sofa bed. There's also a full kitchen, replete with modern appliances and a washer/dryer. The two-level Penthouse Suite is more like a mini-townhome with a loft bedroom. It's very romantic and a perfect place for an away-from-it-all getaway.

1730 Riverside Lane, Courtenay, BC V9N 8C7. *888/703-0202* or 250/703-0202. Fax 250/703-0209. www.oldhousevillage.com. 79 units. July, Aug & Christmas C$149–$C179 suite, C$249 penthouse; Sept-June C$129–C$159 suite, C$199 penthouse. Additional adult C$20. Children 15 & under stay free in parent's room. Golf, kayaking & ski packages available. MC, V. Free parking. **Amenities:** Fitness center; hot tub; sauna; spa. *In room:* A/C, TV/DVD player, hair dryer, Wi-Fi.

Strathcona Park Lodge & Outdoor Education Centre ★★   Perched on the shores of Upper Campbell Lake, just outside the park's eastern boundary, this privately owned lodge provides not only a comfortable place to stay, from lodge rooms and cabins to multi-bedroom chalet-type accommodations, but also a variety of opportunities for exploring the surrounding wilderness. Staying here has been described as a cross between Outward Bound and Club Med, with no Internet access, no TV, and no cellphone service. Everyone, from hard-core outdoor types to parents with young children, can find an educational and adventure program to fit their niche, experiencing activities such as sailing, wilderness survival, rock climbing, backcountry hiking, fishing, swimming, canoeing, and kayaking. Special packages are available, and guides and instructors can be hired by the hour. Unless you know the park well, or are happy trekking through backcountry independently, the lodge is definitely the way to go.

40km (25 miles) west of Campbell River on Hwy. 28; P.O. Box 2160, Campbell River, BC V9W 5C5. ✆ 250/286-3122. Fax 250/286-6010. www.strathcona.bc.ca. 39 units. C$40–C$88 double w/shared bathroom; C$139–C$160 double w/private bathroom; C$175–C$440 cabin. 2–3 night minimum stay in cabins. Adventure packages & off-season discounts available. MC, V. Amenities: Restaurant; babysitting; exercise room; sauna; canoe & kayak rentals. In room: No phone.

Where to Dine

Atlas Cafe Bar ★ 🍴 INTERNATIONAL   From this small restaurant in downtown Courtenay, you can travel the world, food-wise, with large portions of Mexican quesadillas, Greek spanakopita, Japanese nori rolls, Indian samosas, Thai satays, and Italian-style sandwiches on focaccia, as well as a good selection of vegetarian dishes. Nearly all are made with island supplies. Dinner adds more substantial dishes such as stir-fries, noodle creations, fish, and roast beef. The cafe is busy from the moment it opens—locals know where to come for breakfast, and it has specialty coffees that put Starbucks on the back burner. Weekends, breakfast is served until 2pm. Although the wine list is limited, the bar has quite the name on the martini circuit, plus it has a good choice of local beers and non-alcoholic shakes.

250 6th St., Courtenay. ✆ **250/338-9838.** www.atlascafe.ca. Reservations accepted for parties of 6 or more. Main courses lunch C$7–C$15; dinner C$15–C$25. MC, V. Mon 8:30am–3:30pm; Tues–Sat 8:30am–10pm; Sun 8:30am–9pm.

Avenue Bistro INTERNATIONAL   The owners of Atlas operate this Art Deco–style eatery in downtown Comox. The ambiance is a shade impersonal, but the food is excellent. A daily fresh sheet details the selections of the day: always char-grilled steaks, a fish entree—hope for the fresh Pacific halibut with roasted carrot ginger *coulis* when you visit—and a vegetarian option. The Bistro works hard to deliver island products, including wines and beers. The takeout menu is extensive and includes everything from tiger prawn tempura and pork spring rolls with cilantro mango tamarind dip to creative pizzas. On Sunday nights, go for the house specialty: perfectly primed prime rib.

2064 Comox Ave., Comox. ✆ **250/890-9200.** www.avenuebistro.ca. Reservations accepted for parties of 6 or more. Main courses lunch C$9–C$15, dinner C$15–C$27. MC, V. Tues–Fri 11am–9pm; Sat & Sun 9am–10pm. Closed Mon.

Black Fin Pub ★★ PUB FARE/CANADIAN   The view is splendid, stretching from a log-strewn beach, across the water, and on to the distant Beaufort Mountains. The atmosphere is what you want in a stylish pub: dark wood trim complemented by deep blue upholstery with nautical accents. There's a sunken dining area and plenty of chairs against the bar, and the menu includes quality pub dishes like burgers, sandwiches, wraps, and fish and chips, as well as grazing options such as crab and shrimp cakes (they're really worth the trip), a spicy beef satay, and chicken wings.

132 Port Augusta St., Comox. ✆ **250/339-5030.** Reservations accepted for parties of 4 or more in early evening. Main courses C$11–C$25. AE, MC, V. Sun–Thurs 11am–10pm; Fri &Sat 11am–11pm.

Kingfisher Oceanside Restaurant SEAFOOD/CONTINENTAL   Although the food doesn't always match the hyperbole of the menu descriptions, it is still one of the region's better eateries—right on the waterfront, too. Because of its proximity to the spa, the menu includes a number of low-fat, low-calorie options. The poached halibut jardinière with a salad of grilled fruit, roasted nuts, and crumbled Stilton cheese is one of the tastier choices. If lean cuisine's not your thing, there are steaks, schnitzels, and lamb dishes, as well as vegetarian choices such as porcini-mushroom homemade ravioli served with fresh tomato and chipotle-pepper *coulis* with a fresh Asiago crisp. The restaurant is justifiably proud of its all-you-can-eat Sunday brunch and periodic gala seafood buffets. Both are local favorites, so book space in advance.

4330 Island Hwy. S., 7km (4¼ miles) south of Courtenay. ☎ **250/338-1323.** www.kingfisherspa.com. Reservations recommended. Main courses C$20–C$29. AE, DC, DISC, MC, V. Mon–Fri 7am–9pm; Sat & Sun 7am–10pm.

Locals ★★★ 🏠 PACIFIC NORTHWEST   The reason this brilliant restaurant is in a shopping mall is because it receives up to 15 deliveries a day from local farmers. Everything on the ever-changing menu is so fresh that you can taste the minerals in the potatoes that were, more than likely, in the ground that morning. Dishes include a bison carpaccio appetizer; marinated boneless chicken leg stuffed with chorizo sausage meat, served on braised French lentil ragout and seasonal rhubarb compote; and a fresh basil risotto with sundried tomato, organic greens, and toasted pine nuts. The restaurant succeeds in sharing a farm-to-fork ethos beyond the creativity of every dish. Recycled tires produce a more durable, quieter version of hardwood floors; a server's talent for photography showcases suppliers; menu ingredients are identified with their supplier, and wines from local vineyards are superbly paired. Service is attentive without being disruptive.

364 8th St., Courtenay. ☎ **250/338-6493.** www.localscomoxvalley.com. Reservations recommended. Main courses C$18–C$29. MC, V. Tues–Sun 11am–9pm.

Martine's Bistro INTERNATIONAL   This heritage building has been a gathering place since 1886, first as a community hall and today as a chic restaurant with glinting hardwood floors, clean-lined furnishings, and a pretty garden patio overlooking some sculptures. The food runs the gamut from tapas-style sharing dishes to a delicious curried chicken fettuccini, flavored with sweet peppers and a mild mango curry sauce—not a combination you would think of as compatible, but it sure is. The menu also offers seafood, steaks, and poultry dishes; they're best when featured on the daily fresh sheet. The house specialties hint at the owner's Dutch heritage: Try the Bitter Ballen, Dutch meat croquettes which crunch and then melt in your mouth.

1754 Beaufort Ave., Comox. ☎ **250/339-1199.** www.martinesbistro.com. Reservations accepted. Main courses C$15–C$27. MC, V. Daily 5–10pm.

Silverado Steak House STEAK   Lying at the heart of Crown Isle Golf Resort, the atrium-style fine-dining restaurant specializes in AAA-grade steak from Alberta and serves it up alongside some spectacular views of the Beaufort Mountains, as well as the 18th hole. Big eaters can opt for the 567g (20-oz.) Delmonico rib steak chop, while for more modest appetites there's a 170g (6-oz.) filet mignon. Both are exceptionally good with either a red wine garlic or blue cheese cream demi-glace. There's also a good selection of local seafood such as oysters from nearby Talbot Cove, trout, halibut, and salmon.

399 Clubhouse Dr., Courtenay. ☎ **888/338-8439** or 250/703-5000. Reservations recommended. Main courses C$20–C$35. AE, MC, V. Daily 5–10pm.

Toscanos Trattoria ★ ITALIAN   This casual, convivial, licensed bistro is filled with cheerful colors—oranges, yellows, and reds—and wonderfully aromatic smells. The menu includes huge panini, outstanding pastas, and specialty entrees such as chicken breast filled with ricotta, sun-dried tomatoes, and spinach, and served in a basil sauce. Save room for Italian classics such as tiramisu and the mmm, so delicious, Mario Gelato. Toscanos Trattoria is where the trendies on a budget dine.

140 Port Augusta, Comox. ☎ **250/890-7575.** www.toscanos.ca. Reservations required. Main courses C$14–C$25. MC, V. Mon–Sat 11am–2pm & 5–9pm.

HORNBY & DENMAN ISLANDS

A haven for aging flower children and Vietnam draft dodgers who stayed north of the 49th parallel after amnesty, there's a distinct bohemian charm that speaks to 1960s creativity. The beautiful landscapes make the islands one of British Columbia's top beach vacations, drawing flocks of cyclists, though pedaling the hill roads takes a degree of endurance. If you really want to appreciate the rural isolation of these islands, visit in low season; Hornby's year-round population of 1,000 swells to as many as 10,000 in summer.

Getting There

To get there, canoe or kayak across the narrow channel, or hop onto the ferry at Buckley Bay, just north of Fanny Bay. To get to Hornby Island, you must first cross Denman. The dozen daily trips to each island take 10 minutes one-way, and each leg of the journey costs C$9 adults, C$5 children, and C$20 for a standard vehicle.

Visitor Information

On Denman Island, the **Denman General Store** (1069 Northwest Rd.; ☎ **250/335-2293**) acts as the Denman/Hornby Visitor Services. It offers a free island guide, information on the small one- and two-bedroom B&Bs, as well as a brochure listing the *many* small arts and crafts galleries. You can also get information at www.denman-island.com, www.hornbyisland.com, and www.realhornby.com.

Getting Around

Bring bikes on the ferry or contact **Denman Island Hostel** (☎ **250/335-2688**) for bike rentals (C$25/day). If you're staying at the hostel, you can ride the old, road-worn bikes for free.

Exploring the Islands

DENMAN

On Denman, beautiful sandstone and gravel shores are full of life: oysters, rock crabs, clams, eagles, and seabirds. There's good salmon fishing, particularly off the south end. Off the north shores, you can kayak across to **Sandy Island Provincial Marine Park,** a group of beautiful wooded islands with limited camping (☎ **250/334-4600**). **Denman Hornby Canoes & Kayaks** (4005 East Rd.; ☎ **250/335-0079;** www.denmanpaddling.ca) offers rentals (half-day C$50;

full-day C$70) and custom guided excursions ranging from 2½ hours (C$85) to a popular 4-hour trip (C$110) and a full-day excursion (C$130). These folks also offer a modest B&B, geared for paddlers. If nothing else, head for **Fillongley Provincial Park** on the east side of the island. It features an unspoiled sand-and-shell beach, plus fabulous views of Texada Island, and the snow-capped mainland Coast Mountain range with a miles-long foreshore is edged by stands of old growth Douglas and Grand fir and red cedars. The trail is an easy half-hour circuit. Head for **Boyle Point Provincial Park** at the southern end of Denman for a picnic; it overlooks the Chrome Island lighthouse and a variety of seals, sea lions, and seabirds.

HORNBY

You need no other excuse to visit Hornby than **Tribune Bay Provincial Park.** Here, the sea has beaten the soft rock faces into dramatic cave and hoodoo formations. Explore **Helliwell Bay Provincial Park,** both for the trails along the bluff and to see the thousands of nesting birds tucked into the side of the cliffs. Hornby's two claims to fame are as the only spot in Canada where you'll find certain types of butterflies, including Flora Inlet, and outside of the South Pacific it is the only place where divers can count on finding primitive deep-sea six-gill shark swimming in shallow waters.

Where to Stay & Dine

The islands' popularity means that accommodations can be hard to come by, so even if you're sleeping under canvas, book at least 3 months in advance. There are also few places to eat. On Hornby, check out the tiny eatery at Ringside Market or head for the **Thatch Pub** (4305 Shingle Spit Rd.; ☎ **250/335-0136**), open daily and offering casual pub fare. It's the only waterside watering hole on the island, not to mention the only place with ATM access and a liquor store, and it's a popular local nightspot, with live music Friday and Saturday. Notice the tabletops; they represent the work of more than 20 local artists. Look further, and you'll notice imaginative art throughout. There's a wee licensed bistro with very limited open hours at the **Denman Island Hostel & Guest House** (☎ **250/335-2688**) in "downtown." The guesthouse, a 1912 heritage farmhouse, has a mix of accommodations with shared bathrooms, as well as campsites. Rates range from C$17 to C$48 a night, depending on where you hang your shingle. **Bradsdadslad Family Campsite** (2105 Shingle Spit Rd.; ☎ **250/335-0757;** www.bradsdadsland.com) overlooks a child-safe, naturally wild beach along Lambert Channel and has about 50 campsites. Book early to secure your first come, first served spot.

Hornby Island Resort Book months in advance if you want to get a spot at this popular waterfront resort, mainly because it's the only show in town. The rustic cottage rooms are plainly furnished and come with small bathrooms and full kitchen; the campsites are fairly private, separated by roses and honeysuckle plants, and well-maintained. Each has a picnic table, a fire pit, and optional electrical plug-ins. Campground facilities include hot showers and laundry.

4305 Shingle Spit Rd. (next to the ferry terminal), Hornby Island, BC V0R 1Z0. ☎ **250/335-0136.** Fax 250/335-9136. hornbyislandresort@hornbyisland.com. 2 units, 2 cottages, 8 campsites. C$110 double; C$35 campsite; C$135 cabin (in off-season), C$1,100 cabin weekly (in summer). MC, V. **Amenities:** Restaurant; pub; tennis court; Wi-Fi. *In-room:* TV.

CAMPBELL RIVER, GOLD RIVER & TAHSIS, NOOTKA & KYOQUOT SOUNDS

Once you hit mid-island, the entire topography starts to shift. Campbell River (pop. 31,000), is the last major town you come across, and it's the door to Vancouver Island's wilder nature. Head towards Gold River, and you start to see how important the island's inner waterways are to its economy. Go farther to Tahsis, Nootka, and Kyoquot Sounds, and you're in some of the most beautiful coastal waters in the world—the places where the Spanish and Captain Cook first explored—that are now opening up to varied ecotourism activities.

Campbell River

Although you could take the fast inland highway, Highway 19, north from Courtenay for the 48km (30-mile) drive to Campbell River, the scenic and more leisurely route along Highway 19A, also called the **Oceanside Route,** is far more rewarding. Exit Highway 19 at **Miracle Beach** and head north on Highway 19A. Follow the starfish signs past scenic coves and through small, picturesque communities, many of which have small galleries and art studios to browse through. Bring your camera and enjoy weaving along the water's edge. Check out **www.gonanaimo.com/nanaimo/oceanside-driving-tour.html** for details. Once in Campbell River, you'll be in a true North Island community with roots deep in lumber and fishing. Much of this heritage is showcased alongside First Nations exhibits in the **Museum at Campbell River** (470 Island Hwy.; 📞 **250/287-3103;** www.crmuseum.ca). The town center is marked by the high rigger *Big Mike,* a carved wooden lumberjack swinging from a harness at the top of a spar pole. There's also a Torii Gate in Sequoia Park that was a celebratory gift from Ishikari, the city's twin sister in Japan. In Shinto tradition, the gate represents recognition of a special location or place. Although it looks somewhat anomalous, perhaps no more so than the reciprocal gift of a totem pole that now stands in Ishikari.

Tyee Chiefs

The Tyee Club reflects the community's obsession with fishing. Founded in 1924 by Ted Painter, first owner of Painter's Lodge (see "Where to Stay," below), the Tyee Club boasts an elite roster of sport-fishing enthusiasts. Although also the Native word for "chief," in angling jargon, Tyee is the name given to any Chinook salmon weighing 14kg (31 lb.) or more. Hence, club membership is open to anyone who can land a Tyee, but in accordance with club rules.

Requirements include fishing from a guided rowboat in a small, designated area and using a single hook and only certain types of poles and line weights. Between mid-July and mid-September, many try and few succeed. John Wayne, Bob Hope, and Bing Crosby all tried, and failed, to become Tyee members. A Texan named Walter Shutts holds the all-time Tyee record for a 32kg (71-lb.) Chinook, caught in 1968.

The renowned **Tyee Club** attracts fishing enthusiasts from around the world in their pursuit of landing excessively large Chinook salmon. Every year between July and September, the Campbell River, designated a British Columbia Heritage River, swells with both visitors and fish, as salmon pass through the mile-wide passage, known as the **Discovery Channel,** en route to spawning grounds in northerly rivers. The area has historically produced vast hauls of incredibly large fish; thus Campbell River has become known as the "Salmon Fishing Capital of the World."

Today, as salmon numbers diminish, catch-and-release programs are in force, and those leading fishing expeditions are billing them more as wildlife adventures in an attempt to diversify or are reinventing themselves. Examples include rafting tours with **Destiny River Adventures;** day trips aboard the **MV *Uchuck III,*** from Gold River to the Tahsis, Nootka, and Kyoquot sounds; and mini-cruises to Bute Inlet or Kingcome Inlet aboard the **MV *Aurora Explorer***—all reveal parts of British Columbia many visitors never get to see.

ESSENTIALS
Getting There
BY CAR   Driving distances up the center of Vancouver Island are fast and easy with the new inland highway (Hwy. 19) between Nanaimo and Campbell River. Campbell River is 264km (164 miles) north of Victoria (about 2½ hours' worth of driving); 153km (95 miles) north of Nanaimo (about 1½ hours); and 48km (30 miles) north of Courtenay (about half an hour).

BY PLANE   Commercial airlines fly into the Campbell River and District Regional Airport (**✆ 250/923-5012;** www.crairport.ca). **Air Canada Jazz** (**✆ 888/247-2262;** www.flyjazz.ca), **Pacific Coastal Airlines** (**✆ 800/663-2872;** www.pacific-coastal.com), and **Central Mountain Air** (**✆ 888/865-8585;** www.flycma.com), operate daily scheduled flights from Vancouver, Calgary, and Victoria. Car-rental companies at the airport include **Budget** (**✆ 800/668-9688** or 250/923-4283; www.budget.com) and **National Car Rental** (**✆ 800/227-7368** or 250/923-1234; www.nationalvictoria.com). Smaller carriers, such as **Coril Air** (**✆ 888/287-8366** or 250/287-8371; www.corilair.com), provide harbor-to-harbor service between Campbell River and several small island communities. **Kenmore Air** (**✆ 800/543-9595;** www.kenmoreair.com) flies from Seattle Harbor on a seasonal basis.

BY BUS   **Greyhound Canada** (**✆ 800/661-8747;** www.greyhound.ca) runs daily service from Victoria to Port Hardy, stopping in Nanaimo, Campbell River, and other towns along the way. The one-way fare from Victoria to Campbell River is C$62 (refundable) or C$55 (nonrefundable) for adults. From Nanaimo to Campbell River, it's C$39 (refundable) or C$34 (nonrefundable) for adults. Fares for seniors are 10% less than the adult fares; fares for children 2 to 11 are 25% less. The trip from Victoria takes 5½ hours, while the trip from Nanaimo takes 3½ hours. **Island Link Bus** (**✆ 250/954-8257;** www.islandlinkbus.com) runs a passenger express service between BC Ferries' terminals, and Vancouver, Victoria, and Comox airports, and several island hubs as far north as Campbell River. One-way fares are slightly less than Greyhound, but schedules may not be as convenient.

Visitor Information
The **Campbell River Visitor Information Centre** is located at 1235 Shoppers Row (**✆ 866/830-1113** or 250/830-0411; www.campbellriver.travel).

Getting Around

In Campbell River itself, **Campbell River Airporter & Taxi Service** (✆ **250/286-3000**) offers door-to-door service anywhere. Also, **Campbell River Transit** (✆ **250/287-7433**) operates regular bus service.

FABULOUS FISHING

Campbell River is *the* home base for numerous sport-fishing excursions, and there are several quality outfitters and charter-boat companies. These include **Coastal Island Fishing Adventures** (457 Albatross Crescent; ✆ **888/225-9776** or 250/287-3831; www.coastalislandfishing.com). Rates are from C$110 an hour (for up to 3 people), inclusive of gear and tackle, and your choice of a Grady White or Trophy vessel, or a 17-foot open Boston Whaler at C$75 per hour. Going for Tyee fishing? **Sea Beyond Adventures** (526 Thulin St.; ✆ **250/287-4497**; www.seabeyond.ca) charges C$110 per hour for a minimum of 5 hours in a covered 24-foot Grady White, C$600 per day for freshwater fishing. And if you're looking for a Tyee rower, they'll do that too, at C$500 per day or C$150 per tide. Check out **Coastal Wilderness Adventures** (P.O. Box 722, Campbell River; ✆ **866/640-1173** or 250/287-3427; www.coastwild.com) for sky-high heli-fishing, as well as overnight specialty packages such as spa-fishing getaways for ladies.

Virtually every hotel and inn has a recommendation or package to do with fishing, so ask when you make your reservation. The Info Centre has a comprehensive directory to fishing guides. As the largest outdoor store on Vancouver Island, **River Sportsmen** (2115 Island Hwy.; ✆ **800/663-7217** or 250/286-1017) is a one-stop resource for the latest fishing information, as well as offering a huge selection of outdoor, camping, and fishing gear.

Charter companies will handle licensing requirements, but if you decide to fish independently, **nonresident fishing licenses** are available at outdoor recreation stores throughout Campbell River, including **Painter's Lodge Holiday & Fishing Resort,** where you can also watch all the action from beautiful decks (see "Where to Stay," below). Saltwater licenses cost C$13 per day, C$25 for 3 days, and C$37 for 5 days. Freshwater licenses cost C$20 per day or C$50 for 8 days. Fees are reduced for BC and Canada residents.

If private charters are still your preference, be aware that most are geared for fishing. That said, **Rippingale's Fishing** (2330 Steelhead Rd.; ✆ **800/988-8242** or 250/286-7290; www.rippingalesfishing.com) offers all-inclusive 3-night packages ranging from C$1,700 per person.

ECO-EXPLORING

If fishing isn't your thing, or even if it is, riding the rapids along Campbell River or winding down the glacial flow of Southgate River from Bute Inlet is full of hard-to-see, back-country scenery and wildlife. When the salmon are running in their thousands, there's even an opportunity to snorkel and swim alongside them. **Destiny River Adventures** (1630 North Island Hwy; ✆ **877/923-7238** or 250/287-7238; www.destinyriver.com) offers half-day (C$99) and full day (C$139) excursions May to early August, as well as multiple-night camping trips to Nimpkish River—the largest volume river on Vancouver Island. Prices range from C$900 to C$2,300 and include all the gear, from camping stuff and fishing rods to riverside meals and micro-brewed beer.

cruising THE QUEEN CHARLOTTE STRAIT

A rather unique option exists if you want to explore the island's coastal communities. Book a trip aboard the MV *Aurora Explorer*, a 135-foot landing craft that plies the western waterways on 5-day excursions to the remote inlets of the Queen Charlotte Strait. The MV *Aurora Explorer* is the only overnight passenger-freight vessel of its kind, sailing on an itinerary that is set by the tidal currents and the cargo she carries on her open deck. This might include supplies for solitary island retreats, refrigerators for First Nations villages, heavy equipment for a logging outpost, or mail and newspapers for a floating post office.

Passenger quarters, housed just below the main lounge and galley, sleep 12 in cramped but hospitable bunk-style cabins. The crew is friendly, and food is hearty and constant, with a daily supply of fresh-baked cookies and bread. Most passengers are active retirees or 40-something soft adventurers who come from all walks of life, so entertainment relies on conversation, a good book, the awesome scenery, unexpected wildlife, and being part of a working vessel in action, watching the crew on the deck below hoist that winch and tote that bale—sometimes at 4am. Usually, the schedule includes stops at heritage sites, abandoned villages, or even a pebbly beach for an impromptu BBQ (if trolling for supper has proved successful). So, in addition to a seafaring adventure, there are opportunities for shore explorations.

From May to mid-September, all-inclusive fares start at C$2,225 adults; from mid-September through October and from the end of March through April, all-inclusive fares are C$1,690 to C$1,950 adults, minimum age is 16 years. The MV *Aurora Explorer* does not sail November through February. For information, contact Marine Link Tours (P.O. Box 451, Campbell River, BC V9W 5C1; ℭ **250/286-3347**; www.marinelinktours.com).

Want something a little tamer but no less wild? Then **Discovery Marine Safaris** (1003 North Island Hwy.; ℭ **250/287-7008**; www.adventurewhalewatching.com) have it covered with whale-watching expeditions (July to mid-Oct), grizzly bear viewing (Sept to mid-Oct) and a year-round First Nations tour led by a Kwakwaka'wakw (Kwakiutl) Indian who shares his stories, anecdotes, and mythology of the surrounding landscapes and animals, and how they are translated into carvings, paintings, jewelry, and lifestyle. Prices range from C$139 to C$349.

WHERE TO STAY

Anchor Inn & Suites ☺ The inn's five themed suites will satiate the most whimsical dreams with decor that runs from exotic Arabian and wild African to an Arctic-inspired room with igloo-style bed canopy. The English is twee with its carriage bed; the Western will appeal to kids, as they have bunk beds hidden in a "jail cell." More standard rooms are available; each sport ocean views and are comfortably furnished with a choice of queen- or king-size beds. The restaurant serves all three meals, and in the evening, adds a sushi dimension to tried-and-true regular fare of pasta, chicken, and steak.

261 Island Hwy., Campbell River, BC V9W 2B3. ℭ **800/663-7227** or 250/286-1131. Fax 250/287-4055. www.anchorinn.ca. 77 units. C$139 double; C$249–C$289 theme-room double. Additional adult C$10. Theme, honeymoon, golf & fishing packages available. AE, MC, V. Free parking. **Amenities:** Restaurant; lounge; exercise room; hot tub; indoor pool. *In room:* TV, fridge, hair dryer, Wi-Fi.

Coast Discovery Inn & Marina   Adjacent to a busy shopping plaza right on the main drag, this is the only deluxe hotel you'll find downtown. It's a bit noisy by day, but since nothing much happens in Campbell River post-10pm, the location doesn't affect a quiet night's sleep. Guest rooms are spacious, and although they're a shade dated, new linens and a paint job have given them a lift. All guest rooms have views of the harbor, and suites have welcome extras like Jacuzzis. The marina can accommodate 70 yachts of up to 46m (150 ft.), as well as smaller pleasure crafts. Guided fishing tours are also available. There's a restaurant and a pub that features live evening entertainment Thursday through Saturday.

975 Shoppers Row, Campbell River, BC V9W 2C4. ⓒ **800/663-1144** or 250/287-7155. Fax 250/287-2213. www.coasthotels.com. 90 units. May–Sept C$138 double, C$154 superior double, C$230 suite; Oct–Apr C$119 double, C$134 superior double, C$156 suite. Additional adult C$10. MC, V. Free parking. Pets accepted (C$20). **Amenities:** Restaurant; lounge; exercise room; Jacuzzi; room service. *In room:* A/C, TV w/pay movies, hair dryer, minibar, Wi-Fi.

Dolphins Resort ★   Staying at this oceanfront resort is to relax into a 1940s atmosphere of cozy studio, one-, two-, and a four-bedroom log cabins, each self contained with a well-equipped kitchen, fireplace or woodstove, BBQ deck, and private hot tub from which to watch the cruise ships pass by en route to Alaska. There was a time when this was a base camp for anglers (diehards go to the sister resort, Dolphins North), but as families discovered its safe beaches and remote, central location, the demographic has shifted. A highlight here is the Anglers Dining Room, which seats less than 30 and fills up quickly for dinner with resort guests. This is an in-the-know gem of a place for food and low-light ambiance.

4125 Discovery Dr., Campbell River, BC V9W 4X6. ⓒ **800/891-0287** or 250/287-3066. www.dolphins resort.com. 13 units. July–Sept C$230–C$275 cabin; Oct–June C$149–C$199 cabin. Rates include full breakfast. Additional adult C$20. MC, V. Pets accepted. **Amenities:** Restaurant. *In room:* TV/DVD player, fridge, hair dryer.

Haig-Brown House   Prolific writer, avid outdoorsman, and respected judge, Roderick Haig-Brown was also one of British Columbia's most spirited conservationists (check out www.haigbrowninstitute.org). It was largely because of his efforts that the Fraser River, which runs down through the BC interior to Vancouver, was never dammed. From his 1923 farmhouse, set amidst 8 hectares (20 acres) of gardens beside the Campbell River, he wrote ardently about fly-fishing, resource management, and preserving BC's natural environment. Fully restored as a delightful B&B, this BC Heritage Property is a pilgrimage of sorts, especially for anglers. Guest rooms are decorated with comfy furnishings, although nothing too palatial. Guests share bathroom facilities.

2250 Campbell River Rd., Campbell River, BC V9W 4N7. ⓒ **250/286-6646.** www.haig-brown.bc.ca. 3 units. May to end Oct C$90–C$100 double. Additional adult C$20. MC, V. Closed in Nov–Apr **Amenities:** Lounge. *In room:* No phone.

Heron's Landing   A European boutique ambience inspires all the rooms and one-bedroom suites at this lovely hotel, which is decorated with tasteful antiques, hardwood floors, oriental rugs, coordinated linens, and drapes. Many have cozy living areas and full kitchens, making Heron's Landing a good choice for longer stays. Guests have access to the sun-drenched, turfed deck in summer. Across the street, there's a restaurant, pub, and other facilities at the Best Western Austrian Chalet Village (ⓒ **800/667-7207** or 250/923-4231; www.bwcampbellriver.com), a second choice if Heron's Landing is full.

492 South Island Hwy., Campbell River, BC V9W 1A5. ✆ **888/923-2849** or 250/923-2848. Fax 250/923-2849. www.heronslandinghotel.com. 30 units. C$145 double; C$175 suite; C$300 penthouse. AE, MC, V. Free indoor parking. Small pets accepted (C$25). **Amenities:** Restaurant. *In room:* TV, fridge, hair dryer, kitchen, Wi-Fi.

Ocean Resort As more people look to better themselves and their health, resorts like this are coming into their own. Fabulously renovated, it lies near Saratoga Beach in Oyster Bay and exudes a West Coast charm with its timber construction balanced with the clean lines of Asian simplicity. Rooms have hardwood floors, twin beds with brightly-colored throws and hypoallergenic duvets, and a balcony. The resort's main appeal is the space it creates to "naval-gaze." There's a beautifully crafted driftwood labyrinth, a meditation sanctuary, various programs in the healing arts (including regular yoga sessions), and an ocean-view dining room. Rates include a healthy continental breakfast, and for those who just want to stay put, relax, and feel the vibe, meal plans are also offered. Note that although children are accepted, this is an adult-oriented "retreat" resort, so consider the context before bringing the kids along.

4384 Island Hwy., Oyster River, BC V9H 1E8. ✆ **250/923-4281.** www.oceanresort.ca. 28 units, 1 suite. Mid-May to mid-Sept C$125–C$145 double, C$200 suite; mid-Sept to mid-May C$100–C$120 double, C$185 suite. Additional adult C$20. Meal package C$55. MC, V. Pets accepted (C$20). **Amenities:** Restaurant; fitness room; sauna. *In room:* Hair dryer, Wi-Fi.

Painter's Lodge Holiday & Fishing Resort ★★ An international favorite of avid fishermen and celebrities, Painter's Lodge has welcomed the likes of Bob Hope, Julie Andrews, Goldie Hawn, and the Prince of Luxembourg. Its location overlooking Discovery Passage is awesome, and its rustic grandeur has a West Coast ambience, with comfortable lounges, large decks, and roomy accommodations decorated in natural wood and outdoorsy colors. Wrapped in windows, the lodge's restaurant, **Legends,** boasts a view of the Passage from every table (see "Where to Dine," below). One of the neatest dining experiences is to take the speedboat trip (10 min. in each direction) over to **April Point Resort & Spa on Quadra Island** (see p. 200) for a pre-dinner martini at their sushi bar before returning to Legends for the catch of the day. The trip is included in hotel rates.

1625 MacDonald Rd. (P.O. Box 460, Dept. 2), Campbell River, BC V9W 4S5. ✆ **800/663-7090** or 250/286-1102. Fax 250/286-0158. www.painterslodge.com. 94 units. Early Apr–mid Oct C$139–C$159 double; C$219 cabin. Additional adult C$20. AE, DC, MC, V. Closed mid-Oct to early Apr. **Amenities:** Restaurant; pub; lounge; babysitting; children's center; health club; 2 Jacuzzis; heated outdoor pool; 2 outdoor tennis courts. *In room:* TV, hair dryer, Wi-Fi.

Sonora Resort ★★★ A multi-million dollar investment has turned this fishing lodge into a sought-after destination for much more. Fishing is still a primary activity, but with an indoor tennis court, 12-seat movie theater, virtual golf, a luxurious spa, hiking trails, and Zodiac eco-tours, Sonora has high-end appeal. Accommodations include themed-lodge rooms, luxurious multi-roomed cottages, and hotel-like suites. Bedding is plush, bathrooms feature quality amenities, and furnishings are warm and inviting. The all-inclusive rates cover use of all resort facilities, meals, and even alcohol. Spa treatments, fishing trips, and tours are extra, as are its private transfers to the island. Sonora can provide a boat shuttle from Campbell River, as well as direct flights from Vancouver and Seattle via its state-of-the-art Agusta Bell helicopters. **Kenmore Air** (✆ **866/435-9524**) and **SeaAir Seaplanes** (✆ **800/447-3247**) can also get you there from Seattle and Vancouver respectively. Kids are welcome. **Tip:** Be at

Camping

Miracle Beach Provincial Park (© 250/954-4600) is one of BC's best parks. Native legend speaks to a supernatural stranger who appeared on the beach and miraculously transformed a Native princess into Mitlenatch Island. True or not, the beach itself is appropriately named, with countless tidal pools; warm sand; and soft, undulating waves. Add to this roomy campsites beneath tall, sun-dappled trees; forested trails down to the beach; hot showers; and playgrounds, and you've got the makings of a great family camping holiday. A seasonal visitor center has nature displays and park interpreters (© 250/337-8241; www.naturehouse.ca). For reservations, call Discover Camping (© 800/689-9025 or 604/689-9025; www.discovercamping.ca).

dockside when the boats return after a day's fishing; the discards after cleaning the fish attract a gathering of harbor seals all vying for these easy-to-get delicacies.

Sonora Resort, Sonora Island. (Mailing address: 105-5360 Airport Rd. S., Richmond, BC V7B 1B4.) © **888/576-6672** or 604/233-0460. Fax 604/233-0465. www.sonoraresort.com. 87 units. July to mid-Sept C$850/couple, C$545 children 5–18 (C$360 if sharing parent's room); mid-May to June & mid-Sept to Oct C$600–C$675/couple, C$375–C$430 children 5–18 (C$250–C$287 when sharing parent's room). **Amenities:** Restaurant; gym; hot tub; outdoor pool; room service; sauna; spa; indoor tennis court. *In room:* A/C, TV/DVD player, fridge, iPod dock, Wi-Fi.

WHERE TO DINE

Baan Thai THAI   It's so refreshing to find an ethnic eatery away from the big city lights, and this one is as good as it gets. In fact, the menu is so popular it hasn't changed much over the years. You can always judge a quality Thai restaurant by its pad Thai, and this one is extremely flavorful, as are the curries. If your palette isn't up for the fire of Thai spices, all dishes can be modified to suit. The 40-seat saffron-colored restaurant is located over a storefront on Shoppers Row (Campbell River's main drag). The entrance is easy to miss, but let the aromatic smells be your guide. Tables are on the small side, but close quarters simply add to the intimate atmosphere of this eatery. There's also a rooftop patio.

1090B Shoppers Row. © **250/286-4850.** Reservations recommended. Main courses C$12–C$15. MC, V. Mon–Fri 11:30am–2pm; Mon–Sat 5–9pm. Closed Sun.

Dick's Fish & Chips ✦ FISH AND CHIPS   Located beside Discovery Launch near the Quadra Island ferry, Dick's is everything you would wish for in a fish 'n chips shanty. The restaurant floats on a dock brimming with pots of geraniums and overlooking all the boating action; tables inside sit cheek by jowl to a bustling kitchen, and traditional favorites are served in newspaper. There's cod, salmon, and halibut alongside fries (potato and yam), onion rings, mushy peas, and home-style coleslaw. Burgers, chicken, wraps, and hot dogs round out the menu. Call ahead for takeout.

1003B Island Hwy., Campbell River. © **250/287-3336.** www.dicksfishandchips.com. Main courses C$7–C$16. MC, V. Daily 11:30am–9pm.

Fusilli Grill ITALIAN FUSION   Chances are that if you're at any catered event around town, these folks are the cooks behind the scenes; yet their 56-seat restaurant is so unassuming, at first glance, you would have a hard time believing them capable of such fare. But it is the best Italian food in town, with all its pastas, breads, and dressings made in-house, from scratch. Even when they tackle another ethnic cuisine, noodles are usually somewhere on the plate. The Vietnamese-style prawns, chorizo, and scallions with chile, ginger, and fennel is a delicious example, as is the shrimp and scallop stir-fry. The takeout menus are a real value: A three-course pasta lunch is C$8.50; dinner is C$10.

220 Dogwood St. ⓒ **250/830-0090.** www.fusilligrill.bc.ca. Reservations recommended. Main courses lunch C$7–C$12, dinner C$12–C$28. DC, MC, V. Tues–Fri 11am–9:30pm; Sat–Mon 4:30–9pm.

Harbour Grill ★★ FRENCH CONTINENTAL   You wouldn't expect to find the best restaurant in town at a shopping mall, but that's exactly where Harbour Grill set up shop. Thankfully, the restaurant faces the waterside Discovery Harbour Marina, rather that a hoard of retail outlets, so the mall experience doesn't touch on the dining experience one iota—except for always being able to find a parking spot! Grab a window seat, and you're likely to see cruise ships pass by on their way to the Inside Passage. Food-wise, Harbour Grill is classic fine dining with crisp white linens, attentive staff, and traditional French-influenced dishes such as veal Oscar and duck *a l'orange*. Steaks (Alberta grain-fed AAA beef only) are the house specialty: Peppered, béarnaise, *la Wellington*—you name it—and then there's its gi-normous Chateaubriand, done to perfection. The wine list features many VQA wines from BC, as well as a selection from France, Australia, and California.

In the Discovery Harbour Centre, 112–1334 Island Hwy. ⓒ **250/287-4143.** www.harbourgrill.com. Reservations recommended. Main courses C$27–C$38. AE, DC, MC, V. Daily 5:30–10pm.

Legends Dining Room ★ SEAFOOD/CONTINENTAL   Located at Painter's Lodge, this restaurant's open only in season, which is a shame. Floor-to-ceiling windows oversee the comings and goings across Discovery Passage, and the intimate fine-dining area has panache. The menu is varied and, not surprisingly, includes many fish and seafood specialties. This is, after all, a fishing lodge. The perennial favorite? The crab and salmon cakes, with chipotle garlic aioli and sweet-corn vinaigrette. You can't go wrong with the halibut, which always has a different twist, whether it's with purple mustard or sautéed tandoori-spiced almonds. If you've just come off the water and are looking for something more casual, the Tyee Pub is an informal option with an oversize deck offering ringside seats to the water. **Note:** The restaurant often opens at 5am to get fishing enthusiasts off to a good start.

Painter's Lodge, 1625 McDonald Rd. ⓒ **250/286-1102.** Reservations recommended. Main courses lunch C$10–C$18, dinner C$19–C$36. AE, DC, MC, V. Daily 7am–10pm. Closed mid-Oct to early Apr.

Riptide Marine Pub & Grill PUB FARE/REGIONAL   If you're exploring the Discovery Harbour Shopping Plaza, here's where to take time out for lunch, snacks, and dinner, or just a drink over appies. Expect the usual: traditional burgers, salads, and pizza that sit alongside more substantial meals like rack of lamb, filet mignon, salmon, and even lobster tail—an item that seems a bit ambitious for this style of eatery. But its smart-casual style and its location next to the bustling marina attracts boaters, walkers, and folks in transit to another island via water taxi or seaplane. Showers, laundry facilities, and a liquor store are part of the complex.

Discovery Harbour Shopping Plaza, 1340 Island Hwy. ⓒ **250/830-0044.** Main courses C$17–C$23. AE, MC, V. Tues–Sat 11am–1am; Sun & Mon 11am–midnight.

Gold River

The traditional territory of the Mowachaht and Muchalaht peoples, it wasn't until the 1860s, when the Chinese started pulling gold from the river, that Gold River began to find its way onto maps and into public awareness. Even then, when the gold ran out, it would take almost 100 years for lumberjacks to arrive and start harvesting the forested hills. When a pulp mill opened here in 1965, **Gold River** was literally built out of the wilderness—a British Columbia "instant community," whose existence was predicated on forestry and economic need. Gold River was Canada's first all-electric town and the first to have underground wiring. Since the pulp mill closed in 1998, however, Gold River has been forced to reinvent itself in order to survive. Looking to its natural resources once again, the community has a growing ecotourism industry. If you're just passing through, at least try a hike on the **Peppercorn Trail;** it's an easy, well-groomed path that takes about 40 minutes and follows Gold and Heber rivers. Watch for whitewater kayakers taking on the eddies.

ESSENTIALS
Getting There

Aside from Tofino and Ucluelet (see chapter 7), Gold River is the only community on Vancouver Island's west coast reachable by a well-maintained paved road. It's 92km (57 miles) west of Campbell River along **Highway 28;** driving there takes about 1½ hours. You pass through spectacular **Strathcona Provincial Park** and on to the remote **Muchalaht Inlet.**

Visitor Information

For more information and maps on Gold River and the surrounding area, visit the **Gold River Visitor Information Centre** at 499 Muchalat Dr. (© **250/283-2418** mid-May to Labor Day or 250/283-2202 Labor Day to mid-May; www.goldriver.ca).

EXPLORING GOLD RIVER

Sport fishing, rugged scenery, and abundant wildlife have always been the region's trademarks, and since the pulp mill closed in 1998, these natural attractions are becoming the center of a tourist-based local economy. One of the area's largest and most reliable fishing outfitters, particularly for saltwater salmon, halibut, and cod, is **Nootka Sound Sports Fishing Charters** (© **877/283-7194** or 250/338-7679; www.nootkasoundfish.com). Trips start at C$80 per hour for up to two people; 5-hour minimum. Additional passengers incur a nominal extra charge.

If fishing's not your thing, there's kayaking, hiking, and wildlife viewing, as well as spelunking in the **Upana Caves**, 27km (17 miles) northwest of Gold River. A well-marked trail connects the five caves, which include the two-chambered Main Cave, with a waterfall at the end of one passage; the marble-smooth Resurgence Cave, with its toothy outcrops; and the spiraling Corner Cave. There are a number of modest restaurants, B&Bs, and motels, which makes Gold River a good base from which to explore places like **Nootka Sound,** especially if you opt to experience the *Uchuck III,* a working passenger and freight vessel offering scenic tours (see below). Local helicopters (Vancouver Island Helicopters; © **250/283-7616**) and floatplanes (Air Nootka; © **250/283-2255**) provide the closest air access to popular Hot Springs Cove.

WHERE TO STAY & DINE

Ridgeview Motor Inn Clean, simply furnished, and comfortable, this motor inn is pretty standard fare, and while it may not win any awards for style, the folks who run it are friendly and knowledgeable about the area. This is the first choice for most visitors and fishermen since the inn has a fish-cleaning station. Rates include continental breakfast, and some rooms have microwaves, kitchenettes, and valley views. The Ridge Neighbourhood pub/restaurant (© **250/283-2461**) is next door.

395 Donner Court, Gold River, BC V0P 1G0. © **800/989-3393** or 250/283-2277. Fax 250/283-7611. www.ridgeview-inn.com. 44 units. C$99–C$109 double; C$135 suite. Additional adult C$10. AE, MC. **Amenities:** Dining area. *In room:* TV, fridge, Wi-Fi.

Tahsis, Nootka & Kyoquot Sounds

If you decide to venture farther west from Gold River, you'll explore the coastal communities in and around **Tahsis, Nootka, and Kyoquot sounds**—some of the most beautiful coastal scenery in the world. Kyoquot is the ancestral home of the Mowachaht/Muchalaht people of the Nuu-chah-nulth (formerly Nootka) nation. A little farther along, the almost uninhabited First Nations village of historic Yuquot (Friendly Cove) is where British explorer Captain James Cook first came ashore in 1778, making this area, in effect, the birthplace of British Columbia.

Tahsis is accessible only by a well-maintained gravel road, affectionately dubbed the Tree to Sea Drive. Take this road to the Upana Caves that lie just before Bull Lake Summit. As you near Tahsis, you'll find the Leiner River Bouldering Trail, a short loop trail along the narrow valley of Leiner River, as well as a longer (4-hr.) trail to The Lookout over Tahsis Inlet. Typical of those in rugged coastal communities, most visitor services are geared to wilderness tourism. Hiking the rainforests and coastline is big business here, as are fishing and wildlife viewing.

ESSENTIALS
Getting There

Although Tahsis can be reached by land, the best way to visit Tahsis, or explore Nootka and Kyoquot sounds, is aboard the *Uchuck III* (see below) or via seaplane (Air Nootka; © **250/283-2255**). Both operate out of Gold River.

Visitor Information

For maps and information, contact the Gold River Information Centre (499 Muchalat Dr., Gold River, BC V0P 1G0; © **250/283-2418** mid-May to Labor Day or 250/283-2202 Labor Day to mid-May; www.goldriver.ca), or the **Tahsis Chamber of Commerce** (36 Rugged Mountain Rd., P.O. Box 278, Tahsis, BC V0P 1X0; © **250/934-6425**).

EXPLORING THE AREA

Uchuck III ★★★ Exploring this coastline aboard the workboat MV *Uchuck III* is not only a treat for the whole family, but good value for the money. It's a much more cost-effective option than chartering a private boat, and you'll see, hear, taste, and smell more along the way than you will in the more "sanitized" environment of a private vessel. A converted World War II minesweeper, the MV *Uchuck III* sails year-round on day-long and overnight stays. Depending on the day and time of year, your destination might be **Tahsis, Zeballos, Kyoquot,** or **Yuquot** (Friendly Cove).

Nootka Trail

Hugging the west coast of Nootka Island, the Nootka Trail is world-famous for its wilderness hiking experience featuring long beaches, secluded bays, and spectacular headlands jutting into the Pacific Ocean. Unlike the tough West Coast Trail (see chapter 7), this is a relatively easy hike that never rises more than 50m (164 ft.) above sea level. Along the way, you're likely to see whales and old native middens. Hikers can take a water taxi to either trail head (Louie Bay or Friendly Cove) from Tahsis or can arrive by floatplane from Gold River. Purchasing a tide guide before your trip is mandatory, as you can use low tides to follow the beach flats. Most people take 4 days or longer to complete the hike.

As the workhorse of the sounds, and the lifeline of many of these isolated communities, the MV *Uchuck III* also puts in at remote logging camps and fishing ports, picking up passengers and offloading anything from stoves to Oh Henry! bars. In May, the vessel offers a repositioning trip to Victoria for C$425, where it gets refitted for the season, before chugging back to Gold River.

Nootka Sound Services, Gold River. 📞 **250/283-2325.** www.mvuchuck.com. Day-trip rates C$75 adults, C$70 seniors, C$40 children 7–12, free for children 6 & under; overnight trip rates C$240–$335 adults, C$90–C$145 children 7–12, free for children 6 & under.

WHERE TO STAY & DINE

Most of the lodges in Nootka Sound have a definite fishing bent, either floating in protected coves, operating as part homes/part one- and two-bedroom inns, or as small executive-style homes for high rollers. Many close in winter.

Maquinna Resort   Located next door to the Maquinna Mall, this resort offers the conveniences of a tackle and bait store, postal services, a small gallery, and a bakery. It also offers well-maintained, quality hotel rooms, well furnished with comfortable beds, as well as a selection of self-catering one- and two-bedroom condos. The hotel corner rooms are the biggest and have ocean views. The resort has a lively pub (📞 **250/934-5522**) and a licensed bistro-style restaurant serving seafood dishes, steaks, chicken, pasta, and burgers. At press time, the place just went up for sale so double check developments before you book; chances are it will be business as usual. **Nootka Sound Charters** (📞 **250/934-5558**) operates fishing trips out of here. Divers, however, need to head over to **Tahtsa Dive & Kayak Centre** (📞 **866/934-6365** or 250/934-6365), now based on Wharf Street; these folks also offer wildlife tours.

1400 S. Maquinna Dr. (P.O. Box 400), Tahsis, BC V0P 1X0. 📞 **250/934-6367.** Fax 250/934-7884. http://home.cablerocket.com/-maquinna/. 24 units. May–Oct C$115–C$135 double, C$250 condo.. Closed Nov–Apr. MC, V. Free parking. **Amenities:** Restaurant; pub; Wi-Fi. *In room:* TV, no phone.

Tahsis Motel   Very basic, but at least clean, this motel is up to date and provides creature comforts that will probably feel luxurious after a day on the water or trekking through rainforest. The Millhouse Café serves breakfast, lunch, and dinner—the burgers and pizzas are safe bets. They're also available in the Spar Tree Pub. Bag lunches are provided by request.

187 Head Bay Rd., Tahsis, BC V0P 1X0. © **250/934-6318.** Fax 250/934-7808. www.cablerocket.com/
-tahsismotel/. 11 units. C$85 double. Additional adult C$20. MC, V. Pets accepted (C$5). **Amenities:** Pub/
restaurant; Wi-Fi. *In room:* TV, no phone.

QUADRA & CORTES ISLANDS

Affectionately called the Discovery Islands, Quadra and Cortes islands march to the
beat of a different drummer. Both are richly pastoral, with stretches of sandy beaches
to explore and meandering roads that lead to hidden coves, artist studios, and sudden
dead-ends that may or may not have an overgrown path to the beach. Quadra is more
mainstream, probably because of its proximity to Campbell River, while Cortes is a
haven for those walking the talk of living a holistic, alternative lifestyle.

Essentials

GETTING THERE

The islands are accessible only by water. To reach Cortes by public transit, you'll
need to cross to Quadra Island.

    BC Ferries (© **250-386-3431**) operates year-round between these islands with
18 sailings from Campbell River and Quadra Island. The crossing takes 10 minutes
and costs C$8.35 adults, C$4.20 children (5-11 years), and C$20 for a standard-size
vehicle. To get to Cortes Island, you need to travel to Quadra Island for the connector to Cortes. There are half a dozen daily trips both ways between Quadra and
Cortes islands. This crossing takes 45 minutes and costs C$9.75 adults, C$4.90
children (5-11 years), and C$23 for a standard vehicle. All fares are round-trip.
Note: The Ship's crew collects fares, so either pay via credit card for a through fare
from Campbell River to Cortes Island or have enough cash on you to bunny-hop
from Quadra Island to Cortes Island.

VISITOR INFORMATION

There is no visitor center on Quadra, though you can check out www.quadraisland.
ca or the **Campbell River Visitor Information Centre** (© **866/830-1113** or
250/830-1113). For Cortes Island, visit www.cortesisland.com.

Exploring the Islands

QUADRA ISLAND

Touring Quadra Island by car, bike, or scooter (rent the latter from April Point Resort
& Spa—see p. 200) is a delight, with plenty of stop-off points at parks and beaches to
enjoy, as well as a cottage winery. There are over 20 studio locations to visit potters,
carvers, painters, and sculptors; visit www.quadraislandarts.com for more information.
One of the most rewarding destinations is the Nuyumbalees Cultural Centre, formerly
the **Kwagiulth Museum and Cultural Centre**—if it's open. Located in Cape
Mudge Village, the museum drifts from one season to the other—sometimes opening
at odd hours, sometimes not at all. Islanders will have the latest scoop.

CORTES ISLAND

Located at the entrance to Desolation Sound, one of BC's most celebrated cruising
areas, Cortes Island is a beautiful wilderness hideaway. It is a lovely island to wander
through, with breathtaking vignettes of Gorge Harbour Marina, Von Donop Provincial

Marine Park, Squirrel Cove with an anchorage facing Desolation Sound, and 100-hectare (247-acre) Mansons Landing Provincial Marine Park. At Mansons Landing, as well as Smelt Bay and Squirrel Cove, you'll find safe, sandy beaches which are among the few where you can collect shellfish legally. An easy 15-minute walk south from the government float at Mansons Landing leads to Hague Lake, which has a 1km (.6-mile) perimeter trail to the sandspit. Watch your step, it's steep in places. Most walks around Cortes aren't this formal; so if you decide to explore, say, the wilderness of Von Donop Provincial Marine Park, you would do well to create your own marking system. Just be sure to retrieve them all—islanders don't take kindly to eco-unfriendly practices.

Where to Stay & Dine

QUADRA ISLAND

April Point Resort & Spa   The sister resort to Painter's Lodge (see p. 193), April Point caters to a more soft-adventuring crowd with its kayak, bike, and scooter rentals, as well as its Aveda concept spa at the water's edge. Accommodations range from deluxe suites with Jacuzzi tubs to comfortable 1- to 4-bedroom "'woodsy' cabins," all of which have ocean views and decks. The restaurant has floor-to-ceiling windows and serves quality West Coast cuisine from early morning breakfast to fine dining at night, but the sushi bar sometimes steals the show, especially as a prelude to dinner. A free water taxi shuttles guests between April Point and Painter's Lodge.

900 April Point Rd., Quadra Island, (P.O. Box 248), Campbell River, BC V9W 4Z9. ⓒ **800/663-7090** or 250/285-2222. www.aprilpoint.com. 56 units. C$139 suite; C$195–C$209 cabin. Additional adult C$20. AE, DC, MC, V. Closed mid-Oct to early Apr. **Amenities:** Restaurant; sushi bar; lounge; babysitting; bike & scooter rentals; spa; kayak rentals. *In room:* TV, hair dryer, Wi-Fi.

Tsa-Kwa-Luten Lodge & RV Park   Owned and operated by the Laichwiltach (the Cape Mudge Band), here you can enjoy the Native experience with a luxurious twist (hence the Canada Select four-star rating). This modern resort resembles a native Big House, offering lodge suites, waterfront cabins, and two four-bedroom guest houses, as well as an excellent (primarily) seafood restaurant that often stages Native dancing; reservations are recommended. All rooms have an ocean view and either a balcony or patio; contemporary decor balances the earth-tone floors, bedspreads, and walls. Tsa-Kwa-Luten translates as "gathering place" in the Kwak'wala language of the Laichwiltach people, and it's located on the site of the band's original village. There are also 13 RV sites with full hookups.

Nuyumbalees Cultural Centre

The Nuyumbalees Cultural Centre museum (34 WeiWai Rd., Cape Mudge Village, Quathiaski Cove; ⓒ **250/285-3733**; www.nuyumbalees.com) is one of the few places where you can explore the area's Native heritage. On display is one of the world's best collections of potlatch artifacts, ceremonial masks, and tribal costumes, once used by the Cape Mudge Band. Behind the museum is K'Ik'Ik G'Illas, or "The House of Eagles," a longhouse-like structure used to teach carving, dancing, and other traditional skills. There's also an opportunity to make petroglyph rubbings from fiberglass castings of ancient stone carvings.

TRACKING THE wild side

As you travel through the northern regions of Vancouver Island, the richness of the aboriginal and natural heritage becomes increasingly evident. **Aboriginal Journeys** (398-1434 Island Hwy., Campbell River; ☎ **888/455-8101** or 250/850-1101; www.aboriginaljourneys.com) operates wildlife viewing and adventure tours within the traditional territory of the Laichwiltach peoples. This extends from Cape Mudge to the mouth of Bute Inlet, to Smith Inlet and around northern Vancouver Island. Tours include stories, history, and cultural insights alongside whale-watching, grizzly- and black-bear viewing, and other wildlife sightings from a 7.3m (24-ft.) Zodiac or a 17m (55-ft.) classic wooden fishing vessel.

Great Bear Nature Tours (6420 Hardy Bay Rd.; ☎ **888/221-8212** or 250/949-9496; www.greatbeartours.com) are all about bear immersion in the middle of Great Bear Rainforest, 3.2 million hectares (8 million acres) of pristine grizzly-bear wilderness. Hike between monumental cedars to hideaway observing posts, where you can watch bears clambering over rocks to snatch a salmon or tasty bear treats such as salmonberries; even learn how to track scat. Add to this a 10-guest lodge that floats in a serene corner of Smith Inlet, and it's easy to understand why *National Geographic Adventure Magazine* rated Great Bear Nature Tours one of the best adventure companies on Earth. Bear-watching season runs early May through October.

1 Lighthouse Rd. (P.O. Box 460), Quathiaski Cove, Quadra Island, BC V0P 1N0. ☎ **800/665-7745** or 250/598-3366. Fax 250/285-2532. www.capemudgeresort.com. 35 units. C$105–C$145 suite, C$180–C$225 cottage, C$150–C$379 guest house; C$35 ocean-view RV site, C$40 beachfront RV site. Additional adult C$20. Children 11 & under stay free in parent's room. Meal plans available. AE, DC, MC, V. Free parking. Closed mid-Oct to early Apr. Small pets accepted in RV sites. **Amenities:** Restaurant; lounge; free bikes; exercise room; Jacuzzi; sauna. *In room:* Hair dryer, Wi-Fi.

CORTES ISLAND

Cortes is small, so it's a good idea to reserve accommodations. The New Age set tend to head for **Hollyhock** (P.O. Box 127, Mansons Landing, Cortes Island, V0P 1K0; ☎ **800/933-6339;** www.hollyhock.ca), a holistic and spiritual retreat center. The back-to-the-wilderness, kayaking crowd favor **T'ai Li Lodge** (P.O. Box 16, Cortes Bay, Cortes Island, V0P 2K0; ☎ **800/939-6644** or 250/935-6711; www.taililodge.com) staying either in a small cabin or in a platform tent on the beachfront with access to amenities that include a solar hot shower, BBQ deck, and large communal kitchen. **Cortes Island Vacation Rentals** (☎ **888/785-3927** or 250/285-3927; www.cortesislandvacationrentals.com) arranges rentals for several privately owned beach cabins and family homes with rates from C$300 to C$2,500 a week.

EN ROUTE TO PORT HARDY

Trees, trees, and more trees line either side of Highway 19 heading north from Campbell River. The communities along this stretch still have mine- and timber-based economies, and every now and then, the stands of trees break to reveal mountainsides scalded by machinery or fields of blackened stumps, left to rot before replanting. The destinations that follow are listed geographically, heading north from Campbell River along Highway 19.

Paddle & Portage

The Sayward Forest Canoe Route is a spectacular 5km (3.1-mile) portage and canoeing route that will test the power of your stride and stroke. The recently upgraded trail crosses eight lakes with about 48km (39 miles) of paddling, total.

While logging is still the mainstay for communities such as **Port McNeill,** much to the chagrin of environmental activists, smaller hamlets such as **Holberg, Woss, Zeballos, Port Alice** (where you can tour a disused, 1917 pulp mill), **Sayward,** and picturesque **Telegraph Cove** seem to co-exist more peacefully with their lumber-industry environment. As a result, they have developed distinct personalities, whether from the Finnish influence still holding court in **Sointula,** or the richness of First Nations culture in **Alert Bay.**

Essentials
GETTING THERE
BY CAR   Although the singular road north is a well-maintained two-lane highway, it's used by logging trucks, as well as local traffic. Getting stuck behind one of these lumbering vehicles can slow you down, since they aren't always easy to pass. If you're in a camper, try to pull over once in a while to let faster traffic pass. In summer, the road gets busy with ferry travelers heading to and from Port Hardy, so give yourself extra time and avoid frustration by taking detours. The distance from Campbell River to Port Hardy is 238km (148 miles), which could take up to 3½ hours to drive. From Nanaimo to Port Hardy, it's 391km (243 miles)—allow at least 5 hours. For the long haul from Victoria to Port Hardy, it's a whopping 502km (312 miles). For this killer road trip, set aside 7 hours.

BY PLANE   Air Canada Jazz (© 888/247-2262; www.flyjazz.ca) operates daily flights among Vancouver, Victoria, Port Hardy, Comox, and Campbell River, as does **Pacific Coastal Airlines** (© 800/663-2872; www.pacific-coastal.com). **Kenmore Air** (© 800/543-9595 or 425/486-1257; www.kenmoreair.com) flies from Seattle Harbor to Port Hardy, Port McNeill, and Quadra Island.

BY BUS   Greyhound Canada (© 800/661-8747; www.greyhound.ca) runs daily service from Victoria to Port Hardy, stopping in Campbell River. The one-way fare from Victoria to Port Hardy is C$99 (refundable) or C$89 (nonrefundable) for adults. From Nanaimo to Port Hardy, it's C$78 (refundable) or C$70 (nonrefundable) for adults. Fares for seniors are 10% less than for adults; fares for children 2 to 11 are 50% less. The trip from Victoria to Port Hardy is just under 10 hours. From Nanaimo to Port Hardy, it's approximately 7 hours. You can save a couple of dollars by traveling midweek and by booking 7, 14, and 21 days in advance.

BY FERRY   BC Ferries (© 888/223-3779; www.bcferries.com) operates nine crossings daily between Port McNeill and the community of **Alert Bay,** on Cormorant Island, and between Port McNeill and **Sointula,** on Malcolm Island. Round-trip fares are C$9.75 adults, C$4.90 children 5 to 11. Passenger vehicles are C$23. Crossing time is 45 minutes. BC Ferries also operates service between Port Hardy and Prince Rupert, a 15-hour journey via the famed **Inside Passage** (see "The Call of Haidi Gwaii," p. 206). One-way day-sailing fares are C$100 adults, C$50 children 5 to 11. Passenger vehicles are C$200. Overnight and off-season rates are also available. The Discovery Coast cruise to Bella Coola on the mainland costs C$170 adults, C$85 children (5-11 years), and C$350 for a standard vehicle.

VISITOR INFORMATION

There are visitor information centers in several of the communities along the route to Port Hardy, such as **Port McNeill Visitor Information** at 1594 Beach Dr. (© **250/956-3131;** www.portmcneill.net) and **Alert Bay Visitor Information** at 116 Fir St. (© **250/974-5024;** www.alertbay.ca). Once in Port Hardy, head to the **Port Hardy Visitor Information Centre,** 7250 Market St. (© **250/949-7622;** www.ph-chamber.bc.ca). Open daily during normal office hours, these folks also provide an **accommodations reservations service** for Port Hardy and Prince Rupert (for those going to Prince Rupert with BC Ferries). For more information on the north region of Vancouver Island, contact **Vancouver Island North Visitors' Association** (© **800/903-6606** or 250/949-9094; www.tourismni.com).

Zeballos

Located 191km (119 miles) north of Campbell River, at the end of a 40km (25-mile) pitted gravel road off Highway 19, BC's tiniest village, **Zeballos,** once produced more than C$13 million worth of gold. Tailings from the mines were used to build up the roads and led to a local legend that the streets were literally "paved with gold." But when Zeballos lost its Midas touch, logging, fish farming, and tourism became its mainstays. Although still fairly rough and ready, some of the false-fronted historic gold-rush buildings have been spruced up, including the old hospital downtown and the old Privateer gold mine a few minutes up the Zeballos River. Today, this pretty village is also the jumping-off point to an eco-adventurer's dream—everything from kayaking and fishing to diving. Recreational cavers and experienced spelunkers will head to **Little Hustan Caves** for its sinkholes, canyons, and fast-moving river that disappears and reappears in the rock formations. Hikers will find any number of trails including the old logging road down to Little Zeballos and a fairly strenuous climb up Sugarloaf Mountain for amazing views of Little Espinoza Inlet. If you decide to check in with a local outfitter, be sure to ask about the tidal fall change on this inlet. You need a boat to get up close to the swirling waters and an experienced hand at the wheel.

> **Woss's Claim to Fame**
>
> **Woss only changed its status from logging camp to an official community in 1999, and it operates a 122km (76-mile) logging railway—the longest still-working logging railway in North America.**

Zeballos Village Museum (122 Maquinna Ave.; © 250/761-4070 May–mid Sept or 250/761-4229 mid Sept–Apr) doubles as a **Visitors Information Centre** and is your best bet for arranging excursions, since many outfitters are seasonal or seemingly come and go with the tide. The center can also help you reserve accommodations and campsites, both of which are fairly limited, or one of the 30 RV sites. The museum part of the center is filled with old mining equipment and photos of 'old' Zeballos, and is a good starting point to learn about this community that's survived a history of hard knocks, including a tsunami in 1964.

WHERE TO STAY & DINE

Cedars Inn   Built in 1936 during the height of the gold rush, the inn's heritage ambience provides more than creature comforts. Rooms are bright and big enough to have sitting areas, although the public lounge has nice leather-bound chairs to sink into. All rooms have views of the Zeballos River and mountains. All have private baths; some have kitchenettes. **The Blue Heron Restaurant** offers hearty breakfasts (this meal is not included in the room rate), first-rate boxed lunches, local oysters, frothy cappuccinos, and a dinner selection that changes frequently, depending on the catch and the season. True to the multitasking nature of those on the Zeballos tourism scene, you'll find kayak rentals, fishing charters, and water taxi services here.

203 Pandora Ave., Zeballos, BC V0P 2A0. © **866/222-2235** or 250/761-4044. www.cedarsinn.ca. 13 units; 2 cabins. C$105–C$115 double; C$125-C$150 cabins. Additional adult C$20. Children under 12 stay free in parent's room. Off-season discounts available. AE, MC, V. Free parking. **Amenities:** Restaurant; lounge. *In room:* Satellite TV, fridge, hair dryer, kitchenette (in some), Wi-Fi.

Telegraph Cove

A highlight of your trip north must be Telegraph Cove, a picture-perfect village located 239km (149 miles) north of Campbell River. Overlooking Johnstone Strait, it is one of the few remaining **elevated-boardwalk villages** on Vancouver Island. This historic community got its start in 1912 as a one-room telegraph station that marked the end of a cable, strung tree to tree, all the way from Victoria. When messages were received, the operator hopped into a boat and rowed to the community of **Alert Bay,** on Cormorant Island, to deliver the news. Part of the cove's charm is that many of the original buildings still stand, including the telegraph station, an army mess hall, picturesque residences, and cozy cabins perched on stilts over the water's edge and joined by boardwalks. Walk to the end, and you'll find the **Johnstone Strait Whale Interpretive Centre,** (© **250/-928-3129** (mid May to October); © 250/928-3117 (October to mid-May) www.killerwhalecentre.org), dubbed the Bones Project, where they are piecing together the skeleton of a fin whale. You'll also find hands-on displays of the numerous species of marine life populating the area. Across from here, however, is a busy and evolving marina where an expanse of asphalt caters to RVs and roads lead to expensive cliff-hanging lots and even more expensive homes. For many, development is marginalizing something that is still clinging onto "quaint."

Cable Cookhouse

Even if you're not needing a break, a 5-minute detour on the road to Sayward will reward you with a one-of-a-kind cable cookhouse (there is only one road to Sayward, and this is the only building on it!). Owned by the woman whose father built the place some 40 years ago, the Cookhouse serves hearty food with genuine hospitality. Everything's freshly baked, griddled, fried, and tossed. Logging paintings adorn the walls, including original canvasses and cartoons by logging legend Len Whalen. The cinnamon buns are steroid-gi-normous.

Salish Sea

In 2009, British Columbia and Washington State agreed to rename the Strait of Georgia and Puget Sound with the aboriginal-rooted Salish Sea. The 18,000-sq.-km (6,950-sq-mile) area begins south of Telegraph Cove in Desolation Sound and extends through the Fraser River Delta to include all of Puget Sound near Seattle.

OUTDOOR ACTIVITIES

Because of its proximity to Robson Bight Ecological Reserve, whale-watching is big business, though any trip along Johnstone Strait will include sightings of dolphins, seals, porpoises, and eagles. At the end of the boardwalk lies **Stubbs Island Charters** (© **800/665-3066** or 250/928-3185; www.stubbs-island.com), BC's first orca- and wildlife-watching company. The 60-foot boats are equipped with hydrophones so you can listen to the whales' underwater conversations. The 3½-hour cruises run May through late October and cost C$94 adults. Choose either the first or last departure of the day (9am or 5:30pm), and you'll save C$10.

For those who want to stay on land, **Tide Rip Tours** (28 Boardwalk; © **888/643-9319** or 250/339-5320; www.tiderip.com) runs various wildlife-viewing excursions, including seeking out grizzly bears (from C$288).

For kayak rentals and guided multi-day kayaking trips into Telegraph Cove and Johnstone Strait, contact **North Island Kayak** (© **877/949-7707** or 250/928-3114; www.kayakbc.ca) or **Telegraph Cove Sea Kayaking** (© **888/756-0099** or 250/756-0094; www.tckayaks.com). Rentals are C$40 a day for a single; C$65 a day for a double. A 3-day trip runs C$795 adults and includes all camping gear. **Discovery Expeditions** is the company's more adventurous arm and focuses on 4- to 6-day trips, using Sophia Island (across from Robson Bight) as a base camp. A 4-day trip is C$899 adults; a 6-day adventure is C$1,395 adults.

WHERE TO STAY & DINE

Hidden Cove Lodge   Located 6.5km (4 miles) from Telegraph Cove, this 557-sq.-m (5,995-sq.-ft.) retreat lodge exudes an easy-going, West Coast charm. There are cedar beams throughout, floor-to-ceiling windows to take full advantage of the waterfront views, and comfortable furnishings. There are eight lodge rooms and three private self-contained cottages. All accommodations are clean and simply decorated; children are welcome in the cottages only. The licensed dining room, which serves quality international dishes, is open to non-guests by reservation only. Numerous eco-tours, including heli-fishing, can be arranged.

Lewis Point, 1 Hidden Cove Rd., Telegraph Cove, BC V0N 2R0. ©/fax **250/956-3916.** www.hiddencove lodge.com. 11 units. C$155 double; C$199 1-bedroom cottage; C$299 2-bedroom cottage. Double rates include full breakfast. 2-night minimum stay. Additional adult C$25. Off-season rates available. MC, V. Free parking & moorage for boaters. **Amenities:** Restaurant; babysitting; Jacuzzi. *In room:* No phone.

Telegraph Cove Marina & RV Park   The "old" Telegraph Cove still holds its charm of antiquity; the same can't be said of the cove's other side, which is dominated by a 48-space full-hookup RV park. It's part of a larger development program that includes cliff-clinging real estate lots for sale, a recently renovated 130-slip

The Call of Haida Gwaii

Although not technically a Gulf Island, the Queen Charlottes are still part of the same coastal archipelago, albeit strewn further north, with a heritage and natural appeal that leave many awestruck. These are the hereditary lands of the Haida, where pristine rainforest cloaks ancient totem poles and swirling mists often shroud the islands themselves, like Brigadoon. Most lodges, save for the **Queen Charlotte Lodge** (© 800/ 688-8959 or 604/420-7197; www.queen charlottelodge.com), are geared only to serious fishing, and accommodations are secondary. The "Q" however, is the *only*

place where fishing is offered alongside eco-adventures and tours of deserted Indian villages—the only lodge the Haida has sanctioned to do so—as well as gourmet food and spa services. Getting to Haida Gwaii is easiest by air; several charter float planes and helicopters operate between Vancouver and Victoria directly to the islands. The longer, and far more scenic, route is via BC Ferries from Port Hardy to Skidegate via Prince Rupert and the Inside Passage. It's a 15-hour journey that's nothing short of spectacular and at a fraction of the cost of cruise ships.

marina, and Dockside 29, a hotel offering a comparatively luxurious alternative to the 1930s-style structures across the water. Open year-round, the over-the-water rooms and suites are well furnished, clean, and bright, with hardwood floors, small kitchens, and "perfect reception" satellite TV.

P.O. Box 2-8, Telegraph Cove, BC V0N 3J0. © **877/835-2683** or 250/928-3161. Fax 250/928-3162. www.telegraphcove.ca. 29 units, 48 RV sites. C$130–C$160 double; C$35 RV site. Off-season rates available. MC, V. *In room:* TV, kitchen, Wi-Fi.

Telegraph Cove Resorts   The accommodations here are refurbished, self-contained homes from the 1920s and 1930s, and include everything from a converted floating hospital on the boardwalk to a fisherman's cottage. Each has a story to share, and upgrades in decor have managed to combine simplicity with heritage charm. Some homes are cozy enough for two, while others sleep four, six, and even up to nine people. Wastell Manor, a two-level family home built in 1929, is a bit fancier. Because the manor is perched on a bluff, it offers exceptional views of the cove. Some 120 campsites are set back from the village, among the trees; all have water hookups; some also have electrical access, and some have full hookups. Telegraph Cove Resorts also run the Old Saltery Pub (a converted saltery) and the **Killer Whale Café** (© **250/928-3155**). Both are good, which is fortunate, as they really are the only shows in town.

P.O. Box 1, Telegraph Cove, BC V0N 3J0. © **800/200-HOOK** [800/200-4665] or 250/928-3131. Fax 250/928-3105. www.telegraphcoveresort.com. 24 units. Jun–Sept C$115–C$305 cabin/suite; C$273–C$32 campsite. Lower rates May & early Oct. Additional adult C$10. Packages available. MC, V. Closed mid-Oct to Apr. Pets allowed in some cabins (C$5/day). **Amenities:** Restaurant; pub; kayak rentals. *In room:* No phone.

Port McNeill, Alert Bay & Sointula

From Telegraph Cove, it's approximately 40km (25 miles) to **Port McNeill,** a hard-working, hard-edged township founded on logging and fishing. To wit, one of the main attractions is a record-breaking, 500-year-old burl (a dome-shaped tree growth) that weighs in at 21,772kg (24 tons), making it the world's largest, and an old steam donkey engine, circa 1938.

Besides those dubious attractions, Port McNeill has two stellar draws. The first is **Shephard's Garden** (920 Nicholson Rd.; *C* **250/956-4709;** www.shephards garden.ca), a gorgeous sanctuary beside the Nimpkish River. The second is the chance to embark upon whale-watching expeditions. **Mackay Whale Watching** (The Wharf, Port McNeill; *C* **877/663-6722** or 250/956-9865; www.whaletime. com), which uses 17m (55-ft.) aluminum vessels, has been around for more than 25 years and was instrumental in helping to establish the Robson Bight whale reserve nearby. Tours run about 4½ hours, cost C$105 adults, and include a light lunch. **Ocean Rose Coastal Adventures** (Municipal Dock, Port McNeill; *C* **250-902- 9015;** www.orcaadventures.com) is another experienced outfitter that provides an onboard naturalist on its tours and also offers photography safaris for C$150 adults. **Seasmoke Whale Watching** (Government Dock, Alert Bay; *C* **800/668-6722** or 250/974-5225; www.seaorca.com) offers 5- to 8-hour sail-with-the-whales excursions aboard SV *Tuan,* a 12m (40-ft.) craft, for C$95 to C$180 adults.

From Port McNeill, BC Ferries runs nine daily crossings to the 1,800-strong community of **Alert Bay** on Cormorant Island or to **Sointula** on Malcolm Island. Round-trip fares are C$9.75 adults, C$4.90 children 5 to 11. The crossing time is 45 minutes.

A Kwagiulth tribal village for thousands of years, Alert Bay exudes its rich cultural heritage and is most proud of the 53m (174-ft.) cedar totem pole featuring 22 hand-carved figures of bears, orcas, and ravens. It stands outside the Big House at the top of the hill. The modern building is modeled after a Kwakwaka'wakw Big House and, in July and August, hosts performances by 'Na'Nakwala dancers, usually Wednesday through Saturday. The cost is C$15 adults and C$6 children under 12. Near the ferry dock at Alert Bay, at the **U'Mista Cultural Centre** (*C* **250/974-5403;** www.umista.org), you'll find a fascinating collection of carved-wood ceremonial masks, cedar baskets, copper jewelry, and other potlatch artifacts that were confiscated by the Canadian government in 1922 and repatriated in 1980. Although the displays are self-explanatory, try to take a guided tour to really appreciate the stories and folklore that the exhibits represent. Admission is C$8 adults, C$7 seniors and students, and C$1 children 12 and under. The museum is open in summer daily 9am to 5:30pm, and in winter Monday through Friday 9am to 5pm. Call ahead for spring and fall hours. Leave time to browse Alert Bay's newest offering **Culture Shock Gallery** (located 200m (600ft), from the ferry dock on Front St., Alert Bay; *C* **250/974-2484**). Owned and operated by three sisters, each with an individual talent in filmmaking, writing, cedar weaving, or jewelry, they have come together to create a really personal, interative cultural experience.

At the other end of town—about a 15-minute stroll along the waterfront—is the ancient 'Namgis burial ground. It's sacred territory, so don't step over the wall to take photos of the many colorful and unusual totem poles. En route, keep an eye open for the **Anglican Church,** with a graveyard which remembers the arrival of Scottish immigrants into the area at the turn of the 20th century. Erected in 1881, the church's stained-glass windows are an interesting blend of Native Kwagiulth and Scottish design motifs. Also, check out the Ecological Park, a natural wonder that resembles the Florida Everglades without the alligators. An extensive system of trails for hiking and mountain biking crisscross the island. Maps are available at the information center.

Founded by Finnish settlers in 1901, the community of **Sointula,** on Malcolm Island, was to be a Utopian society, "a place of harmony." Although the concept collapsed, you can still feel the peaceful atmosphere of that dream. Finnish was the island's principal language until as recently as 30 years ago. But today, less than half of the 1,000-strong population is Finn. Sointula is a charming fishing village. There's a local gallery, store, and the **Sointula Museum** (© **250/973-6683**) 4 blocks left of the ferry terminal, which tells the Finnish story. The Museum shares space with the library, both in the old Superior School building. Six kilometers (3¾ miles) of gravel road takes you to **Bere Point Regional Park,** a killer-whale rubbing beach over which there's a viewing platform. The park offers two hiking trails of note: The 3.2km (2-mile) Matejeo Heritage Trail is a short walk from the ferry terminal and takes you through bogs, forest, and beside pretty lakes; the 2.5km (1.6-mile) Beautiful Bay Trail is more challenging. It starts at Bere Point and follows the bay to Malcolm Point.

WHERE TO STAY & DINE

Although tourists visit for the fishing, First Nations culture, and outdoor pursuits, Port McNeill, Alert Bay, and Sointula are only now gearing up for visitors. Beyond Port McNeill, accommodations are basic, and restaurants cater to local tastes with burgers, fish and chips, and pasta.

In Port McNeill, the **Dalewood Inn** (1703 Broughton Blvd.; © **877/956-3304** or 250/956-3304; www.dalewoodinn.com) has decent rooms, as well as an on-site pub and restaurant that add good (but nothing to write home about) steaks and chicken dishes to its dinner menu. Rates range from C$90 to C$119 for a double. In the heart of downtown, such as it is, the **McNeill's Inn** (1579 Beach Dr.; © **250/956-3466**) has six small, clean rooms adjacent to **MugZ** (1597 Beach Dr., © **250/956-3466**), the town's only coffee hangout and a stone's throw from a non-descript steak and pizza restaurant. Rooms are C$89 to C$109 double. **The Black Bear Resort** (1812 Campbell Way; © **866/956-4900**; www.port-mcneill-accommodation.com) sounds more stylish than it is. Still, it has all the mod-cons such as Internet, comfortable rooms, and even a spa. Rates range from C$115 to C$160 double.

In Alert Bay, try the **Old Customs House Restaurant & Inn,** (119 Fir St., Alert Bay, BC V0N 1A0; © **250/974-2282**), a 1918 historic building that has three rooms, kitchen facilities, and a deck overlooking Johnstone Strait. Look for rates between C$65 to C$95 for a double. **Alert Bay Lodge** (549 Fir St., Alert Bay, BC V0N 1A0; © **800/255-5057** or 250/974-2026; www.alertbaylodge.com) is more upscale and certainly roomier, in large part because it was once the United Church for Alert Bay. The great room and library feature high, arched cedar beams; the cedar adds a warmth to its five simply furnished guest rooms—that means no TVs or radios. Rates range from C$109 to C$129 per person.

On Malcolm Island, **Sund's Lodge** (445 Kaleva Rd. [P.O. Box 10], Sointula, BC V0N 3E0; © **800/991-SUND** [800/991-7863], or 250/902-1400 Oct–May; www.sundslodge.com) is a fully inclusive "adventure or do nothing" luxury resort located on 16 hectares (40 acres) of unspoiled wilderness on Blackfish Sound. Open mid-June until the end of September, the family-run lodge accommodates up to 20 guests in 12 cabins furnished with overstuffed log chairs and cozy beds with thick down comforters. Food is equally inviting, with an emphasis on local fare with spicy marinades, homemade sauces, and fresh herbs. A 3-night/4-day stay starts at C$2,600 per person and includes accommodations, meals, guided fishing, hiking, and kayaking. **Sea 4 Miles**

KAYAKING adventures WITH A TWIST

Paddling softly through some of the hundreds of islands in the Broughton Inlet must be one of the most magical kayaking experiences available, no more so than when eagles, sea lions, and whales join in the fun. Your "base camp" is a beautifully restored heritage vessel called **MV *Columbia III*** that, 50 years ago, served as a missionary, hospital, and overall life-line vessel to BC's coastal communities. Today, outfitted with half a dozen quality kayaks, the ship travels between different dropoff and pickup paddling points that you could never hope to reach from an on-shore origin. Passenger accommodations comprise five tiny staterooms with extremely comfortable, queen-size bunk beds, a cozy lounge/dining area, and a sheltered deck.

The Campbell family, who own and operate this venture, has pooled their talents to provide expert naturalist and guiding tips, scrumptious food, and informal hospitality that might include an impromptu recital of Irish music after dinner. Passengers range from older teenagers to active retirees, and schedules often include shore stops to explore First Nations communities, a hike through the rainforest, or a beachside picnic of just-caught crab. If ever you get paddle weary, the ship's Zodiac will quickly take you back to the boat. The *Columbia* runs out of Port McNeill June through September; all-inclusive 4- and 7-day trips are C$1,400 to C$3,000 adults. Mothership Adventures, Heriot Bay. ☎ **888/ 833-8887** or 250/202-3229. www.mothership adventures.com.

Cottages (145 Kaleva Rd., Sointula, BC V0N 3E0; ☎ **250/973-6486;** www.sointula cottages.com) are more affordable, as is the seaside campground, Bere Point Park. It has 11 unserviced sites on the waterfront (kayakers take note), plus 11 more sites up the hill in full sun. Here's where you'll find the trail head for Beautiful Bay Trail and a whale-watching platform. Contact the Regional District to reserve a park campsite here or elsewhere in the surrounding area (☎ **250/956-3301**; www.rdmw.bc.ca).

PORT HARDY & CAPE SCOTT PROVINCIAL PARK ★★★

Port Hardy is 44km (27 miles) north of Port McNeill and the final stop on Island Highway. Many visitors, however, come via ferry, en route either to or from **Prince Rupert.** Port Hardy is also the departure point for the Discovery Coast Passage trip to the First Nations communities of Bella Bella, Shearwater, Ocean Falls, and Klemtu, among others. In summer, this tiny town gets so busy with ferry travelers that decent accommodations get full fast, leaving a motley assortment of tired motels to choose from.

Until recently, the town's prosperity was fueled by forestry, mining, and commercial fishing, but the refurbished seaside promenade and the fresh coat of paint here and there are evidence of Port Hardy's efforts to diversify its economic base through tourism. Is this why the timbered **Port Hardy Visitor Information Centre** (7250 Market St. [P.O. Box 294], Port Hardy, BC V0N 2P0; ☎ **250/949-7622**) is the nicest building downtown? If you have an hour to spare, drop into the **Port Hardy Museum** (7110 Market St.; ☎ **250/949-8143**), which has some interesting relics from early Danish settlers,

Why No Grizzly Bears?

According to native legend, there were once many grizzlies and black bears on the Mainland that longed to live on Vancouver Island, but it was too far for them to swim. Finally the Great Spirit announced that if the bears could make the distance in one mighty leap, they might stay there. The catch, however, was that they weren't to get as much as one claw wet, or they would turn to stone. It is said that the mountains and valleys on the mainland were created by the bears digging in for a run at the Island, yet still many black bears tried and failed, as the boulders strewn along the island's shoreline attest. One day, after watching many of his black bear relatives make the jump, a king-sized grizzly boasted he could jump the distance. He went miles back into the mainland to make the mighty leap. Alas, the tide was in, and he landed in the shallow tide, near Campbell River, and was instantly turned to stone. And there he stands today as the Big Rock.

plus a collection of stone tools, found nearby, which date from about 8,000 BC. The **Quatse Salmon Stewardship Centre** (8400 Byng Rd.; ℂ **250/902-0336**; www. thesalmoncentre.org) is a new addition to the scene with a first-rate interpretive display. Crawl inside one exhibit, and you're in the middle of a shoal of salmon—literally!

When you make it to **Port Hardy,** you may feel like you've reached the edge of the world, but in fact, Port Hardy is the jumping-off point for exhilarating, year-round outdoor activities, such as hiking in **Cape Scott Provincial Park** (see below), fishing, kayaking, and diving, as well as to several very remote, very exclusive fishing lodges farther north. **Great Bear Nature Tours** (ℂ **888/221-8212**) are among this group inasmuch as their excursions are based out of a five-room floating lodge in the middle of a rainforest (see "Tracking the Wild Side," p. 201). **North Island Daytrippers** (ℂ **800/956-2411** or 250/956-2411; www.islanddaytrippers. com) is a good option for hikers who would rather not go it alone in these wilderness areas. Based in Port McNeill, these savvy guides offer year-round half-day and full-day hikes to San Josef Bay and Ronning Gardens, Raft Cove, and many of the beaches and coves in between. Fees include lunch and start at C$150 per person for a full day and decrease according to the number of people in the party.

Outdoor Activities

The northern region epitomizes Vancouver Island's wildest (and wettest) coastal country. A lot of it can be enjoyed by visitors who just want a look-see, but you'll quickly learn that the deeper you explore, the greater the rewards. To do that, you should go with an experienced outfitter, unless you are completely at ease when left to your own devices in the great outdoors.

DIVING

Water clarity and tidal action have made this one of the best dive locations in the world. There are more than two dozen outfitters in the area, some of which will provide fully equipped dive boats. A good resource is **Malei Island Dive & Charter**, which operates out of **North Island Dive & Kayak Centre** (8625 Shipley St., Port Hardy; ℂ **250/949-1208**; www.northislanddiver.com). In Port McNeil, check out **Sun Fun**

Divers (445 Pioneer Hill Dr.; © **250/956-2243;** www.sunfundivers.com). Pricing is competitive and varies depending on the type of dive you're looking for, and whether or not equipment is required, but as a guideline, a two-tank dive involving about 6 hours on the water is C$160-C$185 per person, usually with a three-diver minimum.

FISHING

Fishing nirvana awaits, as do several of the local outfitters. Charter trips and self-skippered boat rentals abound. **Catala Charters** (© **800/515-5511** or 250/949-7560; www.catalacharters.net) offers guided fishing trips, as well as diving charters; and **Codfather Charters** (© **250/949-6696;** www.codfathercharters.com) offers year-round fishing, as well as accommodations in a waterfront lodge. If you want to just rent a boat, contact **Hardy Bay Boat Rental** (Quarterdeck Marina, 6555 Hardy Bay Rd.; © **250/949-7048;** www.hardybayfishing.com). Rates start at C$25 per hour and C$200 per day for a 4.9m (16-ft.) covered fiberglass boat and range from C$28 per hour to C$250 a day for a 5.8m (19-ft.) boat.

Port Hardy is the gateway for trips to remote fishing camps, many of which cater to the heavy-wallet brigade with their exclusivity. These include **King Pacific Lodge** (www.kingpacificlodge.com) and **Nimmo Bay Resort** (www.nimmobay.com), where access is by floatplane or boat, and all-inclusive prices start at about C$7,250 for 3 nights.

Duval Point Lodge (© **250/949-6667;** www.duvalpointlodge.com) is an affordable alternative where you can do your own thing without froufrou frills. Located 8km (5 miles) north of Port Hardy (accessed by boat), the lodge has both a floating lodge and land-based log cabins, all of which share a full kitchen (guests do their own cooking) and living area. Some rooms share bathrooms, too. Open May through October, the outfitter provides fishing tackle, bait, and boats for multi-day packages that start from C$970 per person for 3 nights; and less (from C$570) if you bring your own boat. Guests can use the lodge's kayaks at no extra charge.

The MV *Ocean Explorer* (© **877/346-9378;** www.adventurewestresorts.com) takes the best of a resort and puts it at sea, exploring the Inside Passage and fjordic inlets. This 34m (110-ft.) luxury boat is the only fishing experience of its kind, offering nine private staterooms, lounge, a state-of-the-art galley (aka gourmet meals), and a deck-top hot tub. It guarantees your catch or promises your next trip for free. Three-night sports-fishing packages are priced at C$2,995, including roundtrip airfare from Vancouver International Airport, all meals, accommodations, fishing gear, and Cuban cigars.

HIKING

Heavy rainfalls (nearly 500cm/197 in. per year) and violent windstorms predominate in this wild landscape, turning hiking trails into muddy quagmires. But if you thrive on doing things off the beaten track, these trails deliver. The easiest and most popular hike is the 2.5km (1.6-mile) **San Josef Bay Trail,** a fairly easy walk through marshy ferns and skunk cabbage, and along the San Josef River to San Josef Bay, where there's an expanse of sandy beach and the ruins of a Danish settlement.

More experienced and well-equipped hikers can opt for the challenging 24km (15-mile) **Cape Scott Trail.** This grueling trek starts in mud, but once you're on your way, the scenery is pure wilderness: ocean-bay beauty, weathered grass, high-rise canopies of Sitka spruce, and vast stretches of natural beach. Stops along the way include **Eric Lake,** an ideal spot for fishing and warm-water swimming, and **Hansen Lagoon,** once a Danish settlement and now a stopping place for Canada geese and a variety of waterfowl traveling the Pacific Flyway. Allow 3 days of heavy hiking and a good week if you want to explore all the offshoot trails. One suggestion is the fairly new **North Coast Trail** (approximately 44km/27 miles) that ends up at Shushartie Bay. You can catch a land shuttle (📞 **250/949-6541;** www.northcoasttrailshuttle.com) from Port Hardy to the trail head for C$75 provided you can get matched up to make up a minimum party of three, otherwise it's C$225 per person. You can rent a VHF radio from them (C$50), and then organize a water taxi return. Unlike the West Coast Trail (p. 164), hiking reservations aren't required for Cape Scott; however, be sure to book ahead if you require transport. If tackling the North Coast Trail on your own seems daunting, connect with an experienced outfitter like **Sea to Sky Expeditions** (📞 **800/990-8735** or 604/583-3518; www.seatoskyexpeditions.com).

Other than Eric Lake, where there are 11 designated camp pads, camping is unrestricted. You'll find food caches and pit toilets here and at Guise Bay, Nels Bight, San Josef, and Nissen Bight. There's an honor-system backcountry fee (C$8 adults) for overnight camping in effect May to September. Self-registration vaults are located at the San Josef River boat launch and trail head. South of Cape Scott lies Raft Cove Provincial Park, 405 hectares (1,001 acres) of rugged wilderness and wind-swept beaches that make for a good full day's excursion or longer. Campers will find the cove extremely exposed to the Pacific, so even in summer, you can expect temperamental weather systems to dampen your canvas—prepare accordingly. Access to the park by road is on Ronning Main, off the Cape Scott road out of Holberg. Experienced sea kayakers paddle to Raft Cove down the San Josef River and out to the Pacific through San Josef Bay.

Hot News: Plans are finally underway, at least in terms of fund-raising, for a Vancouver Island Spine Trail, which will run from Cape Scott down the center of the island to Victoria. Stay tuned.

KAYAKING

The shores of Hardy Bay are scattered with coves, inlets, and islands to explore and stop at along the way. The major islands are Deer, Peel, Cattle, Round, and Shell islands, all of which you can make into a leisurely day trip or single over-nighter. **Odyssey Kayaking** operates out of **North Island Dive & Kayak Centre** (📞 **250/949-7392;** www.odysseykayaking.com) and offers day-long guided paddles from C$99 per person as well as longer, customized trips. Kayak rentals are from C$45 per day single and C$65 double.

Cape Scott Provincial Park ★★★

Clinging to the northwest tip of Vancouver Island, Cape Scott Provincial Park is 21,840 hectares (53,968 acres) of untamed raincoast wilderness, where the wild Pacific Ocean pounds wide, windswept beaches and crashes against rocky headlands. In the late 1890s, enterprising Danish colonists from the American Midwest carved the tortuous route to Cape Scott itself out of the tangled bush. They hoped to build a community there. But the land was too isolated and the weather too inhospitable to let the settlement grow. Today, their wagon roads are now hiking trails, and heritage markers along the way point out the remains of their endeavors: tumbledown cabins, sun-bleached driftwood fence posts, a dilapidated cougar trap, and cedar planked "corduroy roads."

Getting there is a 2-hour, 67km (42-mile) drive west from Port Hardy down a heavily used gravel logging road (which is still recovering from recent wash-outs) toward2 the tiny town of **Holberg.** A good place to break the journey is at the **Scarlet Ibis**

Pub (© **250/288-3386**). On the outskirts of Holberg, you'll find **Ronning Gardens.** Established in 1910 by Bernt Ronning, a Norwegian settler, the gardens are an extraordinary anomaly of exotic trees and plants from all over the world, including a pair of enormous Chilean Araucario *araucana*—also known as monkey-puzzle trees. These were grown from seedlings, male and female, and have been the starting point of several hundred of the monkey puzzle trees in North America. There is no street address; just watch for the sign. It's a 15-minute walk from the road to the garden.

Then, continue on until the Cape Scott parking lot, where you'll find the trail heads to the rugged 24km (15-mile) **Cape Scott Trail,** with its stunning coastal scenery and some 30km (19 miles) of sandy beach. There's also a more accessible, 45-minute, 2.5km (1.6-mile) hike that leads to scenic San Josef Bay.

Where to Stay

Cluxewe Resort   Owned and operated by the Kwakiutl Band, this year-round resort has a fabulous beachfront location, which includes 14 waterfront cottages and a number of RV and tent sites, most either on or near the beach or estuary—Cluxewe means "changing river mouth." Fully stocked cottages are clean and simply furnished with a BBQ deck, Wi-Fi, and satellite TV; kids will enjoy climbing the ladder to the loft room in cabins 6 and 7. There's a massive wood supply on-site, a decent guest laundry, and washroom/shower facility for campers (both tenters and RVers); a small cafe serving burgers, soup, and sandwiches; a boat/kayak launch—fisherman gravitate towards the estuary waters; a new trail system that's fun to explore; and a wildlife refuge next door. The beach is pebbly and the waters safe.

Located 1km (.6m) off Highway 19, 11 km (6m) NW of Port McNeil (P.O. Box 245), Port McNeil, BC V0N 2R0. © **250/949-0378.** www.cluxewe.com. 14 cabins, 147 campsites. May to mid-Oct C$125–C$165 cabin; C$19 unserviced campsite, C$25 full-hook-up campsite. Winter rates up to 40% less. AE, MC, V. **Amenities:** Restaurant. *In room:* TV, fridge, Wi-Fi.

Eco-Escapes Cabins ★   As one of the more eco-conscious destinations on the island, nearly everything about these new getaway cabins has the health of the planet in mind. Design elements include salvaged timber, environmentally friendly paint and products, low flush toilets, eco-bat (insulation made from repurposed pop bottles), local river rock on bathroom floors, rugs and blinds of renewable bamboo, solar power, recycled water, and other earth-friendly programs. Each studio unit (save one) is small but not at all cramped, even though there's a queen bed, kitchen with tiny eating table, and a lounge area. Decor is tasteful, rustic, and exceptionally cozy. Cabin #1 has the best views; Cabin #2 is the largest, with a loft bedroom that has two queen beds. Landscaping across this rocky hillside, about a 4-minute drive to the ferry north, is taking shape with donated cuttings, self-seeding perrenials, and transplanted trees, which suddenly start to thrive in the organic manure-enriched soil. A nice touch is the complimentary continental-breakfast basket, which is left at your door each morning.

6305 Jensen Cove Rd., Port Hardy, BC V0N 2P0. © **250/949-8524.** www.ecoscapecabins.com. 6 cabins. May–Sept C$80–$150 cabin; Oct–Apr C$100–C$125 cabin. MC, V. **Amenities:** Ferry shuttle. *In room:* TV, fridge, Wi-Fi.

Glen Lyon Inn & Suites ★★   Once you make it past the rather intimidating stuffed eagle showcased in the lobby, you'll find a clean, modern motel. All rooms have an ocean view and decent furnishings, and come in a mix of configurations to match your needs, whether it's a family suite with bunk beds for the kids; an executive-style room; or the honeymoon suite, with Jacuzzi and wet bar. The balconies on the third floor seem custom-designed for eagle-spotting. The family-style restaurant is bright and welcoming (see "Where to Dine," below) and the Glen Lyon pub opens for lunch and is a popular spot until last orders at around midnight. The staff have an "anything we can do?" helpful attitude.

6435 Hardy Bay Rd. (P.O. Box 103), Port Hardy, BC V0N 2P0. 🕾 **877/949-7115** or 250/949-7115. Fax 250/949-7415. www.glenlyoninn.com. 44 units. May to mid-Oct C$110–C$160 double, C$145–C$195 suite; mid-Oct to Apr C$62–C$69 double, C$95–C$125 suite. AE, MC, V. Small pets accepted (C$10). **Amenities:** Restaurant; pub; exercise room. *In room:* TV, fridge, hair dryer, Wi-Fi.

Oceanview B&B ★★ Although it has rather a grandiose exterior, this lovely home extends a warm welcome to weary travelers. Guest rooms have small sitting areas and are quaintly decorated, with brass or wrought-iron beds. All have a private en-suite bathroom. Look for thoughtful touches such as fresh-cut flowers, pillow chocolates, and homemade cookies—baking is this inn's forte. A generous, hot breakfast is served up in a bright, open kitchen. The comfortable sitting room offers various reading materials, a piano, and a fireplace, and is a perfect spot to enjoy afternoon tea. The house has wonderful views of Hardy Bay and the snow-covered mountains on the mainland. An unexpected bonus is free parking for guests who wish to leave their vehicles while they take the ferry to Prince Rupert or to Discovery Passage.

7735 Cedar Place (P.O. Box 183), Port Hardy, BC V0N 2P0. 🕾/fax **250/949-8302.** www.island. net/~oceanvue. 3 units. C$105–C$120 double. Rates include breakfast. Extra person C$15. MC, V. Free parking. **Amenities:** Lounge. *In room:* TV, hair dryer, no phone, Wi-Fi.

Orange Tabby B&B Within steps of the bus depot and within walking distance to downtown Port Hardy, the B&B part of this family home is on the garden level with its own private entrance. Rooms are tastefully furnished with queen-size beds and include pampering robes and extra blankets. One of the owners was a commercial fisherman with plenty of *Perfect Storm* stories; his wife runs a hair-dressing salon upstairs and is into the healing arts. Breakfast is nothing fancy, but just plain good dependables such as pancakes, quiche, and eggs and bacon. ***Note:*** Cash or travelers checks only.

8755 Hastings St., Port Hardy, BC V0N 2P0. 🕾 **250/949-8510.** www.orangetabbybb.com. 3 units. Mid-May to Oct C$140 double; Nov to mid-May C$105 double. 2-night minimum in July & Aug. No credit cards. Free parking. **Amenities:** Lounge. *In room:* TV/DVD player, fridge, hair dryer, Wi-Fi.

Quarterdeck Inn & Marina Resort ★★ A smart, if generic-looking, hotel. Peppermint-green corridors (a favorite color of many Port Hardy buildings—must be something to do with the perpetual grey weather) lead to spacious, pastel-colored rooms with comfortable beds, quality furniture, and ocean views from every window. Some have kitchenettes and DVD players. The hotel is in the midst of a working boatyard and marina, so there's always something to see. The friendly staff can arrange a variety of outdoor activities such as charter fishing, whale-watching, and kayaking, as well as water taxis to Cape Scott.

6555 Hardy Bay Rd. (P.O. Box 910), Port Hardy, BC V0N 2P0. 🕾 **877/902-0459** or 250/902-0455. Fax 250/902-0454. www.quarterdeckresort.net. 40 units. May–Sept C$125–C$145 double; Oct–Apr C$89–C$99 double. Rates include continental breakfast. AE, DC, DISC, MC, V. Free parking. Small pets accepted (C$10). **Amenities:** Restaurant; pub; gym; Jacuzzi; Wi-Fi. *In room:* TV, DVD player (in some), kitchenette (in some), hair dryer.

Quatse River Campground Lying beside the Quatse River, beneath towering old-growth forest, this full-service campsite is one of the nicest in the area. Shaded sites, wooded trails, free hot showers, and plenty of firewood (by donation) are the basics, as is a sun-dappled picnic area near the Quatse River Salmon Hatchery. All profits fun North Island salmon enhancement and habitat rehabilitation projects, including the new, and very nifty, **Quatse Salmon Stewardship Centre** next door (✆ **250/902-0336**; www.thesalmoncentre.org).

8400 Byng Rd., Port Hardy, BC V0N 2P0. ✆ **866/949-2395.** www.quatsecampground.com. 41 RV sites (full hook-ups), 21 tent sites. C$25 RV site; C$20 tent site. MC, V. Pets allowed.

Where to Dine

Harbour View Restaurant CANADIAN   Attached to the Glen Lyon Hotel (see p. 213), this bright and airy restaurant bustles with activity from breakfast in the early morning through to dinner. The extensive menu covers all bases, with salads and burgers by day and dishes such as barbecued ribs, steak, and a very good seafood platter by night, though the fancier dishes can be a bit hit-and-miss. Best to stick to the fundamentals. Families are welcome (kids' portions are available), and all the desserts, whether apple crumble or the surprisingly good tiramisu, are homemade.

6435 Hardy Bay Rd. ✆ **250/949-7115.** www.glenlyoninn.com. Main courses C$7–C$23. AE, MC, V. Daily 6:30am–9pm.

IV's Quarterdeck Pub PUB/CANADIAN   This nautical-style pub-restaurant, situated on the marina, serves fresh halibut and chips, sandwiches, burgers, and other traditional pub fare, as well as standards like steaks and chicken. It's really the only decent eatery in town with evening specials and to-go items, making it a local favorite for both working fisherman and visitors. That, and the variety of beer on tap!

6555 Hardy Bay Rd. ✆ **250/949-6922.** www.quarterdeckresort.net. Main courses C$7–C$20. AE, MC, V. Daily 11am–midnight.

Malone's Oceanside Bistro   Why "oceanside" is included in its name is a puzzle since it's inside a old shopping mall that's trying to be repurposed, in part as a technical college. As a result, the complex feels rather sad. Locals, however, know better; they flock here because the food's decent and the prices are good, as evidenced by the older crowd and young families. The menu has a bit of everything: burgers and steaks, chicken pot pies and wraps, salads and pasta. The bar (and decor, for that matter) is reminiscent of some '60s haunt—all dark mood-lighting and patterned carpets. It can be quite a shock to emerge into daylight.

9300 Trustee Rd. ✆ **250/949-3050.** Main courses C$7–C$20. MC, V. Mon–Sat 11:00am–2pm & 5–8pm.

Oyster Eden

Fanny Bay oysters are served in restaurants from New York to Manila to Beijing. Tasting a little like a cucumber, with a fruity finish, nearly 8.5 million of the mollusks are hauled from the Fanny Bay waters in an average year. Unlike the surrounding farmed salmon, oyster farms are considered environmentally helpful, since they attract and sustain other sealife and birds.

THE GULF ISLANDS

Clustered between Vancouver Island and the mainland, the Gulf Islands are pastoral havens. Their protected waterways provide some of the finest cruising in the world, and their semi-Mediterranean climate is enviable, even by West Coast standards. Add to this sweeping scenes of woods and water, pebble and shell beaches, and placid lakes stocked with bass and rainbow trout ideal for fly-fishing, and you can understand why the Gulf Islands have been described as "fragments of paradise."

9

The raggedly beautiful archipelago, the northern extension of Washington's San Juan Islands, is made up of more than 200 islands. Although most are small, uninhabited, and accessible only by private boat, the five larger islands, off the southeastern tip of Vancouver Island—Salt Spring Island, the Pender Islands, and Galiano, Mayne, and Saturna islands—are home to about 15,000 permanent residents and are served by a regularly scheduled ferry service.

From the beginning, the islands have attracted a diverse set of individuals: writers and artists, poets and cooks, ecologists and escapists. So, far from being an unsophisticated backwater, the region offers the visitor first-class restaurants, as well as heritage B&Bs, galleries, farmhouses, and artisans' studios. In recent years, relocated urbanites have started to gentrify the islands, resulting in an uneasy mix with the existing counterculture. Land values have skyrocketed, and petty crime is on the rise. Only the self-governing Islands Trust holds development in check, although there's creeping evidence that even this influential, tree-hugging group is beginning to lose its grip. Gentrification is happening. One example of the fallout from this concerns the islands' water supply. As more and more city folk migrate to the islands (prompting a population increase of almost 30% in the past decade), resources must stretch to accommodate their city habits. With the onslaught of multi-bathroom homes, dishwashers, and Jacuzzis, fresh water has become a precious commodity. Today, homesteaders must dig twice as deep for water as they did 20 years ago. Boiling and filtering is becoming a way of life, and summer often means water shortages.

That said, the Gulf Islands are still a heavenly place to hike, kayak, and canoe, or simply enjoy a glass of wine from the deck of a cottage. Families usually choose cabins or hotels because many of the islands' inns and B&Bs are geared to adults. When a hotel does welcome children, however, this information is included in the review in this chapter. The islands may lack many urban amenities such as ATMs and laundromats, but they do have a wealth of quirky features that will make your visit memorable. One example is the "honesty stands" that dot the roadsides. You drop your money in the box provided and walk away with honey, flowers, veggies, jams, and whatever else local folk have for sale. Deer are another feature. With no natural predators on the islands, they are free to roam roads, gardens, and forests, so be sure to drive carefully, especially at night.

Of all the islands, Salt Spring is the most dynamic and the easiest to get to from Vancouver Island, especially if you have only a day to spare. Once on a Gulf Island, it is easy to hop to another, arriving in the early morning and departing late afternoon. You're best to incorporate at least one night on each island—it's the only way to experience the very different personality of each, although you might be tempted to stay far longer. After all, they are fragments of paradise.

ESSENTIALS
Getting There

BY PLANE   Seaplanes crisscross the skies above the Gulf Islands at regular intervals, between Vancouver Island, Vancouver on the mainland, and Seattle. **Seair Seaplanes** (© 800/447-3247 or 604/273-8900; www.seairseaplanes.com) and **Harbour Air** (© 800/665-0212 or 604/274-1277; www.harbour-air.com) offer daily flights. One-way fares average C$95. **Kenmore Air** (© 866/435-9524, or 425/486-1257 in Seattle; www.kenmoreair.com) flies from Seattle May through September. One-way fares are US$200 each way, with slight round-trip discounts. Prices are fluctuating, however, with fuel surcharges. There are no areas on the islands that accommodate commercial flights, although some islands have small, grassy airstrips for private aircraft.

BY FERRY   Juggling your schedule with ferry departures is an art that requires patience, if not a master's degree in reading timetables. **BC Ferries** (© 888/223-3779 or 250/386-3431; www.bcferries.com) provides good basic service to the Gulf Islands, with at least two sailings a day from **Tsawwassen,** a 22km (14-mile) drive south of Vancouver on the mainland, and from **Swartz Bay,** 32km (20 miles) north of Victoria on Vancouver Island. Ferries also run frequently between islands. Schedules are available from BC Ferries. One-way fares from Tsawwassen to the Gulf Islands average C$16 adults, C$58 for a standard-size vehicle. One-way fares from Swartz Bay to the islands average C$11 adults; C$32 for a standard-size vehicle. Return fares to Tsawwassen are less, and vary according to which island you are returning from. Return fares to Swartz Bay are free. Inter-island trips average C$5 adults, C$11 for a standard-size vehicle.

Note: Ferry travel can be costly if you're taking a vehicle, and long boarding waits are not uncommon. Ticket prices vary seasonally; mid-week travel is slightly less expensive than that on weekends and holidays, when reservations are essential. During these peak periods, book at least 3 weeks in advance to avoid disappointment. Reservations can be made with BC Ferries by phone or online. **Washington State Ferries**

(📞 **800/843-3779** in Washington, 888/808-7977 in Canada, or 206/464-6400; www. wsdot.wa.gov/ferries) provides daily service from **Anacortes to Sidney,** a short distance from Swartz Bay (see "The Saanich Peninsula," in chapter 6). From Swartz Bay, you can transfer to a BC Ferries ferry to the Gulf Islands. There is only one Anacortes-Sidney crossing daily fall through spring; two in summer, during which vehicle reservations are strongly recommended. Reservations must be made by 5:30pm the day prior to travel. From May to early October, one-way fares are C$16 adults, C$8 seniors, C$13 children 6 to 18, and C$55 for a standard-size vehicle and driver. From mid-October to April, fares remain the same for adults, seniors, and children, but drop to C$50 for a standard-size vehicle and driver. Crossing time is 3 hours.

Gulf Islands Water Taxi (📞 **250/537-2510**) is a local inter-island service that operates June through August on Saturdays. When school is in session, September through June, it operates as a weekday school boat, and adults often hitch a ride for day excursions. The one-way fare between any two points is C$15 adults. Round-trips are C$25 adults. People often transport kayaks for C$5. Transporting bicycles is free.

Visitor Information

Services operate through the local chamber of commerce or general store on individual islands (see "Essentials," throughout the chapter, for the island in question). You can also check out **www.gulfislandstourism.com** or **www.gulfislands.net** for general information. Not all islands have public campgrounds, and moorage facilities for pleasure craft vary in size and amenities considerably.

SALT SPRING ISLAND

Named for the briny springs on the island, Salt Spring Island is the largest and most accessible of the Gulf Islands. Lying just north of Vancouver Island's Swartz Bay, this thriving community is made up of almost 10,500 commuters, retirees, farmers, and artistic free-spirits. You'll come across a number of home-based entrepreneurs: everything from potters and weavers to llama farms and cheese-makers! And make no mistake, Salt Spring is filled with characters, whether dreadlocked or salt-and-peppered, who are as likely to hold a PhD in comparative literature as to be a self-professed expert in UFO technology. Much of the island is considered sacred by the local Coast Salish people. Mount Tuam, the site of a Buddhist Retreat Centre, contains quartz crystal that purportedly infuses those who visit with calm and well-being.

 Collect Island Dollars

Although they're not worth a pinch of salt off the island, Salt Spring Island Dollars are a valued commodity when you're there. They are accepted by most island businesses, some of which have bills on hand to give as change, or they can be purchased dollar-for-dollar at the tourist Information Centre in Ganges. The goal of the local currency is to raise funds for worthwhile community projects while promoting local commerce and good will. Art featured on the back of limited editions of the notes helps to make them collectible after the 2-year expiration date. Legally considered gift certificates, the Salt Spring Island Dollar is Canada's only local legal-tender currency in circulation.

Salt Spring has two golf courses, a small movie theater that substitutes ads and trailers with slides of local people and places, an ice rink, lots of restaurants, and a scattering of hotly debated condominium developments, mostly in the **Ganges** area. As the beating heart of the island, Ganges is where change is most noticeable, especially with the increase in shops and traffic. The island has even introduced a transit system. Tour Salt Spring's pastoral landscape, and you'll quickly see why sheep are Salt Spring's insignia— they're everywhere. You'll also discover any number of lakes (many are good fishing waters) and hiking trails, such as those in **Mount Maxwell Provincial Park,** which includes a 1.5km (.9-mile) trek up to **Baynes Peak.** Rising 595m (1,952 ft.), it is the third-highest mountain on the Gulf Islands. You can drive to the trail head, but go easy; the paved road becomes a narrow, gravel surface that's too rough for RVs to negotiate.

Essentials

GETTING THERE

BC Ferries sails to **Fulford Harbour,** in the southern part of Salt Spring, or **Long Harbour,** toward the north. Seaplanes land in **Ganges Harbour,** in the center of the island. See "Getting There," above, for information about fares and schedules.

If you're arriving via ferry to Fulford Harbour, look out for **St. Paul's Church** (best seen from the water). Founded by a Roman Catholic missionary in 1878, this picturesque tiny stone church was built by immigrants from Hawaii who worked for the Hudson's Bay Company, descendants of whom still live on the island.

VISITOR INFORMATION

Head to the **Salt Spring Island Chamber of Commerce** (121 Lower Ganges Rd.; ℂ 866/216-2936 or 250/537-5252; www.saltspringtourism.com), in the village of Ganges. Open daily, year-round, from 11am to 3pm (10am–4pm in July and Aug). Another good online resource is **www.saltspringtourism.com**.

GETTING AROUND

The introduction of public transit is one of the more significant changes on Salt Spring in recent years. Buses loop around the island with Ganges as the major destination on schedules that are conveniently tied in with arrivals and departures of ferries at Fulford Harbour, Vesuvius, and Long Harbour. **Silver Shadow Taxi** (ℂ **250/537-3030**) services the island. If you want to rent a car, **Salt Spring Marina Rentals** (ℂ **800/334-6629** or 250/537-3122) in downtown Ganges can set you up with a mid-range vehicle for about C$60 a day. This company also rents scooters for C$50 per hour or C$70 for 24 hours. **Salt Spring Adventure Co.,** at Salt Spring Marina, 7-126 Upper Ganges Rd. (ℂ **877/537-2764** or 250/537-2764; www.saltspringadventures.com), rents both bikes (C$25 per day) and kayaks (C$60–C$90 per day), and will deliver them to anywhere on Salt Spring Island for a nominal charge. Although there are no boat rentals available anywhere on the island, **Salt Spring Marina** at Harbour's End (124 Upper Ganges Rd.; ℂ **800/334-6629** or 250/537-5810) does offer fishing charters. Costs start at C$450 for 4 hours for two people.

Exploring Salt Spring Island

GANGES

The bustling seaside village of **Ganges** ★★★ belies the notion that the Gulf Islands are sleepy hideaways. The sheer number of Realtors is a gauge of Salt Spring's

The Gulf Islands

Legend

- Beach
- Ferry Route
- Fishing
- Information
- Mountain
- Winery

Strait of Georgia

DIONISIO POINT PROVINCIAL PARK

Reid Island
Alcala Point
Hall I.
Norway I.
Secretary Islands

Devina Dr.
Porlier Pass Rd.
26
Bodega Beach Dr.
Vineyard Way

Bodega Ridge

Houston Passage

Wallace Island
Retreat Cove

GALIANO ISLAND

Porlier Pass Road

Tent Island
1
Sunset Dr.
North End Rd.
N. Beach Rd.
2 Fernwood
Walker's Hook Rd.

Trincomali Channel

Wise I.
Charles I.
25

Sturdies Bay Rd.
Georgeson Bay Rd.

Parminter Point

Saint Mary Lake

Parker Island

Montague Harbour

BLUFFS PARK

Vesuvius Bay
Vesuvius
Channel Ridge
3
Stark Rd.
Vesuvius Bay Rd.

Julia I.

Mt. Galiano

Georgeson Bay

Stuart Channel

Bullock Lake
4
Robinson Rd.
Mansell Rd.
Long Harbour Rd.
6

Vesuvius Bay / Crofton

Long Harbour

Tsawwassen

Village Bay

MAPLE MOUNTAIN PARK

i 5
Ganges
Fulford-Ganges Rd.

Ganges Harbour

SISTER ISLANDS

Captain Passage

Prevost Island

Maple Mt.
Maple Bay
Maple Bay

Sansom Narrows

Maxwell Lake
Cranberry Rd.
7
Beddis Rd.

Maxwell Rd.

Blackburn Lake
8

SALT

Burgoyne Bay

MT. MAXWELL PROVINCIAL PARK

Cusheon Lake
9
Stewart Road

Weston Lake

RUCKLE PROVINCIAL PARK

Vancouver Island

Fulford-Ganges Rd.

SPRING

Stowell Lake
Beaver Pt. Rd.

Mt. Sulivan
Mt. Bruce

ISLAND

Fulford Harbour

Beaver Pt. Road

Cowichan Bay

Separation Point

Musgrave Rd.

Mt. Tuam

ECOLOGICAL RESERVE 16

Isabella Pt. Rd.

Swartz Bay

Swartz Bay / Tsawwassen

Cowichan Bay

Satellite Channel

Piers Island

PRINCESS MARGARET PROVINCIAL MARINE PARK
Portland Island

Anne's Oceanfront Hideaway B&B **1**
Blackberry Glen **6**
Blue Vista Resort **20**
Bodega Ridge Resort **26**
Breezy Bay B&B **15**
Corbett House Country Inn **10**
Cottage Resort **3**
Cusheon Lake Resort **9**
Driftwood Village Resort **22**
Galiano Inn & Spa **23**
Hastings House **5**
Inn on Pender Island **11**
Lyall Harbour B&B **17**

Mayne Island Eco Camping **21**
Monivea B&B **7**
Oceanwood Country Inn **18**
Poets Cove Resort & Spa **12**
Rocky Ridge B&B **25**
Sage Cottage **19**
Sahaali Oceanfront B&B **14**
Salt Springs Spa Resort **2**
Saturna Lodge **16**
Shangri-La Oceanfront B&B **13**
Sky Valley Inn **8**
Whaler Bay Lodge **24**
Wisteria Guest House **4**

Bellhouse Provincial Park
Georgina Point Lighthouse

Strait

of

Georgia

Waugh Rd.
Oyster Bay
Tsawwassen

24
23

22

---*Miners Bay*

21

Campbell Bay

Wilkes Rd.

MAYNE

MT. PARKE PARK
Fernhill Rd.

Bennett Bay
20 **19** *Curlew I.*

ISLAND

Mariners Way
East West Rd.

18
Dinner Bay
Horton Bay

Piggott Bay

Navy Channel

Samuel

WINTER COVE PROVINCIAL MARINE PARK

Island

Port Washington

Veruna Bay

Swartz Bay / Tsawwassen

Lyall Harbour

East Point Rd.

Russell Reef

Tumbo Island

Hope Bay

10

Port Washington Rd.

Saturna Pt.

East Point Rd.

17

Saturna Island Vineyards

Tumbo Channel

Tumbo Channel Rd.
Cliffside Rd.

East Point Regional Park

Otter Bay

Bedwell Harbour Road

Morning Bay Winery

15 **16**

Harris Rd.

SATURNA ISLAND

ECOLOGICAL RESERVE

Narvaez Bay Rd.

NORTH PENDER ISLAND

11

Breezy Bay

Warburton Pike

Medicine Beach

Browning Harbour

Magic Lake

MT. NORMAN REGIONAL PARK

Pirates Rd.

BEAUMONT MARINE P.P.

Canal Rd.

12

Spalding Rd.

SOUTH PENDER ISLAND

Brookes Pt.

13 **14**

Boundary Pass

Swanson Channel

Moresby Island

0		2 mi
0		2 km

"love-at-first-sight" appeal. Historic buildings and bright new commercial structures harbor banks and shopping malls, liquor stores, cafes, bakeries, and a busy marina. A favorite stop is **Sabine's** (115 Fulford-Ganges Rd.; © 250/538-0025), one of the best fine used book stores in the Pacific Northwest. Two floors are filled to the rafters with contemporary used and antiquarian books in all categories, and is home of the works of Nick Bantock, creator of *Griffin & Sabine* (Raincoast Books), among others, and who is often on hand to chat and sign books. As the cultural center of the island, Ganges also offers several quality galleries of locally crafted goods. In spring, this showcase expands into **Artcraft,** an exhibition of more than 250 Gulf Island artisans. Housed at Mahon Hall, Artcraft runs May through September daily from 10am to 5pm (© 250/537-0899). **A Studio Tour** (www.saltspringstudiotour.com) explores all manner of studios scattered among nooks and crannies on the island, letting you chat with the artists, view their work, and watch them create. Although officially tour season is from mid-May to the end of September, many sites are open year-round. Keep a lookout for the blue "sheep" signs for participating studios. Be warned, it can take about a week to visit them all!

Salt Spring's Saturday **farmers' market,** held in Centennial Park in the heart of Ganges, is another summer must-see. This weekly gathering is a glorious melee of islanders and visitors, dogs and children, craftspeople, food vendors, jugglers, and musicians. Everything for sale must be handmade or homegrown, so it's as much a feast for the eyes as for the stomach. If you're looking to snatch up some of the freshly baked goods, arrive before 10am, as they're often sold out within an hour or so of opening. And be prepared to find a few items that are unexpected, whether it's an alpaca throw, hand-painted Wellington boots, a pottery apple-baker, or whimsical jewelry. It's *the* place to shop if you're heading out for a weekend picnic or sail. The crowds stay until late afternoon, when fresh-produce vendors, having sold their lot, start to drift away. Go to **www.saltspringmarket.com** for more information.

As good as it is, the farmers' market pales in comparison to the **Salt Spring Island Fall Fair,** an annual weekend event held toward the end of September at the Farmers' Institute Fairgrounds (351 Rainbow Rd.). Filled with all the sights, sounds, tastes, and smells of a good old-fashioned country fair, it showcases award-winning livestock and home-baked pies, alongside rides and classic games like balloon darts. The gymkhanas are fun, and the sheepdog trials are superb, with hardworking collies maneuvering bundles of sheep from one corner of the field to another, all to the command of a whistle. A shuttle runs from Ganges to the fairgrounds; call © 250/537-2484 for fair information.

RUCKLE PROVINCIAL PARK ★★

This 433-hectare (1,070-acre) park starts out along 8km (5 miles) of shoreline around **Beaver Point** and sweeps up to an expanse of open and grassy meadow. Once owned by the Ruckle family, Irish immigrants in the late 1800s, part of the park is still operated as a sheep farm by the Ruckle family. Several of the original buildings, including a barn and an old residence, still stand. Ruckle Park is by far the easiest hiking ground on Salt Spring Island, offering more than 15km (9.3 miles) of trails, the favorite being a shoreline trail than runs 4,400m (14,436 ft.) from the heritage farm area right through to Yeo Point. Another trail, about the same distance but with some hills to climb, leaves from the park headquarters and heads inland in a loop around Merganser Pond. Trail maps are available at the park's visitor center. Do remember your binoculars so that you can enjoy the abundance of wildlife. You're also likely to see scuba divers in the waters off Ruckle Park, where castle-like underwater caves and a profusion of marine life create intriguing dives.

The park has 75 walk-in campsites with fire pits (firewood is provided in the summer), 8 RV sites without hook-ups, plus some group sites, a picnic area, a large kitchen shelter, drinking water, several pit toilets, and a security patrol for the entire camping area. The park attracts eco-adventurers and families alike, though for young children, you would be better off heading for **Cusheon Lake.** Ruckle Park has no designated swimming and playground areas, and no interpretive programs. From mid-March to October, a camping fee of C$16 per day applies, and you must reserve your campsite in advance. Camping is free from November to mid-March, on a first-come, first-served basis. No firewood is supplied November through mid-March. Call (✆ **877/559-2115** or 250/539-2115) for local reservations and information, or log on to www.discovercamping.ca.

VESUVIUS

Located at the western edge of Salt Spring Island, the village, which consists of old seaside cottages knitted together by twisting lanes, was named for its wonderful sunsets, made all the more dramatic by the clouds of smoke that spew forth across the Stuart Channel, from a pulp mill in Crofton on Vancouver Island. Unfortunately, this artistry also carries an off-putting pulpy odor, though that's not putting off a remake of the area. It started with the closure of one of the island's time-honored drinking establishments, the Vesuvius Inn, rumored to be morphing into a jazz bar, and continues with the development of the Vesuvius Villas, a modish vacation condominium complex. **BC Ferries** (✆ **888/223-3777** or 250/386-3432; www.bcferries. com) runs a regular service—almost every hour—across the Stuart Channel to Crofton. Return fares are C$9 adults, C$4.50 children, and C$29 for a standard-size vehicle. The crossing takes 20 minutes.

OUTDOOR ADVENTURES

As is their nature, the islands have been slow on the uptake when it comes to developing tourism-related products. Finally, however, there are signs of a mini-eco-activity industry that goes beyond bicycling and hiking. Although sea kayaking has always been popular, now it proliferates professionally. **Island Escapades** (163 Fulford Ganges Rd.; ✆ **250/537-2553;** www.islandescapades.com) offer harbor tours (from C$50 adults) to full day paddles, including lunch, for C$150 adults. At the north end of Salt Spring, **Andale! Kayaking** (1484 North Beach Rd.; ✆ **250/537-0700**) is another reliable outfitter.

If letting the topsails catch the wind is your preference, **L'Orenda Sailing** (Moby's Dock; ✆ **250/538-0084;** www.lorenda.ca) offers daily afternoon sails aboard a 12m (39-ft.) Classic North Sea double-ended yawl. Sailors can help hoist the sails or do nothing but enjoy the passing scenery. Sails cost C$69 adults; children 12 years and under are half price. One of the more unique land tours is with the **Sidecar Touring Company** (✆ **250/538-7981**), which really feels like a throwback to the 1940s. One passenger rides the sidecar, the other takes the pillion seat behind the driver. Tours are C$65.

Where to Stay

Anne's Oceanfront Hideaway B&B   Decor at this oceanfront inn ranges from French country to Queen Anne elegance, often appealing to those on a romantic getaway. Perched on the edge of a cliff, Anne's provides sweeping views of the island

PALATABLE diversions

Treats for your taste buds, here are some of Salt Springs' top culinary diversions:

- Big Foot Organic Herb Farm (104 Eagle Ridge Dr.; © **250/537-4466**): Unusual varieties of fresh and dried herbs, along with salsas, jams, jellies, chutney, flavored vinegars, honeys, and mustards.
- Salt Spring Cheese Company (285 Reynolds Rd.; © **250/653-2300**) and Moonstruck Organic Cheese (1306 Beddis Rd.; © **250/537-4987**; www.moonstruck cheese.com): Artisan goat cheeses and a gourmet selection of blues, savory, and ash-ripened Camembert cheeses.
- Salt Spring Vineyards & Winery (151 Lee Rd.; © **250/653-9463**; www.saltspringvineyards.com), Garry Oaks Vineyard (1880 Fulford-Ganges Rd.; © **250/653-4687**; www.garryoakswine. com) and Mistaken Identity (164 Norton Rd.; © **250/538-9463**; www.mistakenidentityvineyards. com): Cottage wineries with wine tasting and retail sales

of Pinot Gris, Pinot Noir, Pinot Rose, Blackberry port, and Gewürztraminer. The Oaks even offers a labyrinth to walk.

- Sacred Mountain Lavender Farm (401 Musgrave Rd.; © **250/653-2315**; www.sacredmountain lavender.com): A "boutique" lavender farm that grows more than 60 varieties of the plant, from which are made specialty and custom-made products, from lavender salts and scrubs to lavender coffee and chocolates.
- Gulf Islands Brewery (270 Furness Rd.; © **250/653-2383**; www.gulf islandsbrewery.com): Producer of golden ales and an Irish-style extra stout; it's the only brewery in the Gulf Islands.

And for those who would rather not go it alone, **Island Gourmet Safaris** (© **250/537-4118**; www.islandgourmetsafaris. com) hosts year-round tours to discover Salt Spring through its art and cuisine. Tours are 6 hours long and start at C$500 for one to four people, including lunch, which features only Salt Spring Island produce.

and sea; both the library-lounge and the den are perfect spots to take in the dramatic vistas. Thoughtful touches include free soft drinks, slippers and robes for when you want to head outside to the Jacuzzi, and evening turndown service. All rooms have ocean views and fireplaces. Four-course breakfasts are elegantly served and include items such as a salmon scramble wrap, a Portobello Benedict, and an artichoke and pimento frittata. The inn prides itself on being completely free of allergens, if indeed such a thing is possible.

168 Simson Rd., Salt Spring Island, BC V8K 1E2. © **888/474-2663** or 250/537-0851. Fax 250/537-0861. www.annesoceanfront.com. 3 units. C$185–C$225 double. Rates include breakfast. AE, MC, V. Children 15 and under not accepted. **Amenities:** Lounge; Jacuzzi. *In room:* Fridge, hair dryer, no phone, Wi-Fi.

Blackberry Glen ★ 🛏 An idyllic setting sets the tone for this stylish inn. The orchard gardens are gorgeous, and the rooms are finessed with tasteful color schemes, luxurious linens, and hardwood floors. All have queen beds, except the Long Harbour Suite, which has its own terrace balcony, cathedral ceilings, and a sitting area in front of a wood-stove fireplace. The Fulford Suite has a private bathroom across the hall. Refreshments and cookies are always available in the tiny library, and there's a main floor lounge crammed with books and DVDs. For breakfast, you may have orange-liqueur French toast or stinging nettle quiche and lemon balm tea. At press time, two cabins were under renovation: One floats on a tranquil pond, decorated with colorful art and vintage nautical pieces; the other cabin has a more lodge-style ambiance with gorgeous fir floors and elegant furnishings.

156 Quebec Dr., Salt Spring Island, BC V8K 2P4. ⓒ **877/890-0764** or 250/537-0764. www.blackberryglen. com. 6 units. May–Sept C$99–C$169 double; Oct–Apr C$89–C$149 double. Rates include breakfast. MC, V. Children 12 & under not accepted. **Amenities:** 2 lounges; hot tub. *In room:* Hair dryer, no phone, Wi-Fi.

Cottage Resort ☺

Accommodations at this resort are a mix of snug studios and small one-, two-, and three-bedroom cabins appointed with country-style furnishings, kitchens, and small private decks. Most cabins have an electric or wood-burning stove. All units are within a few steps of St. Mary Lake, where the entire family can enjoy free use of canoes and row boats; life jackets are provided. Watch for stray chickens roaming beneath the rhododendron bushes and bring carrots to feed the horses. You can even try your luck fishing for smallmouth bass, yellow perch, and rainbow trout.

175 Suffolk Rd., Salt Spring Island, BC V8K 1L8. ⓒ **888/537-4854** or 250/537-2214. 9 units. May–Aug C$115–C$150 double & 1-bedroom cabin; C$210–C$375 2- & 3-bedroom cabin; Oct–Apr C$95–C$150 double & 1-bedroom cabin; C$165–C$375 2- & 3-bedroom cabin. Additional adult C$20. MC, V. Pets accepted (upon approval). **Amenities:** Internet; free canoes & row boats. *In room:* TV/DVD player, fridge, hair dryer, kitchen, no phone.

Cusheon Lake Resort ☺

With its location right on the shores of Cusheon Lake, this family-oriented resort has a holiday-camp feel. The one- and two-bedroom log cabins and A-frame chalets are spotlessly clean and furnished in a no-nonsense style that suits families and people who want a self-catering, un-froufrou getaway. The kitchen is well stocked with all the essentials, including coffee filters. Beach towels are also part of the deal because there's so much to do in and around the lake: canoeing, swimming, rowing, picnicking, and lawn games. Although there's generally a 2- or 3-night minimum stay, if there's an opening, they'll accept 1-night stands!

171 Natalie Lane, Salt Spring Island, BC V8K 2C6. ⓒ **250/537-9629.** www.cusheonlake.com. 16 units. Mid-May to mid-Oct C$154–C$232; mid-Oct to mid-May C$120–C$188. Additional adult C$20. 2-night minimum stay; 3-night minimum July & Aug. Weekly rates available. MC, V. **Amenities:** Outdoor hot tub; canoes & rowboats; Wi-Fi. *In room:* Fridge, kitchen, no phone.

Hastings House ★★★

A member of the exclusive Small Luxury Hotels of the World, this sophisticated inn overlooks Ganges Harbour and lies an olive pit's throw from the village itself. First a Hudson's Bay Company trading post, then a farm, and then the homestead of Warren Hastings and his bride, Barbara Wedgwood, the British pottery heiress, the property and magnificent orchard gardens were transformed into a replica of a 16th-century Sussex estate. Since then, the Tudor-style manor house, farmhouse, barn, and trading post have been turned into cottages and suites, each charged with character and filled with original art and antiques, and all the modern luxuries of a first-class hotel (including bathrooms large enough for deep soaking tubs). A two-room spa, with steam shower, offers quality treatments. A somewhat incongruous sculpture garden gives purpose to a wilder part of the property. When it comes to dining here (see "Where to Dine," below), reserve 6 months in advance for summer visits and check out the "Catch your own Dungeness crab" add-on package. After you trap your crab, you have the option of either learning to clean and prepare the crab yourself, or have the chef create a crab specialty for you to enjoy.

160 Upper Ganges Rd., Ganges, Salt Spring Island, BC V8K 2S8. © **800/661-9255** or 250/537-2362. Fax 250/537-5333. www.hastingshouse.com. 18 units. July–Sept C$495–C$895 double; early-Apr to June & Oct C$395–C$715 double. Closed Nov to early-Apr. Rates include afternoon tea, & breakfast. Additional adult C$75. AE, DC, MC, V. Children 16 & under not accepted. **Amenities:** Restaurant; lounge w/honor bar; spa. *In room:* CD player, fridge, Wi-Fi.

Monivea B&B 🎁 Located within an easy walk of Ganges, this beautifully furnished inn offers three self-contained artisan suites, each with private entrance, en-suite bathroom, and decor that's a comfortable mix of antiques, heritage quilts, and island art. Locally, the inn is known as the Starry Night Artisan Gallery, which in 2010, opened a tiny gallery at the top of the property—the owners are both artists. There's also a new, equally intimate, Aveda spa. Both overlook Monivea's stunning garden that overflows with flowering perennials, ponds, and fountains. Enjoy it from the main deck, which offers peek-a-boo ocean views, or the conservatory, where breakfast is served (if the weather's good, try breakfast on one of the garden's private patios). The inn uses only organic produce and even has its own laying hens for fresh eggs.

420 Fulford Ganges Rd., Salt Spring Island, BC V8K 2K1. © **888/537-5856** or 250/537-5856. Fax 250/537-5856. www.moniveasaltspring.com. 3 units. Apr–Sept C$159–C$179 suite; Oct–Mar C$123–C$133 suite. Rates include breakfast. Additional adult C$35. MC, V. **Amenities:** Lounge; spa. *In room:* TV, no phone, Wi-Fi.

Salt Springs Spa Resort This spa resort is the only spot where the island's salty spring waters can be enjoyed. The 12-room day spa offers a variety of facials, body wraps, and massages, as well as some exotic Ayurvedic therapies and yoga sessions. Even if the spa isn't your thing, Salt Springs is a great getaway; choose from several one-, two-, and three-bedroom A-frame chalets. A handful are in the forest, but most sport an ocean view, looking across Trincomali Channel to Wallace Island, a marine park. All chalets have full kitchens; wood-burning fireplaces (including complimentary supplies of firewood); wide porches with BBQs; and an oversize, two-person mineral tub, in addition to a regular bathtub. Wi-Fi access is a bit "iffy" in the perimeter units. Clamming gear and crab traps are available for those wanting to try their luck on the beach across the road.

1460 North Beach Rd., Salt Spring Island, BC V8K 1J4. © **800/665-0039** or 250/537-4111. Fax 250/537-2939. www.saltspringspa.com. 13 units. Late June to Aug C$199–C$299 chalet; mid-Feb to late June, Sept & Oct C$135–C$219 chalet; Nov to mid-Feb C$109–C$199 chalet. Additional adult C$20. Weekly rates & packages available. AE, MC, V. Free parking. Children 12 & younger not accepted. **Amenities:** Bikes (free); spa; badminton court; rowboats (free); Wi-Fi. *In room:* Fridge, hair dryer, kitchen, no phone.

Sky Valley Inn 🎁 With a touch of Provence in every renovated corner, Sky Valley is more like an old French country retreat nestled on 4.5 gated hectares (11 acres), with outstanding views to neighboring islands. The inn sits along high mountain ridges, so unless your pedals have wing power, make the climb here by car. Each of the three guest rooms is distinctly decorated with hardwood floors, French toile wallpaper, and wainscoting. The king- and queen-size down-feather mattresses are topped with down duvets and crisp white linens for a luxurious feel. Each room has a private entrance; the Garden Room is completely separate from the main house. Amenities even include hand-crafted, homemade soap. Full breakfasts are served in an open French-style country kitchen and will likely feature cheese blintz crepes, and a frittata or soufflé, as well as lavender scones with peach and lavender jams that have won first prizes in the Salt Spring Island Fall Fair.

421 Sky Valley Rd., Salt Spring Island, BC V8K 2C3. ℂ **866/537-1028** or 250/537-9800. www.skyvalley inn.com. 3 units. C$170–C$220 double. 2-night minimum stay in summer. MC, V. Children 12 & younger not accepted. **Amenities:** Lounge; outdoor swimming pool; Wi-Fi. *In room:* No phone.

Wisteria Guest House ★   Located within a 10-minute stroll of Ganges, this charming inn is so full of color and character, it's hard to believe that it was once a nursing home. Its renaissance has certainly created something for everyone. The main guest house has six vibrantly decorated rooms: two with en-suite bathrooms and four that share two bathrooms, making them a good choice for friends and family traveling together. The two studios are the most romantic. Each has a private entrance, French doors leading onto a sunny patio, and a well-equipped kitchenette. One has a king, the other a queen-size bed. If you want to be totally independent, go for the private cottage; it has twin beds, a fully equipped kitchen, cable TV, and private patio. In winter, only a cold breakfast is served, though that's not the drawback it sounds. One of the owners was a pastry chef at the Westin New York, so breakfast is still a pretty lavish affair of home-made Swiss-style muesli and almond croissants. In summer, enjoy additional items such as savory egg strudels, bramble crumbles, or baked eggs.

268 Park Dr., Salt Spring Island, BC V8K 2S1. ℂ **250/537-5899.** Fax 250/537-5644. www.wisteriaguest house.com. 9 units. Mid-May to mid-Oct C$165–C$190 double w/private bath, C$120–C$150 double w/ shared bath; mid-Oct to Mar C$119–C$129 double w/private bath, C$99–C$109 double w/shared bath; Apr to mid-May C$150–C$165 double w/private bath, C$120–C$130 double w/shared bath. Additional adult C$10–C$15. AE, MC, V. Pets accepted. **Amenities:** Lounge. *In room:* No phone, Wi-Fi.

Where to Dine

Auntie Pesto's Café ECLECTIC/REGIONAL   With a lovely view of Ganges Harbour and a waterfront patio, this tiny eatery is busy all day long, whether because of its hearty soups and over-stuffed sandwiches on fresh-baked breads, or its excellent pasta dishes (including wheat-free) that come with a choice of toppings such as marinated tofu, prawns, meatballs, and homemade sauces. The dinner menu features steak and seafood specials that may include Thai-prawn stir-fry or grilled halibut with salsa topping. The latter is homemade, using whatever is in season. *Tip:* For many, sitting up at the bar, for coffee or wine, is the best seat in the house.

2104-115 Fulford-Ganges Rd., Grace Point Sq. ℂ **250/537-4181.** www.auntiepestos.com. Reservations accepted only for dinner July & Aug. Main courses lunch C$8–C$12, dinner C$10–C$20. MC, V. Daily 8am–9pm.

Bruce's Kitchen 🍴 CANADIAN   Chef-owner Big Bruce loves his trade, which he applies with gusto in this open kitchen. Diners sit at communal tables so that the entire atmosphere takes on the conviviality, aromas, and relationship of a neighbor's kitchen. Dinner revolves around three courses of local food with wine pairings, and menus vary week to week. Items have included roast prime rib with Bruce's Mom's Yorkshire pudding; quiche with Tuscan ham, caramelized onions, local chevre; and vegetarian chili with house-made cornbread. Pot pies are a classic; breads and scones are baked daily. The place is so popular, and so small (it seats only 20 people), that most items are available as take-out.

149 Fulford-Ganges Rd. (aka Gasoline Alley). ℂ **250/931-3399.** 3-course table d'hôte C$50; take out C$5–C$12. Sept–June Mon–Thurs 11am–7pm, Sat 8am–4pm; July & Aug Mon–Thurs 11am–7pm, Sat 8am–4pm, Sun 11am–3pm.

Hastings House ★★ PACIFIC NORTHWEST   Impeccable cuisine, attentive service, and a gracious setting have made Hastings House one of the most sought-after destination restaurants—and inns—in the Pacific Northwest (see "Where to Stay," above). In addition to a la carte selections, there's a superb, multi-course menu that changes daily; many of the ingredients come from the estate itself. Dinner can be an elegant, evening-long affair with an excellent wine list. The choice of entrees nearly always features Salt Spring lamb, the house specialty (try it grilled with rosemary spaetzle and a grainy mustard jus). Wild spring salmon, perhaps with a sweet soya emulsion, or a pan-seared duck breast with port wine jus and filet of Alberta beef, with duck liver and apricot mousse, are other possibilities. In warm weather, the best tables are on the veranda overlooking the gardens and harbor.

160 Upper Ganges Rd. © 250/537-2362. Reservations required. Main courses C$12–C$48; 3- to 4-course prix fixe dinner C$65–C$80. AE, DC, MC, V. Mid-Mar to mid-Nov daily 6–10pm. Closed mid-Nov to mid-Mar.

House Piccolo ★ CONTINENTAL   This small blue-and-white heritage farm-house-turned-restaurant is wonderfully intimate. Two-person tables are scattered through two connecting country-style dining rooms accented with copper kettles set high on shelves. Everything on the European-style menu is enticing, particularly the fresh bread, broiled prawn and sea-scallop brochettes, and wiener schnitzel. Save room for homemade ice cream or the chocolate terrine, both of which are Piccolo institutions. House Piccolo is a member of Chaine des Rôtisseurs, an international gastronomic society dedicated to the promotion of fine dining around the world.

108 Hereford Ave. © **250/537-1844.** www.housepiccolo.com. Reservations recommended July–Sept. Main courses C$25–C$36. DC, MC, V. May–Sept daily 5–10pm; Oct–Apr Wed–Sun 5–8pm.

Moby's Marine Pub PUB FARE   A local favorite, this multilevel marine pub sports big beams, wood floors, and cathedral-size windows for views of Ganges. On nights when there's live entertainment, it could R&B, folk, jazz, or rock that takes the stage. If it's a local headliner such as aging rocker Randy Bachman performing, get there early for a table. Jazz on Sunday nights is a dinner tradition. The menu includes burgers and fajitas, alongside savory entrees like Caribbean fish pot (to die for) and Louisiana lamb curry. Ten beers are on tap. Bask in the sun and sup a cold one on the deck that hangs within inches of bullwhip kelp and minnows.

124 Upper Ganges Rd. © **250/537-5559.** www.mobys.ca. Main courses C$8–C$24. MC, V. Sun–Thurs 10am–midnight; Fri & Sat 10am–1am.

Raven Street Market Café Pizza PIZZA   The thin-crust, wood-fired pizzas here are among the best and most creative you'll find anywhere. Made in the tra-ditional Neapolitan way, they include combinations such as roasted pepper chicken, basil, cilantro, and fresh tomatoes; herbed lamb and artichoke pesto; and "the Canadianne": real back bacon, chorizo sausage (or substitute with crab meat), mushroom, white mozzarella, black olives, and green pepper. Other dishes include a delicious seafood and sausage gumbo; a spicy, very good curried chicken mulli-gatawny; as well as focaccia sandwiches, burgers, and salads. Love the kids menu, too, because it's uncluttered: simple cheese pizza, chicken strips, and a 4-ounce cheeseburger. This is a grocery and deli market as much as it is an eatery, which makes the atmosphere a tad busy; so the wait staff may not be as attentive as you might like. The cafe runs the **North Island Coffee House** (325 Fernwood Rd., © 250/931-7207) next door, where organic coffee brands are served, enjoyed in oversized armchairs with sea views.

321 Fernwood Rd. © **250/537-2273.** www.ravenstreet.ca. Main courses C$10–C$18. Daily noon–8pm.

Tree House Cafe CAFE   Set in the heart of Ganges, this 12-seat cafe spills over onto a larger patio that stakes its claim around and beneath a sprawling old plum tree. In summer, the place is jammed, in part because of the folksy musical entertainment, but also because of the cool food that includes everything from Thai peanut tofu and vegetarian chili to burgers and BLTs. The organic Salt Spring coffee sidelines Starbucks.

106 Purvis Lane, Ganges. ℂ **250/537-5379.** Main courses C$5–C$7. MC, V. Oct–May daily 8am–3pm; June–Sept daily 8am–11pm.

THE PENDER ISLANDS

Known for their secluded coves, beautiful beaches, and islets, the Penders are a tranquil escape, and a boater's nirvana. With a population of barely 2,000, they remain small enough that, as one resident says, "The sight of another human being still conjures up a smile!"

The Penders are actually two islands, linked by a short wooden bridge that spans a canal between **Bedwell and Browning harbors.** Until 1903, when the canal was dug, island pioneers were forced to haul their boats laboriously over a wide neck of land known as "Indian Portant." Centuries before, the Coast Salish, a local First Nations group, used to set up seasonal camps in the area, and several shell middens (refuse heaps), some dating from 4500 B.C., have revealed thousands of artifacts, including carved spoons and lip ornaments. With several parks, picnic areas, and overnight camping facilities, the Penders are threaded with meandering, illogical roads that are a delight to tour by car or bicycle. The Penders have more public beach access points for their size than any other Gulf Island—37 in all, with plenty of picturesque cottages, orchards, and a dozen or so artisans' home galleries to enjoy en route. The well landscaped, 9-hole golf course is a pleasant diversion (it also has a cute cafe), as is the golf Frisbee–throwing park, where the "tees" are metal poles tucked in between trees. The real trick is to keep your Frisbee from ricocheting off the trees on its flight to the target.

Essentials

GETTING THERE

BC Ferries sails to **Otter Bay,** on the northwest side of North Pender Island. Pleasure boats can dock at **Bedwell Harbour,** on the southern cove where North and South Pender meet. See "Getting There," at the beginning of this chapter, for information on ferry fares and schedules.

VISITOR INFORMATION

There is no formal visitor information center on Pender Island, although you can pick up brochures at the "mall," **The Driftwood Centre** (4605 Bedwell Harbour Rd.; ℂ 250/629-6555). Or contact the **Pender Island Chamber of Commerce** (ℂ 866/468-7924; www.penderislandchamber.com).

GETTING AROUND

Pender Island Cab Company (ℂ **250/629-2222;** www.penderislandcab.com) provides service to various points around the islands. Bike and scooter rentals are available in season at **Otter Bay Marina** (ℂ 250/629-3579) at a daily rate of C$25 and C$85, respectively. Hourly rentals are C$8 for bikes and C$25 for scooters.

Exploring the Penders

NORTH PENDER

The larger of the two islands, **North Pender** is more populated and more developed than its southerly neighbor. There's no real town center in the traditional sense on North Pender, so the modern **Driftwood Centre** (4605 Bedwell Harbour Rd., near Razor Point Rd.), in the center of the island, is the nucleus of island life. Here's where to stock up on groceries and gift items, and indulge in your sweet tooth at the must-visit **Pender Island Bakery** (© **250/629-6453**; www.penderislandbakery. com). It's also excellent for picnic supplies, as well as for an easy lunch with home-made soups, sandwiches, and salads. Call ahead for specialty items. The **Saturday Market** (May–Oct 9:30am–12:30pm) is a fine place for mixing with the locals, sampling island-grown produce, and browsing through artisan stalls. Continue on along Razor Point Road toward Browning Harbour, and you'll find **Morning Bay Vineyard** (6621 Harbour Hill Dr.; © **250/629-8352**; www.morningbay.ca). Overlooking Plumber Sound and with a main building designed to look like a barn, it features 20 terraces that climb up the south side of Mount Menzies. In 2007, the vineyard delivered its first estate wines: Pinot Noir, Pinot Gris, Maréchal Foch, and Schonberger. Its Gewürztraminer-Riesling (the first vintage) has since won a silver medal in the 2008 All-Canadian Wine Championships, and its Reserve Merlot was awarded a bronze medal at the prestigious New York–based Finger Lakes competition. Tastings are Wednesday through Saturday, 10am to 5pm.

Away from the Driftwood, most activity happens around **Otter Bay,** where the ferries arrive; **Port Browning;** and **Hope Bay.** At **Port Washington,** northwest of Otter Bay, you'll find orchards and charming old cottages reminiscent of a turn-of-the-20th-century coastal village; the village has a pretty dockside, a couple of galleries and a water's-edge bistro cafe. Check out **Pender Island Kayak Adventures** at the Otter Bay Marina (© **250/629-6939**; www.kayakpenderisland.com) for kayak rentals, and guided kayaking tours and lessons in and around island coves and to neighboring Mayne and Saturna islands. Everyone from beginners to advanced kayakers are welcome. Two-hour guided tours are C$45 adults, C$30 children 11 and under; 3-hour guided tours are C$60 adults; and all-day paddles are C$105 adults. *Tip:* Mondays are geared for family outings: Pay for your first child, and the second paddles for half price. **Port Browning Marina** (4605 Oak Rd.; © **250/629-3493**), on the northern cove where North and South Pender meet, is an inviting "watering hole" with First Nations decor, including a totem pole. This marina is cheerfully downscale from Bedwell Harbour, on the other side of the narrow neck of land that separates the two islands, where Poets Cove Resort has made its mark. (see "Where to Stay," below). North Pender parks include **Medicine Beach,** one of the last wetlands in the Gulf Islands, and home to many native plants once used for food and medicine. The beach is within walking distance of **Prior Centennial Provincial Park,** a forest of cedar, maple, fir, and alder trees. Located 6km (3¾ miles) from the ferry terminal, Prior Centennial can also be reached off Canal Road. **Roesland** is a 230-hectare (568-acre) park that includes a headland, Roe Lake, a freshwater lake, beaches, and lots of forest. The site was once a summer cottage resort, and has an original farmhouse dating back to 1908 that now serves as a tiny museum. Take the trail past the Davidson home to the headland to see the rotting remains of a 220-year-old **Indian canoe** that lies 6km (3¾ miles) from the Otter Bay ferry terminal off Canal Road.

SOUTH PENDER

This remote part of the island has always attracted independent, sometimes eccentric, fun-loving spirits who don't mind the isolation. Although the only services to be found are at the **Poets Cove Marina** (9801 Spalding Rd.; © 250/629-3212), there are lots of beaches, parks, and trails to enjoy. Hikers should head for **Mount Norman Regional Park** (www.britishcolumbia.com/parks). At 244m (801 ft.), Mount Norman is the highest point on the Penders.

The gravel access road up to Mount Norman is uninteresting, but the 1km (.6-mile) hike to the summit is well worth the effort. It starts at the Ainslie Point Road trail head, and as the trail begins to climb, the landscape changes from wetlands to forests of Douglas fir and western red cedar, and ends with lichen-covered bedrock up top, where the panoramas are stunning. From Mount Norman Regional Park, you can access **Beaumont Marine Provincial Park,** without a doubt the prettiest marine park in the Gulf Islands, its picturesque coastal wilderness seemingly tamed by gentle waters, moss-covered rocks, and grassy verges. It's now a part of the **Gulf Islands National Park Reserve** (© 250/629-6139; www.pc.gc.ca/eng/pn-np/bc/gulf/index.aspx) and is a moderate, 40-minute hike from Mount Norman.

Unlike the limited facilities of most of these parks, nearby Prior Centennial (also a part of the Reserve) includes 17 vehicle/tent sites, pit toilets, water, fire pits, and picnic tables operated by Parks Canada (© 877/737-3738 for reservations; www.pccamping.ca). Sites average C$36 per day, depending on the site size required, plus a nonrefundable reservation fee of C$11. Another favorite recreation area, **Brookes Point,** is one of the last undeveloped headlands in the Gulf Islands. The coastal bluff is ecologically important, as it hosts rare types of native grass and more than 100 bird species, some of which are endangered. Large pods of **killer whales** sometimes swim right under the point in the nearby kelp beds, as do mink, seal, otter, and Dall's porpoises. Tidal pools contain abalone, sea anemones, and coral. If you have good shoes, the walk along the shoreline from here to Gowlland Point is captivating.

Where to Stay

Corbett House Country Inn New owners have breathed new life into this lovely wisteria-covered heritage home so that the hardwood floors, trim, and furnishings sparkle with care, attention, and comfort. Located in the middle of an orchard, with sheep grazing in fields beyond, the inn serves as an escape into the heart of the country. Two rooms have queen-sized beds; though each has a basin and toilet, the rooms share a shower. The third room has a king-sized bed, private balcony, and en-suite bathroom with claw-foot tub. Breakfast is generous, with traditional favorites served with fine china and silverware. Check out the impressive art displays of photos and paintings. Hope Bay is within an easy 15 minute country walk.

4309 Corbett Rd., Pender Island, BC V0N 2M1 © 250/629-2022. Fax 250/629-2032. http://corbett housecountryinn.com. 3 units. Apr–Nov C$135–C$155 double. Open by request Dec–Mar. **Amenities:** Lounge. *In room:* TV/DVD player, hair dryer, Wi-Fi.

Inn on Pender Island ★ 🦆 Situated next to Prior Centennial Provincial Park, this modest inn offers a choice of nine motel-style lodge rooms or three studio log cabins, many with ocean views and some with private Jacuzzis. Lodge rooms are clean and roomy; cabins have fireplaces and deck swings. Children and pets are welcome. **Memories at the Inn** is a fully licensed restaurant, and although the decor's a bit plain, it's a popular choice for affordable dining. Menu items include pastas, fish and chips, pork ribs, and chicken. The homemade pizza is exceptionally good.

4709 Canal Rd. (P.O. Box 72), Pender Island, BC V0N 2M0. © **800/550-0172** or 250/629-3353. Fax 250/629-3167. www.innonpender.com. 12 units. May–Sept C$79–C$99 double, C$159 cabin; Oct–Apr C$69–C$89 double, C$149 cabin. MC, V. Small pets accepted. **Amenities:** Restaurant; Jacuzzi. *In room:* TV/DVD player, fridge, Wi-Fi.

Poets Cove Resort & Spa ★★ ☺ As one of the most upscale, year-round destinations in the Gulf Islands, this resort offers so much to do that you never have to leave its confines. Accommodations range from 22 modern lodge rooms (they all face west to catch glorious sunsets) to deluxe two- and three-bedroom cottages (best for romantic getaways), and spacious and family-oriented villas complete with kitchens, dining rooms, living rooms with fireplaces, balconies, and BBQs. Most have private hot tubs. Children's programs and a 110-slip marina make Poets Cove popular with families and boaters. The bright, airy **Aurora Restaurant** (see "Where to Dine," below) features French-influenced fine dining, and Syrens Lounge & Bistro offers casual dining inside or on the enormous deck. The menu includes kid-friendly burgers and pint portions of other selections for smaller appetites. If you're staying in a cottage or villa, you can order items from the "raw menu" to barbecue yourself. The Susurrus Spa is a destination unto itself, with six large treatment rooms, a steam cave, and oceanfront Jacuzzi.

Tip: The "Poets Cruises" is an excellent 3-hour island hop and eco-adventure (C$109) with different itineraries that include stopovers at historic Hope Bay on North Pender, the vineyard on Saturna Island, and places to spot wildlife in the area.

9801 Spalding Rd., South Pender Island, BC V0N 2M3. © **888/512-7638** or 250/629-2100. Fax 250/629-2105. www.poetscove.com. 22 rooms, 15 cottages, 9 villas. C$189–C$299 double; C$359–C$699 cottage; C$239–C$529 villa. Children 17 & under stay free in parent's room. AE, MC, V. Pets accepted (C$50 per stay). **Amenities:** Restaurant; pub; large heated outdoor pool; spa; 2 outdoor tennis courts. *In-room:* TV/DVD player, fridge, hair dryer, Wi-Fi.

Sahaali Oceanfront B&B New owners have restyled this B&B into a luxurious, pampering retreat. Its two guest rooms suites and 2-bedroom cottage getaway feature richly furnished queen-sized beds, wood burning fireplaces, private decks with hot tubs, and wraparound-windows. Breakfast is delivered to your door in hampers, pretty much to order, and filled to the brim with home-baked goodies, granola mixes, fruit compotes, and even snacks for the road.

5915 Pirates Rd., Pender Island, BC V0N 2M2. © **888/724-4254** or 250/-629-3756. www.pender-island-bedandbreakfast.com. 3 units. June–Sept C$275–C$295 double, C$235 cottage; Mar–May & Oct C$225–C$245 double, C$180 cottage; Nov–Feb C$205–C$225 double, C$150 cottage. 2-night minimum. Weekends C$30 extra each night. MC, V. Children accepted in cottage only. **Amenities:** Bike rentals. *In room:* TV/DVD player, fridge, hair dryer, Wi-Fi.

Shangri-La Oceanfront B&B Perched on Pender's Oaks Bluff with 4 hectares (10 acres) of wilderness at its feet, this sprawling house is the only B&B on the island with 360-degree views and 511 sq. m (5,500 sq. ft.) of wraparound balconies from which to drink it all in: a panorama that stretches across Swanson Channel to Washington State's Mount Baker and the Olympic Range, to the coastal mountains on the mainland. Staying here is like nesting in your own aerie, complete with private deck and Jacuzzi. Guest rooms aren't overly fancy but have all the extras such as fireplaces, queen-size beds with foam toppers, and down duvets for extra comfort. The Lost in Space Suite even has glow-in-the-dark planetary murals, and because of its extra size and BBQ, it's good for longer stays. A range of in-room spa services is available, from massage to Reiki.

5909 Pirates Rd., Pender Island, BC V0N 2M2. © **877/629-2800** or 250/629-3808. www.penderisland shangrila.com. 3 units. May to mid-Sept C$200–C$235 double; mid-Sept to mid-Jan C$145–C$165 double; mid-Jan to Apr C$145–C$185 double. Rates include full breakfast. Additional adult C$35. MC, V. Pets accepted (C$20). **Amenities:** Lounge; Jacuzzi. *In room:* TV, fridge, no phone; Wi-Fi.

Where to Dine

Aurora ★ PACIFIC NORTHWEST   By far the most sophisticated dining room you'll find anywhere on the Penders, Aurora serves food to match the great marine views. There's a French influence to the menu items, which lean to local produce. Standouts include the Salt Spring goat-cheese tart and herb salad, seared Qualicum scallops (the catch of the day is always a good choice), and Pender Island lamb. For dessert, sample local creations on the cheese plate. The restaurant is romantic, whether you sit by the huge stone fireplace that dominates an entire wall or beside the floor-to-ceiling windows. If you're an oenophile, you'll probably prefer a table near the wall of wine bottles—the wine list is extensive.

In Poets Cove Resort & Spa, 9801 Spalding Rd. © **250/629-2100.** Reservations recommended. Main courses C$24–C$35. AE, MC, V. Daily 5:30–10pm.

Fish On Pender 🐟   The restaurateurs who run the highly successful Fish on 5th in Sidney (p. 112) have repeated their formula here. Traditional cod and halibut come with regular or yam fries, though the calamari dinners, rock fish tacos, and hot Thai wraps are so good, you'll be tempted to digress from regular fish and chips. Burgers, soups, salads and veggie options are on the menu if fish isn't your thing. All entrees come with home-cut fries and coleslaw.

Driftwood Centre, 4605 Bedwell Harbour Rd. © **250/629-3232.** Main courses C$8–C$15. MC, V. Daily 11am–8pm.

GALIANO ISLAND

Galiano Island is a magnet for outdoor enthusiasts. It's a long, skinny island that stretches more than 26km (16 miles) from top to bottom, and is no more than 2km (1¼ miles) across. Two harbors and several parks provide abundant opportunity to hike, camp, fish, boat, and bird-watch—activities that have, in fact, been hard won. Logging was once Galiano's biggest industry, and when clear-cutting almost destroyed the wilderness, the community rallied, purchasing key tracts of land that have now returned to wilderness. Remnants of lumber operations are still evident in parts, including a shoreline strewn with salt-laden, sun-bleached logs. In spite of their activism, the folks on Galiano are actually very laid-back. It's as if they've not quite outgrown their obsession with growing marijuana back in the '70s. For boomers, this may be strangely comforting.

Most of the 1,100 or so permanent residents live on the southern part of the island, close to **Sturdies Bay,** which, for all intents and purposes, is the island's downtown. So, it's here that you'll find most of the accommodations and a handful of restaurants and stores, as well as in the surrounding areas of **Georgeson Bay, Montague Harbour,** and **Spotlight Cove.** North Galiano is much wilder, and although there are pockets of housing, the country is dense with cedar and fir trees, maple and alder stands.

Essentials

GETTING THERE

BC Ferries sails to **Sturdies Bay** on the southern tip of the island. Boaters and floatplanes dock at **Montague Harbour,** on the west coast, about a 20-minute drive from Sturdies Bay.

VISITOR INFORMATION

Contact the **Galiano Chamber of Commerce** (2590 Sturdies Bay Rd.; ℭ **250/ 539-2233;** www.galianoisland.com). It's open in July and August daily from 9am to 5pm and September to June on occasional weekends from 9am to 5pm. Pick up a self-guided **Galiano Art Guide** here or on the ferry.

GETTING AROUND

Taxi Galiano (ℭ 250/539-0202) provides year-round land-based taxi service You can also rent boats and mopeds from **Galiano Adventures,** at Montague Harbour (ℭ **250/539-3443;** www.galianoadventures.com), and bicycles from **Galiano Bicycle** (36 Burrill Rd., Sturdies Bay; ℭ **250/539-9906**). Boats and mopeds are available from May to September and cost C$18 and C$20 per hour, respectively. Bike rentals are C$35 for a 24-hour period.

Exploring Galiano Island

In and around **Sturdies Bay,** you'll find picturesque B&Bs, a few galleries, and a handful of shops. Nearby, **Bellhouse Provincial Park** is one of the prettiest settings on the island, with a rocky, moss-covered peninsula, sculpted sandstone, and magnificent groves of copper-red arbutus trees. Situated at the entrance to **Active Pass,** here's where to linger for an hour or two over a picnic, watching the myriad kinds of wildlife. Tides run up to 5 knots here, and the shoreline drops sharply into deep water, making it an excellent point to spin-cast for salmon.

    Galiano Bluffs Park, another favorite area, is also at the entrance to Active Pass but sits 120m (394 ft.) above it. The views from the bluffs deserve rave reviews. Watch BC Ferries' largest ships rumble past and grab your binoculars to see eagles riding the updrafts, as well as seals, sea lions, and other marine life. Seasonal wildflowers are an equal delight. Go easy on the approach road; it has some serious potholes. **Montague Harbour Marina** (ℭ **250/539-5733**) is a fun place to visit, if only to yacht-watch or catch a light meal in the marina restaurant. While there, check out **Galiano Island Kayaking** (ℭ 250/539-2442; www.seakayak.ca). The 3-hour rentals are C$55 a person; full-day paddles are C$85 a person. You can also rent canoes. **Gulf Island Safaris** (ℭ **888/656-9878**) runs wildlife and whale-watching tours that get you up close with marine life aboard rubber Zodiac boats, with pre-arranged pickups from Galiano.

Montague Harbour Provincial Marine Park ★★

One of the Gulf Islands' most popular provincial parks, Montague Harbour is where to watch giant American yachts arriving and chattering kingfishers diving for salmon. Swim and beach comb to your heart's content along gorgeous shell and gravel beaches, enjoy a picnic on the bluff, and search through shell middens dating back 3,000 years. The protected waters are perfect for beginner rowers, and hiking trails include an easy 3km (1.9-mile) forest and beach walk that loops around Gray Peninsula, originally inhabited by First Nations peoples. Along the northwest edge of the peninsula are spectacular rippled rock ledges, as well as white shell beaches, and along the southern shore are two caves that can be reached by foot at low tide, or by boat.

If you want to stay awhile, the park has two year-round campgrounds: one with 15 walk-in sites for boaters and cyclists, another with 25 drive-in sites for motorists. **Note:** There are no RV hookups. There's a boat ramp, 35 mooring buoys, and a store. Free interpretive talks are offered during July and August. Check the **Nature House** for schedules. Buoys are C$12 per vessel; campsites are C$21 a day. Call **Discover Camping** at ✆ **800/689-9025** or 250/391-2300 for information and reservations, or go online to www.discovercamping.ca. For a more rustic camping experience, head up to the northern tip of Galiano, where you'll find Dionisio Point Provincial Park. Sitting at the entrance to Porlier Pass, it is accessed only by water. Take care to approach it at slack tide, as the currents can be unruly. There are 30 first-come, first-served walk-in campsites. Even if you're not overnighting here, the park's beaches are strewn with shell middens to comb, making them a good pit stop for day-tripping kayakers.

Where to Stay

Bodega Ridge Resort ★ ☺ 🍴   Located near Spanish Hills, at the island's northern end, this hilltop resort and sheep farm is a rambling collection of hand-hewn cottages, offering majestic views and basic comforts. The immaculate two-level log chalets are simply decorated and have full, well stocked kitchens, making them just right for families, while no. 7, the only single-level building, is a cozy hideaway for romantics. They feature stained-glass doors and tasteful wood furnishings. Kiwi and grape vines clamber over the main farmhouse, and landscaped gardens are sprinkled with Celtic standing stones, ponds, and kilometers of hiking trails. The resort offers mountain bike rentals and exclusive guided tours through the network of private trails.

120 Manastee Rd. (P.O. Box 115), Galiano Island, BC V0N 1P0. ✆ **877/604-2677** or 250/539-2677. Fax 250/539-2677. www.bodegaridge.com. 7 units. Apr to mid-Oct C$150–C$200 cabin; mid-Oct to Mar C$125 cabin. Additional adult C$25. MC, V. Pets accepted (C$15). **Amenities:** Lounge; mountain bike rentals; Wi-Fi. *In room:* TV/DVD player (upon request), kitchen, no phone.

Driftwood Village Resort ★ ☺ 🍴   Set in a delightful garden filled with fruit trees, the Driftwood Village Resort epitomizes Galiano's easy-going attitude, making for relaxed, stress-free family vacations. Each of the studio, one-, and two-bedroom cottages is charming, cozy, and decorated with original artwork. While various bed-linen combinations give each cabin a different feel, all have oceanfront views, private bathrooms, well-equipped kitchens, and private decks with barbecues. All but one of the cottages have wood-burning fireplaces. There's a Jacuzzi in the center of the garden from which to stargaze or watch deer meandering by. A footpath leads down to a sandy beach on Matthews Point, one of Galiano's many bird-watching spots. The "Ocean" cottages, which come with skylights and a private Jacuzzi, are especially nice.

205 Bluff Rd. E., Galiano Island, BC V0N 1P0. ✆ **866/502-5457** or 250/539-5457. www.driftwoodcottages. com. 10 units. Mid-June to mid-Sept C$129–C$160 cottage; mid-Sept to mid-June C$85–C$135 cottage. Additional adult C$10–C$20. Children 12 & under stay free in parent's cottage. MC, V. Pets accepted (C$10). **Amenities:** Jacuzzi; Wi-Fi. *In room:* TV, DVD player (in some), kitchen, no phone.

Galiano Inn & Spa ★★★   A cosmopolitan boutique destination spa resort, every room is its own tranquil, eco-conscious retreat overlooking Active Pass. Each room is invitingly uncluttered with open-beam ceilings and decor that includes chocolate-brown cork floors and a ledge-rock wood-burning fireplace that conceals a plasma

TV/DVD player. At a push of a button, a hidden table emerges from the cherry-wood wall for intimate, in-suite dining. A push of another button reveals a massage table for in-room spa services. All beds have silk stuffed duvets (versus allergenic down duvets). En-suite bathrooms feature heated floors, air-jetted Jacuzzis or soaker tubs, separate showers—and 24-karat gold fixtures. New 1-bedroom villas have virtually doubled the inn's capacity. The Atrevida! restaurant is an island favorite (see "Where to Dine," below), and the Madrona del Mar Spa, with its Zen garden, showcases exclusive hemp-inspired spa treatments, which give a whole new dimension to the infamous BC bud. Rates are consistent year-round. In winter, however, they include several extra-value items, such as certificates to the spa. *Tip:* The inn is a 5-minute walk from the ferry terminal, so if you're staying here, leave your car behind and explore the island using one of the resort's Smart Car runabouts.

134 Madrona Dr., Galiano Island, BC V0N 1P0. ✆ **877/530-3939** or 250/539-3388.. www.galianoinn. com. 18 units. July to mid-Sept C$249–C$299 suite, C$425 villa; mid–May to June & mid-Sept to Oct C$199–C$249 suite, C$299 villa; Nov to mid-May C$179–C$199 suite, C$199 villa. Rates include break-fast. Additional adult C$25. MC, V. **Amenities:** Restaurant; lounge; hot tub; room service; spa. *In room:* TV/DVD player, hair dryer, Wi-Fi.

Rocky Ridge B&B Although it's only 13km (8 miles) from the ferry, the last couple of kilometers is on an unpaved road that traverses a spectacular cliff-side location overlooking Trincomali Channel. Drive carefully, and you'll find a modern, wood-beamed B&B that's one of the more relaxing stays on the island. All rooms boast comfortable queen-size beds and plenty of personal amenities, from choco-lates to binoculars. Two of its three rooms are oceanfront with wraparound windows; the larger Yellow Room has a full en-suite bathroom and sitting area, while the Blue Room has a small en-suite bathroom and shares the shower with the back-of-house twin-bedded African Room. You can get a game in on the pool table in the upper lounge; enjoy the library, fireplace, and expansive views on the main level; or watch a favorite movie in a small theater/TV room. Breakfast is substantial and tasty.

55–90 Serenity Lane, Galiano Island, BC V0N 1P0. ✆ **250/539-3387**. www.galianorockyridge.com. 3 units. C$110–C$120 double. C$15 extra for 1-night stay. No credit cards. Children 12 and under not accepted. **Amenities:** Lounge; hot tub; sauna. *In room:* Hair dryer, phone (on request), Wi-Fi.

Whaler Bay Lodge Lying at the end of a dirt road—pay attention to directions, or you'll miss the place—picturesque Whaler Bay is the backdrop to this secluded get-away. There's no doubt that it's a home-turned-B&B and, with only two (quite sumptu-ous) rooms, staying here feels like being a house guest. Fortunately, you have complete freedom to enjoy the living room, heated outdoor pool, gazebo garden, and private beach access. The owner is a jazz buff and sometimes hosts informal concerts, which puts the grand piano to work, and if you're lucky, you can sample his impressive 900-bottle wine collection. Other amenities include a private 9.7m (32-ft.) dock and the free use of kayaks, canoes, and rowboats. Keep your eyes open for eagles, since the bay is a known nesting area.

725 Cain Rd., Galiano Island, BC V0N 1P0. ✆ **877/539-3199** or 250/539-2249. Fax. 250/539-2257. www. whalerbaylodge.com. 2 units. C$175–C$195 double. MC, V. **Amenities:** Pool. *In room:* TV/DVD player, hair dryer, Wi-Fi.

Where to Dine

Atrevida! ★ PACIFIC NORTHWEST Galiano Island's only oceanfront restaurant is a treat. Watch the ferries ply through Active Pass as you enjoy rock crab croquette with cilantro chipotle tamarind; grilled beef tenderloin with green peppercorns, crème fraîche, and lobster sweet-pea risotto; or sandalwood-smoked salmon with brown butter. The vegetarian Moroccan *tajine* is rich and aromatic, served in the traditional pottery *tajine* with eggplant, zucchini, and red peppers, butternut squash, couscous, garbanzo beans, carrot, grape tomatoes, almonds, and spices of every description. It's a very exotic, flavorful experience. The wine list focuses on special orders from British Columbia, some of which you can purchase from the wine store. If you've a ferry wait, park your car in the lineup and head over to the outdoor patio to chill out over a cold drink.

In the Galiano Inn, 134 Madrona Dr. *€* **250/539-3388.** Reservations required. Main courses C$18–C$29. MC, V. Daily 5:30–9:30pm.

Hummingbird Pub PUB FARE   Serving hearty pub grub (burgers, fish and chips, steaks, and pasta) at reasonable prices, the Hummingbird is *the* local boozer and tempts with ales on tap from Vancouver Island Brewery on Salt Spring Island and wines from Saturna Island. The classic West Coast cedar-and-beam architecture creates a warm atmosphere for playing pool and darts, and although there's no water view, the decor and perennial garden more than make up for it. From mid-May to October, this resourceful pub runs its own shuttle bus to the ferry at Sturdies Bay, and from the Montague Park Marina. The pub could be of particular interest to boaters seeking some liquid libations on dry land.

47 Sturdies Bay Rd. *€* **250/539-5472.** Main courses C$7–C$17. MC, V. Sun–Thurs 11am–midnight; Fri & Sat 11am–1am.

La Berengerie ★ FRENCH   Shrouded by evergreen clematis, this tiny log cabin is a jewel in the forest. Floral linen tablecloths, soft classical music, and watercolor paintings by local artists set a romantic tone. The food rarely disappoints. Described as French-Algerian, the cuisine uses herbs to bring Middle Eastern flavor to classics such as duck *a l'orange, coq au vin,* and red snapper with gingered tomato sauce. La Berengerie also does an excellent bouillabaisse. The seafood gratiné is delicious— creamy and light, with a host of delicate flavors. A four-course menu features a choice of appetizers, entrees, and desserts. The homemade breads and comfort desserts are yummy. In July and August, the vegetarian sundeck opens up, as does a garden patio. The drawback is that it closes in winter. *Tip:* There are three quaint bedrooms upstairs, often available for rent.

2806 Montague Harbour Rd. *€* **250/539-5392.** www.galianoisland.com/laberengerie/. Reservations recommended on weekends. Main courses C$15–C$22; 4-course prix-fixe dinner C$31. MC, V. July & Aug daily 5–9pm; Apr–June & Sept–Oct Fri–Sun (call for hours). Closed Nov–Mar.

MAYNE ISLAND

Mayne has always been a transfer point between islands. This began in the 1860s, when prospectors rested up in Miners Bay before crossing the Georgia Strait on their way to the gold mines in the Fraser Valley and the Cariboo. Back then, this rowdy social and drinking hub was known as "Little Hell," but as gold fever faded, so did Mayne's importance. Today, stopovers are much tamer. The 900 permanent residents like it this way, as it's enabled the island to retain much of its charm and heritage.

Because most of Mayne Island is privately owned, there are few public trails, so walkers and cyclists take to the network of hilly roads, traveling past 19th-century buildings, farms, beaches, and home studios. Cyclists could complete Mayne's

25km (16-mile) circuit in a day. Some of the more "natural" walks are along the pathways of yet-to-be-developed areas, where locals have created impromptu trails through the forest. Hendersen Hills is one example. There are numerous sheltered bays, including **Village Bay, Miners Bay,** and **Horton Bay,** all with docking facilities and accommodations that run the gamut from bare bones to luxurious.

Essentials

GETTING THERE
BC Ferries sails to **Village Bay,** on the northwest side of the island. Pleasure boaters dock at **Horton Bay,** at the southwest corner of the island. Floatplanes arrive at the docks at **Miners Bay.**

VISITOR INFORMATION
Mayne Island Community Chamber of Commerce (*©* **250/539-5034**) doesn't have a bricks-and-mortar headquarters but does maintain a resource site at www.mayneislandchamber.ca. Useful maps and event information are usually posted on bulletin boards in the windows of the gas station (which doubles as a video-movie rental place) and the grocery store. This is where you can also purchase a copy of *The Mayneliner* (C$3.50), a monthly publication of gossip, happenings, and island issues.

GETTING AROUND
You need to be self sufficient on this island since there isn't transit or a taxi service. Hitchhiking is a common alternative; look for car stops along the way.

Exploring Mayne Island

Miners Bay is the hub of Mayne, housing a surprisingly well-stocked supermarket, a small library, and a bakery-cafe. The liquor store, which is actually only a counter with a separate till, is part of a store that has sold goods and groceries since World War I. On summer Saturdays, a small farmers' market is held outside the **Agricultural Hall,** which on other days doubles as a theater, bingo hall, and exhibition center. The fairly new community center, the venue for ongoing programs such as yoga, choir, and drop-in Tai Chi, also has outdoor tennis courts. The **Mayne Island Museum** is in a former one-room jail dating from 1896 and displays all manner of local artifacts from the early 1900s. Located on Fernhill Road, just up from the Springwater Lodge (see p. 241), it usually opens on July and August weekends, as well as holiday weekends, from 10am to 3pm. Admission is by donation; C$2 is suggested. Kayak and canoe rentals are available at **Mayne Island Kayaking** (*©* **250/539-0439**) which launches from Bennett Bay and Oyster Bay. Rates range from C$48 adults for a 2-hour rental to C$78 adults for a 24-hour rental of a fiberglass kayak, with an option to extend the rental. Guided tours include a 2½-hour Discovery tour (C$49), and a 5-hour paddle to Saturna's winery for a tasting (C$110). The company also offers bike rentals at C$18 for a half-day or C$25 for a full-day. Travel up Fernhill Road to **Fernhill Centre,** at the top of the hill. This hub of activity has a gift store, restaurant, art gallery, and a tiny day spa; Vancouverites often make the day trip for its facials. Local scuttle suggests the spa may be moving to a more expansive island location.

The road from Miners Bay to **Georgina Point** and the **Active Pass Lighthouse** is the most picturesque on Mayne Island. En route, you'll pass **St. Mary Magdalene Anglican Church,** built in 1898, on a hill amid a grove of red arbutus trees.

The steeple of the church overlooking Active Pass has been a landmark for sailors for more than a century. Many of the headstones in the mossy graveyard are silent testament to Mayne Island's pioneers, whose names are also reflected in the names of the coves and streets of the island. Established in 1885, the lighthouse marks the entrance to Active Pass and, now automated, is open daily from 9am to 3pm, with free admission. You'll likely see seals, seabirds, and the occasional whale.

Although many islanders have "back routes" to the top of **Mount Parke Park** (www. crd.bc.ca/parks/mountparke)f, officially, there's only one public hiking trail up, and it's a fairly strenuous 30- to 40-minute uphill hike. (Cyclists must leave their bikes at the trail-head rack.) At 255m (837 ft.), the end of the trail is the highest point on Mayne, and if you can forgive the obligatory antennae towers, you'll be rewarded with wonderful views and maybe an air show of soaring eagles and turkey vultures. Six beaches on the island are open to the public, but since a distinct lack of signs to access points makes them easy to miss, keep your eyes peeled for road markers that lead down to the shoreline—and avoid tromping on private land. Two of the best beaches for picnics are at **Georgina Point** and **Dinner Bay,** so-called because it once teemed with fish and shellfish. "When the tide goes out," the old prospector's slogan goes, "the table is laid for breakfast." A **Japanese Garden** is a part of Dinner Bay and commemorates the Japanese who settled and worked on the island between 1900 and 1942. Admission is free. **Bennett Bay,** now a part of the Gulf Islands National Park Reserve, has an undisturbed waterfront that is home to herons, kingfishers, and unusual pink seashells. When the tide goes out far enough (which doesn't seem to happen often), the pebbly beach eventually gives way to fine sand. **Oyster Bay, Piggott Bay,** and **Campbell Bay** are good for swimming. The latter has eye-catching rock formations that served as models for the artificial rocks around the killer whale pool in the Vancouver Aquarium.

Where to Stay

Blue Vista Resort Blue Vista's updated one- and two-bedroom cabins are good value for family vacations. Comfortable, but not fancy, each of the blue-painted, wood-framed units comes with a fully equipped kitchen, private bathroom, fireplace (the first batch of wood is free), deck, and barbecue. Until recently, this was a popular spot for kayakers; however, that part of the business has moved elsewhere, so the resort's now a much quieter, low-key place. Families looking for value and self-catering vacations are still its main focus, and the open, park-like setting really encourages children to play with newfound friends.

Respites from Bully Birds

The nest boxes you'll see mounted on pilings in the water in Bennett Bay, beside the Mayne Inn's dock and in front of the Springwater Lodge, are all part of a stewardship and recovery program for the Purple Martin. Muscled out of their traditional nesting areas by house sparrows and starlings, the Western Purple Martin is at risk in British Columbia. Placing these boxes over water minimizes competition from the "bully birds" and is working. In 2006, Mayne Island welcomed their first nesting Purple Martin pairs, and 3 years later, the count was somewhere between 6 and 10, depending on whom you speak to.

563 Arbutus Dr., Mayne Island, BC V0N 2J0. ℭ **877/535-2424** or 250/539-2463. Fax 250/539-2463. www.bluevistaresort.com. 9 units. June–Sept C$99–C$150 cabin; Oct–May C$85–$115 cabin. Weekly rates & yoga packages available. MC, V. Pets accepted w/prior approval (C$15). **Amenities:** Free shuttle. *In room:* TV/DVD player, kitchen, no phone.

Mayne Island Eco Camping   Of the two campsites on Mayne, this is by far the superior, with waterfront sites, outdoor hot and cold showers amid the trees, out-houses, a communal fire pit, and even a hot tub. Many kayakers choose to paddle right up to the beach—a pretty but pebbly cove near Miners Bay—or take advantage of the free pickup and delivery service to and from other islands.

359 Maple Dr., Mayne Island, BC V0N 2J0. ℭ **250/539-2667.** www.mayneisle.com/camp. May–Sept C$12; Oct–Apr C$10. Children 13 years & under half price. **Amenities:** Hot tub; kayak rentals.

Oceanwood Country Inn ★   This waterfront English country inn is as posh as it gets on Mayne. New owners have enhanced the old charm with a contemporary feel. The living room features a crackling fireplace, full bookshelves, a DVD library, board games, and a nice selection of music. Each guest room is as comfortable as ever. Most are romantic, with deep-soaker bathtubs and private balconies. Many have fireplaces. The Wisteria Suite even has a sunken living room and private outdoor soaking tub—perfect for a moonlit soak *à deux*. The Geranium is particularly large and also has a private outdoor soaking tub—on a rooftop deck, no less. Continental breakfast includes hot-from-the-oven croissants, homemade granola, and exotic fruit juices. Dining at Oceanwood continues as a grazing experience through the afternoon and into dinner (see "Where to Dine," below). This is a gated property, so the deer haven't ravaged the gardens of tulips, irises, and other tasty morsels, as they have most Mayne gardens.

630 Dinner Bay Rd., Mayne Island, BC V0N 2J0. ℭ **250/539-5074.** Fax 250/539-3002. www.oceanwood. com. 12 units. Mid-June to mid-Sept C$125–C$250 suite; mid-Sept to mid-June C$110–C$225 suite. 2-night minimum. Single nights C$40 extra. MC, V. Children 12 & under not accepted. **Amenities:** Restaurant; lounge; complimentary bikes; hot tub; sauna. *In room:* TV/DVD player, fridge, hair dryer, iPod dock, no phone, Wi-Fi.

Sage Cottage   The two oceanfront bedrooms are plush, decorated in neutral earth tones of sand and sage, and with all the trimmings of luxurious bathrobes, toiletries, duvets, and a satellite TV and DVD player with a growing title list to choose from. A shared deck overlooks a picturesque beach and boat launch. Rates include a huge breakfast that might include Brie-stuffed French toast or an herb-flavored egg soufflé. Scones and jams are homemade and usually made in such abundance that guests depart with a doggy-bag of snacks for the road. Custom-made picnic lunches can be ordered, too, for a nominal additional charge. If you would like to eat dinner in, this can also be arranged. The cost is a reasonable C$30 and includes a full three-course meal such as a mixed green salad, BBQ pork tenderloin, and a lemon cheesecake pie.

782 Steward Dr., Mayne Island, BC V0N 2J0. ℭ **250/539-2859.** www.sageonmayne.com. Mid-Nov to Apr C$95–$125 double; May to mid-June & Oct to mid-Nov C$125–C$135 double; mid-June to Sept C$125–C$150 double. V. **Amenities:** Lounge. *In room:* TV/DVD player, no phone, Wi-Fi.

Where to Dine

Oceanwood Country Inn ★★ PACIFIC NORTHWEST   Now that Ocean-wood has a patio license, it's become the "in" place for sharing ocean-view sunsets and a glass of wine—BC vintages, as well as labels from Italy, Chile, France, and California. Add a variety of tapas plates and quesadillas (lobster with black bean puree and chile sauce is a winner), and it's the only elegant inside/outside locale on the island for stylish afternoon munchies. Come dinner, a new a la carte menu is presented every day. Past menus have included goats cheese ravioli, basil infused rack of lamb with olive sauce, and prosciutto crusted halibut. It's casual, but for dinner and Sunday brunch, you might want to doff your muddy Reeboks for something a little smarter—or at least wear clean jeans.

In the Oceanwood Country Inn, 630 Dinner Bay Rd. ✆ **250/539-5074.** Reservations recommended. Main courses C$11–C$28. MC, V. Mon & Thurs–Sat 11:00am–9:30pm; Sun 11am–3pm.

Springwater Lodge PUB FARE/PACIFIC NORTHWEST Built in the 1890s, this pub and restaurant is the heart of the Mayne Island community. In summer, people crowd the flower-brightened outdoor decks to watch the boats thread through Active Pass. In winter, the pub overflows with boisterous gossip. Live bands are often featured on Saturday nights. On the whole, food is good, though sometimes the restaurant specials are overly ambitious and don't live up to their promise. Go for the fish and chips or thickly battered, deep fried onion rings—the best. Despite service that's rather offhand, it's a lazin' place to kick back and grab a meal. This good review doesn't extend to the guest rooms. Despite what you might hear, they are nothing to write home about. The beach cabins have been given a facelift, but at C$40 a day, you still get what you pay for: the basics.

400 Fernhill Rd. ✆ **250/539-5521.** Reservations accepted. Pub main courses C$8.50; restaurant main courses C$19. MC, V. Mid-May to mid-Sept daily 9am–9pm; mid-Sept to mid-May Mon–Thurs 11am–8:30pm & Fri–Sun 9am–8:30pm. Pub may be open later.

Wild Fennel Food & Wine Located in the middle of the island at Fernhill Centre, the funky ambiance here, never mind the terrific food, will brighten your day. The wine list features mostly local ciders, micro-brewed beer, and BC wines; try Bad Dog Blonde, a private-label house wine that's become a bestseller largely because of its whimsical label. The menu changes weekly according to food availability and freshness, but the crab cakes are amazing. And hope that when you visit one of the shellfish soups—or the plum-glazed Pacific salmon with house-made *udon* noodles, *sashi* broth, and water chestnuts—is in the kitchen. There's a strong seafood focus here, but meat eaters will find lamb, pork tenderloin, or steak, alongside comfort foods such as macaroni 'n' cheese, sweet 'n' sour apple pie, and portions geared for children. The small deck and garden fill up fast on sunny days.

574 Fernhill Rd. ✆ **250/539-5987.** Reservations accepted. Main courses lunch C$9, dinner C$15. MC, V. Wed–Sat 11:30am–2:30pm & 5:30–9pm.

SATURNA ISLAND

Time seems to have bypassed Saturna Island, making remote tranquility the island's star attraction. Home to approximately 350 permanent residents, Saturna is still fairly primitive. There are no banks, no pharmacies or drug stores; the library's located in the church basement, and the general store doubles as a tiny coffee shop. In fact, Jose Maria Narvaez would probably still recognize the forests and shorelines of the island named after his ship, Santa Saturnina, even though his last visit was in 1791. The Gulf Islands National Park Reserve protects some 44% of Saturna's 49 sq. km (19 sq. miles), earning the island an elevated status for hiking, boating, and communing with nature. Of all the Gulf Islands, Saturna is the most ecologically vigilant. For such a small island, there are some surprisingly nice places to stay in terms of cottage rentals and single waterfront suites, usually part of a home. It also boasts one of British Columbia's largest estate wineries, Saturna Island Vineyards, which alone is worth the ferry trip.

Visitors may quickly note the island's drawbridge mentality, but Saturna people aren't unfriendly—they just prefer to keep their own company.

Laced with trails through mixed forest and marshland, hikers rarely tire of this island's topography. Most head for **Winter Cove Marine Park,** a sanctuary to eagles, shorebirds, kingfishers, seals, and otters; or up to the summit of Mount Warburton. Kayakers will prefer **Thomson Park** or **Cabbage Island Marine Park,** near **Tumbo Island,** and **Veruna Bay** and **Russell Reef** are the hot choices for family swimming. What commerce there is happens around the community center at **Lyall Harbour,** where the ferry docks. Here, you'll find a grocery store, pub, gas station, kayak rentals, and a gallery, as well as a couple of B&Bs. *Note:* There are no public campgrounds.

Essentials

GETTING THERE
BC Ferries sails to **Lyall Harbour.** Most trips involve a transfer at Mayne Island. Boaters dock at **Winter Cove Marine Park,** north of Lyall Harbour. Seaplanes can dock at Lyall Harbour.

VISITOR INFORMATION
Head to the **Saturna Island General Store** (101 Narvaez Bay Rd.; (C) **250/539-2936;** www.saturnatourism.com). Wi-Fi hot spots are sporadic; your best bets are the **Recreation & Cultural Center** (104 Harris Rd.) and the library at **St. Christopher's Church** (140 East Point Rd.; (C) **250/539-5312**). The latter offers terminals but is open only Wednesday and Saturday 11am to 3pm. The **Saturna Point Lighthouse Pub** ((C) **250/539-5725**) at the Ferry Dock is home to the island's only ATM.

GETTING AROUND
The island has no pickup or touring service, although your B&B may step in to fill this need on an as-required basis. Bring your own bike (there are no rentals) or come to

 Saturna Island Vineyards

The location is idyllic and offers visitors more than just a taste of wine. Nestled among the Pacific Ocean, a soaring granite cliff face, and picturesque Campbell farm, these south-facing vineyards are a pleasure to explore. The first wines from the 1998 harvest were released to critical acclaim and just keep getting better, garnering a silver medal in 2008 for the Vintner's Select Chardonnay in the All Canadian Wine Championships and a gold for their Pinot Noir. Look, also, for good Pinot Gris, Merlots, and Gewürztraminers for less than C$20 per bottle in the wine shop, as well as other merchandise. The small terraced bistro is big on taste: recommended items include the halibut ceviche with its jalapeno miso-citrus dressing, the West Coast bouillabaisse, and the charcuterie plate of local cheeses, house-made pickles, and cured meats. The vineyards are at 8 Quarry Rd. ((C) **877/918-3388** or 250/539-5139; www.saturnavineyards.com). They are open daily May through October from 11am to 4:30pm and through the winter by appointment. Tours and tastings are free. Take East Point Road from Lyall Harbour, and then Harris Road for 2.5km (1½ miles).

Island Legend: Warburton Pike

Mount Warburton Pike is named for the legendary English "gentleman adventurer," the biggest property-owner on Saturna at the turn of the 20th century. A member of the British gentry and an Oxford graduate, Pike was temperamentally better suited to life in the great outdoors and much preferred to sleep under a large maple tree in the yard than in his pretty, well-furnished bungalow. During his life, Pike was a big-game hunter, a Wyoming cowboy, an Arctic and Icelandic explorer, a businessman and community benefactor, a mining and railroad promoter, a Yukon gold prospector, a sheep rancher, and an author of two books on the North. Among many stories about this elusive adventurer is the one tale about how Pike used the ocean as his washtub. He just tied his clothes to a long rope and trailed them behind his sailboat *Fleetwing* while he stretched out and relaxed on the gunwale.

kayak. **Saturna Sea Kayaking** (© 250/539-5553) is located in the village and can fit you out with single and double fiberglass kayaks from C$30 to C$65 for 2 hours, C$40 to C$70 for 4 hours. Multiple-day rates are available. **Discovery SeaTours** (© 250/539-3211 or 604/377-5385) offers 2½- to 5-hour sightseeing tours of the neighboring islands with the added bonus of circumnavigating Saturna. Rates are C$100 adults, C$80 children under 12. Group size is limited to eight passengers; departure points include Lyall Harbour on Saturna Island, as well as Hope Bay on Pender Island and Horton Bay on Mayne Island.

Exploring Saturna Island

East Point Regional Park ★★, on the island's southeastern tip, is a naturalist's delight. It starts with the ocean views from the sculptured sandstone headlands and just gets better. Strong tides curl around the point to create back eddies where salmon and small fish congregate; rocks, honeycombed by wind and waves, form tidal pools filled with starfish, limpets, spider crabs, and more; and waving kelp beds attract cormorants, oystercatchers, eagles, seals, and even whales. Take the very short trail down to the **East Point Lighthouse,** built in 1888, and you'll be standing at the easternmost edge of the Gulf Islands, looking over to **Patos Island Lighthouse,** on the U.S. side of the border. Together, the lighthouses guide large vessels through the channel's surging waters. Some of the area is on private land; be careful not to trespass off the trails. A longer trail (300m/984 ft.) leaves the parking lot and heads north to a viewpoint of Tumbo Channel and the Strait of Georgia.

If you've time, make the 4.5km (2¾-mile) drive or hike up to the 497m (1,631-ft.) summit of **Warburton Pike.** If you can disregard the unbecoming sprawl of TV towers, the sweeping vistas from the top are nothing short of fantastic. The way up is via a winding gravel road that's narrow and sometimes slippery in wet weather, but the beautiful Douglas fir forest more than makes up for the occasional rough patch of road. Look out for feral goats, wild descendants of domestic goats imported here in the early 1900s, along the paths at the edge of the bluff.

Where to Stay & Dine

Breezy Bay B&B ★ ☺ This charming 1890s heritage house, Saturna's oldest home, lies at the heart of a 20-hectare (49-acre) farm approximately 2km (1¼ miles) from the ferry dock. You enter beneath a canopy of century-old Lombardy poplars that gives way to gardens filled with trees: walnut, maple, scented linden, and hawthorn. Inside, you'll find architectural details such as Victorian wainscoting and period wood paneling. The guest library is full of assorted titles, from nature books to historical novels, while the piano lounge is comfortable without being pretentious. The four guest rooms are small, simply furnished, but inviting; they share one bathroom. On the first floor, an outside veranda runs the length of the house and overlooks the orchard, waterfowl pond, and pastures of sheep and llama. The beach at the end of the garden is ideal for swimming and launching kayaks. The kids will love it.

131 Payne Rd., Saturna Island, BC V0N 2Y0. © **250/539-5957** or 250/539-3339. www.saturnacan.net/breezy. 4 units. May–Sept C$75–C$95 double. Rates include full breakfast. 2-night minimum July & Aug. No credit cards. Closed Oct–Apr. **Amenities:** Lounge. *In room:* No phone.

Lyall Harbour B&B ★ Three points are in its favor: The home epitomizes the West Coast, with a ton of windows and views; it's within walking distance of the ferry terminal, a big incentive to leave your gas-guzzling car behind; and it's one of the only B&Bs that's open year-round. All three guest rooms have queen-size beds and 425-thread-count linens, full en-suite bathrooms, views, and private decks; and while there's no air-conditioning per se, overhead vents and a return-air system keep the inside temperature comfortable, even on the hottest of days. The house is filled with original art by owner-artist Donna Digance; her adjoining studio welcomes visitors. Her husband, Len, is a potter with his own on-site studio and also just happens to be a professional chef who turns breakfast into a gourmet affair. The West Coast Smoked Salmon Benny is the house specialty.

121 East Point Rd., Saturna Island, BC V0N 2Y0. © **877/473-9343** or 250/539-5577. www.lyallharbour.com. 3 units. C$135–C$140 double. Rates include full breakfast. Additional adult C$30. 2-night minimum stay in peak season. MC, V. Children 12 & under not accepted. **Amenities:** 2 lounges. *In room:* No phone, Wi-Fi.

Saturna Lodge Set amid the rustic, rural charms of the island, a stone's throw from the Saturna Island Vineyards, this casual country inn is an unexpected delight. Guest rooms are named after wine grapes and are comfortably appointed with duvet-covered queen-size beds (twin beds in the Ambrosia Suite) and private en-suite bathrooms. This and the Napa Suite share a bathroom and can be joined for family accommodation. All have views of Plumber Sound (though some more than others), and the Riesling Suite has a private deck. TV-hungry urbanites can cozy up in front of the fireplace in the downstairs lounge, or pick a DVD/VHS title from the lodge's small library. In shoulder season, the lodge discounts its rate by C$20 per night.

130 Payne Rd. (P.O. Box 54), Saturna Island, BC V0N 2Y0. © **866/539-2254** or 250/539-2254. Fax 250/539-3091. www.saturna.ca. 6 units. June to early Sept C$119–C$169 double; Apr, May, Sept & Oct C$99–C$135 double; Nov–Mar C$79–C$119 double. Rates include full breakfast. Additional adult C$35. Discounts for longer stays. MC, V. **Amenities:** Restaurant; lounge; complimentary bikes; Jacuzzi; Wi-Fi. *In room:* TV/DVD player (on request), no phone.

THE SAN JUAN ISLANDS

Beckoning just off the coast of Vancouver Island, south of the Gulf Islands, the San Juan Islands are a mostly blue-sky oasis in a region better known for its clouds. Like their island neighbors, they provide mariners with spectacular waters, hundreds of small, protected coves, and a landscape where stands of coastal trees give way to grassy meadows and gardens. It's a landscape that earned the number-four spot in *Travel & Leisure's* list of "Top 5 Islands in North America." The ferry trip between the San Juan Islands and Sidney, on Vancouver Island, is a delightful 1½-hour mini-cruise and provides the opportunity to create a really diverse islands adventure. From Sidney, you can choose to explore Vancouver Island or take a ferry to the Gulf Islands, creating an itinerary that can stretch from a few days to a few weeks. The alternative trip is via the Washington State Ferries out of Anacortes; the crossing time is about an hour.

For years, the San Juans' pastoral tranquility was a favorite getaway for Washingtonians, but this is now taking its toll. Today, land deals for would-be homeowners are long gone. There are more than 30 different real-estate dealers on the San Juans—that's one for every 40 residents; and assessed property values are almost three times the state average. Although development is controlled somewhat by the San Juan Preservation Trust, monumental homes are appearing in what was once humble rock and farmland.

In the 1800s, because of their proximity to British Columbia (San Juan Island lies only 26km/16 miles from Sidney), many British settlers moved to the islands alongside their American counterparts. Remnants of those pioneering years are seen throughout the islands, and many landmarks are listed in the National Register of Historic Places. On San Juan Island, in particular, you'll find the Anglo-American rivalry especially well documented in the American and English camps.

The three largest islands, San Juan, Orcas, and Lopez, are home to about 15,000 people. For much of the year, the residents' easygoing lifestyle is quite solitary, but when summer arrives, the population triples with the arrival of eco-adventurers and vacationers. **Note:** If you're traveling with children, be aware that family fun is derived mainly from beachcombing, kayaking, hiking, and some horseback riding. Also, despite the annual influx of visitors, accommodations on the San Juans are limited, and prearranged accommodations are highly recommended. Touring all three islands can be done in 3 or 4 days, but chances are that you'll acclimatize to "island time," slow down, and wish you had set aside a day or two longer. But leave your jet skis at home. When locals complained that the incessant buzzing of city folk zipping around their waterfront was disrupting the serenity and marine habitat of the islands, San Juan County promptly outlawed the noisy watercraft. The only wild time you'll find on the San Juan Islands is pretty much what nature provides.

ESSENTIALS

Getting There

BY PLANE **Kenmore Air Seaplanes** (© 800/543-9595; www.kenmoreair.com) provides daily flights from **Seattle** to the three major San Juan Islands May through September. One-way fares range from US$130 for mid-week travel to US$160 for weekend trips. Kenmore Air also offers daily departures from Seattle to Victoria. Fares vary, depending on travel day, but one-way fares average US$120, US$240 for round-trip. Day trips to the San Juans from Victoria are US$199. **San Juan Airlines** (© 800/874-4434; www.sanjuanairlines.com) has daily land plane flights from **Anacortes** and **Bellingham** at US$68 adults and offers charters that start from US$85 adults. Locally-owned **Island Air** (© 888/378-2376 or 360/378-2376; www.sanjuan-islandair.com) offers on-demand and scenic flights at US$250 per hour for a 3-person aircraft—you can see the entire San Juan archipelago and Vancouver Island in that time. **Northwest Sky Ferry** (© 360/676-9999; www.skyferrynw.com) has a flight pooling program from Bellingham, which offer one-way tickets as low as US$39, depending on the number of passengers. Small public airstrips on San Juan, Orcas, and Lopez islands accommodate these flights and private plane arrivals.

BY FERRY **Washington State Ferries** (Column Dock/Pier 52, Seattle; © 888/808-7977 or 206/464-6400; www.wsdot.wa.gov/ferries), offers multiple daily sailings between **Anacortes** and the San Juan Islands, and limited service from **Sidney**, on Vancouver Island. From Anacortes, loading is on a first-come, first-served basis. It's a good idea to get in line about 30 minutes in advance of the scheduled sailing. If you bring a vehicle, allow for at least an hour's wait—up to 3 hours at peak travel times on summer and holiday weekends. Also, be sure to fill your tank in Anacortes. Gas stations on the islands charge at least 30% more for gas than on the mainland. Some food service and a picnic area are available near the terminal. Check out **www.ferrycam.net** to see live images of the ferry lanes.

One-way passenger fares during the high season (from May to mid-Oct) Wednesday through Saturday are US$13 adults, US$11 children 6 to 18, US$7 seniors, and US$36 to US$53 for a driver and standard-size vehicle. Fares are slightly less Sunday to Tuesday. Inter-island travel is US$23 for a driver and standard-size vehicle; passengers and bicycles are free.

Ferry foot-passengers are charged only in the westbound direction; eastbound travel within the San Juan Islands or from the San Juan Islands to Anacortes is free (the only exception to this is for travelers leaving from Sidney, BC). If you're planning to visit all the San Juan Islands, save money by heading straight to Friday Harbor on San Juan Island, the most westerly of the islands, and work your way back through the others at no additional charge.

Twice a day in summer (once a day in winter), the ferry continues to Sidney, 26km (16 miles) north of Victoria, and returns. Summer vehicle reservations are recommended to and from Canada, and must be made by 5:30pm the day prior to travel, at least 24 hours in advance. One-way passenger fares from May to mid-October are US$16 adults, US$8 seniors, US$13 children 6 to 18, and US$55 for a driver and standard-size vehicle. From mid-October to April, fares remain the same for adults, seniors, and children, but reduce to US$44 for a driver and standard-size vehicle. Crossing time is 3 hours. From the San Juan Islands to Sidney, one-way fares are US$6 adults, US$3 seniors, US$5 children 6 to 18, US$28 for a standard-size vehicle and driver. Fares are lower October through April.

Victoria Clipper (© 800/888-2535 or 206/448-5000; www.clippervacations.com) is a popular way to reach the San Juan Islands from either **Seattle or Victoria.** This passenger-only catamaran departs from Seattle's **Pier 69** daily and has a number of hotel and attraction packages. Adult fares from Seattle to Friday Harbor, on San Juan Island, are US$75 adults one-way during the week and US$120 adults on weekends; same-day returns are US$100 adults. Tickets for children 11 and under cost about 50% less. Reservations originating in Victoria should call © 250/382-8100. A sister company runs daily passenger-only sailings between Port Angeles and Friday Harbor aboard the **Victoria Express** (© 360/452-8088 from the U.S. or 250/361-9144 from Canada; www.victoriaexpress.com). The cost is US$43 each way; bikes and kayaks cost an additional US$5. **Puget Sound Express** (© 360/385-5288) offers passenger-only service between **Port Townsend,** northwest of Seattle, and Friday Harbor. The captain takes the 3-hour scenic route. Round-trip fare is about US$79 adults. All of the above operate May through September. The **Island Express** (© 877/473-9777 or 360/299-2875; www.islandexpresscharters.com) runs a year-round passenger taxi from downtown Anacortes to the three major San Juan Islands, and many of the smaller ones, too, that are so popular for kayakers. Fares are based on the number of passengers sharing a common destination and generally range from US$38 to US$95 adults. Bicycles are US$6 and kayaks are US$15 extra. Check out **Outer Island Expeditions** (© 360/376-3711; www.outerislandx.com) for a similar service.

Visitor Information

The **San Juan Islands Visitor Information Service** (640 Mullis St., Building A, Ste. 210, Friday Harbor, San Juan Island; © 888/468-3701 or 360/378-6822; www.visitsanjuans.com) offers a range of maps and information throughout the islands. For live images of the San Juan Islands, check out **www.islandcam.com.**

10

THE SAN JUAN ISLANDS | Essentials

The San Juan Islands

Aleck Bay Inn **1**
Bird Rock Hotel **10**
Cascade Harbor Inn **5**
Doe Bay Resort & Retreat Center **4**
Edenwild Country Inn **3**
Friday Harbor House **12**
Lakedale Resort at Three Lakes **13**
MacKaye Harbor Inn **2**
Orcas Hotel **9**
Outlook Inn **7**
Roche Harbor Resort **15**
Rosario Resort & Spa **6**
Tucker House Inn **11**
Turtleback Farm Inn **8**
Wildwood Manor B&B **14**

Legend

✈ Airport
▲ Mountain
[📷] Winery
--- Ferry Route

San Juan Trivia

- There are no traffic lights anywhere in the islands. People don't even honk.
- San Juan County has more miles of marine shoreline (657km/408 miles) than any other county.
- The marine highway that follows the historic canoe route of the Coast Salish peoples, from Anacortes to the San Juans, is Phase One of Washington State's newest legislated Scenic Byway.

- Phase Two continues around San Juan Island, and Phase Three follows the country roads on Orcas Island.
- There are no rivers in the islands but several waterfalls on Orcas Island.
- There are 83 National Wildlife Refuge sites in the San Juans. A number are clustered on the southern coast of Lopez Island, and near Spieden and Waldron islands.

San Juan, Lopez, and Orcas islands also operate visitor services through their local chambers of commerce (see "Essentials," in the sections devoted to each island).

SAN JUAN ISLAND

Compared to sleepier Orcas and Lopez islands, San Juan Island is "downtown central." Home to almost 8,000 people, most of whom prefer this island's quicker pace, and covering over 142 sq. km (55 sq. miles), San Juan is a popular holiday destination, offering visitors the most in terms of urban amenities, relaxing hideaways, and wilderness hikes. For those who like to fill their days with a variety of activities, San Juan is your best bet. It is also the most practical destination in the San Juan Islands if you're traveling without a car, since restaurants, shops, and museums are within walking distance of the ferry landing. Car and moped rentals are available, all the same. The island even has a small winery, the **San Juan Vineyards** (3136 Roche Harbor Rd.; ℭ **360/378-9463;** www.sanjuanvineyards.com), housed in a century-old schoolhouse, as well as an alpaca farm, **Krystal Acres Alpaca Farm** (152 Blazing Tree Rd.; ℭ **360/378-6125;** www.krystalacres.com); both are near **Roche Harbor.**

San Juan Island has historic appeal, too. Its colorful past stems from a boundary dispute between the U.S. and Great Britain when, from 1860 to 1872, both countries occupied the island. In one of the stranger pieces of history, the killing of a British homesteader's pig by an American settler nearly sent the two countries to the battlefield. Fortunately, cooler heads prevailed, so what is now referred to as the Pig War of 1859 resulted in only one casualty: the pig. The San Juan Islands were eventually declared American territory.

The history of this little-known war is chronicled through the interpretive centers in **San Juan Island National Historical Park,** divided into **English Camp** and **American Camp.** The Pig War was the last time that Great Britain and the U.S. opposed each other in war. General George Pickett, of the famed "Pickett's Charge" at the Civil War's Battle of Gettysburg, was commander of U.S. forces during the Pig War.

Essentials
GETTING THERE
Washington State Ferries arrive at **Friday Harbor** on the island's eastern coast. See "Getting There," above, for information about fares and schedules.

VISITOR INFORMATION

The **San Juan Island Chamber of Commerce** (135 Spring St. [P.O. Box 98], Friday Harbor; ✆ **360/378-5240;** www.sanjuanisland.org) will be happy to tell you what you need to know about the island. For information on accommodations, contact the **Bed & Breakfast Association of San Juan Island** (✆ **866/645-3030;** www.san-juan-island.net).

GETTING AROUND

There are several island taxi services, **Bob's Taxi & Tours** (✆ **360/378-6777**), **Classic Cab** (✆ **360/378-7519**), **Friday Harbor Taxi** (✆ **360/378-4434**), and **San Juan Taxi** (✆ **360/378-3550**). In summer months, **San Juan Transit** (✆ **800/887-8387** or 360/378-8887) provides bus transportation. Rental cars are available year-round from **M&W Auto** (725 Spring St., Friday Harbor; ✆ **800/323-6037** or 360/378-2886; www.sanjuanauto.com). Rates for a mid-size car are US$60 per day mid-May through September, US$10 less per day October through mid-May. Touring the island via bicycle, scooter, or moped is great fun. Rent bikes at **Island Bicycles** (380 Argyle Ave., Friday Harbor; ✆ **360/378-4941;** www.islandbicycles.com). Rates for mountain and hybrid bikes are US$38 per day. Hourly and multiple-day rates are available. Burley "tail wagon" bike trailers are also available for small dogs. Rent mopeds and "Scootcars" (an inventive composite of a car and scooter) at **Susie's Mopeds** (125 Nichols St.; ✆ **800/532-0087** or 360/378-5244; www.susiesmopeds. com), located 2 blocks up from the ferry landing at Friday Harbor. Moped rentals are US$30 per hour; Scootcars are US$65 per hour; Scootcoups (a flashier looking Scootcar) are US$70 per hour. Per-day rates are available. **Friday Harbor Marine** (4 Front St.; ✆ **360/378-6202;** www.sjimarine.com) has boat rentals that start at US$150 for 2 hours for a 4.9m (16-ft.) Duffy and US$200 for a 6.7m (22-ft.) Boston Whaler.

Exploring the Area

FRIDAY HARBOR

The busy fishing village of **Friday Harbor** was first populated by a feisty bunch of scalawags in the mid-1800s and gained respectability only when it became the county seat in 1873. Today, it encompasses 259 hectares (640 acres), which, as the bustling business center of the San Juan Islands, the National Trust for Historic Preservation added to its 2008 list of Dozen Distinctive Destinations. Its harbor teems with commercial fishing boats and pleasure craft.

FISHING & WILDLIFE

From the docks of the Friday Harbor marina, **Trophy Charters** (✆ **360/378-2110;** www.fishthesanjuans.com) runs salmon fishing trips, starting from US$98 adults. **Western Prince Wildlife Cruises** (✆ **800/757-6722** or 360/378-5315; www.orcawhale watch.com) offers nature and **whale-watching** expeditions from US$76 adults, US$49 children 12 and under. The 14m (46-ft.) vessel accommodates up to 30 passengers; and with plenty of indoor and outdoor seating, inclement weather is no deterrent. Tours are 3 to 4 hours. **Maya's Whale Watch Charters** (✆ **360/378-7996;** www.mayaswhale watch.biz) take out smaller groups (six passengers); 3-hour tours are US$75 adults and US$65 children 12 and younger. Guides are exceptionally wildlife-savvy, having written several wildlife books. They are also accomplished photographers who will give you tips beyond just point and shoot. Although the resident whales are a much smaller population than those found off British Columbia's coastline, whale-watching here usually delivers results. In fact, **San Juan Excursions** (© 800/809-4253; www.watchwhales. com) stands by a guarantee "to see whales or go again for free," and since they keep racking up various kudos for their successes, they've earned inclusion here.

KAYAKING

Kayaking has blossomed here in recent years, as have many good outfitters. Consequently, pricing is competitive from one to the other, so your choice boils down to convenience, experience, and attitude. **Crystal Seas Kayaking** (© 877/SEAS-877 [877/732-7877]; www.crystalseas.com), which provides complimentary shuttle service over to Snug Harbor, offers a variety of tours from a 3-hour sampler or sunset paddle to various multi-day, multi-actioned tours involving kayaking, biking, camping, and hiking. **San Juan Outfitters** (© 866/810-1483; www.sanjuanislandoutfitters.com) operate out of Roche Harbor with hourly rentals and guided tours. **San Juan Kayak Expeditions** (© 360/378-4436; www.sanjuankayak.com), which has been in business over 30 years, will set you up with multi-day expeditions, as well as with kayak-sailing, a combination of sail, paddle, and a following wind that has you traveling up to three times the speed of just paddling. They also rent standard double kayaks.

HORSEBACK RIDING

Horses graze in fields seemingly in every vista on San Juan Island, but only recently has a bona fide ranch come along with gentle horses, a learning corral, and sufficient trail rides to cater to riders of all ages and abilities. **Horseshu Ranch** (131 Gilbert Lane; © 360/378-2298; www.horseshu.com) is a 5-minute drive from Friday Harbor. Rides start at US$35 for a 30-minute mini-trail for youngsters (children must be at least 8) and US$55 for a 1-hour forest ride. There's a spectacular rental hacienda overlooking the ranch that's great for families. Kids can roam safely with the horses below, help with stable care, enjoy a free daily ride, and even gather fresh eggs for breakfast, all under the watchful eye of adults. You can even bring your own horse on vacation.

ATTRACTIONS

San Juan Historical Museum   Housed in an 1890s wood-frame farmhouse, the museum includes a crowded collection of antiques, old photos, and American Indian artifacts, plus intriguing old farm equipment that makes you wonder how on earth they did what they purport to have done. Unless you're really into maritime "stuff," save your visit for a rainy day, though the other buildings—a carriage house, a pioneer cottage, and what was once declared the "worst county jail in the state of Washington"—are fun to wander around. On Friday nights, July through August, the museum stages musical evenings on the lawn—bring a blanket and a picnic.

405 Price St., Friday Harbor. © **360/378-3949.** www.sjmuseum.org. Admission US$5 adults, US$4 seniors, US$3 children 6 to 18. May–Sept Wed–Sat 10am–4pm, Sun 1–4pm; Apr & Oct Sat 10am–4pm; Nov–Mar by appointment.

The Whale Museum   Although the maritime displays (other than the whale skeleton) are on the ho-hum side, a visit does give you a good insight into whale behavior: Learn the difference between breaching, spy hopping, and tail lobbing, as well as the many vocalization patterns; listen to their songs on the Whale Phone Booth. If whale-watching is on your agenda, check out the photo collection with the names and identification markings of some of the 90 or so resident orcas in the area. The museum has an orca adoption program to help fund ongoing research and operates a **24-hour hotline** (© 800/562-8832) to report whale sightings and marine mammal strandings.

Orcas roam between 97 and 129km (60–80 miles) per day in Puget Sound and the Salish Sea, following a feeding route through the islands and up the west coast of Vancouver Island to northerly feeding grounds. For 30 years, San Juan Islands' Ken Balcomb, an ex-marine biologist, has observed, photographed, and catalogued the three pods that make up the southern resident killer whales. His work proved that high-powered sonar is harmful to the hearing of cetaceans (thus halting the device from being used in local waters) and helped convince the federal government in 2005 to declare the southern resident killer whales endangered, in part because of the dwindling King salmon runs throughout the Pacific Northwest on which they are so dependent.

62 1st St. N., Friday Harbor. © **360/378-4710.** www.whalemuseum.org. Admission US$6 adults, US$5 seniors, US$3 children 5 to 18. May–Sept daily 10am–5pm. Oct–Apr hours vary (call to confirm).

American Camp ★

When British and American settlers were tilling the soil of San Juan Island, soldiers on both sides attempted to stake a national claim to these fertile lands. Sovereignty was eventually settled and, although not entirely accurate, today Americans refer to that time as the British occupation. However you view it, the American Camp, 10km (6¼ miles) south of Friday Harbor, serves as an historic reminder of those early days. The windswept grassy peninsula is a wonderful place to spend a sunny summer afternoon. On any other day, though, the winds make it barren and rather inhospitable, though some might say deliciously lonely. Two buildings remain, an abandoned officers' quarters and a laundresses' quarters, along with a cemetery and a defensive fortification built by Henry M. Roberts, of *Roberts Rules of Order* fame. A white picket fence circles the grounds, which include a Hudson's Bay Company farm on Grandma's Cove at the southern border of the park, along the water.

American Camp is really all about the great outdoors and limited facilities—you'll find a pit toilet along the way, but little else. The approach road, Cattle Point Road, can get pretty busy with cyclists heading for the southernmost tip of the island, and trails throughout the park are popular for hikers, though none of them seem to get overcrowded. An on-site **Visitor Centre** (© **360/378-2902**) is open year-round daily 8:30am to 4:30pm. Admission is free.

HIKING HIGHLIGHTS

There are various routes to gain beach access, the easiest and most direct being from the respective parking lots and a 5- to 10-minute walk. These include **South Beach,** the longest public beach on San Juan Island, and a great place to see shorebirds and whales. The beach is mainly gravel, so shoes or sandals are a must. It's a short walk to reach the secluded **Fourth of July Beach** where, appropriately, eagles nest nearby. Getting to **Picnic Cattle Point,** arguably the prettiest beach on the island, is a precarious scramble down a rocky ledge, but again, only minutes from the parking lot. **Grandma's Cove** is a downhill stroll for half a kilometer (¼ mile) to a picturesque beach. Use caution in descending the bluff: The gravelly soil gets very dry in summer, and it's easy to lose your footing.

Prairie Walks are primitive tracks that crisscross the prairie and trace the bluff from Grandma's Cove. It feels wild, and on a clear day, you can see views of Mount Baker, the Olympic and Cascade ranges, Vancouver Island, and even Mount Rainier, 209km (130 miles) up Admiralty Inlet. Mind your step; watch for rabbit warrens. A more protected walk is the 2.4km (1.5-mile) **Jakle's Lagoon Trail,** which travels along the old roadbed beneath a canopy of Douglas fir, cedar, and hemlock trees.

Hardy hikers usually opt for the upward trail to reach **Mount Finlayson**—90m (295 ft.) from where you can see the Coastal Mountains—as well as the Olympic and Cascade ranges on the horizon and seascape below. *Tip:* From the parking lot, follow the trail along the ridge; you have a dense evergreen forest to your left and a prairie of golden grass down to the beach on your right. From the summit, choose the well-worn path on the east side of the bluff and you descend into a cool, thick forest and a network of trails that twist and turn along the shore of Griffin Bay and pass two saltwater lagoons. You can enjoy the best of both worlds—different as night and day—as the two trails connect in a 4km (2.5-mile) loop. Birders come to the camp to catch a glimpse of the only nesting Eurasian skylarks in the U.S.

English Camp ★★

In sharp contrast to American Camp, English Camp is located in an area of protected waters, with maple trees spreading out overhead. About 16km (10 miles) from Friday Harbor, the site includes a restored hospital, a commissary, an impressive formal garden, and small white **barracks,** which are open to the public mid-May through Labor Day. The blockhouse, built right on the beach, served to protect the marines from marauding Natives, not Americans, and was later used as a guard house for miscreant troopers. You'll find interpretive displays on a hillside terrace overlooking the camp, close to where the officers' quarters were built. A small cemetery holds the graves of six British Marines who died accidentally during the occupation from 1860 to 1872 (there were no war-related casualties, other than the pig), and a trail leads through second-growth forests up to **Mount Young,** a fairly easy 198m (650-ft.) ascent. A **Visitor Centre** (✆ 360/378-2902) operates June through August daily from 8:30am to 4:30pm. It is housed in what was once the officer's mess hall and is staffed by rangers in period costume. At opening and closing times, these rangers create a fair to-do about raising the British flag, although it's lower than the American flag just up the hill. For information at any time of year for English and American Camps, contact the **Park Headquarters** (125 Spring St., Friday Harbor; ✆ 360/378-2240). Admission is free.

HIKING HIGHLIGHTS

Hiking here is not as rigorous as in American Camp. The easiest trail is the **Bell Point Trail,** a 1.5km-long (.9-mile), fairly level walk to Bell Point—it's a 3.2km (2-mile) loop—for a view of Westcott Bay. If you like to harvest shellfish, check with the park ranger at the visitor center for locations, daily limits, and red tide warnings, when the growth in algae is so prolific that they render shellfish unsafe to eat. Red tides usually occur from May to August. Conversely, the **Young Hill Trail** climbs 198m (650 ft.) to the top of Young Hill for a panoramic view of the island's northwest corner. Novice walkers should take care to pace themselves, as most of the gain is in the last half-kilometer (¼ mile). **Royal Marine Cemetery** is located about 46m (151 ft.) off the Young Hill Trail, about a third of the way up. Five Royal Marines are interred here, and a memorial stone is in place for two other marines.

Roche Harbor ★★

Roche Harbor is a heritage destination resort about 14km (8¾ miles) away from Friday Harbor, San Juan's commercial center. A favorite getaway of the late John Wayne, Roche Harbor is a mix of historic buildings, modern conveniences, and marine-related activities. Listed on the National Register of Historic Places, Roche Harbor was once the home of lime and cement tycoon John S. McMillin. In its heyday during the 1890s, the town had the largest lime works west of the Mississippi, operating kilns that each burned 10 cords of wood every 6 hours—just to keep functioning. The remains of several kilns are still visible. Much of the lime sweetened the huge salt marsh that was filled in and became the tulip fields of the Skagit Valley.

The renovated **Hotel de Haro** still maintains much of its historic character, and a number of the heritage cottages used by workers in the lime kiln business have been converted to overnight lodgings (see p. 256).

The resort has some walks to enjoy: through pretty Victorian gardens beside the hotel, along the docks, and on some heritage trails that take you through the old lime quarries; past historic sites such as the wood yard, the site of the original company cottages; and onto the hillside, where you can take in views of the Spieden Channel and small San Juan Islands. Some of the paths are paved with the same bricks that lined the original lime kilns. Pick up a trail map (US$1) at the hotel. The one walk you don't want to miss is to the **Mausoleum**, a bizarre McMillin family memorial that's about 20 minutes from the harbor. The structure itself is covered with Masonic symbols: an open, Grecian-style columned complex surrounds six inscribed chairs, each containing the ashes of a family member, set before a round table of limestone. Rumors abound as to why the seventh chair and column have been removed. Some say it was part of Masonic ritual, others believe a family member was disinherited. Or was it because the seventh member considered life to be everlasting?

Although open year-round, the resort is at its best in summer, not only for the landscaping but for the activities. Sea kayaking and whale-watching expeditions are available through the **Marine Adventure Centre**, and a naturalist guide hangs around to answer any questions about the local wildlife and terrain. The resort also becomes a showcase of local talent. By day, the resort's pathways and docks fill up with artists' booths displaying watercolors, oil paintings, photography, jewelry, knitted products, alpaca yarns, handmade handbags, and pottery. You can even get your portrait painted. By night, **Island Stage Left**, a local outdoor theater company, takes to the boards with productions such as *Henry V*, *The Tempest*, and *The Merchant of Venice*. It can get a bit chilly by final curtain, so dress warmly, and bring bug spray and a blanket to sit on. Performances are free.

Lime Kiln Point State Park ★

Head due west from Friday Harbor, through the center of the island, and you'll wind up at Lime Kiln State Park. Named for an early lime-kiln operation on site (remnants of its old structures are still evident), this is the only park in the world dedicated to whale-watching. Researchers use the **Lime Kiln Lighthouse**, built in 1914 and listed on the National Register of Historic Places, to watch for whales and to determine whether passing boats are affecting their behavior. Other whale-watching enthusiasts crowd the bluff or set up camp around picnic benches scattered along the beach. Your chances of sighting success are especially good in late August and early September, when major

Field of Sculptures

The Westcott Bay Reserve (www.sjima. org) is an 8-hectare (20-acre) nature interpretive park filled with a rotating exhibit of more than 100 modern sculptures in bronze, stone, wood, metal, glass, and ceramics. The park is part of the San Juan Island Museum of Art, and although individual sculptures are on loan, many individual pieces can be purchased from the artists.

salmon runs head for the Fraser River spawning grounds. En route, they pass through **Haro Strait** in front of the park, along the west side of San Juan Island, attracting whales, which feed on them. You might spot orca, Minke, and pilot whales, or their smaller cousins, harbor and Dall's porpoises. Bring your binoculars and cameras with telephoto lenses. There are 12 picnic sites and decent washroom facilities, so it's a good family destination, especially since the trails are short (from less than .8km/.5 mile to the longest at 2.5km/1.6 miles) and easy to navigate. The park is open year-round daily from 8am to dusk. It operates a recorded information line at ℭ **360/378-2044.**

Pelindaba Lavender Farm

Located on Wold Road, a half-mile north of Bailer Hill Road (which cuts across the island just south of Lime Kiln Point), the farm (ℭ **866/819-1911** or 360/378-4248; www.pelindabalavender.com) boasts more than 10,000 lavender plants that grow in scenic rows, providing a fragrant stroll on a hot summer's day. Admission is free, just be sure to close the gate behind you or wild deer might follow. Designated "certified organic," the plants are transformed into essential oils, processed on site in a custom-built distillery, along with handcrafted perfumes, soaps, pet grooming products, jewelry, candles, truffles, and other foodstuffs. True to its name, which is the Zulu word for "gathering place," Pelindaba's store (daily 10am-5pm, closed October to April) is the place to shop for everything lavender, including a first-class lavender lemonade and ice-cream. It also operates a lavender store in Friday Harbor, which is really just a taste of what you'll find out on the farm, but is your only option in winter when the fields close.

Where to Stay

Bird Rock Hotel   A half-million-dollar makeover has transformed the historic inn (ca. 1891) into a sassy boutique hotel that maintains the gracious atmosphere of yesteryear while still appealing to the Gen-X crowd. Guest rooms are decorated in rich colors against light walls, with a blend of modern and period furnishings, some swishier than others. Every room is a different size and shape, as might be expected in an old building, but that's part of its quirky charm. Four of the rooms share two bathrooms; 11 have private en suite bathrooms. All bathrooms have heated floors. The Marrowstone Suite has a private outdoor Jacuzzi, and the Bainbridge Suite can sleep six and has three flat-screen TVs. Top choice is the San Juan Suite near the top of the house, offering a kitchen, a private deck, and a bird's-eye view of the harbor. *Note:* Guests have access to the pool, hot tub, and sauna facilities at the nearby Earth Box Motel & Spa.

35 1st St. (P.O. Box 2023), Friday Harbor, WA 98250. ℭ **800/352-2632** or 360/378-5848. www.bird rockhotel.com. 15 units. June–Sept US$227–US$297 superior, US$177–US$197 standard, US$127–US$157 simple; Oct–May rooms are US$30–US$40 less. Rates include continental breakfast. Additional adult

US$20. Children 3 & under stay free in parent's room. AE, MC, V. **Amenities:** Lounge; complimentary bikes; room service. *In room:* TV, iPod dock, no phone, Wi-Fi.

Friday Harbor House ★ This elegant hotel on the harbor bluff offers the finest modern accommodations on San Juan Island—and the best views of the harbor, to boot. Guest room interiors are distinctly West Coast, with lots of windows, wood, slate tiles, and carpets. A double-person Jacuzzi is strategically situated so that you can see through into the bedroom, enjoying the views beyond. It's also within sight of the fireplace, so you can enjoy its warmth. All rooms have queen-size beds, save for three, which each feature a king. The continental breakfast includes home-baked scones and muffins. If you're on the early morning ferry, park your car in the lineup and return to enjoy these goodies; and be sure to ask for a treat box "for the road." The revamped Bluff Restaurant is earning a solid reputation for a creative fine-dining restaurant.

130 West St., Friday Harbor, WA 98250. ℭ **360/378-8455.** www.fridayharborhouse.com. 23 units. Mid-May to Sept US$320–US$380 double, US$460–US$529 suite; Oct to mid-May US$150–US$180 double, US$200–US$265 suite. Rates include continental breakfast. Additional adult US$35. Children 17 & under stay free in parent's room. 2-night minimum in summer & on weekends. AE, MC, V. **Amenities:** Restaurant. *In room:* TV/DVD player, fridge, Wi-Fi.

Lakedale Resort at Three Lakes Surrounded by three fresh spring-water lakes, on 33 hectares (82 acres), this resort is a rarity in that it has something for everyone: a waterfront lodge; cabins; and glamping (glamorous camping), tent, and RV sites. Lodge rooms have double French doors that open onto a private deck, with fireplaces and comfortable furnishings. The self-contained two-bedroom cabins (and one three-bedroom cabin) are tucked away in the woods, complete with large decks and full kitchens. From May through September, the glamping canvasses are the most exotic; although they have no electricity or running water, they're only a short walk to the showers. Besides, these 21-sq.-m (226-sq.-ft) structures have wood floors, proper beds, warm duvets, linens, and a cordless lantern just in case the moon and stars aren't lighting the way. Rates include a continental breakfast that's served in the Mess Tent. The regular tent sites are nicely laid out, too, with easy access to fishing in the well-stocked lakes, swimming areas, and paddle-boat and canoe rentals.

4313 Roche Harbor Rd., Friday Harbor, WA 98250. ℭ **360/378-2350.** www.lakedale.com. 10 lodge rooms, 18 cabins, 86 campsites, 6 RV sites. May–Sept US$249 double, US$379–US$539 cabin, US$149 glamping canvas, US$57 RV site (power/water), US$32–US$45 tent site; Oct–Apr US$179 double, US$249–US$439 cabin, no glamping/camping. Children 15 and younger not accepted in lodge. **Amenities:** Lounge; Wi-Fi. *In room:* TV/DVD player, fridge, full kitchen (some).

Roche Harbor Resort ★★ ☺ A village unto itself, Roche Harbor offers accommodations, as well as a marina large enough for 377 vessels, for seafaring guests. First, there is the century-old Hotel de Haro, where lace-trimmed beds, antiques, and roaring fireplaces transport you back to an earlier time. Originally a log bunkhouse, which sports the occasional slanting floor and crooked window, the hotel evolved into the distinctive three-story structure you see today, sophisticated enough to entertain company brass and dignitaries, including President Theodore Roosevelt (look for his signature in the guestbook). Suites have killer views, big beds, and large, claw-foot soaking bathtubs. Some single guest rooms share a bathroom. The one on the second floor contains John Wayne's custom over-size bathtub. In addition, nine former workers' cottages have been converted into two-bedroom units close to the swimming pool, as well as one- to three-room condominiums and carriage houses. These, and the ultra-deluxe spa suites, all have contemporary furnishings, full kitchen facilities, and of course, great views. Dining options include **McMillin's Restaurant** (✆ **360/378-5757**), housed in the former home of John S. McMillin, Roche Harbor Lime & Cement company president. The menu is expensive enough that you would expect the prime rib to be outstanding or presented with designer panache. It's good, but for better value for the money, opt for the less formal Madrona Grill downstairs. *Note:* Both restaurants are grandstand locales to watch the nightly closing taps ceremony and lowering of the flags.

4950 Reuben Tarte Memorial Dr., Roche Harbor, WA 98250. ✆ **800/451-8910** or 360/378-2155. www. rocheharbor.com. 80 units. Mid-May to Sept US$109–US$139 double w/shared bathroom, US$209–US$229 double w/private bathroom, US$269–US$799 condo & carriage house, US$339–US$449 suite, US$319–US$339 cottage; Oct to mid-May US$79–US$99 double w/shared bathroom, US$99–US$149 double w/private bathroom, US$129–US$249 condo & carriage house, US$99–US$199 suite, US$129–US$199 cottage. Children 18 & under stay free in parent's room. AE, MC, V. **Amenities:** 3 restaurants; lounge; large outdoor heated pool; spa; 2 tennis courts; Wi-Fi (in cafe). *In room:* TV, DVD player (in some), fridge (in some), kitchen (in some), Wi-Fi (in some).

Tucker House Inn ★　Spread over two corner lots, Tucker House comprises two heritage homes and two Victorian cottages, all woven together with decks, stone pathways, and garden walkways. Stay in the Upper Tucker House, and you'll have a lounge, full kitchen, and Wi-Fi laptop outside your bedroom door; stay in the Lower House or one of the cottages, and you'll have sun-drenched decks and a hot tub within steps. The entire place is dressed with polished hardwood floors, understated antiques and furniture, lovely linens, and top-of-the-line bedding (feather mattresses and feather quilts). Breakfast is served family-style in the third building, sometimes in two shifts (8:30 and 9:30am); menus always include dessert. Stay at one of the cottages or in **Harrison House Suites** (✆ **360/378-3587**) next door, and there'll be a breakfast hamper at your door. If you have your dog in tow, expect a basket of dog biscuits.

235 C St., Friday Harbor, WA 98250. ✆ **800/965-0123** or 360/378-2783. www.tuckerhouse.com. 15 units. June–Sept US$180–US$310 double; US$260–US$385 suite; Oct & Mar rates are 20% less; Nov–Feb US$120–US$185 double, US$160–US$280 suite. Pets accepted (in cottages only; US$25 per pet per stay). **Amenities:** Lounge; refreshment bar; hot tub. *In room:* TV/DVD player, no phone, Wi-Fi.

Wildwood Manor B&B　This elegant Queen Anne–style home has so many comfort touches that it ranks with the best. A winding drive leads you through a canopy of evergreens to a picture-book country manor. The surrounding woods offer easy trails on which to wander, and the views roll down the hills to the San Juan Channel. A large living room has oversized lounge chairs, floor-to-ceiling bookshelves lined with books and movies, hand-painted murals, a large Georgian fireplace, and a refreshment station that includes candies, specialty coffee, and home-baked cookies. Leave your shoes at the door because your feet will sink into high-grade carpeting up the stairs and in every guest room. Beds have down duvets and high-quality linens, and furnishings include antiques alongside flat-screen TVs. Bathrooms are stocked with everything from Q-Tips to robes. Breakfasts are stellar, changing to guest preferences, and may include items such as vanilla bean *panna cotta* with fresh strawberries, or wild rice and goat cheese frittata. The inn's genuine hospitality even extends to a deer-feeding station near the front drive, frequented by entire families of deer for some good Kodak moments.

5335 Roche Harbor Rd., Friday Harbor, WA 98250. ✆ **877/298-1144** or 360/378-3447. www.wildwood manor.com. 4 units. May–Sept US$205–US$275 double; Oct–Apr US$170–US$210 double. **Amenities:** Lounge; refreshment bar; Wi-Fi. *In room:* TV/DVD player, iPod dock, no phone, Wi-Fi.

Where to Dine

Backdoor Kitchen 🎁 PACIFIC NORTHWEST This kitchen is not only a discovery for its cuisine, it's a find geographically. Traipse through a parking lot and past some shipping containers, and this garden oasis and welcoming bistro unfolds with a menu of scrumptious food. Start with homemade flatbread with albacore tuna, slightly spicy tomato-garlic sauce, feta cheese, and sautéed seasonal greens. Then choose a New York steak topped with caramelized onions, or perhaps the mahi-mahi baked in a Spanish-style tomato-saffron broth and served with cheese stuffed roasted Anaheim chili, fresh avocado, cilantro, and orange segments. Vegetarian options are excellent, especially the East Indian Platter of homemade crepes. Winter hours vary, call ahead to confirm.

400b A St., Friday Harbor. ⓒ 360/378-9540. www.backdoorkitchen.com. Reservations recommended. Main courses US$24–US$32. MC, V. Daily from 5pm.

Coho Restaurant ★ PACIFIC NORTHWEST With only eight tables, the place fills up quickly, and is a popular venue for intimate tête-à-têtes and group celebrations. The owner-chefs actually run two B&Bs, Harrison House Suites and Tucker House Inn (see "Where to Stay," above), each set in an historic building nearby, and this restaurant (also housed in a craftsman house) expands their horizons beyond breakfast. Both are big in the Slow Food movement, so dinner plates are packed with local fare. Try the roasted-beet and goat-cheese salads, Westcott Bay oysters, ivory salmon with homemade ricotta gnocchi, and homemade pasta tossed in a fresh tomato-basil sauce. The hazelnut-encrusted lavender chicken is exceptionally flavorful, as are the homemade ice creams and sorbets. Even the art on the walls is by local artists. Book a table between 5 and 6pm if you want to try the chef's three-course tasting menu (US$35), wine included.

120 Nichols St., Friday Harbor. ⓒ 360/378-6330. www.cohorestaurant.com. Reservations recommended. Main courses US$24–US$36. AE, MC, V. Apr–Sept daily from 5pm; Oct–May Thurs–Mon from 5pm.

Duck Soup Inn 🎁 PACIFIC NORTHWEST Set in the woods overlooking a pond, this former woodworking shed now presents an intimate atmosphere with private booths and small tables, a fieldstone fireplace, local art, and hurricane-lamp sconces. The menu changes daily around the best island produce, meat, and poultry; the surrounding garden, a stunning sight in its own right, provides most of the herbs, fruits, and edible flowers. Choices usually include only four appetizers, two or three entrees, and a handful of decadent desserts. But this really is a case where less is definitely more. It's the innovative breads and creative combinations that set this restaurant apart. There might be a roasted-chili and cocoa-rubbed duck breast; or tempura squash blossoms stuffed with goat cheese and thyme, served with tangy apricot-orange jam.

50 Duck Soup Lane, Friday Harbor. ⓒ 360/378-4878. www.ducksoupinn.com. Reservations required. Main courses US$25–US$36. AE, MC, V. Apr Fri–Sun from 5pm; May Thurs–Sun from 5pm; June & Oct Wed–Sun from 5pm; July & Aug Tues–Sun from 5pm. Closed Nov–Mar.

Vinny's Ristorante ITALIAN/PACIFIC NORTHWEST The elegant atmosphere lends itself to smart-casual dining and special occasions with service. Menu selections celebrate popular Italian cuisine, as in veal Marsala and chicken piccata, alongside Dungeness crab cakes with sweet chili sauce and a seafood pasta filled with everything West Coast—clams, mussels, scallops, oysters, prawns, and halibut—in a delicious, light garlic cream sauce. Pasta dishes are so generous that there's a split charge of $4 so smaller appetites can share dishes. In winter, half portions are a real winner so more menu items can be enjoyed. Sadly, this restaurant has lost its water view to a new condo development, which seems to have rocked the restaurant's psyche from being consistently great to being occasionally so-so. That said, it's still worth a visit.

165 West St., Friday Harbor. *℃* **360/378-1934.** www.vinnysfridayharbor.com. Reservations recommended. Main courses US$14–US$33. MC, V. Oct–June Tues–Sat 4–9pm; July–Sept daily 11am–9:30pm.

ORCAS ISLAND

Named for the viceroy of Mexico in 1792—not, in fact, for the orca whales common to its waters—Orcas Island is the largest (148 sq. km/57 sq. miles), hilliest, and most beautiful of the San Juan Islands. Half the fun of exploring this island is traveling its roads, which, in addition to going up and down, twist and turn among hedgerows, fields, and orchards. Around any bend might lie a jewel of a bay or an unexpected hamlet filled with quaint cottages and wildflower gardens. You can climb to the top of **Mount Constitution** in **Moran State Park,** where the panorama stretches from the North Shore Mountains over Vancouver to Mount Rainier, south of Seattle, or stroll down lanes that give way to picturesque havens such as **Deer Harbor** and **Orcas Landing.** Early settlers logged, fished, and farmed, but today, most of the island's 5,000 population are artisans, entrepreneurs, retirees, and eco-adventurers. In **Eastsound,** the heart of "commercial" activity on Orcas, you'll find kayaking excursions, galleries, restaurants, and some shops. The **Rosario Resort,** an elegant mansion that regularly graces the pages of travel magazines, is probably the island's most prominent landmark (see "Where to Stay," below) and even though much smaller than it once was, it is still a showcase of island history.

Essentials

GETTING THERE

Washington State Ferries dock at **Orcas Landing,** at the central southern peninsula of the island. See "Getting There," at the beginning of the chapter, for information about fares and schedules.

VISITOR INFORMATION

Stop in at **Orcas Island Chamber of Commerce** (65 North Beach Rd. [P.O. Box 252], Eastsound, WA 98245; *℃* **360/376-2273;** www.orcasislandchamber.com), which operates from June to Labor Day (first Mon in Sept) daily from 8:30am to 4:30pm. The **Orcas Island Lodging Association** operates a web-based accommodation booking alliance at **www.orcas-lodging.com**.

GETTING AROUND

Once there, **Orcas Taxi** (*℃* **360/376-TAXI** [360/376-8294]) provides pickup and drop-off service throughout the island, year-round. From May to September, **Orcas Island Shuttle** (*℃* **360/376-RIDE** [360/376-7433]; www.orcasislandshuttle.com) offers rental cars for about US$60 a day—US$99 for a convertible—as well as a summer-time shuttle service. The website offers self-guided audio tours, which you can download onto a CD, MP3, or iPod for US$15. **Orcas Mopeds** (*℃* **360/376-5266**), near the ferry landing, rents mopeds for US$25 per hour or US$65 per day, Scootcars for US$40 per hour and US$110 per day. Bike rentals are available from **Wildlife Cycles** (350 N. Beach Rd., Eastsound; *℃* **360/376-4708;** www.wildlife cycles.com). Mountain bike and hybrid bike rentals are US$30 to US$45 per day. If time is of the essence, why not opt for a vintage biplane tour with **Magic Air Tours**

(© **800/376-1929** or 360/376-2733; www.magicair.com) and get the lay of the land from the air? Trips are US$299 for two people, US$249 for a single.

Exploring the Area

EASTSOUND VILLAGE

From the ferry dock, head due north 23km (14 miles) to **Eastsound Village,** at the center of the island. This is the commercial hub of Orcas Island, and it's both lovely to look at and a delight to stroll through. Catering to backpackers and the well-to-do alike, Eastsound sports galleries, potteries, and a charming village green that hosts a number of special events. Check out the **Saturday morning market** or watch a craftsperson whittle all manner of furniture and kitchen utensils with a foot-powered lathe at a pioneer display.

Eastsound is also where you'll want to base most of your **activities.** Most outdoor outfitters are headquartered here, though you'll also find them in other parts of the island. These include **Orcas Outdoors** (© **360/376-4611;** www.orcasoutdoors.com), which has a booking shack at the ferry dock where it offers stand-up paddle boards alongside 1-, 2-, and 3-hour kayaking trips (US$30, US$45, US$60, respectively) as well as multi-day excursions. **Eclipse Charters** (© **360/376-6566;** www.orcasisland whales.com) also offers departures from the ferry dock; 4-hour excursions cost US$72. Head to **Shearwater Adventures** (138 North Beach Rd.; © **360/376-4699;** www. shearwaterkayaks.com), which operates launch points from Deer Harbor, Rosario, and Doe Bay. Three-hour trips cost US$65, full-day trips cost US$159. The sunset tour (US$80) is highly recommended. Family-owned **Orcas Island Trail Rides** (168 Burl Hall Rd., Olga; © **360-376-2134**) has horses for kids 7 and over. Prices vary considerably by season; at the height of a summer weekend, expect to pay US$69 per hour.

Once in a Blue Moon Farm (412 Eastman Rd.; © **360/376-7035;** www. onceinabluemoonfarm.com) is a 1915 farmhouse that a former owner, a wealthy oil heiress, converted into a 465-sq.-m (5,005-sq.-ft.) villa. Mediterranean influence aside, the farm is a delight to visit; tours include petting llamas (guardians of the farm's sheep and chickens), gathering eggs, enjoying the lovely gardens, and picking fruit in the orchards and strawberry fields.

The Orcas Island Historical Museum (181 N. Beach Rd.; © **360/376-4849;** www.orcasmuseum.org) makes for a brief diversion, mainly for a look at the building itself. It comprises six one-room log cabins constructed by homesteaders in the 1880s. Between 1951 and 1963, cabins were disassembled and transported to Eastsound Village, where they were painstakingly reconstructed and connected to create the museum you see today. Admission is US$5 adults, US$4 seniors, and US$3 students. Children 12 and under get free admission. The museum is open June through September Saturday to Thursday from 11am to 4pm, Friday 11am to 7pm.

MORAN STATE PARK

A favorite destination for visitor and islander alike, Moran State Park's 1,864 hectares (4,606 acres) offer a number of outdoor recreational activities, including camping, picnicking, canoeing and kayaking, hiking, horseback riding, and more. Over 48km (30 miles) of hiking trails, most built by the Civilian Conservation Corps (CCC), cover everything from easy nature loops like the 4.3km (2.7-mile) walk around Cascade Lake to challenging out-of-the-way hikes such as the 7.6km (4.7-mile) Mount Pickett Trail that ascends 338m (1,109 ft.) through part of the largest tract of unlogged, old-growth forest in the Puget Sound Trough. Pick up a trail map from the Park Office at Cascade Lake. Unlike quieter Mountain Lake (that's where to put in for a quiet paddle and where fishing enthusiasts angle for trout), Cascade Lake gets a little like Grand Central Station in summer with canoe and paddleboat renters, picnickers, swimmers, day hikers setting off from the lakeside's many trail heads, and overnight campers. It's the only place in the park where you'll find bathhouses, kitchen shelters, and a sani-station. Call ✆ **888/CAMPOUT** (888/226-7688) or 888/226-7655 for campsite reservations or visit www.parks.wa.gov. The park's landmark, **Mount Constitution,** is the highest point in the islands. Rising 734m (2,408 ft.) above sea level, the summit is reached by a steep, paved road, where you'll discover a 16m (52-ft.) stone tower patterned after a 12th-century fortress. You can drive to the top; if you take your bike, you'll find the hard ride up rewarded with an exhilarating ride back down. Because the gradient is so steep, the road is generally closed from mid-November to mid-April, as it can get slick and dangerous. Information on trails, campsites, and activities in the park is available from **Moran State Park** (✆ **360/376-2326;** www.moranstatepark.org).

DEER HARBOR

Lying at the end of a winding country lane, Deer Harbor has some of the best marine views in all of the San Juans, as well as a marina with showers and a laundry, boat charters, gift shops, and a new waterfront park. **Deer Harbor Charters** (✆ **800/544-5758** or 360/376-5989; www.deerharborcharters.com) offer year-round 4-hour marine wildlife tours with a professional naturalist at US$69 adults and US$42 children under 14, while **Deer Harbor Marina** (✆ **360/376-3037;** www.boattravel.com/deerharbor) can arrange for kayak tours with Shearwater Adventures (see "Eastsound Village," above), as well as small boat and bicycle rentals. **The Resort at Deer Harbor** (✆ **888/376-4480**), which lies just above the marina, is a complex of deluxe timeshare cottages, some of which are in a rental pool, so the only place left to stay in the area is the **Deer Harbor Inn**

 GET potted

In operation for more than 60 years, **Orcas Island Pottery** (338 Old Pottery Rd, Eastsound; ✆ **360/376-2813;** www.orcasislandpottery.com) is one of the oldest potteries in the region and represents the work of almost two dozen potters. Look for a weathered log cabin festooned with colorful oversize pottery plates, and jewel-tone glazed vases in the garden. Inside is a working studio with artists throwing pots on the wheel, hand-building and glazing. **Crow Valley Pottery & Gallery** (2274 Orcas Rd., Eastsound; ✆ **360/376-4260;** www.crowvalley.com) is also housed in a log cabin, built around 1866, and showcases the

works of more than 70 artists and craftspeople. Located in a renovated strawberry-packing plant, **Olga Artworks** (11 Point Moran Rd., Olga; ✆ **360/376-4408;** www.orcasartworks.com) is just east of Moran State Park and features the work of more than 60 local artists displayed in a fashion almost as creative as the pieces themselves: on shelves made of railroad ties, benches of driftwood, and tree-stump pedestals. **Café Olga** (✆ **360/376-5098**) is also located here, legendary for its crab quesadillas, lemon shaker pie tart (made with the entire lemon), and homemade cinnamon rolls, which tend to sell out pretty quickly.

10

THE SAN JUAN ISLANDS | Orcas Island

(© 877/377-4110 or 360/376-4110; www.deerharborinn.com). This charming, family-run operation offers both lodge and private cottage accommodations, with country quilts on the beds and paper cups in the bathroom, versus down duvets and glasses, and only peek-a-boo harbor views. The Inn runs a casual restaurant in the original 1915 building, serving mostly comfort foods and seafood, inclusive of salad and soup, so there's a real sense of value for money.

Where to Stay

Rosario Resort & Spa ★   This turn-of-the-20th-century mansion, originally the private residence of shipping magnate Robert Moran, is the crown jewel of Orcas Island. In the last 2 years, new ownership has downsized the resort from a 122-room sprawling destination to a 22-room boutique resort that is reconnecting with its historical roots. Listed on the National Register of Historic Places, the original mansion has been beautifully restored. Walls are 30cm thick (12 in.) and paneled with mahogany. Windows are 2.5cm-thick (1 in.) plate glass. And teak parquet floors, covering some 557 sq. m (5,995 sq. ft.) took craftsmen more than 2 years to lay. The music room features a Tiffany chandelier and a working 1,972-pipe Aeolian organ, which, when installed in 1913, was the largest organ in a private home in the United States. Don't miss the free hour-long concerts held daily—they're entertaining and reminiscent of when Moran used to play the complicated organ for his guests—only the real secret is, he never knew how to play. In winter, concerts are performed on Saturday evening only. The mansion is one of several buildings that make up the Rosario Resort & Spa, which is spread out over 3 hectares (7½ acres) and surrounded by several more acres of countryside. Guest rooms vary from standard accommodations, either scattered along the waterfront in motel-style buildings or near the mansion, to four-bedroom suites, with kitchens and private balconies, perched on the hillside overlooking Cascade Bay. The **Spa Rosario** offers facials, massage, and other personalized body treatments. There are two restaurants: **The Marina Grill** is geared to the boating community with simple fare, breakfast, and burgers; and the **Quilted Pig,** which the resort has high expectations will become *the* destination restaurant of choice. Its chef traded a roaringly successful venture on San Juan Island to help recreate the "new" Rosario persona, so it deserves a try based on reputation alone.

1 Rosario Way, Eastsound, WA 98245. © **800/562-8820** or 360/376-2222. www.rosarioresort.com. 22 units. July–Sept US$129–US$169 double, April–June & Oct US$109–US$149 double, Nov–Mar US$89–US$129 double; year-round US$259–US$279 suite. Additional adult US$20. Children 17 & under stay free in parent's room. AE, DC, DISC, MC, V. Some pets accepted. **Amenities:** 2 restaurants; lounge; health club; 1 indoor & 1 outdoor pool; sauna; spa. *In room:* TV, Wi-Fi.

Cascade Harbor Inn   Situated among madroña trees, across the bay from Rosario Resort, accommodations here are a bit motel-like, with private balconies and views of Cascade Bay. Studios, and one- and two-bedroom suites come with fully equipped kitchens, making them a good choice for families and those indulging in longer island stays. The studio Murphy beds are surprisingly comfortable, as are the sofa pullouts for additional guests. Summer rates include continental breakfast. Moran State Park is literally a stone's throw away, making the Inn a convenient home-base for the park's hiking and water activities.

1800 Rosario Rd., Eastsound, WA 98245. © **800/201-2120** or 360/376-6350. Fax 360/376-6354. www.cascadeharborinn.com. 44 units. July to Labor Day US$129–US$149 double, US$199–US$399 suite; Apr, May & Sept US$90–US$104 double, US$139–US$279 suite; Oct–Mar US65–US$75 double,

US$139–US$199 suite. Additional adult US$25. AE, DISC, MC, V. Free parking. **Amenities:** Breakfast lounge; Wi-Fi. *In room:* Fridge, kitchen (in suites).

Doe Bay Resort & Retreat Center   Spread over 12 hectares (30 acres) of waterfront property, this resort is a throwback to the congenial, New Age 1970s, complete with impressive organic garden. There's a wide range of accommodations: rustic cabins (one-, two-, and three-bedroom configurations; some with no running water, others with fully equipped kitchen), yurts (canvas and wood structures) with skylights, tree houses (kids and romantics love them), greenhouse cabins, geodesic domes, tents, limited RV sites, and a hostel. There are shared central bathrooms and a community kitchen. The fully equipped, self-contained "retreat house" accommodates 10. A wonderful, clothing-optional, three-tiered sauna and a creek-side mineral springs Jacuzzi perch on a covered deck. Bring an oversize towel or two, and a flashlight. Sea kayak tours are available. **The Cafe Doe Bay** (*C* **360/376-8059**) is a wood-paneled bistro, full of windows and water views. It dishes up good vegetarian and seafood selections, although you might have to wait a bit because service can be casual. The cafe is housed in a former general store and post office (built in 1908 and listed in the National Register of Historic Places). It's open daily in summer for breakfast, brunch, and dinner, with restricted hours in winter. Call to confirm. It's also one of the few Wi-Fi hot spots at the resort.

107 Doe Bay Rd. (P.O. Box 437), Olga, WA 98279. *C* **360/376-2291.** www.doebay.com. 64 units. July & Aug US$55–US$125 tent, dome, yurt & hostel bed; US$130–US$275 cabin w/kitchen; US$650 cabin. Sept–June rates up to 30% lower. Minimum 2-night stay. MC, V. Pets accepted (US$20). **Amenities:** Restaurant; lounge; Jacuzzi; sauna; limited watersports rentals; Wi-Fi. *In room:* No phone.

Orcas Hotel ★   Built in 1904 as a boarding house, this restored Victorian home is on the National Register of Historic Places and overlooks the ferry terminal. Guest rooms aren't deluxe, but they're clean and comfortable, decorated with faux country quilts and period furniture that provides a simple, old-world appeal. Some share bathrooms; others have private toilets but shared showers. The newer guest rooms have private balconies and Jacuzzis. In the summer, there's a tiny attic room—a great find for the budget conscious. Rates include a continental breakfast in the Orcas Café, which also has a grandstand veranda to wait out the ferry with a beer or a sandwich later on in the day. **Octavia's Bistro** adjoins the hotel and serves a good selection of seafood, steaks, and pasta.

Orcas Ferry Landing (P.O. Box 155), Orcas, WA 98280. *C* **888/672-2792** or 360/376-4300. Fax 360/376-4399. www.orcashotel.com. 12 units. June–Sept & holiday weekends US$89–US$185 double, US$218 double w/Jacuzzi; Nov–Apr US$89–US$145 double, US$176 double w/Jacuzzi. Additional adult US$15. MC, V. **Amenities:** Restaurant; pub; lounge. *In room:* TV/DVD player (on request), no phone, Wi-Fi.

Outlook Inn   The only hotel on Eastsound's village waterfront, this Inn has been in business since 1888 and today is more like three hotels in one. The heritage building has completely updated its 14 original rooms with modern colors and crisp linens that enhance the old-fashioned European charm. These rooms are smallish but certainly not claustrophobic with sinks, shared baths, and phones but no TVs. The East Wing has 10 modern, traditional hotel rooms with en-suite bathrooms, quaintly decorated with a country-cottage feel. The Bay View Building, completed in 1995, is where to find 16 deluxe suites with king beds, sunken living areas, kitchenettes, fireplaces, radiant bathroom floor heating and whirlpool tubs. **The New Leaf Café** (see "Where to Dine," below) occupies the street-side atrium and is exceptional, whether for brunch, dinner, or a glass of wine.

171 Main St., Eastsound, Orcas, WA 98245. © **888/OUTLOOK** (888/688-5665) or 360/376-2200. www. outlookinn.com. 40 units. Mid-June to Labor Day US$289–US$309 Bay View, US$189–US$199 East Wing, US$84–US$99 Main; Sept to mid-Oct, Apr & May US$189 Bay View, US$109 East Wing, US$66 Main; mid-Oct to mid-June US$165 Bay View, US$89 East Wing, US$60 Main. Additional adult US$15 (Bay View); US$10 (East Wing); US$5 (Main). MC, V. **Amenities:** Restaurant; pub; lounge. *In room:* TV/DVD player (in Bay View & East Wing), Wi-Fi.

Turtleback Farm Inn ★★ The pastoral setting of Turtleback Farm is refreshingly bucolic, with its lush meadows, duck ponds, and forests. Originally constructed in the late 1800s, the farmhouse has been completely redone, and yet still retains a heritage feel, with lots of wood paneling, antiques, comfortable lounge chairs, and a living room that boasts a Rumford fireplace. Bedrooms tend to be on the small side but exude such charm that you'll want to nest. Linens include woolen comforters and down pillows. Most en-suite bathrooms have claw-foot tubs. Orchard House, separate from the farm, resembles an upscale barn from the outside. Surrounded by an apple orchard, it has four largish rooms with king-size beds, complete with gas fireplaces and private decks from which you can watch the farm's handful of sheep and cows, including some Scottish Highlanders, set the pace for the day. Wi-Fi is available as a must-have concession "for a farm on an island in the middle of nowhere."

1981 Crow Valley Rd., Eastsound, WA 98245. © **800/376-4914** or 360/376-4914. www.turtlebackinn.com. 10 units. US$115–US$195 double; lower rates Nov–May. Additional adult US$35. MC, V. Children 7 & under not accepted in Farmhouse. 2-night minimum stay June–Sept. **Amenities:** Lounge. *In room:* No phone, Wi-Fi.

Where to Dine

Alium PACIFIC NORTHWEST With a waterfront location and a chef who has a fine-dining pedigree from Seattle, Alium creates a fine-dining experience within a casual atmosphere and with as many local ingredients as is possible. For example, fresh scallops and prawns for a clam chowder with saffron, line-caught lingcod served with Oregon hazelnut barley and bay-roasted eggplant puree, as well as farm-raised chicken and a tangy-sweet rhubarb meringue pie. Most diners head for the oversized deck at the water's edge, but if there's any chance of rain, especially in winter, grab a seat in the tiny and oh-so-snug back bar.

310 E. Main St., Eastsound. © **360/376-4904.** www.aliumonorcas.com. Reservations recommended July–Aug. Main courses US$17–US$29. AE, MC, V. Wed–Sun noon–10pm (variable).

New Leaf Café ★ STEAK/REGIONAL When you hear a Texan talk about his mouth-watering, best-ever steak, you know this restaurant is doing something right. And

 Blue Marbles for Bluer Water

If a translucent, azure marble makes its way into the palm of your hand, commit a random act of ocean kindness. Introduced in 2010, on World Oceans Day and in celebration of what would have been Jacque Cousteau's 100th birthday, Orcas Island was among the first communities to get with the wave of blue marbles and a growing worldwide movement to save our oceans—one marble at a time. Look out for buckets of blue marbles throughout Orcas Island and beyond, and be prepared to act green for blue, and then pass your marble along. Visit **www.bluemarbles.org** for kindness ideas and program details.

steak isn't even a specialty of the house. Menu items are as playful as they are delicious: three-cheese fondue with chicken-apple sausage, roasted vegetables, and artisan breads (all home-baked); mangoed mahi-mahi tacos with a cumin-scented radicchio slaw and avocado salsa; and Korean-style BBQ short ribs with grilled scallion and apple-corn salad. The atrium setting fills the room with light, and the chef frequently swans around the restaurant with such genuine hospitality for his craft, you can't help but catch his enthusiasm. Don't be surprised if he appears at your table with an *amuse-bouche* or a small taster scoop of his latest dessert. *Tip:* Afternoon tea here is a delight.

At the Outlook Inn, 171 Main St., Eastsound. ℂ **888/OUTLOOK** (888/688-5665) or 360/376-2200. Main courses US$15–US$34. Daily 8am–10pm.

LOPEZ ISLAND

Laced with country lanes, picturesque farms, and orchards, Lopez Island is just about as bucolic and pastoral as it gets. Cows and sheep are a common sight, as are bright fields of daffodils, tulips, lilies, and delphiniums. Home to approximately 2,400 people, and covering 76 sq. km (29 sq. miles), Lopez has a rich agricultural heritage. Once known as the "Guernsey Island" for its exports of cream, eggs, and poultry, the land now supports more than 50 working farms. In summer, cyclists flock to the gently rolling hills, hikers explore the trails and bluffs of county parks, and birdwatchers take to the expanses of protected tidal flats to watch a myriad of shorebirds: horned grebes, double crested cormorants, yellow legs, peeps, ospreys, and peregrine falcons.

Spencer Spit State Park is a 56-hectare (138-acre) marine and camping park, named for the lagoon-enclosing sand spit on which it lies. Clamming, crabbing, and saltwater fishing are among the park's most popular activities. It's also a sun-drenched picnic area with 37 sought-after standard camping sites at US$17 to US$26 per night March through October. Call ℂ **888/CAMPOUT** [888/226-7688] for reservations or visit www.parks.wa.gov. **Lopez Farm and Cottages** (ℂ **800/440-3556**) is a private, alternate camping spot for tents only and is the only site on the island with showers. **Shark Reef Recreation Area** is a favorite spot from which to watch harbor seals, sea lions, and bald eagles diving for dinner. Or you can head for **Agate Beach,** one of the few beaches open to the public, and one of the most romantic places to watch the sun go down. The southernmost point, Iceberg Point, is another easy trail to the bluffs that edge the shore.

Come winter, Lopez Island seems to go into virtual hibernation, save for a fairly recent phenomenon: When one of the original Microsoft team built his compound here a few years back, techies followed, and vacation mega-houses have been popping up all along the waterfront ever since. Real-estate prices are soaring. Lopez village has developed a new gentrified air and now has street names and sidewalks. Lopez is, however, still the friendliest of the San Juan Islands. Waving to passing cars and cyclists is a time-honored local tradition.

Essentials
GETTING THERE
The ferry arrives at the northerly tip of the island. See "Getting There," at the beginning of the chapter, for information about fares and schedules.

VISITOR INFORMATION

The **Lopez Island Chamber of Commerce** (P.O. Box 102, Lopez, WA 98261; ✆ **360/468-4664;** www.lopezisland.com) distributes literature and maps in shops and galleries throughout the island.

GETTING AROUND

Folks on foot could be out of luck. Taxi service is an on-off affair (at time of printing, there was none available, although there's continued talk about starting some sort of bus service). Call the Chamber of Commerce (above) to get the latest scoop. One of the best bike routes around the island is a 48km (30-mile) circuit that can be done in a day and is suitable for the whole family. If you don't have your own wheel power, here are some rental options: **Lopez Bicycle Works & Kayaks** (2847 Fisherman's Bay Rd.; ✆ **360/ 468-2847;** www.lopezkayaks.com) and **Cascadia Kayaks & Bikes** (135 Lopez Rd., Building A; ✆ **360/468-3008;** www.cascadiakayaktours.com) offer mountain bikes, tandems, and children's bikes, as well as kayak rentals. The latter outfitter also does guided kayak tours, from mellow half-day excursions to multi-day adventures.

Exploring the Area

Lopez Village is the business center of the island and has a scattering of cafes, shops, a charming farmers' market (held Wed and Sat), and of course, real-estate offices. The **Library** (2225 Fisherman Bay Rd.; ✆ **360/468-2265**), housed in a bright-red and white 19th-century schoolhouse, is the *only* place to get the Sunday *New York Times, Los Angeles Times,* and *Wall Street Journal.* Copies are donated, which might mean you're reading 2-day-old news. Well, call it being on island time. Nonresidents pay a refundable US$10 fee to check out books while on the island. This is also where you can find computer and Internet access.

When you're browsing through Lopez Village, be sure to drop in to the **Soda Fountain & Pharmacy** (✆ **360/468-4511;** www.lopezislandpharmacy.com), where you'll find an old-fashioned ice-cream parlor with a slew of fountain treats: killer banana splits, hand-dipped malts, and suck-'til-your-brain-hurts thick-and-creamy milk shakes. The place is a bit scruffy, but the lunch counter is gossip central for Lopez locals, just in case you're interested in the lowdown on island life. For picnic supplies of rustic breads, pizzas, and sweet treats, visit **Holly B's Bakery** (✆ **360/469-2133;** www. hollybsbakery.com), open April through November. The **Lopez Historical Museum** (28 Washburn Place; ✆ **360/468-2049;** www.lopezmuseum.org) houses artifacts such as a foot-powered cow-milking machine and a 1903 Orient buckboard—the first car driven on the island. The museum puts out an island tour map of historic landmarks that, believe it or not, has 34 destinations! You have to be a history nut to really appreciate this, though. Museum operating hours are sporadic, particularly in winter, although in the summer, you can usually count on Wednesday through Sunday from noon to 4pm. It's a fun 20-minute visit while you're wandering around the village. Admission is US$1.50 adults, US$1 children 18 and under. **Tip:** The museum's map of the island's Historic Homes adds a neat touring dimension. Download a copy or pick one up on-island. Touring island farms is another fun excursion, especially if you're into market produce, herbs, or hand-woven blankets. Call the **Lopez Community Land Trust** (✆ **360/468-3723**) for information. If you're a wine lover, or are even just learning to love it, pay a visit to **Lopez Island Vineyards** (724 Fisherman Bay Rd.; ✆ **360/468-3644;** www.lopezislandvineyards.com). This small, family-owned winery is the oldest in San Juan County, producing organically grown grapes and some pretty drinkable wines. Until recently, if you bought any wines with labels stating an origin of Friday Harbor or Orcas Island, they were tourist gimmicks. The wine was actually made in the Yakima Valley. These folks, however, have matured their early-ripening vines from the mid-1980s, so they now produce grapes that create more flavor. In addition to a Cabernet and Merlot, there's a medium-dry white apple-pear wine, as well as a full-bodied blackberry dessert wine, all of which are made on the premises. The vineyard is open for tastings year round, though hours and days vary by month, so call ahead. In July and August, the sure bet is Wednesday through Friday noon to 5pm.

Where to Stay

Aleck Bay Inn With its location right on Aleck Bay, early risers could well be greeted at this inn with sights of eagles, sea otters, and seals—perhaps even passing whales (especially in spring). Add to this the deluxe comforts of well-appointed rooms, beautiful gardens, and attentive innkeepers, and it's a winning combination. Each of the four rooms has romantic appeal, and they seem in competition as to the number of wedding proposals each can claim. Although only the Morning Glory room has a fireplace, all the rooms have either a private sun room or patio, breathtaking views, and en-suite bathrooms. Breakfasts are hearty and generous without being fancy, and offer extra scones to take on the road. A three-course dinner is also offered for US$20. *Tip:* The nearby beaches are kayak-friendly.

45 Finch Lane, Lopez Island, WA 98261. ℂ **360/468-3535.** http://home.centurytel.net/abi. 4 units. May–Sept US$149–US$189 double; Oct–Apr US$129–US$169 double. Rates include full breakfast. MC, V. Children under 12 not accepted. **Amenities:** Lounge. *In room:* No phone, Wi-Fi.

Edenwild Country Inn ★ Set away from the water, this is the Victorian centerpiece of Lopez Village, complete with picturesque flower garden and large wraparound porch from which to view San Juan Channel. Pleasant antique furnishings decorate refurbished rooms, and there are quality bathroom amenities and delicious Bavarian chocolates at your bedside. Three guest rooms have large wood-burning fireplaces; all have private bathrooms, some with deep-soaker, claw-foot bathtubs. Room no. 2 is the most comfortable, notable for its size and cozy sitting area, the family heirlooms (ca. 1920), and vistas of Fisherman's Bay. In answer to the island's lack of cable TV, there are books everywhere—you can actually take them home thanks to Lopez's phenomenal recycling program. The European-style breakfast is generous, with plenty of cold cuts, cheeses, bread varieties, eggs, and fresh fruit.

132 Lopez Rd. (P.O. Box 271), Lopez Island, WA 98261. ℂ **800/606-0662** or 360/468-3238. www.edenwildinn.com. 8 units. May–Sept US$170–US$195 double; Oct–Apr rates 20% lower. Rates include full breakfast. Additional adult US$25. AE, MC, V. Children under 12 not accepted. **Amenities:** Lounge. *In room:* No phone, Wi-Fi.

MacKaye Harbor Inn Originally built in 1904 and dramatically rebuilt 20 years later, when it was the first island homestead to have electricity, the upgraded farmhouse still retains much of its homey style. Rooms are large, ceilings are high, picture windows overlook the bay, and there's a long porch. Decor and furnishings are unassuming but comfortable, and an enclosed garden gazebo is a private sanctuary where guests can read, meditate, enjoy watching the hummingbirds at the feeder or arrange for a spa massage. Rates include truffles and port in the evening, and a large continental breakfast with very wholesome muffins, hard-boiled eggs, fresh fruit, and granola. Guests have free use of 21-speed mountain bikes and can rent kayaks for US$25 per day, US$35 for their entire stay.

949 MacKaye Harbor, Lopez Island, WA 98261. © **888/314-6140.** www.mackayeharborinn.com. 4 units. US$135–US$235 (rates are less in early spring). Rates include breakfast. Retreat packages available. MC, V. Closed mid-Oct to late Apr. **Amenities:** Lounge; complimentary mountain bikes; kayak rentals. *In room:* No phone, Wi-Fi.

Where to Dine

The Bay Cafe ★★ 🏠 PACIFIC NORTHWEST   Located at the entrance to Fisherman's Bay, this bright, airy restaurant is a delight. Colorful and contemporary art adorns the walls, while row upon row of windows give way to terrific sunsets and waterside views. The views are only outdone by the food: the ever-changing selection of seafood tapas is imaginative (the shrimp cakes with a citrus-sesame soy sauce are to die for), and the entrees cover all the bases, with dishes to please carnivores, herbivores, and everything in between. The Thai curry is exceptionally good, as is almond-crusted Alaskan halibut with gingered boysenberries and the sesame-crusted pork tenderloin medallions with a Szechwan hoisin BBQ sauce. Homemade soup and salad are included with your meal, which makes the menu a particularly good value. There's a patio in summer. In winter, call ahead.

9 Old Post Rd, Lopez Village. © **360/468-3700.** www.bay-cafe.com. Reservations required July & Aug. Main courses US$17–US$27. AE, DISC, MC, V. May–Aug daily 5:30–10pm; Sept–Apr Wed–Sun 5:30–10pm (variable).

Love Dog Café 🏠 ECLECTIC   Its name is derived from a 13th-century poem by philosopher Rumi: "There are love dogs in this world no-one knows the names of, give your life to be one." The chef-owner-storyteller is (self-)named White Bear for her white hair and somewhat stocky appearance. The food is some of the best Italian fare in the San Juan Islands—there are always half a dozen pasta specials (pray that you're there for the pesto capellini) usually served family-style, as well as a couple of fresh-fish features. In the morning, the cafe serves some of the best breakfasts, too, and true to its eclectic nature is able to transform from an eatery serving burgers, quiche, and good salads by day, to quite a romantic spot at night, especially if you hit an evening with live jazz. Service can be on the slow side, but it's worth the wait. All the basics and baked goods are made from scratch, and the desserts are delicious, especially the pot au chocolate or bread pudding with whiskey sauce.

1 Village Center, Lopez Island. © **360/468-2150.** Main courses US$6–US$14. MC, V. Daily 8am–8pm (variable in winter).

FAST FACTS: VANCOUVER ISLAND, THE GULF ISLANDS & THE SAN JUAN ISLANDS

Area Codes Numbers are made up of the 3-digit area code and the 7-digit local number. On Vancouver Island and the Gulf Islands, this prefix is 250. For the San Juan Islands, the area code is 360.

Business Hours In Victoria and other major urban centers, banks are open Monday through Thursday from 10am to 3pm, Friday from 10am to 6pm, and sometimes on Saturday mornings. Stores typically open Monday through Saturday from 10am to 6pm. Stores in Victoria are also open Sundays in summer. Although business hours on the San Juan Islands and Gulf Islands tend to follow this pattern, you may come across unexpected closures of individual stores, especially early in the week when tourist traffic is slower.

Cellphones (Mobile Phones) See "Staying Connected," p. 44.

Drinking Laws In British Columbia, the minimum drinking age is 19. Liquor is sold only in government-run liquor stores, although in the larger communities such as Victoria and Nanaimo, you may find beer and wine sold from independent, government-licensed specialty shops. In the Gulf Islands, liquor is sold over a specific counter in one of the local stores.

In Washington State, the legal age for purchase and consumption of alcoholic beverages is 21; proof of age is required and often requested at bars, nightclubs, and restaurants, so it's always a good idea to bring ID when you go out. Spirits, wine, and beer are available for purchase in most grocery stores and at outlets adjoining bars. Closing time is usually earlier than you would find in big cities, at around 11pm to midnight.

Do not carry open containers of alcohol in your car or any public area that isn't zoned for alcohol consumption. The police can fine you on the spot. And nothing will ruin your trip faster than getting a citation for DUI ("driving under the influence"), so don't even think about driving while intoxicated.

Driving Rules See "Getting There and Getting Around," in chapter 3.

Electricity The United States and Canada use 110 to 120 volts AC (60 cycles), compared to 220 to 240 volts AC (50 cycles) in most of

Europe, Australia, and New Zealand. Downward converters that change 220–240 volts to 110–120 volts are difficult to find in Canada and the United States, so bring one with you.

Embassies & Consulates   The **United States** Embassy in Canada is in Ottawa at 490 Sussex Dr. (© **613/688-5335**); it has a consulate office in Vancouver, at 1095 West Pender St. (© **604/685-4311**).

In Canada, the **Australian Consulate** is at 50 O'Connor St., Ste. 710, Ottawa, Ontario, K1P 6L2 (© **613/236-0841**), with the nearest location located in Vancouver at 1075 West Georgia St., Ste. 2050 (© **604/684-1177**).

The embassy of **Canada** in the U.S. is at 501 Pennsylvania Ave. NW, Washington, DC 20001 (© **202/682-1740;** www.canadainternational.gc.ca/washington). Other Canadian consulates are in Buffalo (New York), Detroit, Los Angeles, New York, and Seattle.

The embassy of **Ireland** in the U.S. is at 2234 Massachusetts Ave. NW, Washington, DC 20008 (© **202/462-3939;** www.embassyofireland.org). Irish consulates are in Boston, Chicago, New York, San Francisco, and other cities. See the website for a complete listing.

The embassy of **New Zealand** in the U.S. is at 37 Observatory Circle NW, Washington, DC 20008 (© **202/328-4800;** www.nzembassy.com). New Zealand consulates are in Los Angeles, Salt Lake City, San Francisco, and Seattle.

In Canada, the **New Zealand High Commission** is at Metropolitan House, 99 Bank St., Ste. 727, Ottawa, K1P 6G3 (© **613/238-5991**). A consulate office is in Vancouver: 1200-888 Dunsmuir St. (© **604/684-7388**).

The embassy of the **United Kingdom** in the U.S. is at 3100 Massachusetts Ave. NW, Washington, DC 20008 (© **202/588-6500;** http://ukinusa.fco.gov.uk). Other British consulates are in Atlanta, Boston, Chicago, Cleveland, Houston, Los Angeles, New York, San Francisco, and Seattle.

The **British High Commission** in Canada is at 80 Elgin St., Ottawa, Ontario K1P 5K7 (© **613/237-1530**). The nearest office is in Vancouver: 1111 Melville St., Ste. 800 (© **604/683-4421**).

Emergencies   Call © **911** for fire, police, or ambulance in either the U.S. or Canada. This is a toll-free call. (No coins are required at public telephones.) In British Columbia, the Royal Canadian Mounted Police (RCMP) administer a **Tourist Alert** program by posting emergency notices at visitor information centers, at provincial park sites, and on BC ferries.

To report a forest fire in any wilderness area, or even the suspicion of one, call © **5555.**

Gasoline (Petrol)   At press time, the cost of gasoline (also known as gas, but never petrol) is abnormally high, and in many cities and towns, it's not unusual to see per-unit prices fluctuate by the day. Gas is certainly more expensive in the rural areas, particularly on the relatively isolated San Juan and Gulf islands. Taxes are already included in the printed price. One U.S. gallon equals 3.8 liters or .85 imperial gallons. Canadian gas is sold by the liter and by law must be paid for in advance of purchase.

Holidays   Banks, government offices, post offices, and many stores, restaurants, and museums are closed on the following legal national holidays.

In the **United States,** the national holidays are January 1 (New Year's Day), the third Monday in January (Martin Luther King, Jr., Day), the third Monday in February (Presidents' Day), the last Monday in May (Memorial Day), July 4 (Independence Day), the first Monday in September (Labor Day), the second Monday in October (Columbus Day), November 11 (Veterans' Day/Armistice Day), the fourth Thursday in November (Thanksgiving Day), and December 25 (Christmas). The Tuesday after the first Monday in November is Election Day, a federal government holiday in presidential-election years (held every 4 years, and next in 2012).

In **British Columbia,** there are nine official public holidays: New Year's Day (Jan 1), Good Friday Victoria Day (the Mon on or preceding May 24), Canada Day (July 1), BC Day (first Mon in Aug); Labor Day (first Mon in Sept), Thanksgiving (second Mon in Oct), Remembrance Day (Nov 11), and Christmas Day (Dec 25).

For more information on holidays, see "Calendar of Events" chapter 3.

Hospitals Most major cities and towns, such as **Victoria, Nanaimo,** and **Campbell River,** have hospitals. These include **Royal Jubilee Hospital** (1952 Bay St., Victoria; ✆ **250/370-8000)** and **Lady Minto Hospital** (135 Crofton Rd., Salt Spring Island; ✆ **250/538-4800).** On the Gulf and San Juan islands, however, there are only medical clinics; for life-threatening situations, airlift services are used.

Insurance Although it's not required of travelers, **health insurance** is highly recommended. Most health insurance policies cover you if you get sick away from home—but check your coverage before you leave.

For information on **traveler's insurance, trip cancellation insurance,** and **medical insurance** while traveling, please visit www.frommers.com/tips.

Internet Access Although you'll find Wi-Fi and Internet cafes in Victoria, public Internet access becomes increasingly scarce away from the city center. Except for most hotels and inns, access can be spotty on the Gulf Islands and San Juan Islands.

Also see "Staying Connected," p. 44.

Legal Aid If you are "pulled over" for a minor infraction (such as speeding), never attempt to pay the fine directly to a police officer; this could be construed as attempted bribery, a much more serious crime. Pay fines by mail or directly into the hands of the clerk of the court. If accused of a more serious offense, say and do nothing before consulting a lawyer. In both the U.S. and Canada, the burden is on the state to prove a person's guilt beyond a reasonable doubt, and everyone has the right to remain silent, whether he or she is suspected of a crime or actually arrested. Once arrested, a person can make one telephone call to a party of his or her choice. The international visitor should call his or her embassy or consulate.

Mail At press time, domestic U.S. postage rates were US28¢ for a postcard and US46¢ for a letter. For international mail, a first-class letter of up to 28g (1 oz.) costs US95¢ (US75¢ to Canada and US79¢ to Mexico); a first-class postcard costs the same as a letter. For more information go to **www.usps.com** and click on "Calculate Postage."

Within Canada, the postal rates are C57¢ for standard letters and postcards, C$1 to the U.S., and C$1.70 overseas. For more information, including postal codes, go to www.canadapost.ca.

Passports See "Embassies & Consulates," above, for whom to contact if you lose your passport while traveling in the U.S. or Canada. For other information, contact the following agencies:

For Residents of Canada   Passport applications are available at travel agencies throughout Canada or from the central **Passport Office,** Department of Foreign Affairs and International Trade, Alberta, ON K1A 0G3 (✆ **800/567-6868;** www.ppt.gc.ca). **Note:** Canadian children who travel must have their own passport.

For Residents of Australia   Contact the **Australian Passport Information Service** at ✆ **131-232** or visit www.passports.gov.au.

For Residents of Ireland   Contact the **Passport Office,** Setanta Centre, Molesworth Street, Dublin 2 (✆ **01/671-1633;** www.foreignaffairs.gov.ie).

For Residents of New Zealand   Contact the **Passports Office,** Department of Internal Affairs, 47 Boulcott St., Wellington 6011 (✆ **0800/225-050** in New Zealand or 04/474-8100; www.passports.govt.nz).

For Residents of the United Kingdom Visit your nearest passport office, major post office, or travel agency, or contact the Identity and Passport Service (IPS), 89 Eccleston Sq., London, SW1V 1PN (© **0300/222-0000;** www.ips.gov.uk).

Police Call © **911** for emergencies.

Smoking British Columbia by-laws prohibit smoking in a public place, including restaurants, offices, shopping malls, and even transit shelters. There is also a 3m (10-ft.) smoke-free zone around most public and workplace doorways, open windows, and air intakes. Although this is adhered to in the larger cities, individual pubs and bars in the island communities sometimes turn a blind eye to the legislation. Ask before you light up publicly anywhere in the province. No smoking is also the "norm" in most public places in Washington State.

Taxes British Columbia charges a harmonized provincial and federal sales tax (HST), meaning you will pay an additional 12% on most purchases. In San Juan County, the retail sales tax is 7.8%, with an additional 2% on lodging.

Telephones See "Staying Connected," p. 44.

Time British Columbia and Washington State are in the Pacific Time Zone, 3 hours behind Eastern Standard Time. **Daylight Saving Time** is in effect from 1am on the second Sunday in March to 1am on the first Sunday in November. Daylight Saving Time moves the clock 1 hour ahead of Standard Time.

Tipping Tips are a very important part of certain workers' income, and gratuities are the standard way of showing appreciation for services provided. (Tipping is certainly not compulsory if the service is poor!) Tipping etiquette is the same in Canada and the United States. In hotels, tip **bellhops** at least $1 per bag ($2–$3 if you have a lot of luggage) and tip the **chamber staff** $1 to $2 per day (more if you've left a disaster area for him or her to clean up). Tip the **doorman** or **concierge** only if he or she has provided you with some specific service (for example, calling a cab for you or obtaining difficult-to-get theater tickets). Tip the **valet-parking attendant** $1 every time you get your car.

In restaurants, bars, and nightclubs, tip **service staff** 15% to 20% of the check, tip **bartenders** 10% to 15%, tip **checkroom attendants** $1 per garment, and tip **valet-parking attendants** $1 per vehicle.

As for other service personnel, tip **cab drivers** 15% of the fare; tip **skycaps** at airports at least $1 per bag ($2–$3 if you have a lot of luggage); and tip **hairdressers** and **barbers** 15% to 20%.

Toilets You won't find public toilets or "restrooms" on the streets, but they can be found in hotel lobbies, bars, restaurants, museums, department stores, railway and bus stations, and service stations. Not all the islands have all these facilities; on the San Juans, for example, you're more likely to find an outhouse or two, strategically placed at a trail head or public beach.

Visas For information about U.S. visas, go to **http://travel.state.gov** and click on "Visas." Or go to one of the following websites:

Australian citizens can obtain up-to-date visa information from the **U.S. Embassy Canberra,** Moonah Place, Yarralumla, ACT 2600 (© **02/6214-5600**) or by checking the U.S. Diplomatic Mission's website at **http://canberra.usembassy.gov/consular**.

British subjects can obtain up-to-date visa information by calling the **U.S. Embassy Visa Information Line** (© **0891/200-290**) or by visiting the "Visas to the U.S." section of the American Embassy London's website at **www.usembassy.org.uk**.

Irish citizens can obtain up-to-date visa information through the **U.S. Embassy Dublin,** 42 Elgin Rd., Ballsbridge, Dublin 4 (© **353/1-668-8777; http://dublin.usembassy.gov**).

Citizens of **New Zealand** can obtain up-to-date visa information by contacting the U.S. Embassy New Zealand, 29 Fitzherbert Terrace, Thorndon, Wellington (📞 **644/472-2068; http://newzealand.usembassy.gov**).

Like Canada, Australia and New Zealand are members of the British Commonwealth, and therefore need no special visas to travel between their respective countries, only a valid passport.

Visitor Information A great source for information on British Columbia is **Tourism British Columbia (**P.O. Box 9830, Parliament Building, Victoria, BC V8V 1X4, or P.O. Box 9830 Stn. Prov. Government, Victoria, BC V8W 9W5; 📞 **800/HELLOBC** [800/435-5622]; www.hellobc.com). Be prepared for lots of glossy magazines to whet your appetite.

For Vancouver Island specifics, contact the **Tourism Association of Vancouver Island** (501-65 Front St., Nanaimo, BC V9R 5H9; 📞 **250/754-3500;** www.vancouverisland. travel). Another useful website is **www.vancouverisland.com**. There is a central reservations service for hotels and B&Bs in the Gulf Islands. Call 📞 **877/537-9934** or 250/537-9933. You can also check out **www.gulfislandsguide.com** for general information.

For the San Juan Islands, contact **San Juan Islands Visitor Information Services** (P.O. Box 1330, Friday Harbor, San Juan Island, WA 98250; 📞 **888/468-3701** or 360/378-9551; www.visitsanjuans.com). All these resources also provide excellent destination-specific maps, and many have lively travel blogs.

Wi-Fi See "Staying Connected," p. 44.

AIRLINE WEBSITES

MAJOR AIRLINES

Aeroméxico
www.aeromexico.com

Air France
www.airfrance.com

Air New Zealand
www.airnewzealand.com

Alaska Airlines/Horizon Air
www.alaskaair.com

American Airlines
www.aa.com

British Airways
www.british-airways.com

China Airlines
www.china-airlines.com

Continental Airlines
www.continental.com

Delta Air Lines
www.delta.com

Frontier Airlines
www.frontierairlines.com

JetBlue Airways
www.jetblue.com

Hawaiian Airlines
www.hawaiianair.com

Japan Airlines
www.jal.co.jp

JetBlue Airways
www.jetblue.com

Korean Air
www.koreanair.com

Lufthansa
www.lufthansa.com

Qantas Airways
www.qantas.com

United Airlines
www.united.com

US Airways
www.usairways.com

Virgin America
www.virginamerica.com

BUDGET AIRLINES

Aer Lingus
www.aerlingus.com

AirTran Airways
www.airtran.com

Frontier Airlines
www.frontierairlines.com

Southwest Airlines
www.southwest.com

WestJet
www.westjet.com

Index